D0919776

Wenger

THE MEN FROM WENGEN

AND

AMERICA'S AGONY

THE MEN FROM WENGEN

AND

AMERICA'S AGONY

The Wenger-Winger-Wanger History

including

Christian Wenger, 1718

By

John E. Fetzer

with additional family notes
on
Barnhart, Barr, Brandon, Coble, Deitrick, Dittmore, Eby,
Evans, Fetzer, Foster, Geaubaux, Gilbert, Hager, Hess,
Hoenie, Keeler, Lawrence, Limes, Marker, McGrew, McKee,
Mendenhall, Passwater, Pierstorff, Pyle, Ribble, Robinson,
Sipes, Smith, Thomas, Watters, Woods and Yeager.

Published
by
JOHN E. FETZER FOUNDATION, INC.
of
Michigan

Copyright ©, 1971
John Earl Fetzer

*All rights reserved. No part of this book
may be reproduced in any form, except
for short passages quoted by reviewers,
without permission from the publishers.*

Library of Congress Catalog
Card Number 79-179875

Printed in United States of America

TO MY MOTHER

BORN

DELLA FRANCES WINGER

AND

THOSE WENGER PATRIARCHS

WHO BUILT AN ETERNAL GARDEN OUT

OF A WILDERNESS

THE MEN FROM WENGEN

CONTENTS

PART I

AMERICA'S AGONY

CONTENTS

PART II

Foreword

It was with great personal and professional pleasure that I learned of John Fetzer's intention to produce another volume to complement his previously published chronicle of the Fetzer family, entitled ONE MAN'S FAMILY, by paying equal homage to those interesting and rather accomplished Swiss forebears on his mother's side, the Wengers.

My satisfaction is considerably increased by the fact that Mr. Fetzer is a personal friend. I met him first in Paris in 1944 where I was then serving as Commanding Officer of the American Forces Radio Network. He and a group of other distinguished American broadcasters had been invited by General Eisenhower to come to Europe so that the Supreme Commander and members of his staff might have the benefit of their valuable guidance. Mr. Fetzer was of enormous help to me, and there then began a friendship which has continued uninterrupted through the years.

My assignment in Bern obviously calls for a somewhat more than casual interest in the relationships between Switzerland and the United States, and to the events and activities which influence them. Thus I am especially aware of the pride and affection with which the Swiss people recall such illustrious fellow countrymen as statesman Albert Gallatin, engineer Othmar Ammann, and pioneer John A. Sutter. These together with thousands of other Swiss emigrated to the United States, there to become distinguished American citizens who made giant contributions to their adopted homeland.

I heartily welcome John Fetzer's new addition to the recorded history of ties between the two countries. It appropriately augments the proud record of official relations which have flourished without interruption since the first representative of the President of the United States was appointed to Switzerland 117 years ago.

JOHN S. HAYES
United States Ambassador to Switzerland

Bern, Switzerland
May 8, 1969

Prologue

This line of Wengers could qualify as the "Clan in Mobility." They started to move toward America in the 18th Century and they have been moving ever since. Long before that, in feudal times and later in the Reformation period, they moved constantly in Switzerland to avoid the persecutions of that day. They were not wanted due to their religious differences and so they moved to the Rhineland and then to Holland. They moved to America where they were welcome.

Then came the madding rush for land. Usually the oldest son acquired the homestead and the rest of large families scattered, some from eastern Pennsylvania to the western part of the state and Canada. Some went south but, for the most part, they went to Ohio, Indiana, Illinois, Iowa, Nebraska, across the plains and the mountains and to the West Coast of the continental United States.

The name of Wenger somehow managed to surround the globe in every direction. The writer has traveled the world and has found the name in most lands — the Middle East, the Far East, South America, South Africa, the North Countries — everywhere in Europe. It is estimated that there are more than 150,000 Wenger families in existence today.

This effort to document the descendants of Christian Wenger, who came to America in 1718 and settled in Leacock Township of Lancaster County, Pennsylvania, is the first comprehensive attempt to establish this family line of more than 500 years. We consider this account long overdue, and the record shows this family to be among the first of scores of Wenger families who have come to America from the 16th to the 20th Centuries.

By contrast, Christian Wenger (C), who came to Lancaster County in 1727 a decade later, is well established in authenticated material. There were also many other Wenger families in Lancaster County at an early day. Some of these may have been identified with our brothers, Henry Wanger (A1) of Montgomery County and Christian Wenger (A2) of Lancaster County, Pennsylvania.

It has taken the writer more than 30 years to collect the parts of this puzzle. Family research requires infinite patience and a driving desire to delve into the past. The pathway to success is long and arduous due to family indifference and sometimes traditions which have no basis in fact.

On the other hand, one of the grandchildren of Joseph Wenger (A22269) remembered that around the year 1895 he received a notice from a lawyer near Philadelphia stating that the Wenger family at one time had owned a farm in eastern Pennsylvania concerning which there was a title in dispute. The attorney was looking for Peter Henry Wenger (A2226) or one of his heirs to sign a right of title to one of the owners at that time. Checking this bit of family information led for the first time to research in the county records of three or four of the eastern counties of Pennsylvania. As a result, in Chester County, Pennsylvania, documents were found which led to a solution of the complete ancestral line of Peter Henry Wenger (A2226), my great-grandfather. One must conclude, therefore, that family traditions and stories and rumors must be pursued to outer limits, in spite of their limitations, if material facts are to be discovered.

This account is a chronicle of a family that was victimized by a tide of history which swept Switzerland and Europe during the 16th Century. It is not intended to cast deprecation upon the Swiss or any other people of Western Europe who are the root ancestors of the majority of Americans. Americans of Swiss extraction have reason to be proud of the sturdy heritage each has received from his ancestors in the mother country. The vicissitudes in Switzerland in that earlier day served to bring a race of people, tried in the crucible of discontent, to these American shores. Here they helped to build a great nation under conditions of adversity because they had the fiber to persevere.

I assume complete personal responsibility for all interpretive conclusions indicated herein. This is particularly true in European generation analysis which is based upon the isolated work of several historians. In my view no single researcher can always exercise the intuitive options required, as one deals with data from multitudinous quarters. In our case we had to deal with records in four different countries, some of which involved extreme language difficulties. Hence the responsibility was mine to pull all the diverse sources together in order to find the whole, as I see it.

For the most part, reasoned conclusions based on cause to effect or vice versa have been categorically outlined in their procession. It is left to the reader to judge the quality of such conclusions. I have no fixation concerning pride of my composition.

In the assembly of the family trees herein, I have given all details available for those generations that follow the family member, around which a full chapter has been developed. The first nine Swiss generations are for optional use only, since American genealogical research affirmatively follows that of the first ancestor to come to these shores. This avoids the repetition of family lines contained in preceding chapters. It is hoped this technique will avoid confusion that otherwise might develop.

Thucydides, the Greek historian, tells us that "both justice and decency require that we should bestow on our forefathers an honorable remembrance." Macaulay, the British essayist, declared that "a people that take no pride in the noble achievements of their remote ancestors will never achieve anything to be remembered with pride by their remote descendants." These challenges are removed for this present generation, many members of whom will question their validity.

The purpose of this historical treatise is to establish the continuity of life. We have looked back as far as we are permitted to see. At the present time we are moving through an accelerated world upheaval. It is history in the making, but it is part of the continuous life story. The Wenger family history, past and present, is tied together in fairly clear tones as it relates to these eventful times. The future and its uncertainties are also a significant part of the continuity of life, in its ebb and flow from eternity to eternity. The individual participation in this drama should cause one to seek his identity through self-examination. As one looks within, one must identify with this link from the past, the present and the future. From our sires we must extend it through our lifetimes and beyond, a Segment Eternity. I have chosen this form of treatment because of my concern about the relevancy of our present sociological environment which, out of necessity, must undergo extensive reform.

Therefore, this is more than a numbers game which is so often the case with genealogies. It is an attempt to link a fascinating element of historical research to a modern social need. I can only hope that my belabored work, as recorded in Part II, expressing "America's Agony," will partially meet that challenge.

For easy reference to each American Wenger descendant, a York number has been assigned. For an explanation of the York System, I suggest that you turn to the Appendix. Such an understanding will greatly add to your comprehension of this story.

I am grateful to many members of the Wenger families, regardless of branch, who have significantly contributed to Part I of this material. I absolve them, of course, from any responsibility for Part II, which is solely my personal viewpoint. Rev. Roger Winger of Omaha, Nebraska, the author of Wenger Clan Notes, has gone the last mile to be helpful. Norman Wenger Nauman, family historian of Lancaster, Pennsylvania, who has collected the history of hundreds of collateral Wenger families, has gone far beyond the call of duty. Samuel S. Wenger, Attorney at Law of Lancaster, Pennsylvania, has searched out the records in minute detail. His contributions have been many. The well-known publications of Dr. John C. Wenger have been most helpful.

Others in Lancaster are Ira D. Landis, Secretary of The Lancaster Mennonite Conference Historical Society, M. Luther Heisey, historian, Grace W. Wenger, Maude Yuninger, Luella Wenger, Clair McCollough, President of The Steinman Stations, and a host of others have made considerable material available. Moreover, the documental story of many Wenger families in the State Archives of Bern, Switzerland, prepared by Gottlieb Kurz under the direction of Henry E. Wenger of Detroit was most significant. Dr. Robert Oehler, noted Swiss genealogist and historian, and Fritz Allimann, an outstanding and authoritative historical researcher, brought together a multiplicity of evidence from parish and other records throughout the Bernese territory.

In Kaiserslautern and Zweibrücken, Palatinate, West Germany, the officials gave significant help. This includes Richard B. Hudet, Director of the Archives for the City of Zweibrücken, and Dr. Fritz Braun, Director of Heimatstelle Pfalz in Kaiserslautern.

To Madelene Howland of Swarthmore, Pennsylvania, goes well-earned plaudits. It was she who discovered the missing link between my great-grandfather, Peter Henry Wenger (A2226), and his father, Abraham Wenger (A222).

In Ohio and Indiana, numerous cousins contributed their family patterns and, of course, without the contributions of my mother, Della Frances Winger Fetzer, and my sister, Harriett C. Thomas, this history would not have been possible.

I want to emphasize my thanks and appreciation to my friend of a quarter century, The Honorable John S. Hayes, United States Ambassador to Switzerland. He not only accepted my invitation to write the Foreword, but was most helpful in establishing genealogical expertise in the Wenger research in that delightful little country.

Finally, let me say that I have enjoyed great psychological insight as the compiler of this history. Most of the characters of this drama have been actors on the stage of time. I have lived with many of the principals hundreds of hours, while each took his place, front and center stage. At times I have had to play the part of producer, choreographer, art and technical director, stage manager and artist. Our association has been intimate — a rare privilege, indeed, for one who usually has only a three score and ten years exposure to his ancestors. Mine has been more than 500 years!

JOHN E. FETZER

CHAPTER ONE

Derivation of the Wenger Name

THE WENGER family name finds its origin following the same pattern that has characterized the development of all surnames. In the dim ages of the past, communications necessitated that a designation be attached to tribes, clans and races. In early times, first or given names were the only designation; however, as time passed society became more complicated and a need arose for more specific identification which, of course, led to the development of surnames. In Europe these began to appear in the 11th Century. In the beginning, after the father adopted the surname, his sons and daughters used some form of diminutive such as "son of." Offices, trades and occupations made a definite contribution toward surnames. The use of such names as knight, marshal, constable, carpenter, mason, etc., are typical examples. Baptismal names, bodily or personal characteristics, or derivatives from the locality or place of residence were in wide use quite early in Europe. These locality designations seem to have been the direct result of the feudal system. Examples of these are suffixes such as "ton," "ford," "ley," "ham," etc. It is in this latter category that we find the derivation of the surname of Wenger.

Swiss Archives

The archives of Switzerland indicate numerous localities in German-speaking Switzerland that suggest the origin of the Wenger name. Some of these are Wang, Wangi, Wengi, Wangen, Wengen, etc. All these names mean approximately the same: "extensive meadow" located on a hill or spreading over a side of the valley. Wengen, a world famous resort village in the vicinity of Lauterbrunnen and often referred to as the Wengern-Alp, is the best known locality suggesting the Wenger name. The mountain village of Wengen marks the beginning of the Wenger families. From it is derived the title of this book.

The village of Wengen on the mountainside which bears its name. The Men from Wengen found their origin here.

Early records give an insight into names to come. In 1303 Johannes von Wengi, Nicolaus de Wengi, and Peter von Wengi were recorded. Heinricus de Wengen and Kristan de Wengi appeared in the 1340s. Around 1350 such names as Christian Wenger, Uelli Wenger, Conrad Wenger, Peter Wenger and Hans Wenger were in the records. After that, as more records were kept in the parishes, the Wenger name became prolific.

With so many localities precipitating the origin of the name of Wenger, it is apparent that present-day descendants of those early families did not all spring from the same cradle and, while it cannot be concluded that all Wenger families descended from a common ancestor, it becomes apparent that scores of present Wenger families are descendants of the family line reported herein.

Swiss-American Nomenclature

In Switzerland, the records show, for the most part, that the name was spelled W-e-n-g-e-r, although the name of many families was spelled W-ä-n-g-e-r. However, today in the United States we find the name has been changed so much that it is almost impossible to trace it to the founding families. The most prominent variation is W-i-n-g-e-r, which is used extensively by the descendants of this family line, not only in Pennsylvania, but in Canada and Ohio as well. Some other variations are Wengar, Weinger, Weingher, Weiniger, Wengert, Wingert, Wingaart, Wengerd, Wingerd, Wangerd, Wengerdt and many others. Most of the variations were anglicized by English school teachers who had language problems with these early families of Swiss-German extraction. Today in the United States many families spell the name W-e-n-g-e-r which, of course, is the proper context on both sides of the Atlantic.

The old Bernese custom of the right of preference in inheritance, which was later practiced in America, played the principal part in the indicated changes in dwelling places. When the older sons had no desire other than to remain in the single bliss on the patriarchal estate, the younger sons sought their fortunes elsewhere. In studying Swiss archives from the 13th to 16th Centuries, it becomes apparent that leaving their birthplaces the Wenger families, known at home as Wengi or Wengen, were soon called Wenger at the new dwelling place.

The Wenger family name originated in the 13th Century but was not fully established for 200 years. That was just as well, because citizens of the state were not at that time listed in public records. Not till the establishment of parish records after the Reformation did family names gradually assume a degree of permanence.

Wenger Coat of Arms

As one might expect, there are several versions of the Wenger Coat of Arms. From the standpoint of European orthodoxy, it would be easy to establish the quality of the various Wenger Arms which have been used by a number of Wenger families; however, in the view of many Americans, such consideration, while necessary, is only a part of the story. A goodly number of our people entertain the idea that adopting a coat of arms can be effectuated in any family line in accordance with the aim, desires and ideals of the founder. It is contended that arms' development is evolutionary and that changes in design and interpretation are perfectly in order.

Conversely, some people feel that heraldry is so intimately connected with aristocracy that it has no connection with a democratic age or nation. It is claimed that this is disproved by the interest shown in this subject by leadership in the United States and in small American republics, as well as in Germany, France and Switzerland. Some of the most striking and most ancient coats of arms in these countries have been and are borne by families who are distinguished neither by titles nor by possessions.

From this it can be construed that the display of a coat of arms, even though open to interpretive discussion, and rightly so, is a discretionary matter with the individual. I would caution, however, that such arbitrary powers should be exercised only after most careful consideration of all the historical background surrounding this complicated subject. In Switzerland an official coat of arms book for the Bernese gentry has never been published and, according to the Swiss, probably never will be published. In the Swiss view, the display of a coat of arms is a matter of private concern. There is, however, one reference source of quality, namely *Schweizerich-Biographisches Lexicon.*

The Early Designs

In early times each Swiss city had its own coat of arms and qualified citizens of that city were permitted to use it as a personal coat of arms. In the rural areas, however, people were free to adopt a coat of arms in accord with their own sentiments. Many people of the rural areas did adopt their own coat of arms, but for the most part the plain and sober people (Anabaptists), principally on the left bank of the River Aare, considered such arms insignificant and of no practical value. This attitude prevailed even though many of them came from ancestral lines whose predecessors had adopted a coat of arms. (See Appendix.)

Melchior Wenger of Wattenwil, a carpenter by trade, adopted his coat of arms in 1758. The symbols of his arms became standards for most Wenger families. The emblem consists of a black eagle in gold above and a golden lion in red below. Both are separated by a silver crossbeam. This is depicted in a stained glass window at the Bern Historical Museum. A similar design was chosen by Christian Wenger of Uttigen who was master of a house of weavers in Bern. The figures in the escutcheon are like those in the Melchior Wenger coat of arms except the crossbeam is silver-white.

Some Swiss records indicate three branches of Wenger families that have adopted a similar coat of arms. These families are located in Buchholterberg (Solothern), Blumenstein (Bern) and Thun

(Bern). There is a family "wappen" for each branch; however, all branches have the same symbols, the eagle and the lion. The description is substantially the same as described for Melchior Wenger of Wattenwil and Christian Wenger of Uttigen, namely a black eagle in a gold field above and a golden lion in a red field below. Genealogists in Switzerland state that all three of these insignias are authentic.

From family to family these fields seem to be varied in color, and some have a silver-white crossbar between the two fields. Any of the Wenger families may use the "Berner Wappen." We have chosen to display an approximation of the Wattenwil Coat of Arms in the frontispiece because our branch of the Wenger family was intimately identified with that area.

The coat of arms of Melchior Wenger, a carpenter of Wattenwil, which he adopted in 1758. This is now in a glass window in the Bern Historical Museum. This is a direct photograph of the window.

CHAPTER TWO

The Reformation

IN ORDER to bring into focus subsequent events in Switzerland, it is necessary to look at the broad spectrum of events in Europe. More particularly, I refer to the Protestant revolt from the church.

The Reformation, as commonly understood, means the religious and political revolution of the 16th Century which caused a disruption of the mother church and the establishment of various national and territorial churches. The effect was to repudiate the long established doctrines which speedily merged into chronic political rivalries, domestic and foreign. Religious considerations played a very important part in diplomacy and war for at least a century and a half, from 1530 to 1690. Protestantism was born out of bitter antipathies engendered by a period of fervid religious dissention. Even to this day, the old issues are by no means dead, and recent events foreshadow for all organized churches a new revolt in religious concepts which will differ radically with traditional approaches.

In Switzerland, early opposition to the church was made manifest through the Waldensian movement in the 13th Century and through many religious leaders in dissent. However, Martin Luther in Germany was beyond doubt the most important single figure in the Protestant revolt from the church. Recklessly impetuous, he was no statesman, yet Luther's writings showed him to be deeply spiritual, completely imbued with genuineness of purpose. In 1520 he boldly repudiated the papal government under which Europe had lived for centuries. Selective masses of people rallied to his support.

Within a generation after this proclamation, North Germany, Scandinavia, England, Scotland, Holland and portions of France and Switzerland, each in its own way, had permanently seceded from the papal monarchy.

The Anabaptists

A fundamental aspect of the revolution from the church was the development in Zurich of opposition groups known as Anabaptists. These religionists denied the validity of infant baptism. Therefore the Anabaptists baptized those whom they quite logically regarded as not having received any Christian initiation. There were several known sects of Anabaptism which developed a multitude of followers.

One sect not only advocated religious reform but its members were outright social and political revolutionaries. This movement created general havoc in Europe, particularly among the peasants, who were prone to destructive revolt. After these energies were spent, harassed remnants of the Anabaptists were gathered together under Menno Simons. His moderation and piety held in check the turbulence of the more fanatical.

Menno Simons, as shown in the Mennonite Encyclopedia.

Menno and his followers expressly repudiated the social and political aims of this fanatical sect. Conversely, the aims of the church established by Menno Simons and his followers in Zurich were the antithesis of discord.

The Mennonite Church

The Mennonite Church, named after Menno, the Anabaptist, accepted no authority outside the Bible. It limited baptism to the believer and stressed those precepts which vindicated the sanctity of human life and of man's word. Menno's church discipline was not unlike that of the Swiss Baptists. Sermons were without texts and silent prayer was a feature of worship. Oaths and military action were forbidden.

The Unkown Martyr, as shown in the Mennonite Encyclopedia.

Menno denied the Christian character of the old church and its civil authority, a position regarded subversive by civil and church authorities alike. Hence, bitter persecutions followed which made martyrs of these humble people. The horrors of the spectacle became a byword of Anabaptism all over Europe.

Persecutions

In France an imperial mandate in 1529 demanded the execution of all Anabaptists. From time to time French officialdom would moderate, only to change later. As late as 1712, strict orders were given in the districts in which Mennonites lived to expel them and not permit them to settle in any province under French rule.

In Alsace, a province of the German Empire, Strasburg became a center of the Swiss Anabaptists. A mandate against them was published in 1527 forbidding the populace to give them shelter or food. Subsequently, a decree was issued requiring the banishment of all

Anabaptists. After banishment, if any returned to the city, they were to be imprisoned for a period of four weeks. If they returned a second time, they were punished by the amputation of fingers and by being branded on the cheek with a red hot iron. Anyone returning the third time was to be drowned.

When persecution was in full sway in Holland, faithful Anabaptists were burned at the stake within a week after sentence had been pronounced.

In the Austrian Tyrol a great number suffered martyrdom. In 1530 the government of Tyrol reported to the Austrian authorities in Vienna that more than 700 persons, men and women, had been executed as Anabaptists in the province, and a greater number had fled the country. The report continued that the obstinacy of the Anabaptists in the face of cruel punishment and death only served to strengthen their faith to the bitter end.

In Switzerland the Council of Zurich decreed that anyone that would henceforth perform the act of re-baptism should be "drowned without mercy," without trial or further hearing.

A large number of Anabaptists in Bern in 1530 were "held under water." They were submerged in the river until life was almost extinct, a form of punishment which in the opinion of many was more cruel than actual drowning. After this, they were released with the threat that they would be "drowned until dead" if they were found again in the Canton of Bern.

The trials and tribulations and the severity of human punishment suffered by these gentle people were almost beyond the pale of endurance. They wanted only the opportunity to live a life far removed from the calloused world they found around them.

George Wanger

No better illustration of the extreme persecution suffered by many of the Anabaptists can be found than that suffered by George Wanger, a tailor, who was executed August 5, 1591. This account is recorded in *Martyr's Mirror* by Thieleman J. Van Braght. George Wanger, prior to his execution at Lorenzi in Pusterthal, in the earldom of Tyrol, was apprehended in 1590 and confined in prison for more than a year.

At Lorenzi Wanger was brought to the bailiff's house where the bailiff, the judge, the clerk, and the priest queried him concerning his activities. He answered, "God keep me from this evil; we do not betray our enemies; should I then betray my friends and dear brethren? By the help of God I shall not do this, for it is contrary to the love for our neighbor." The judge strenuously assailed him with smooth and hard words; but the brother said, "I received my sound members from God; to Him I will offer them up again, and this with a good conscience."

Having been confined long at Lorenzi and examined three times by the authorities, he was taken to the castle of Michelsberg, placed upon the rack, and when he would not surrender to their demands and tell what was contrary to God, his conscience, and neighborly love, he was tortured so severely that the marks could be seen on his body for thirteen weeks.

Michelsberg Castle and Brixen

Confined in the castle of Michelsberg for two weeks, on September 16, he was taken to Brixen, and put in chains in the tower, where there were many vermin. Scorpions crawled about his head, on his bed, and on the walls. He could barely turn over; because of the vermin, he had to keep his head covered. During the 19 weeks that Wanger was imprisoned at Brixen, his death was announced to him twice, and he was at the same time earnestly admonished to recant. But he said, "I have no desire to go to this people to whom you want to drive me, but to amend my life, if I err, and to exhort others that have not yet amended their life, to repentance, this I consider a work of God, and will gladly do it, and keep to God what I promised Him in baptism, to my soul's salvation."

Back to Lorenzi

Having been imprisoned at Brixen seven weeks, George Wanger was taken back to Lorenzi, where he was to be executed after two nights. However, this was frustrated by the death of the Bishop of Brixen. Wanger was taken back to Michelsberg, and imprisoned in the castle until the 5th day of August. Again he was brought to Lorenzi to the judgment hall where the priests held judgment over him, first trying to make him apostatize. When they could not, he was sentenced to death by imperial mandate.

He was led out to the place of execution, where the commander of Lorenzi again earnestly admonished him to recant; the commander would give Wanger so much that he should have enough all the days of his life; he would, moreover, be surety for Wanger at the last day, if he did wrong in it. But George Wanger said, "If I did this, and were to accept you as my surety, and the devil should first make off with the surety, where should I then have to go and seek my surety and pledge?" Thus the commander was made ashamed, and desisted from him.

Many people were present. Some of them wept. Wanger asked that his hands be released a little, that he might lift them up to God, to thank and praise Him, and to ask Him, that He would give him strength to resist the false prophets and evil spirits. Finally, he commended his spirit into the hands of God, and was at last beheaded for the Word of God and His truth.

The doom that plagued George Wanger was not typical for all of the oppressed. The narrative does serve, however, to remind us of how fortunate we are today in that we enjoy the freedom that was fought and paid for by our fathers of the past. The compassion found today in peaceful Switzerland and elsewhere in Europe has overtones of an environment born out of the blood and tears of the past.

This Gürbetal map of 1731 gives an excellent topographical view of the Wenger area. Note its reversal of directions to that of present-day maps.

CHAPTER THREE

The Bernese Wengers

The Veneration of Values

OUR WENGER ancestors have long believed that the clan predated the time of Kristian von Freutigen who served under Charlemagne in the 8th Century and was of Celtic extraction in Switzerland. Members of the family state that the Wengers, centuries later, were brought out of the State Church originally by the Waldeneses and subsequently by the Anabaptists. Many a patriarch of our family has said that "martyrs' blood of the centuries flows through our veins and we have reason to be proud of our forefathers." For the most part, simple farmers participated in the religious reforms of early times. Family tradition repeatedly stated that "bitter persecution caused our Swiss ancestors to take refuge in the highlands of the country." This tradition concerning the Waldeneses and the Anabaptists was handed down through the families of Henry Wenger (A1) and Christian Wenger (A2), the two brothers who emigrated to America. It will be seen hereinafter that these family disclosures reinforce our data that many of our branch of the Wengers were of the agricultural class. The first known records indicate that they originally lived in or near Blumenstein, Thun, and later in or near Wattenwil, Seftigen. The family, including Christian Wenger (A2), later lived in or near Uetendorf, Thun, and the nearby territory of Buchholterberg. Finally, the hamlet of Martisegg in the Signau Emmental was the temporary abode of Henry Wenger (A1).

In the year 1399 there were more than 130 known Waldeneses in the Bernese territory. These hardheaded farmers were taught the tenets of their beliefs from father to son for generations. Many historians believe that the Bernese Anabaptists had pre-Reformation connections with the Waldeneses. Members of our family have long alluded to their beliefs, which did not conform with the State Church of an early day. Great pride was taken in the fact that certain members of our family, particularly those of the clergy, knew the New Testament from memory, "just as the Waldeneses."

Many Wenger families during the 16th Century went as interlopers to the Upper Emmental region. The security of the area made possible a continuous organization of the Anabaptists for more than three centuries, while the rest of the countryside slowly but surely annihilated and exiled large numbers of Mennonites.

The Emme River near Eggwil showing the hills and valleys where many early Anabaptists found security.

The conduct of these people was beyond the reproach of those who knew them. They were described as "quiet, retired people with a clean conscience. They pray much, give alms, fast often, pay their taxes and bless their persecutors." Many were poor and unlearned farmers and hard workers "who often had no more than two books beside the Bible, but could preach with more earnestness and get more results than the learned ministers of the State Church."

Early Families

It should be recognized also that the time factor takes our known Wenger historical background to the secular and civil environment of the pre-Reformation era, when the Swiss were drawing together parts of each of the imperial kingdoms of Germany, Italy and Burgundy. Unification was necessary for the common defense against the House of Hapsburg. In the 15th Century the armies of Bern, Zürich and Luzern occupied the territory of the Duke of Austria known as "Unteraargau and Freiamt." That was in 1415. Switzerland was in the throes of a civil war, 1440-1450, and the

Harvest time near Wattenwil.

eight states of the confederation ended bitter hostilities when the Duke of Burgundy won complete victory at Grandson, Murten, and Nancy. The Wenger families, during these benchmarks of Swiss history, took their turn at breaking the shackles of feudalism.

As early as 1310 the Gürbe valley was beset with over-population problems. Large families were the rule and land was scarce. Forests were cut down and meadows were plowed. As hunger for land continued, the farmers spread to higher, more hilly areas and small lonesome valleys. Dairies and alpine houses and barns were built. Officials became protectors of the forest and new Hapsburg laws had to be enforced.

In the 14th Century many Wenger families were among these peasant farmers. They discovered the black soil and succeeded in cultivating and harvesting golden wheat. Numerous native-born Wengers were industrious at plowing, sowing, making hay, harvesting, threshing and many other tasks of the agricultural class. They led their fat young cattle to market at such places as Thun, Bern, Freiburg, into the Waadtland and even over the mountains to Italy.

The locale of Wenger families was numerous small Swiss com-

In the Gürbe Valley near Blumenstein where many Wenger families lived.

munities on both sides of the Rivers Aare and Gürbe. About a half-dozen districts located in the Canton of Bern were seats of origin of many Wenger families in the districts of Thun, Seftigen, Schwarzenburg, Bern, Signau and Grindelwald.

To market in Thun.

The Secular and Civil Setting

Since our principal interest lies largely in the Seftigen district surrounding Wattenwil on the north and the Thun district in the neighborhood of Blumenstein on the south, I will relate two amusing civil cases involving Hans Wenger and Barbara Wenger.

In 1518 there was recorded a lawsuit before the little court in Bern. There appeared Hans Wenger from Wattenwil who charged the following: "Antoni Jost has slandered me. This court in its capacity as arbitrator has previously ordered Jost to take back his words. But he doesn't want to do that. I request that he be arrested." Jost, who also appeared, defended himself. "I question the jurisdiction of the court and contend that this body of gentlemen has taken advantage of me and has done me wrong. To be specific, it is known and proven that Hans Wenger has possessed a calf which did not belong to him. He has refused to return it to me as the rightful owner. I request, therefore, that the before-mentioned decision be revoked and that I be allowed to bring the case before the court in my own behalf."

The court, however, gave Hans Wenger the decision and fined the defendant for all expenses. Antoni Jost refused to comply with the judgment whereupon the court proceeded to assess him a "pile of gold." He was fined for all the court costs and legal expenses but, of course, there is no record that he appealed the case. What the lawsuit settled is difficult to surmise. Probably Jost called Hans Wenger a "calf stealer."

In 1526 there was a civil proceeding involving a broken engagement. In Thun County, Hans Studer and Barbara Wenger, believed from Blumenstein, were engaged to be married. The boy's parents, who had not agreed to the marriage, protested. The government of Bern, in view of the fact that the boy was still under 16 years of age, considered the grounds sufficient to dissolve the engagement. Further, the court decided that each one of them could marry whomever he or she chose! However, the government concluded that if the parents of Barbara Wenger felt her honor had been spoiled in some way, they could summon Hans Studer before a higher court. As to whether this momentous question was satisfactory settlement remains somewhat in doubt. Since the court decreed that the couple could marry anyone of their choice, it does not require much imagination to reflect that the choice was to complete the original marriage contract in spite of parental protest.

In the Beginning

In spite of extensive material, much of the story we should like to know concerning our branch of the Wengers is lost in the past. Many records have disappeared through the ravages of war and the time — evolutionary environment. Thus in some cases, out of necessity, we have accepted meager but satisfactory data to establish conclusions based on the rule of reason. It would be classically advantageous if we could deal only in the absolute. If, on the other hand, we must exclude partial documentary proof, given names, names of godfathers and godmothers, evidentiary material, local history and credible family traditions, then this account, along with many other family histories, could not have been prepared.

Therefore the acceptability of the following evidential account must be left to the discretion of the reader. The research reported herein sifts through a maize of evidence by the use of reasoned elimination. This method has led us to a qualitative and plausible report which can be considered completely authentic.

Blumenstein Castle, Thun

The Village of Blumenstein in the district of Thun is located at the foot of the beautiful Stockhorn mountain. Blumenstein was established prior to 1285 and is only nine kilometers from the City of Thun where forms a gateway to the Oberland in Stockental.

Of prime interest is the Gothic Church of Blumenstein which was established more than 700 years ago. The choir and the tower were donated by the knight Johann von Weissenburg, who had it built in the second half of the 13th Century. The church was first named for the parish of the Dechanet of Bern under the name Blomensten in the year 1361. The nave was built in 1505. The main point of interest is the choir which is separated from the nave by a pointed arch. The windows of the nave emit a rich glow of colors. The magnificent glass painting of the choir is a jewel of medieval art.

The first documentary evidence (Fontes Rerum Bernensium VII, 343) shows that the Blumenstein Castle was built during the Hapsburg dynasty in the early middle ages before the year 1000 on the ruins of a Roman Watch Tower. It is indicated that on May 18,

Blumenstein — The famous Stockhorn is in the center of the Alp background.

1348, a young Welsh nobleman, Peter of Raron, sold Blumenstein Castle and environs "with all mastery over the Church" in Blumenstein to the City of Bern for 400 gulden. The instrument of sale enumerates a series of farm estates and land properties surrounding Blumenstein. Wenger's Hill is specifically mentioned in the land descriptions. Apparently our first Wenger of record in 1348 held Wenger's Hill and surrounding property as fief from the nobility. In assuming this tenure of land, he pledged himself to pay a yearly land tax of two pfund pfennigen and eight large sacks of German corn.

This Wenger's Hill property is also mentioned in the Spiez Feudal Holder's Register of Lands from 1488/1514. Blumenstein (meaning "flower stone") Castle and Wenger's Hill were located about two kilometers northeast of Blumenstein in the direction of Forst and Längenbühl. By coincidence, the hamlet of Mettlieggen is located about one and one-half kilometers west of the site of Blumenstein Castle. The former is believed to be among the first homes of our branch of the Wenger family.

It is thought that Blumenstein Castle came into the hands of

This Blumenstein church, founded about 1330, contains a heraldic glass window with the inscription "Johannes of Weissenburg of a noble family of the lower Simmental founded this church."

Peter of Raron through marriage. The Rarons were allied to the nobles of Ringgenberg on the lake of Brienz. Apparently after Peter of Raron sold the castle to Bern in 1348, it was resold to the knights of Burgistein (over Thurnen and Wattenwil) and then passed by marriage to the nobles of Münch of Münchenstein. By 1642 the property was owned by the noble Franz of Wattenwil who a short time later sold the complete property to the City of Blumenstein. By 1782 the castle was in ruins. Twenty years later the natives had used all the stone to build their own houses and there was no remaining evidence of this edifice of feudal times.

Castle of Thun is located less than nine kilometers from the site of Blumenstein Castle.

Medieval Times

We cannot be totally sure that the Wenger or his descendants who held Wenger's Hill might have had an alternative status in the feudal system. In medieval times there was, as alluded to above, an institution that survived the age of chivalry known as the fee tail. A fee tail or male fief was a portion of real estate including tillable land. It was rent free and tendered as a leasehold right to the recipient. For all practical purposes, it was the recipient's land but without actual title, contrary to the custom in more recent times in most democratic states. The holder could dispose of it at will, sell it, rent it or give it away. He could bequeath it by will with the proviso that the recipient be of male gender.

With every change of hands, the new possessor had to receive the fief from the seignor or feudal lord. Undoubtedly Wenger's Hill passed from father to son through many generations. If a landholder had no male heirs, the lord of the castle usually acted out of benevolence and permitted the fief to go into a woman's hands. Since the transfer of a fief was always a ceremonial event held in the castle and presided over by the lord, there were certain traditions. If the heir were male, he appeared in person and was duly honored. If the recipient were female, she could not appear in person but could be represented by a male relative or guardian.

In feudal times the lord of the castle had to defend his stronghold estates from outside aggressors. This necessitated the maintenance of armed guards and warriors. After a victorious confrontation, the lord of the castle often would reward his vassals and warriors with field, meadow or pasture land which, of course, was a fee tail or male fief. If a warrior recipient was an outstanding hero in his last conflict, he was rewarded by being exempted from further military duty. Sometimes such a hero was given an official title of Bailiff. As such, he became a representative of the lord and usually was in charge of collecting revenue taxes. From this it seems altogether fitting that we should conclude that the original holder of Wenger's Hill, prior to 1348, earned his right as a landholder or Bailiff because he was a warrior in the battalion of the lord of Blumenstein Castle, Peter of Raron, or his predecessor.

Wenger References

In the 15th Century Christian Murer of Tannenbrehl, as male fief, received Arolf's Mill near the present Blumenstein mineral bath. The description of the transfer instrument states that the mill bordered "the Wenger estates."

At the town limits of Blumenstein flows the stream from the mineral spring near the "Wenger Estates."

In 1449 at Blumenstein, Conrad Wenger was mayor of the village and was described as "the most esteemed man in Blumenstein." As such, he was charged with collecting a "weekly farthing" tax from the people of the community. Often he would send his manservant, a neighbor, or his son, Christian Wenger, to Bern to make the funds available to the officials there.

Later in the same century it was recorded in the archives at Bern that Jacob Wenger as Mayor of Blumenstein dedicated his coat of arms dated 1755. After this, official records referenced Wenger families as landlords. To this day the arms may be seen cut in glass in the windows of the Historical Museum in Bern.

During the course of the Huguenot Wars in France, Bern was forced to undertake military preparations. The muster rolls show Wenger representation from the area between Wattenwil and Blumenstein. It would appear that these early branches of the Wenger family had attained more than a superficial status in their relations with the feudal system surrounding Blumenstein Castle.

Many more Wenger families in subsequent years occur in the records of a dozen communities near Blumenstein and Wattenwil. Since so many Wenger families find their origins in this area, it is only reasonable to assume that some of them, including our own clan which lived within the environs of the castle, conclude their root ancestors sprang from Wenger's Hill near Blumenstein prior to 1348.

The Gürbetal Ancestors

In the Gürbetal, Wattenwil is one of our focal points of interest. This beautiful Swiss community surrounded by the hills and valleys of the Seftigen district with the background of the Swiss Alps, particularly the Stockholm, gives a pastoral setting of unusual distinction; it is a picture post card landscape.

Wattenwil as it appears today.

In this district there are two parish registers of concern. Prior to 1659 these records were kept at Thurnen. After that, they were located at Wattenwil. Thurnen is about eight kilometers north of Wattenwil and 15 kilometers south of Bern. These communities are close to all of the early records of the first Wenger families. In these two parishes alone are records of many Wenger people, including five generations previous to our American immigrants, Henry (A1) and Christian (A2). There are over 50 entries directly and indirectly related to the families of these two brothers. There are a number of volumes of parish registers at Thurnen and Wattenwil covering a period of time beginning in 1550. These communities are reference points for much of the material which follows.

Mayor Wenger, Esq.

One of the first Wengers of distinction from whom the remainder of our family descends was mayor of his village which we believe was Wattenwil. From later parish records at Thurnen and from Blauen Hefte (Blue Books) in the archives of Bern, we learn that he was probably born about 1510. Mayor Wenger had a son, Hans Wenger, who was born about 1530. This son, Hans Wenger, and his wife, Dichtle (Benedicta) Wenger (maiden name), christened their fourth son Christian Wenger on March 19, 1559, in the Church at Thurnen. (Th. I, p. 58) The record of that baptism states that this Hans Wenger, the father of Christian, was "des Ammann Sohn" or "son of the Mayor." (Th. I, p. 58) This Swiss dialetic term "Ammann" freely translated means "first in rank in civil authority." Depending upon usage, it could mean lord mayor, ensign, chairman, bailiff, mayor, baron, magistrate, governor, etc. We believe that early English interpretation dictates the term "mayor" probably would be the correct translation. Hence, we conclude that Hans Wenger representing the sixth generation was a son of the mayor of his village.

As the result of a chain of circumstantial evidence, we believe that the Mayor was Ruff (Rudolfus) Wenger. Here we recite the facts as reported in *Blauen Hefte* and *Stift DOC. BUCH* III 518. The Castle of Burgistein near Thurnen and Wattenwil in the 14th and 15th Centuries was under the dominion of the von Muleren family. Rudolf von Muleren was councilor of Bern in 1352. Sir Urban von Muleren, his grandson, was councilor in Bern in 1455 and was considered one of the wealthiest men in the State of Bern. Sir Urban was Bailiff at Aarwangen in 1456 and at Lenzburg in

1465. After the victory at Murten in 1476 in the war with the Duke of Burgundy, he became bailiff of the latter community.

During these years, among the assets of his estate he held the house, mill, sawmill and dam on a farm rivulet in the village of Wattenwil. On June 9, 1487, he granted Hans Wenger of Blumenstein as a male fief the entire land establishment as a condition of "good maintenance" to which Hans Wenger agreed. It should be emphasized that this estate, by terms of the agreement, was a quality operation and should not be confused with numerous small mills which were under government surveillance.

From Father to Son

Hans Wenger held this fee tail for 11 years. On May 10, 1498, it was transferred to his son, Hans Wenger. Since this family was from Blumenstein, we are led back to Wenger's Hill. Moreover, the evidential Wenger relationship between Blumenstein and Wattenwil becomes material. Previously we reported that in 1642 Blumenstein Castle including Wenger's Hill was sold to the noble of Wattenwil; a short time later he sold it to the community of Blumenstein. Thus the nobility of Blumenstein and Wattenwil engaged in property interchange and the Wenger fiefs went with these estate transfers.

On January 18, 1519, Nicholas Wenger, son of the late Burkhard Wenger of Forst, acquired the Wattenwil estate and mill. Forst was within the environs of Blumenstein Castle. By reconstructing the records, we believe Burkhard Wenger, the father of Nicholas and Peter, was the son of Hans, the original fief holder and brother of Hans, the second owner.

Five years later, on July 18, 1523, Nicholas Wenger transferred the estate and mill to his brother, Peter Wenger. The latter died within three years and the land and mill passed on July 31, 1526, to Peter's son, Peter Wenger. Peter Wenger, the younger, held this Wenger estate in Wattenwil for 24 years, and it was passed on to his son Ruff (Rudolfus) Wenger on May 6, 1550. The latter held the property for 17 years before it was passed to his son, Peter Wenger, on May 15, 1567.

This fief was an important property in Wattenwil and was held by a long line of Wengers since 1487. It is probable that the Wen-

This old mill operates on a farm rivulet like many fed by the mountain waters. The Castle of Burgistei under the dominion of the vo Muleren family held a similar Wat tenwil mill until 1487 at which tim it was granted as a male fief to Han Wenger.

This old mill near Büren is a museum relic of the distant past. It is one of many in the Bernese area having a single mechanism housed in a complete building.

Another view of the water wheel co structed of wood. Under the roof you ca see the wooden water channel which co ducted the water over the wheel. Oft these water channels were hundreds feet long bearing the water from t mountainside to turn the wheel in clockwise motion.

gers were a well-to-do family in 15th Century terms. From the time the property became a fief to the Wengers from Sir Urban von Muleren, it is within reason that originally Hans Wenger from Blumenstein became a bailiff, as was often the case when a male fief was granted. It will be recalled that Conrad Wenger, "the most esteemed man in Blumenstein," was mayor of that community in 1449. Hans Wenger and his sons, Hans and Burkhard, who came to Wattenwil from the Blumenstein area, could have been members of the Mayor Conrad Wenger family. We must speculate on this because Hans had sufficient status to become a fief of the Wattenwil estate. That distinction could have resided in prior as well as the descending generations.

At the time Hans Wenger "des Ammann Sohn" was designated as such in 1559, Ruff (Rudolfus) Wenger was the male fief of the Wenger estate in Wattenwil. Hence, even though we do not have precise documentary evidence, it is altogether appropriate to believe that he had all of the accepted qualifications of that day to be mayor of Wattenwil. The estate which he held must have given him primary status in Wattenwil and this distinction usually resided in the mayor of the village.

The First Five Generations

There is further confirmatory evidence that the mayor, believed to be Ruff (Rudolfus) Wenger, had at least three sons, two of whom were Ruff and Peter Wenger, the mill fiefs. After the death of Mayor Wenger, his son Peter received the mill and estate on May 15, 1567. We believe that our Hans Wenger who was recorded as "des Ammann Sohn" was the third son, and consequently was a brother to Ruff and the abovementioned Peter for the following reasons:

Hans Wenger "des Ammann Sohn" was born about 1530. He married his cousin, Dichtle (Benedicta) Wenger, about 1550. They had their first child, Hans, in 1551. Peter Wenger, who acquired the mill in 1567 from his father Ruff (Rudolfus) Wenger, was born within a year or two of Hans "des Ammann Sohn" for Peter was married, probably in 1551, and had his first child in 1552. He also married a cousin, Margreth Wenger.

Hans "des Ammann Sohn" had his second child, Uli, christened on April 23, 1553, and Margreth Wenger, the wife of Peter Wenger, the miller, was the child's godmother. (Th. I, p. 46) Likewise, when

Peter Wenger had his second child, Margareth Wenger, christened on October 22, 1554, Dichtle (Benedicta), the wife of Hans Wenger "des Ammann Sohn," was godmother. (Th. I, p. 13) If both couples mutually gave their wives as godmothers in 1553 and 1554, it is reasonable to think that Hans and Peter were brothers. For this and the other general citations, we conclude that this is another link in this chain of evidential material.

Peter, who had received the fief from his father, believed to be Mayor Wenger, took his brother Ruff as a partner on August 17, 1583. It is assumed Ruff was identified as a worker at the mill many years prior to 1583 because we believe he was born about 1531. After the death of his brother Ruff, Peter Wenger at an advanced age secured another partner in the estate, namely Bendicht Zimmerman. That was on December 17, 1605.

We believe the two Wenger men, Ruff and Peter, the brothers of Hans Wenger "des Ammann Sohn" have further identification in

The village of Thurnen under the tremendous shadow of the Alps.

the parish records at Thurnen, which were first compiled in 1550. Ruff Wenger married Lena (Magdalena), the daughter of Peter Bruni, about 1550. At the christening of their first child, Anna Wenger, January 19, 1551, the record refers to Ruff Wenger as "Müller zu Wattenwil." Apparently Anna died soon after for a second Anna was christened on July 3, 1552, at which time Ruff Wenger was recorded "der Müller." (Th. I, pp. 37, 46)

Peter Wenger, the brother and partner of Ruff "der Müller" had two children. David was christened March 31, 1566, and Elsbeth January 30, 1569. Peter Wenger, the father, was recorded "Müller zu Wattenwil." (Th. I, pp. 135, 163)

Significant History

As stated above, Hans Wenger "des Ammann Sohn" married Dichtle (Benedicta) Wenger (maiden name), whom we have called his cousin. It seems evident that Dichtle (Benedicta) Wenger also came from a long line of Wengers in the Seftigen and Thun districts. An examination of the later church records shows many inter-Wenger family relationships. Marriage, godmother and godfather records show multitudinous connections between alternate family lines in the Wenger ancestral chain.

Hence, our Rudolfus Wenger of the seventh generation of Switzerland, who descended from two separate lines of Wengers, in all probability carries his ancestry twice over, in both the paternal and maternal families to Wenger's Hill near Blumenstein.

This formulates a long history of the Wattenwil mill estate passing from father to son in the Wenger family. The circumstantial evidence of the father-son-brother-cousin relationship is most convincing in that the fiefs of Wenger Mill are one and the same as our Wenger line.

It is interesting to note that the mill tradition was carried forward by Henry Wenger (A1) and Christian Wenger (A2), our two brothers, after they came to America. Henry (A1) operated a mill on the Schuylkill River in what is now Montgomery County, Pennsylvania; Christian Wenger (A2) had his home on Mill Creek near the famous Eby Mills in Lancaster County. The Ebys and Wengers intermarried and descendants of Christian (A2) owned and operated mills on Mill Creek. John Wenger (A2211) and his wife, Susana Eby Wenger, sold their last Lancaster County grist, saw

The parish church at Thurnen where scores of Wenger children were baptized.

and merchant mill in 1836. (Lancaster County Deed Book E6, 238) Since the descendants were mill owners, we conclude that Christian Wenger (A2) also had mill involvements. Thus we have a record of our Wenger clan as being "millers" for nearly 350 years.

Summary

Even though our evidence ranges from hard-core to passive, we believe our thesis is reasonable. The records in *Blauen Hefte* — The Blue Book has 15 to 20 unbound sheets covering Wenger documents — at the Bern Historical Archieves, plus the parish records at Thurnen, and later American records establish what we believe is a plausible family report. These data cover more than a century preceding the available parish records. As this is written, I consider the postulation of this account in credible stance even though additional documentary material would prove salutary. Therefore, our thesis leads us to the conclusion that Hans Wenger, born about 1430 and who acquired the Wattenwil estate from Sir Urban von Muleren in 1487, represents the first generation. The line would be as follows: Hans (1), Burkhard (2), Peter (3), Peter (4) and Rudolfus (5). The latter is believed identified as Mayor of Wattenwil. Hence, with Ruff (Rudolfus) as the ascribed first name, we conclude with the verified fact that Mayor Wenger, Esq., born about 1510, was a descendant in the fifth generation in Switzerland. Five more generations in Switzerland will be outlined hereafter from the parish records at Thurnen and Wattenwil and the Reformed Church records at Zweibrücken, Germany.

Thus we start this family treatise first with Wenger's Hill in 1348 and collaterally with Hans Wenger of Blumenstein about 1430, shortly after Zwingli Protestantism found its way into Swiss history. Moreover, this was long before the discovery of the American New World, a land which was to contribute so much to future members of the Wenger family.

The Descending Generations

Hans Wenger, the son of the Mayor of Wattenwil and of the sixth generation, was born in or near Wattenwil, Seftigen, about 1530. He married Dichtle (Benedicta) Wenger, a cousin, during the time of the Peasant War about 1550. They had eight children of the seventh generation, all recorded at Thurnen. Hans Wenger was christened September 20, 1551; Ulli Wenger, April 23, 1553; Peter Wenger, September 20, 1556; Christian Wenger, March 19, 1559; Anna Wenger, January 9, 1561; Rudolfus Wenger, who died in infancy September 3, 1564; *Rudolfus Wenger was christened April 5, 1566*, and Benedicta Wenger, June 11, 1570. (Th. I, pp. 37, 46, 58, 80, 120, 136 and 177.)

Rudolfus Wenger, of the seventh generation, the seventh born child of Hans Wenger, was christened at Thurnen April 5, 1566. He married Gredy Pfister. This was the generation that experienced the great floods of the Gürbe River in 1575 and again in 1589. The water reached both sides of the valley and resembled a large inland sea. Great devastation resulted.

This wooden bridge near Wattenwil is a prototype of many built by Swiss-Americans throughout Pennsylvania and elsewhere in America. The great floods often give these ancient bridges a severe test, but many have survived through the decades.

Rudolfus and Gredy Pfister Wenger had eleven children of the eighth generation, all recorded in the parish of Thurnen, as follows: Hans Wenger was christened November 14, 1591; Rudolfus Wenger, April 15, 1593; Rudolfus, June 30, 1594, and Jost, March 27, 1596. The latter three died in infancy. Triny Wenger was christened November 6, 1597; Jost Wenger, February 10, 1600; Peter Wenger, December 13, 1601, who died in infancy; Anna Wenger, christened August 7, 1603; Melcher Wenger, December, 1605; *Peter Wenger, December 13, 1607,* and Dichtle Wenger, November 18, 1610. (Th. II, pp. 137, 151, 163, 182, 196 and Th. III, pp. 16, 42, 67, 89, 121, 150 and 183.)

The eighth generation, as it relates to our line, was represented by the tenth-born child of Rudolfus and Gredy Pfister Wenger, namely Peter Wenger, christened December 13, 1607, at Thurnen. (Th. III, p. 67.) He married Salome Blatter during the Thirty Years' War which was to bring the downfall of the Hapsburgs. Peter and Salome were married before 1625 at Thurnen.

They had eight children of the ninth generation, all christened at Thurnen, as follows: Elsbeth Wenger, December 4, 1625; Peter Wenger, July 13, 1628; Melcher Wenger, January 24, 1630, and died

The Wattenwil Parish Church where all the tenth generation of Wengers were baptized.

in infancy; Melcher Wenger, christened April 1631; *Hans Wenger, May 30, 1633*; Margreth Wenger, November 29, 1635; Peter Wenger, April 22, 1638; and Veronica Wenger, January 13, 1640. (Th. IV, pp. 44, 65, 75, 85, 102, 119, 140 and 157.) For additional lineal descendants of Jost Wenger, christened February 10, 1600, and Melcher Wenger, christened in April, 1631, see the Genealogical Chart at the end of this chapter. Note that Jost Wenger married Verena Tschäppeler and thereafter had eleven children. When their third child was christened, Christina Tschäppeler, Ursula Schnell and Sir Rudolf von Luthernau were sponsors.

Hans Wenger of Wattenwil

Of prime concern to us is the fifth-born child of Peter and Salome Blatter Wenger, representing the ninth generation of our family line in Switzerland. Hans Wenger was this son who was to see Switzerland gain its independence from the Empire. Hans Wenger was christened May 30, 1633, at Thurnen. (Th. IV, p. 119.) He married Verena Krebs June 17, 1662, recorded at Wattenwil. (Wa. I, p. 259.)

They had the following children representing the tenth generation, all recorded at Wattenwil: Hans Wenger was christened September 13, 1663; Anna Wenger, February 4, 1667; Barbara Wenger, November 22, 1669; Verena Wenger, November 1, 1672; Heinrich Wenger, June 18, 1675, who died in infancy; Elsbeth Wenger, August 4, 1676; Heinrich or Henry Wenger (A1 in the York System), February 13, 1680, and Maria Wenger, January 18, 1684. *Christian Wenger (A2 in the York System), the ninth child, was born about 1688 in the territory of Buchholterberg near Uetendorf, Switzerland,* after Hans and Verena Krebs Wenger, the parents, had fled their Gürbetal home after 1684. (Wa. I, pp. 18, 42, 62, 83, 102, 110, 132 and 163.) (Church Archives, Rieschweiler-Zweibrücken IV, 258)

The records at Rieschweiler, Zweibrücken, specifically state that Christian Wenger (A2) was of Uttendorf (Uetendorf) and alternatively indicate the territory of Buchholterberg. The latter territory refers to the mountain range and hills back of Uetendorf. Buchholter is the name for the plant, hemlock. Hence, Buchholter-Berg means the mountain covered with hemlock.

The name often has been applied to settlements on or near the mountain and as early as 1261 documents refer to this territory as

The mountain territory of Buchholterberg taken from Heimenschwand. Christain Wenger (A2) was born in this general area. The hamlet of Badhus is in the foreground.

Bucholtron. The general area became a parish in 1860 encompassing such communities as Uetendorf, Heimschwand, Wachseldorn and Oberdiesbach. The parish church is located in the latter community. Buchholterberg is not a political territory or state. It simply is the mountain territory back of Uetendorf.

We believe Hans and Verena Krebs Wenger of the ninth generation originally lived three kilometers south of Wattenwil near the village of Mettlen at a hamlet called Mettlieggen, as mentioned previously. Many years later Melchior Zaller, a Mennonite leader, stated that Henry (A1) was originally from a place called "Moglenberg." This was probably an error in translation. The name Mettlen (Mettlein-Eggen, meaning a small hill,) could have been confused with the mountain named Macolin in French. Berg could be a German translation from Mont, accounting for the berg being added to the mistranslation of Mettlenberg. A meticulous search shows there is no such community or hamlet in Switzerland as Moglenberg. Hence we come to the conclusion that Mettlen or Mettlieggen was the actual habitat of the Hans and Verena Krebs Wenger family. When we visited this hamlet in 1970 there were two Wenger fam-

The hamlet of Mettlieggen is within the environs of the Blumenstein Castle site. Mettlieggen (Mettlein-Eggen, meaning a small hill) is in the foreground.

The 300-year-old house in Mettlieggen said to be at one time a Wenger home.

ilies still residing there. While Mettlieggen has always been in the parishes of Thurnen and Wattenwil in the district of Seftigen, just across the Gürbe River is the Blumenstein Castle site located in the district of Thun. Mettlieggen is within sight of the castle, about one and one-half kilometers away.

The parish records of Wattenwil, as seen by the writer in 1952 and 1970, show Hans Wenger of the ninth generation and members of his family as Anabaptists. When Hans, the first-born child, was christened September 13, 1663, the record states that "The father of this child is a very disobedient Anabaptist." (Wa. I, p. 18) Since the children were christened in the State Church, we believe that while Hans was an Anabaptist, his wife, Verena Krebs, was not. It probably was she who insisted that the children be baptized.

It was from this entry alone, indicating Hans Wenger as "a disobedient Anabaptist," that we can project the past Swiss History as well as what follows.

To Uetendorf and Buchholterberg

Hans Wenger resided in or near Wattenwil for over 50 years before he and his family moved. His son, Henry (A1), who was christened February 13, 1680, became a weaver in Wattenwil as we believe his father, Hans, was before him. Since this was an Anabaptist family, they were subject to the persecutions of the day and, as all families of that faith, were considerably dislocated. It is believed that after 1684 when Maria, their last recorded child, was born in or near Wattenwil, Hans and his wife, Verena Wenger, along with scores of other Anabaptists, went to the right bank of the River Aare in the Emmental region. As shown by later records in Zweibrücken, Germany, Hans and Verena Krebs Wenger went to or near the community of Uetendorf, Thun, and the nearby territory of Buchholterberg above the district of Thun. The parish archives at Oberdiessbach indicate marriage and baptismal records covering, among others, the community of Uetendorf, Thun, as well as many persons from the territory of Buchholterberg. Since there is no record at Oberdiessbach of our Hans Wenger family including Christian (A2), we conclude that they were in hiding in the hills and mountain of Buchholterberg as Anabaptists and had finally burned all their bridges with the State Church. Hence we rely upon

46

the Zweibrücken account which we believe is confirmatory. Christian Wenger (A2) was born in the territory of Buchholterberg near Uetendorf about 1688. The record further shows he did not marry in Switzerland but did so later in Germany. (Church Archives, Rieschweiler-Zweibrücken IV, 258)

Mr. and Mrs. Ernest Wenger standing in front of their present-day home at the hamlet of Badhus, Buchholterberg. They display the Blumenstein Coat of Arms of 1755.

Henry Wenger (A1) to Martisegg

In the meantime Christan's (A2) brother, Henry Wenger (A1), of the tenth generation married Elsi (Elizabeth) Blum about 1705 in Wattenwil. They had two children of the eleventh generation. Hans (A11) was born in 1706 and Heinrich (A12) in 1708. Both were born in or near Wattenwil. During the 16th Century, the upper Emmental had become a refuge and asylum for many Anabaptists of the Bernese territory. The inaccessible highland farms and the deep valleys made it possible to evade the police. In February 1709, Henry (A1) and his wife, together with their two children, went to the Emmental hamlet of Martisegg in the Rothenbach parish. The parish records in Wattenwil show that Hans (A11) and Heinrich (A12), the children of Henry (A1), were christened February 17, 1709, at Rothenbach. Hans (A11) was sponsored by Hans Schindler, Hans Straam and Elsbeth Schindler. Heinrich (A12) was sponsored by Andres Straam, Benedicht Schindler and Babi Müller.

Han's (A11) sponsor, Elsbeth Schindler, and Heinrich's (A12) sponsor, Babi Müller, were living at the hamlet of Martisegg.

The parish church at Rothenbach where Henry (A1) and Elizabeth Wenger baptized their two sons, Henry (A11) and Hans (A12) Wenger, in 1709.

In 1709 Jakob Dürr, the pastor at Rothenbach, reported the christenings in his church of Hans (A11) and Heinrich (A12) Wenger, the sons of Henry (A1), to the pastor of Wattenwil (Wa. II, p. 24.) The local recorder noted, "If these children are still citizens of our community (Wattenwil), their status will have to be decided by our most honorable governor because the father has left our community as an Anabaptist."

Since the canton of Bern had declared that every inhabitant was a citizen of the place in which he lived and that this "right of citizenship" was made hereditary, the citizenship fate of the children, Hans (A11) and Heinrich (A12), was somewhat in doubt. The father had left Wattenwil because he was an Anabaptist, therefore only the governor could decide whether these children were citizens of that community.

At that precise time, in 1709, Henry (A1), the father, was in hiding in a Martisegg home to which he went after leaving Wattenwil.

The hamlet of Martisegg where Henry Wenger (A1) arrived in 1709.

It could have been that he and his wife had the children christened to confuse knowledge of his whereabouts, or perhaps his wife insisted on a baptism in the State Church.

Many families from the area in which Martisegg is located had children christened at the mother parish at Rothenbach. The records there show some of these were Christian and Peter Stauffer, Hans Broennimann and Hans and Ulli Gerber. Of the latter, Ulli Gerber's wife was Anna Wenger. When their child, Hans, was christened at Rothenbach February 8, 1705, Peter Saugg, Madle Rupp and Christian Wenger were the sponsors. Christian Wenger (A2) was 17 years old at that time. Ulli Gerber later was to become the hired man of Hans Burkholder, the Mennonite committeeman identified with the tide to America. Moreover, Gerber and Burkholder, along with many others, were identified with a confrontation with the authorities as will be reported later. (Rb. V, pp. 117, 118, 129, 133, 141, 145, and 172.)

The records at Rothenbach show that Melchior Zahler from Frutigen had married Dichti (Benedicta) Gerber, the widow of

Peter Stauffer. She probably was the sister of Ulli Gerber. They had a child, Anna, who was christened April 30, 1699, and a child, Melchior, who was christened February 4, 1706. Melchior Zahler, Sr., along with Hans Burkholder and Benedict Brackbill, were to serve on the principal Mennonite committee that brought scores of the exiles, including Henry Wenger (A1) and Christian Wenger (A2), to America. (Rb V, pp. 129, 145.)

These baptisms in the State Church only show the serious family divisions that existed at that time. Many times the husband was Anabaptist, the wife was not, and vice versa.

The oldest house at Martisegg, said to be several hundred years old. We speculate that this could have been the Henry Wenger (A1) abode.

In Bern

In March 1709, Bern authorities announced from the pulpits that anyone giving aid to Anabaptists would have his possessions confiscated and would be deported from the country. Informers were offered rewards of 50 to 100 thalers of the realm for each person apprehended. Permission was granted to confine captured prisoners in private homes or elsewhere and that they should be bound and placed in captivity. We conclude that in January 1709, Henry Wenger (A1) arrived in Martisegg. On February 17 the children were baptized. This act may have led to Henry Wenger's (A1) apprehension. Through an informer, Henry (A1) was arrested at Martisegg in March for his Anabaptist faith. Many, including Henry (A1), were deported from Switzerland in the fall of that year. Others voluntarily fled the country. Some went to Alsace and the Zweibrücken while many others went to Mompelgard and Neuenburg.

By 1710 Henry (A1), lonesome to see his wife and children, had returned to Switzerland. Soon after he and many others were arrested again and imprisoned, suffering much persecution. There was no mention of Christian (A2), but he is presumed to have been in similar circumstance. Since Henry (A1) would not repent, the Bernese government gave orders February 19, 1710, to hold him until such time as a larger group of Mennonites could be collected so that deportation could be effectuated.

The prison tower in Bern where Henry Wenger (A1) was imprisoned in 1709. Note the bars over the windows above the arch.

In the meantime the Bernese Ambassador in Amsterdam, Francois Louis Pesme, Lord of St. Saphorin, via diplomatic exchange with Dutch Ambassador Runckel in Bern, secured tentative permission to send a ship-load of "the undesirables" across Holland to Amsterdam and thence to America.

The Mennonite Chamber, a committee charged by the Bernese government to deal with the Mennonite problem, decided to look into the wealth of Henry (A1) while he was being held. The policy was to impound, wherever possible, all wealth of Mennonite prisoners. Henry Wenger (A1) after the investigation was stripped of all his possessions. Within a short time the authorities at the Bern prison tower placed many of its prisoners, who had been there since 1708, in a dungeon. Others were placed in a separate "Hole" and were secured with iron shackles. All lived on bread and water and worked on wool processing from 4 o'clock in the morning until 8 o'clock at night.

Aboard Ship

There were 57 exiled Mennonites aboard the ship which left Bern March 18, 1710. Captain Schinder was given 130 thalers for the maintenance of a sergeant and soldiers to guard the exiles. The Bernese government was so determined to be rid of the Anabaptists that it outfitted the ship and agreed to pay a man by name of Ritter 45 thalers for each person delivered to America. Of the 57 confined, three were deacons of the church who previously had been to the Palatinate but had returned and were captured. Melchior Zaller (Zahler), originally of Frutigen and later reported near Rothenbach, Benedict Brackbill (Brechbüehl), a native of Trachselwald in the Emmental, and Hans Burkholder (Burki) of Langnau were a constituted committee in charge of the banished. These three men had undergone all the trials and more during the imprisonment in Bern. Melchior Zaller had lost his five children and all other blood ties, including his estate and 15000 florin. Benedict Brackbill was apprehended at the point of a bayonet under a hay stack and thrown in prison because he was a preacher. He lost his entire estate. Hans Burkholder was betrayed by a so-called friend, imprisoned in the Castle of Trachselwald, then brought by two provosts to the prison in Bern.

Intercession

Hearing that the Bernese authorities were seeking permission for the ship to cross Holland, the Committee communicated with their fellow churchmen in Holland and the authorities there. On March 22, 1710, influential local members of the church interceded with the Netherlands authorities in Amsterdam, requesting them to prevent the forceful transportation of Mennonites across the country. They stated that the ship was filled with old and sick persons who would surely die on the high seas. As a result of this negotiation, the Netherlands authorities through diplomatic channels denied the request of the Bernese government for the right to cross Holland. The negotiation also clarified, in the minds of the Dutch, the status of the Mennonites. They were no longer considered enemies of the government. A degree of compassion was precipitated.

As a result of this intercession, the Dutch Ambassador in Bern on March 22, 1710, wrote the Bernese government the following letter:

> In religion, freedom must be allowed to every man to believe and profess that which in his judgment is necessary to his salvation. No one may be persecuted and punished for such faith and such profession if his life and doctrines do not tend to the injuring of the state.
>
> And as to these Mennonites, it is well known that they have at all times conducted themselves as good inhabitants and subjects. Therefore, the Holland authorities cannot in any way lend a hand to the forcible transportation and banishment of Mennonites to America; nor do anything whereby they might give color of approving, even indirectly, such proceedings as have been inflicted upon the Mennonites in the Canton Bern.
>
> (Signed) *Ambassador Runckel*

At Mannheim

After a delay in Basel, the ship arrived at Mannheim, Germany, on March 28, 1710. Here 32 of the infirm and feeble, including Henry Wenger (A1), were taken off the ship and set free. Since they were destitute, they were left at the mercy of the Mennonites in Germany.

The ship continued down the River Rhine with its cargo of the 25 or so "less infirmed." On April 6, 1710, they landed at Nijmegen, Holland. They were met by the local Mennonite group. Their number had declined from 25 to about 20. Here those on board ship learned from the members of the local congregation of Mennonites that the ship would not be permitted to cross Holland. All were released at once by the Dutch authorities except the Committee of Brackbill, Zaller and Burkholder, who were taken before the authorities to render a report. They were released April 9, 1710. Mr. Ritter, who headed the mission, was without money or friends as a result of his failure. The boatman was compensated with 130 thalers by the Bernese consul at The Hague to aid him to return to Switzerland.

The Sick Removed

Many of the sick were removed from the ship and taken to the Mennonite hospital by Henrik Laurens, a concerned minister and teacher. Several of the congregation saw the plight of the voyagers and immediately took steps to supply needed nourishment. All on board were brought into town and advised not to return to the boat.

On April 7, 1710, the condition of some of the group had improved, but "many could walk only with extreme difficulty, suffering with a large variety of infirmities to limb and body. Their long imprisonment of almost two years amid suffering and intense cold, shackled their feet with fetters." For the most part, they were confident and of good cheer even though they were sick and had lost all their worldly goods. Through it all, they were sturdy, hardened people, capable of enduring great hardships and privations. Most of them had long unshaven beards and wore disordered clothing and heavy shoes. To converse with many of them was difficult, because in Switzerland they had lived in or near the mountains far from the villages and cities, and had had little intercourse with other people.

Laurens, the minister and schoolteacher, secured funds from his church to help them and on April 9, 1710, walked with them for an hour and a half outside of town, "then with tears of joy and cheerful minds they embraced each other and parted with the kiss of peace."

At Large

All of them, including the Committee, stayed together and arrived at Crefeld by way of Clevel. Here further help was extended and it was learned that of the 20, about 17 of them were married. They longed for their families after the long and grievous separation. However, none wanted to return to Switzerland. They preferred to settle where they were or nearby. The Swiss ambassador in Holland had arranged a temporary stay for the Mennonites. He said, "They cannot be expected to go back to Bern to be killed." He wrote the English Ambassador at The Hague, Lord Townsend, and tried to make arrangements to send the refugees to Pennsylvania. Nothing was timely.

For seven years, many of them endured the extreme hardship of moving from place to place, a complete charge on society. They spread over Holland and to the south where they re-entered the Palatinate, Alsace, Germany, and some relented and returned to Switzerland to find their wives and children. As early as 1711 some arrived in the Emmental region. Among those who returned was Hans Burkholder. On July 11, 1711, he and his children in company with his hired man, Ulli Gerber (referred to in Rothenbach), along with Daniel Grim and his ten children, and Christian Neuenschwander armed themselves. They procured pitchforks, sticks and clubs and through force made a stubborn resistance with the Bernese authorities. They strongly protested the treatment of Hans Burkholder. This led to the threat to place Hans Burkholder in irons.

The confrontation only stirred the determined authorities to exile many more Mennonites. Over 340 persons were exiled, including a few by the name of Wenger.

Christian Wenger (A2) in Switzerland

It is not known whether Henry (A1) who had been away since 1710 returned to Switzerland during this time. With some degree of certainty, we believe that Christian (A2), who was eight years younger than Henry (A1), remained in the territory of Buchholterberg in or near Uetendorf, Thun, Switzerland, with his mother, Verena Krebs Wenger, until 1713, at least.

Müller gives a group of miscellaneous items on page 252 in which he refers to Hans Wenger who had been a weaver of Wattenwil. We believe this Hans Wenger to be the same as Hans Wenger, the father of our Henry (A1) and Christian (A2). The items state that since Hans Wenger and some 15 others in the "Upper Jail on the Island" were not able to do galley service, Bern had asked the Baptist Chamber to see that they were all sent to the East or West Indies and Pennsylvania. If old Hans, the father, called "the disobedient Anabaptist," and Henry (A1), his son, were in the hands of the authorities, most certainly the rest of the family, including Christian (A2), were in jeopardy.

Bern, Switzerland, as it appears today. In the right foreground, "the upper jail" may have been on the Aäre River island above the two-arch bridge.

Christian Wenger (A2) at Zweibrücken

We shall never know how many members of the family made their way to the German Palatinate. Several Wenger families have been recorded there, particularly in the Zweibrücken area. Benedict Wenger from Wattenwil was the first of record, having gone to Hornbech, Zweibrücken, in 1694. It was near there that many Anabaptists settled, some permanently, others only as a temporary respite from their persecution and escape from Bern.

Ernest Drumm, Archivist of the City of Zweibrücken, prepared a manuscript which was later published by the City under the direction of Karl Jost. The latter succeeded Ernest Drumm as Archivist. This publication in 1962 entitled *Zur Teschichte der Mennoniten im Herzogtum Pfalz-Zweibrücken* gives us the first insight as to the whereabouts of Christian Wenger (A2). On pages 32 and 33 we learn that by 1713 the Governor of Zweibrücken through the good offices of Duke Christian IV decreed that the Mennonites could own and work on the land. The German people had begun to recognize that the Anabaptists were desirable farmers and had the capacity to develop the land for increased output.

The pastor of the parish church in Rieschweiler, 1661-1695, was Isaac Isemann who came from Switzerland. After the Ryswyker-Peace in 1697 he had great influence in the migrations from Switzerland. In particular, he sought the Mennonite farmers who were so adept at rehabilitating the land which had been devastated during the Thirty Years' War. During the war, practically every hamlet and village was overrun and left in smoking ruins. The land was depopulated. All of the cattle in the barns and fruit in the fields were taken. The Mennonite farmers were needed. On page 36 the names are given of Anabaptist families, including the Wengers, Reutigers and Ebys who were among the first arrivals.

We believe Christian Wenger (A2) arrived in Zweibrücken in 1713. He, like the others, was a young man 25 years of age who worked to clear the land. Ernest Drumm says the following: "Only 4 years later, in 1717, the Anabaptist Christian Wenger, born in

The City of Zweibrücken where the offices of the City Archivist contain all the early records of some Swiss emigrants who came in search of a better life.

the Bernese territory (Buchholterberg), lived as a subtenant in a barrack on the Huberhof (farm) in the municipality of Nünschweiler and shared with Christian Schneider house and land. *He is officially listed as an Anabaptist in the books of the Hornbacher monastery.*"

Again on page 55 he says, "The first appearance of the Anabaptist farmers in the principality of Zweibrücken only too clearly shows the poverty of the early persecuted Anabaptists. Among the earliest settlers is Christian Wenger, who as a subtenant shared on the Huberhof near Dusenbrücken with Christian Schneider, house and land, like so many new settlers at the beginning of the 18th Century. Unfortunately, Wenger's tracks get lost in the documents. His development and movement could greatly illuminate our research."

On page 86, Drumm says "Christian Wenger, born in the area of Buchholterberg in Bernese territory about 1688, lived in 1717 in a barrack on the Huberhof, sharing with Christian Schneider house and land." (Church archives Rieschweiler-Zweibrücken, IV/258)

From further references (Church archives Zweibrücken, IV/2058 and 2060), we find Jakob Weiss and Jakob Steinmann who, in 1742, had been tenant farmers on Bickenaschbacherhof took over the leasehold rights of Huberhof from Johannes Baer who came to America that year. By coincidence these names later were to become prominent in the affairs of Lancaster County, Pennsylvania.

The Family of Christian Wenger (A2)

The office of Richard B. Hudet, Director of the Archives for the City of Zweibrücken, directed us to the Reformed Church records of the parish of Rieschweiler. There we found the family pattern of Christian Wenger (A2). Christian (A2) was married at Huberhof (sometimes Hubenberg) on January 16, 1714, to Anna Catharina Bertschy. She was the daughter of Peter Bertschy, farmer, who came to Zweibrücken from the village of Saanen near Bern, Switzerland. The Bertschy family left Switzerland as members of the Reformed Church in opposition to the State Church. They settled on Fauenerhof, a farm near the hamlet of Ludwigswinkel. Here Peter Bertschy was steward of the farm in the territory of the Counts of Hanau. This is now the district of Pirmasens of the Palatinate, West Germany. Anna Catharina had a brother, Johannes, who died in

1712 at the age of 22. As was the case with a number of Mennonite young men who found their wives in the Reformed Church, so it was with Christian Wenger (A2). It should be noted that this marriage record specifically states that Christian Wenger's (A2) father was Hans Wenger of Uetendorf (South of Bern, District of Thun), thus reinforcing our Wattenwil conclusion which was reported previously. There is some indication, but not verified, that the mother of Christian (A2), namely Verena Krebs Wenger, was also at Huberhof. Hans Wenger, the father, was still believed to have been in custody in Bern.

It is apparent that after his marriage Christian (A2) and his wife, Anna Catharina (Barbara in America), continued to live at Huberhof because their first three children were born there. Johannes Jacob Wenger (A21) was born July 29, 1715; Johannes Henrich Wenger (Henry Wenger, Sr. A22) was born July 26, 1716, and Anna Catharina (A23) was born August 21, 1718. The record of the last-born child is the last entry of the Christian Wenger (A2) family of the parish of Rieschweiler in Zweibrücken. Thereafter they came to America.

The oldest house in Huberhof. It could well have been there during Christian Wenger's (A2) time.

The Huberhof Cloister

In consultation with officials of the Archives Department of the City of Zweibrücken and the parish records at Rieschweiler (2058-61, IV), it was learned that the Huberhof Cloister was destroyed

By the side of the road at Huberhof.

during the Thirty Years' War. The Cloister and surrounding land were attached to the Hornbacker Monastery near Zweibrücken. Generations later the land and buildings were acquired by private owners.

Mennonite farmers in the Palatinate who, for the most part were destitute, were attracted to these community farms in order to live. While they did not receive net compensation, these farmers did receive a place to eat and sleep. They worked to clear the land and were required to furnish produce from the farm to the owner at specified times. The worker, as a subtenant, could retain a small income from the sale of certain products on which he was required to pay a tax.

On October 18, 1970, my wife and I visited Zweibrücken, Nünschweiler, Düsenbrucken and Huberhof. Zweibrücken is the center of all records pertaining to the Zweibrücken district. Nünschweiler is the central municipality of the district which contained Huberhof as taxable property. Düsenbrucken is a hamlet of three houses next to Huberhof. The latter has four family homes consisting of 21 people. There are not more than half a dozen buildings at

The site of the Huberhof Cloister. Christian Wenger (A2) and his family had lived in this vicinity since 1714. They departed for America in 1718. Karl Bähr, who resides at Huberhof during this present day, is pointing out the exact location where the cloister once stood.

Huberhof today. There are 275 acres (130 morgens) of land surrounding Huberhof which is maintained by these resident farmers. When Christian Wenger (A2) was there, over 2,000 acres were attached to Huberhof (1,100 morgens; one morgen equals about 2.1 acres).

We were fortunate to speak to one local farmer, Karl Bähr, a descendant of Johannes Baer and his father, Melchier Baer, who came from Ottenbach, Switzerland, in the 1690's. Johannes Baer migrated to America. It is believed that he was the forebearer of a long line, some of whom intermarried with later Wenger families in America. Karl Bähr knew the exact location of the Huberhof Cloister. It has long since been ruined by time and war and is now a peaceful valley. Mr. Bähr stated that many years ago a search was made on the site of the cloister for its foundation or other remains of the building. Certain material items were found but apparently there is no precise record of the discoveries of this expedition. This search may have been the one which was made by Heinrich Bachman who built his Huberhof home at an early day. Mr. Bähr now lives in this home. The cloister site is now called Monchhoferfeld. In English, "The Field of the Farm that once belonged to the Monks."

The Lehemann Report

From the Rieschweiler records (2058-61, IV), we learned that in 1698 the government in Zweibrücken gave an assignment to the renovator Lehemann to search out the cloister of "Höfe Rupertsbronn" and make a report concerning its location and boundaries. Lehemann's report indicated the location to be near a "spring of fine mountain water." He described the surrounding area as grown up with large oaks and other trees containing some swamp-like marshy areas with a cover of underbrush and that there had been no farming there for over 400 years. His report stated that the land

Nünchweiler, where the early records indicate that Huberhof was made available to the Swiss as subtenants.

surrounding the cloister site was in a poor location and would be unprofitable until cleared. The record shows that Heinrich Bachmann also discovered the building foundations which he said were located in the Huberhof basin. ("Lehmekaut")

The Lehemann report did outline the fact that Huberhof had a good meadow and considerable undeveloped farmland of the

We depart Huberhof via nearby Dusenbrücken.

"Grosse Hub." As a result, many of the Swiss applied for land grants, but the city fathers of Nünschweiler thought otherwise. Instead of land grants, the land was made available to the Swiss as subtenants. They suffered from excessive fees profiteering as a result. (The government at Zweibrücken stopped this exploitation in 1724.) Between 1705 and 1720, all the work at Huberhof was devoted to the difficult tasks of clearing the land and building wooden huts and barracks.

It was during this period that Christian Wenger (A2) lived here (1713-1718). In this environment, it is little wonder that he decided to make it a temporary stopping-off place and that he would find a better opportunity in America.

From the above we conclude: Christian (A2) must have been a good worker and farmer to have had a stake in Huberhof. Since Drumm regrets his absence from the records after 1718, we conclude that he had a good estimate of Christian Wenger (A2) as a man. Drumm must have been impressed with this record. (Later records in Lancaster County, Pennsylvania, reveal Christian (A2) to have been a Mennonite preacher.) This also affirms the fact that Christian did in fact leave Huberhof; probably arriving in America late in 1718. Christian's (A2) brother, Henry (A1), arrived in America a year earlier.

Zweibrücken and the Palatinate

After the Thirty Years' War, Zweibrücken had a shortage of men and Duke Christian IV of the principality sent word to the Swiss Government to send their surplus of men to his state. This may have encouraged the Swiss during the next half century to exile the Mennonites in increased numbers. So many Swiss came, either voluntarily or involuntarily, that three-quarters of the Zweibrücken population today is of Swiss extraction.

Even so, during those early times religious differences continued and the Anabaptists continued to see trouble. For many, the Zweibrücken was only a temporary abode. Circumstances kept them on the move.

Coincidently during this period of activity in Zweibrücken, the Committee of Burkholder, Zaller and Brackbill continued to seek help for the Palatinate exiles. They appealed to the Dutch for help by making journeys to Amsterdam and Rotterdam. They went to Northern Germany and Lithuania. Upon their return, they were received by King Frederick I. He offered them 62 farms. The Committee had mixed feelings about this proposal, and the exiles were too exhausted to reach a better solution to their problem. The Palatinate Swiss had to endure more and more intolerance. Poverty, floods, failure of crops, and the billeting of foreign soldiers contributed to make their lot overwhelming. They seemed ready to go to America for better or for worse!

At Nijmegen

In February 1717, the elders of the church in Nijmegen decided to call upon the Netherlands authorities to aid in removing the Swiss Mennonite exiles to America. Their pleas were heard and aid was forthcoming. Movement was in the air. Hundreds of the oppressed were going to Pennsylvania which was the asylum for the persecuted of a large body of defenseless Mennonites who had fled from the Cantons of Bern, Zurich and Schaffenhausen.

One of the more imaginative advertisements of the period which was posted in the streets of Dutch towns helped the Anabaptists to make up their minds to go to America. It read: "Many men in Pennsylvania own 500 geese. Bison deer roam the forest. Giant deer stalk the woodland lanes; two hunters stagger beneath the weight of a wild turkey. Indian corn grows free for the taking. Rye heads of prodigious size vie with beets and cabbages of tremendous proportions, and fish struggle to impale themselves on the hook."

The Voyage to America

Events brought Martin Kindig, who substituted for his aged bishop Hans Herr, Sr., of Lancaster County, Pennsylvania, to the Palatinate to extend the invitation to the oppressed to come to that colony. He had retained nearly 10,000 acres in Conestoga, now Lancaster County, to sell to his countrymen at 32¢ an acre and the payment of quitrent .

In February 1717 as a result of Kindig's visit, the Committee of Benedict Brackbill, Hans Burkholder and Melchior Zaller and others held a conference with the Mennonites at Mannheim. They pointed out that the Holland authorities were permitting the Mennonites to cross Holland. As a result, funds were raised and it was decided to provide transportation for all who wanted to go to America. Surnames of many families which came in that year have been available, although passenger lists of specific ships have not been uncovered.

In 1717 and 1718, hundreds came to America. On one voyage three vessels, with 363 passengers, traveled in tandem.

On March 31, 1717, a large group left Mannheim bound for the new country. Dielman Kolb, a Mennonite preacher, headed one of the first groups to undertake the voyage. They arrived in Philadelphia after many heartbreaking delays.

Henry (A1) and Christian (A2) sailed for America in 1717-1718.

The Committee of Brackbill, Burkholder and Zaller were joined by Hans Rub, Peter Donens, and Henry Wenger (A1), as well as scores of others, on a ship which left Mannheim the last week in May. They went down the River Rhine across Holland to Rotterdam, through the English Channel and across the Atlantic, arriving in Philadelphia 12 weeks later on August 24, 1717. The exact date Christian Wenger (A2) and his family, including his mother Verena Krebs Wenger, arrived is unknown. Certainly, it must have been in 1718, since he disappeared from Zweibrücken at that time. One unconfirmed report stated that the third Wenger brother, Hans, also started for America but died at sea. This may or may not be true. There is some indication that Hans, who was 44, arrived in America at a later date. It is definitely known that a Hans Wenger family did reside in Zweibrücken and later came to America. Henry (A1) was 37 and Christian (A2) was 29 years of age. "Old Hans," the "disobedient Anabaptist" father, was 84 at the time and probably remained in Switzerland.

There is considerable confusion surrounding the crossing of ships during this time. Some left Rotterdam, passed through the English Channel and directly across the Atlantic. Others, particularly English ships, stopped at English ports. This created long delays. Some ships, after leaving Gravesend in England, joined the Russian fleet at Harwich which served as an escort as far as the Shetland Islands. This took two weeks. One diary describes the trip as troublesome, not only on account of the many dangers, the tempestuous ocean, the hidden cliffs, sandbanks, and the roving sea robbers and pirates, but because of the hard unhealthy ship's food, intolerable to many, from which people became sick and even died.

In approaching the American shore, the ships always tried to enter the Delaware River as soon as possible to avoid attacks by pirates. One account describes the ship stuck on a sandbank opposite Newcastle. Some passengers went ashore for the first time and met friendly people. They were delighted to receive apples and peaches to take back to the ship. Through it all these humble people always thanked God for a safe arrival in the new country.

This chronicle of Henry (A1) and Christian Wenger (A2) is a composite of the reporting of *The Lancaster County Historical Society Notes*, Vol. 31, p. 59; *Pennsylvania Magazine of History*, Vol. 2; *Swiss and German Pioneer Settlers of Southeast Pennsylvania*, by H. Frank Eshleman and the *Bernese Anabaptists*, by Delbert Gratz, as well as *History of the Franconia Conference and Brief Notes on the Bernese Wengers*, by Dr. John C. Wenger; Müller's book, *Geschichte der Bernischen Taufer*, and the genealogical research in Switzerland by Dr. Gottlieb Kurz, Dr. Robert Oehler and Fritz Allimann.

All were exceedingly useful. Probably the most valuable document in Germany was the Ernest Drumm manuscript, *Zur Teschichte der Mennoniten im Herzogtum Pfalz-Zweibrücken,* compiled by Karl Jost. The Reformed Church records in Zweibrücken were significant and served to totally sustain American and Swiss data. The officials of the Archives in Zweibrücken and the Heimatstelle Pfalz in Kaiserslautern were most helpful. Other invaluable sources were the *Mennonite Research Journal,* particularly, October 1960, and January 1961; Samuel S. Wenger in the *Pennsylvania Dutchman,* July 1949, and the files of Norman Wenger Nauman and those of Rev. Roger D. Winger. All disclosed excellent material.

Genealogical Chart of Henry (A1) and
Christian (A2) Wenger
Projected by John E. Fetzer from
Qualitative Research in Switzerland

1st Hans Wenger (b. About 1430) Blumenstein, Thun

2nd Burkhard Wenger (b. About 1450) Forst, Thun

3rd Peter Wenger (b. About 1470) Wattenwil, Seftigen

4th Peter Wenger (b. About 1490) Wattenwil, Seftigen

5th Rudolfus Wenger, Esq. (b. About 1510)
Wattenwil-Thurnen, Seftigen

6th   B-1 Hans Wenger
            b. About 1530, Wattenwil-Thurnen, Seftigen
            m. Dichtle (Benedicta) Wenger
            about 1550, Thurnen

        C-1 Hans Wenger
            Ch. Sept. 20, 1551, Wattenwil-Thurnen
            Sp. Hans Nussbaum, N. Eyer, Christina Bäler

        C-2 Ulli Wenger
            Ch. April 23, 1553, Wattenwil-Thurnen
            Sp. D. Bäler, Ruff Bernhart, Margreth Wenger

        C-3 Peter Wenger
            Ch. Sept. 20, 1556, Wattenwil-Thurnen
            Sp. Peter Henni, Urs Krenger, Anna Krenger

        C-4 Christian Wenger
            Ch. Mar. 19, 1559, Wattenwil-Thurnen
            Sp. Hans Brönnimann, Peter Springen,
                Madlen Bäler

        C-5 Anna Wenger
            Ch. Jan. 9, 1561, Wattenwil-Thurnen
            Sp. Anna Aebischwiler, Barbli Kükler,
                David Bäler

C-6 Rudolfus Wenger (Died in infancy)
     Ch. Sept. 3, 1564, Wattenwil-Thurnen
     Sp. Christian Krebs, Benedict Messerli,
     Benedicta Schmid

7th   C-7 Rudolfus Wenger
     Ch. April 5, 1566, Wattenwil-Thurnen, Seftigen
     Sp. Thomas Schmidt, Melchior Kunkler,
     Anna Wenger
     m. Gredy (Margreth) Pfister,
     June 5, 1590, Thurnen

     D-1 Hans Wenger
         Ch. Nov. 14, 1591, Wattenwil-Thurnen
         Sp. Batt Erb, Hans Krebs, Barbli Spring

     D-2 Rudolfus Wenger (Died in infancy)
         Ch. April 15, 1593, Wattenwil-Thurnen
         Sp. Ruff Bachman, Melcher Wyniger,
         Christini Bulffer

     D-3 Rudolfus Wenger
         Ch. June 30, 1594, Wattenwil-Thurnen
         Sp. Hans Biller, Lienhart Nunouw,
         Vroneg Erb

     D-4 Jost Wenger (Died in infancy)
         Ch. Mar. 27, 1596, Wattenwil-Thurnen
         Sp. Hans Jacob Mueller, Hans Bulffer,
         Christine Wyniger

     D-5 Triny Wenger
         Ch. Nov. 6, 1597, Wattenwil-Thurnen
         Sp. Bernhart Künkler, Triny Beller,
         Barbli Bachmann

     D-6 Jost Wenger
         Ch. Feb. 10, 1600, Wattenwil-Thurnen
         Sp. Jorg Krenger, Hans Baumgart, Voerely
         m. Verena Tschäppeler, March 2, 1629,
         Thurnen

       E-1 Anna Wenger
            Ch. Aug. 21, 1631, Wattenwil-Thurnen
            Sp. Benedict Marti, Susanna Michel,
            Margreth Byland

E-2 Hans Wenger (Died young)
    Ch. Jan. 15, 1632, Wattenwil-Thurnen
    Sp. Benedicht Bäler, Jonas Jordi,
        Barbil Kisling

E-3 Christina Wenger
    Ch. Jan. 26, 1634, Wattenwil-Thurnen
    Sp. Sir Rudolf V. Luthernau,
        Christina Tschäppeler and Ursula Schnell

E-4 Christian Wenger
    Ch. Mar. 6, 1636, Wattenwil-Thurnen
    Sp. Christian Wichtermann, Hans Wenger,
        Madlen Berner

E-5 Verena Wenger
    Ch. Aug. 19, 1638, Wattenwil-Thurnen
    Sp. Ulli Nurger, Anna Kohler,
        Elsbeth Balsiger

E-6 Elsbeth Wenger
    Ch. Dec. 19, 1641, Wattenwil-Thurnen
    Sp. Hans Springer, Salome Kunkler,
        Elsbeth Buchi

E-7 Jost Wenger
    Ch. Oct. 22, 1643, Wattenwil-Thurnen
    Sp. Pastor David Rämerstal, Jost Springen,
        Elsbeth Bulfer
    m. Anna Messerli
        Ch. June 30, 1673, Wattenwil-Thurnen

  F-1 Elsi (Elsbeth) Wenger
      b. June 24, 1674, Wattenwil-Thurnen
      Sp. Hans Wichtermann, Anna Bulfer,
         Elsi Schappeler

E-8 Christian Wenger
    Ch. Dec. 13, 1646, Wattenwil-Thurnen
    Sp. Christian Spring, Ruff Zender,
        Vroenek Zingenberg, pastor's wife

E-9 Cathrin Wenger
    Ch. Sept. 10, 1648, Wattenwil-Thurnen
    Sp. Melcher Kunkler, Anna Wenger,
        Elsbeth Springen

E-10 Salome Wenger
Ch. Nov. 30, 1651, Wattenwil-Thurnen
Sp. Bendicht Zender, Anna Zender,
Verena Messerli

E-11 Hans Wenger
Ch. June 14, 1657, Wattenwil-Thurnen
Sp. Hans Springer, Uli Messerli,
Elsbeth Tischer

D-7 Peter Wenger
Ch. Dec. 13, 1601 (Died in infancy),
Wattenwil-Thurnen
Sp. Peter Zender, Hans Erismann,
Maria Steinmann

D-8 Anna Wenger
Ch. Aug. 7, 1603, Wattenwil-Thurnen
Sp. Peter Balsinger, Elsbeth Balsinger,
Anna Zeender

D-9 Melcher Wenger
Ch. Dec. 1605, Wattenwil-Thurnen
Sp. Melcher Billet, Felix Tschäppeler,
Anna Mischler

8th   D-10 Peter Wenger
Ch. Dec. 13, 1607, Wattenwil-Thurnen,
Seftigen
Sp. Wolf Hofmann, Baschi Messerli,
Barbara Glantzmann
m. Salome Blatter before 1625, Thurnen

E-1 Elsbeth Wenger
Ch. Dec. 4, 1625, Wattenwil-Thurnen
Sp. Jost Wenger, Elsbeth Balsinger,
Barbel Nussbaum

E-2 Peter Wenger
Ch. July 13, 1628 (Died young)
Sp. Wolfgang Schnell, Hans Nussbaum,
Anna Berger

E-3 Melcher Wenger
 Ch. Jan. 24, 1630 (Died in infancy)
 Wattenwil-Thurnen
 Sp. Melcher Nussbaum, Jacob Langhans,
  Salome Düggeli

E-4 Melcher Wenger
 Ch. Apr. 1631, Wattenwil-Thurnen
 Sp. Melcher Kunkler, Peter Winzenried,
  Christina N.
 m. Barbar Wenger before 1658

 F-1 Peter Wenger
  Ch. May 23, 1658, Wattenwil-Thurnen
  Sp. Melcher Mettler, Benedict Baeler,
   Elsbeth Meyer

 F-2 Madlena Wenger
  Ch. May 26, 1661, Wattenwil
  Sp. Nans Mettler, Madlena Blatner,
   Madlena Portner
  m. Benedict Wenger, 1681, Wattenwil

  G-1 Barbara Wenger
   b. 1683

9th E-5 Hans Wenger
  Ch. May 30, 1633, Wattenwil-Thurnen,
   Seftigen
  Sp. Adam Wysshan, Christian Dällenbrack,
   Anna Wenger
  m. Verena Krebs, June 17, 1662,
   Wattenwil-Thurnen

 F-1 Hans Wenger
  Ch. Sept. 13, 1663, Wattenwil
  Sp. Peter Wenger, Hans Kisslig,
   Elsbeth Wenger

 F-2 Anna Wenger
  Ch. Feb. 4, 1667, Wattenwil-Thurnen
  Sp. Daniel Zimmermann, Elsbeth Doeni,
   Barbara Jausi

F-3 Barbara Wenger
      Ch. Nov. 22, 1669, Wattenwil-Thurnen
      Sp. Daniel Baeler, Barbara Baeler,
      Anna Karebs

F-4 Verena Wenger
      Ch. Nov. 1, 1672, Wattenwil-Thurnen
      Sp. Bendicht Megert, Barbara von
      Niderhuesern, Verena Zimmerman

F-5 Heinrich Wenger (Died in infancy)
      Ch. June 18, 1675
      Sp. Bendicht Gilgen, Hans Kisslig,
      Barbara Wanger

F-6 Elsbeth Wenger
      Ch. Aug. 4, 1676, Wattenwil-Thurnen
      Sp. Bendicht Juentzi, Christina Roth,
      Catharina Loew

10th   F-7 Heinrich (Henry A1) Wenger (10th generation in Switzerland, 1st generation in America)
      Ch. Feb. 13, 1680, Wattenwil-Thurnen, Seftigen
      Sp. Christen Baeler, Hans Cappeler, Verena Wanger
      m. Elsi (Elsbeth) Blum before 1705

11th   G-1 Hans Wenger
        b. 1706, Wattenwil-Thurnen
        Ch. Feb. 17, 1709, Rothenbach
        Sp. Hans Schindler, Hans Straam, Elsbeth Schindler

11th   G-2 Heinrich Wenger
        b. 1708, Wattenwil-Thurnen
        Ch. Feb. 17, 1709, Rothenbach
        Sp. Andres Straam,
          Benedicht Schindler, Babi Müller

F-8 Maria Wenger
      Ch. Jan. 18, 1684, Wattenwil-Thurnen
      Sp. Christen Freyenberg, Anna Rohr,
      Verena Stuedler

10th   F-9   Christian Wenger (A2) (10th generation in Switzerland, 1st generation in America)
                   b. About 1688,Territory of Buchholterberg, Thun
                   m. Catharina (Barbara) Bertschy, Jan. 16, 1714, at Huberhof, Zweibrücken, Germany

11th   G-1   Johannes Jacob Wenger
                   b. July 29, 1715, Huberhof, Zweibrücken

11th   G-2   Johannes Heinrich Wenger (Henry Wenger, Sr. A22)
                   b. July 26, 1716, Huberhof, Zweibrücken

11th   G-3   Anna Catharina Wenger
                   b. Aug. 21, 1718, Huberhof, Zweibrücken

     E-6   Margreth Wenger
            Ch. Nov. 29, 1635, Wattenwil-Thurnen
            Sp. Rudolf Stüerler, Margreth Funerer, Elsbeth Steiner

     E-7   Peter Wenger
            Ch. April 22, 1638, Wattenwil-Thurnen
            Sp. Hans Wenger, Jost Wenger, Margreth Leuw

     E-8   Veronica Wenger
            Ch. Jan. 13, 1640, Wattenwil-Thurnen
            Sp. Christoffel Zender, Veronica Zingenberg, Barbli Krebs

   D-11 Dichtle Wenger
            Ch. Nov. 18, 1610, Wattenwil-Thurnen
            Sp. Peter Schnell, Dichtli Wuel, Susanna Glanzman

   C-8   Benedicta Wenger
            Ch. June 11, 1570
            Sp. Benedicta Baler, Margreth Krebs, Hans Messerli, Ammann zu Hasli

CHAPTER FOUR

In the New Land

THE YEARS 1717-1718 were times of destiny for the scores of banished Anabaptists. Through all of the turmoil of dislocated and lost families, to say nothing of a hazardous sea voyage, many made a successful landing in Philadelphia. Such familiar names as Shallenberger, Stauffer, Binkley, Frei, Hoffman, Zimmerman, Meier, Kratzer, Roth, Sommer, Stettler, Haldiman, Strohm, Eschback, Huber, Rohrer, Sherk, Wisler, Burkholder, Kindig, Zaller, Brackbill and Wenger were among several hundred that found a welcome in the New World.

Henry Wenger (A1) and Christian (A2), our two brothers from the left and right banks of the rivers Aare and Gürbe in Switzerland, made successful crossings in 1717 and 1718.

The young men must have looked forward to the bounty of the new land. William Penn had described southeastern Pennsylvania as having "living creatures," such as "fowl, and the beasts of the woods of diverse sorts, some for food and profit. . . . the elk, as big as a small ox; deer bigger than in England; beaver, raccoon, rabbits, squirrels and young bear." He stated there were 40-pound turkeys, pheasants, heath birds, pigeons, and partridges in abundance and described eight different kinds of fish.

Another writer said, "The fruits which I find in the woods are the black and white mulberry, chestnut, walnut, plums, strawberries, cranberries, burtleberries, and grapes of diverse sorts."

Advanced billing such as this was a major incentive to make for the land posthaste.

Henry (A1) to Hanover

From Philadelphia Henry (A1) made his way westward along the Schuylkill River to a location in Hanover Township in what is now the borough of Pottstown at the junction of Montgomery, Chester and Berks Counties, Pennsylvania. At that point he pondered sites for prospective farm land. Having been a weaver in Wattenwil and a farmer in the Palatinate, Henry (A1) liked the wide open spaces in that locality because the trees were smaller and it was easier to clear the land. He knew there would be hard manual work, in contrast to working as a weaver, and his experience as a farmer told him to be selective with the workload. He may have been influenced also by Preacher Dielman Kolb who also came from Mannheim in 1717. The preacher was to establish a Mennonite parish at nearby Solford. On September 15, 1718, a year after his arrival in Philadelphia, Henry (A1) bought 100 acres from Ludwig Christian Sprogell. This parcel is now a part of the borough of Pottstown.

Henry Wenger (A1) was christened February 13, 1680, in the parish of Wattenwil, Switzerland. He married Elsie Blum prior to 1705 in the same parish. They had two children, born in or near Wattenwil. Hans Wenger (A11) was born in 1706 and Heinrich (A12) in 1708.

It is not known if Hans (A11) and Heinrich (A12) Wenger, the sons of Henry (A1), were brought to America or whether they grew to manhood. So many of the Mennonite families were dislocated that death often took the young. It is known, however, that Wengers by the name of Hans and Heinrich did come to America later in the 18th Century.

Henry (A1) was the founder of a long line of Wenger families which is well documented in local county histories in Eastern Pennsylvania. He died in 1753 and was buried in the Mennonite graveyard, East Coventry. He was survived by nine known children who married into the Brower, Switzer, Heistand, DeHaven, Souder and Wisler families. A partial family tree may be found in the Library of Congress in Washington and in the Appendix here. For further references, see Biographical Sketches, Berks County, Pennsylvania; also Chester County Biographical Sketches, Honorable Irving Price Wanger, p. 56, and Wanger Family in the History of Chester County, Pennsylvania, p. 756.

A drawing of an original believed to be Christian Wenger (A2).

Christian Wenger (A2) to Lancaster County

Mennonite tradition states that the families of Henry (A1) and Christian (A2) Wenger did not all come to America at the same time. This is certainly true with Henry (A1) whose Swiss-born sons do not appear in American records, but in Christian's (A2) case, we believe he brought his mother, wife and three children with him. A traditional story from Ohio states that "one ancestor was brought to America when he was two years old." Indeed, this has proved to be accurate. Christian's (A2) second son, Johannes Heinrich (Henry Wenger A22), was born in Zweibrücken. Since Christian (A2) and his family disappeared from the Zweibrücken records in 1718, we believe this pinpoints the fact that all of the family came in that year, bringing with them their two-year-old son, Henry Wenger (A22), who was born in 1716.

In Lancaster County there is also a traditional story that a third brother of Christian (A2), namely Hans, started for America but died en route. This has not been confirmed. At least two Hans Wengers are recorded as having arrived in the forepart of the 18th Century. Both are known to have lived in Zweibrücken and are indicated as having been born in Switzerland. They came to America in 1737 and 1748 and may have had some relationship with this family line. In Zweibrücken certain correspondence in German gives a rather

78

nebulous substantiation to the prior reference that Christian Wenger (A2) brought his family, including his mother, Verena Krebs Wenger, to America. It was inferred that she left Switzerland after the imprisonment of Christian's (A2) father, Hans Wenger, and joined the family at Huberhof, Zweibrücken.

Verena Krebs Wenger, mother of Christian Wenger (A2), an original drawing by Elaine Journet.

It is believed that Christian (A2) and his family, after their arrival in 1718, settled for a short time with Henry (A1) in Hanover Township in the Pottstown area. In any event, Christian's (A2) descendants in Ohio often said that "one Wenger ancestor of German origin came to Lancaster County from a place called Hanover."

In due course Christian Wenger (A2) decided that he would travel farther west where he was to find sugar maple, hickory, and black and white walnut trees in abundance. He felt that in spite of the additional hard work, the soil would be so enriched by the humus from these trees that he could develop a more productive farm, particularly wheat. He found 100 acres between the "Conestoga and Mill Creeks," which is now Upper Leacock Township, Lancaster County, Pennsylvania. Here, probably in 1719, he staked his claim for land. His first Taylor Survey was completed in 1721 and duly recorded in 1735. (C234-255 Land Office, Harrisburg.)

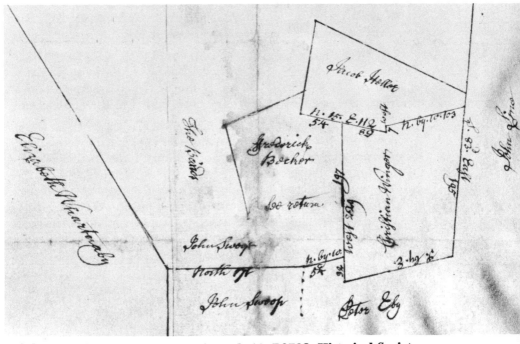

**The original Taylor survey made June 22, 1721, covering land be-
tween "Conestoga and Mill Creeks," for Christian Wenger (A2).**

**A later Taylor survey, recorded in Vol. 13, P2738, Historical Society
of Pennsylvania.**

Our records, as previously reported, confirm the fact that Christian Wenger (A2), founder of our American Clan in Lancaster County, married Anna Catharina Bertschy on January 16, 1714, at Huber-hof, Zweibrücken, Germany. They had three children, all born at

Barbara Catharina Bertschy Wenger, wife of Christian Wenger (A-2).

Huberhof. Johannes Jacob Wenger (A21) was born July 29, 1715; Johannes Heinrich (Henry) Wenger (A22) was born July 26, 1716, and Anna Catharina (A23) was born August 21, 1718.

The Zweibrücken correspondence referred to above indicates that Johannes Jacob Wenger (A21) died at the age of thirteen and Anna Catharina (A23) died at the age of five. If this unconfirmed report is true, these children would have been buried in the family cemetery on the Upper Leacock farm.

The Wengers had at least three more sons and possibly additional daughters, all born in America. The additional three known children were Abraham (A24), Christian (A25) and Michael (A26). Of the six known children of Christian (A2), with the exception of Henry (A22), very little is known about Johannes Jacob (A21) and Anna Catharina (A23), and practically no signficant information has been preserved concerning Abraham (A24), Christian (A25) and Michael (A26). With the exception of John Henry (A22), all had passed away before 1762.

As discussed earlier, Christian (A2), in addition to his brother, Henry (A1), had another brother Hans (b. 1663) and five sisters as follows: Anna (b. 1667), Barbara (b. 1669), Verena (b. 1672), Elizabeth (b. 1676), and Maria (b. 1684). All these were born at or near Wattenwil. It is known that there were at least three single women by the name of Elizabeth and two by the name of Anna Wenger who at one time or another were in the Palatinate. In Lancaster County there was an Elizabeth Wenger who was a Sister at the Ephrata Cloister, the first Protestant monastery in America. She died about 1745. We speculate that she could have been Christian Wenger's (A2) sister, Elizabeth, who was born in 1676 in Switzerland. The original Society at Ephrata started in 1708 in Germany and after much persecution emigrated to America in 1719. After 1723 a congregation was established at Mill Creek not far from the Christian Wenger (A2) homestead.

Conrad Beissel, a native of Eberbach, not far from Huberhof where Christian Wenger (A2) lived in Germany, became a militant leader of the sect at Mill Creek. He published a tract which caused considerable controversy and, as a result, a congregation was established at Ephrata.

Mill Creek, an environment of Wenger action.

Anna and Mary Eicher and many others of the Mill Creek congregation followed to Ephrata. Elizabeth Wenger, referred to above, could have been in the Mill Creek congregation since her brother,

Christian Wenger (A2), was in that area. It should be noted that the Ephrata Cloister was similar to the Huberhof Cloister which was affiliated with the Hornbacker Monastery in Zweibrücken, the German home of Christian Wenger (A2).

We cannot with certainty identify any of the sisters or brothers of Christian (A2) as having come to America with the possible exception of Elizabeth. Again, according to the unconfirmed Zweibrücken correspondence, Elizabeth, Christian's (A2) sister, was reported as being in Pennsylvania.

Problems of Given Names

One of the difficult problems in family research among the German families was the habit of naming several children with a common first name, followed by a distinctive second name. This practice of using two given names, particularly the name of Johannes for the boys and Anna for the girls, stems from a custom in vogue before the Reformation. Saint Johannes (St. John the Baptist) was regarded as a very influential and helpful Saint. Thus Johannes was chosen as first patron for each male child. Saint Anna, the Mother of Holy Mary, was similarly regarded and was often chosen as the first patron for each female child. Later, the children chose freely between the use of the first and second names for common designation. Sometimes the children, particularly the girls, used altogether different first or second names in an attempt to end the conflict of designations. A classic example is the case of Henry Wenger (A1). When he was married in Switzerland his wife was designated as "Elsie." In America she was called "Elizabeth." Christian Wenger (A2) married in Huberhof, Zweibrücken, "Anna Catharina" Bertschy, according to the records there. After their arrival in America "Anna" became "Barbara" and "Catharina" disappeared. The birth records in Zweibrücken record the name "Johannes Heinrich Wenger" (A22). In America most of the family knew him simply as Henry Wenger (A22). Johannes was not a name known by many of his descendants.

Some members of the family had transmuted "Johannes" to "Hans." Thus Henry Wenger (A22) became Hans Heinrich Wenger (A22) in some quarters. Indeed, some of our Canadian descendants insist that John Henry Wenger's (A22) son, Adam Wenger (A221), was the son of "Old Hans" Wenger. Since "Old Hans" has been freely assigned to several old patriarchs, more than a little confusion has resulted. All this disorder required meticulous search for additional evidential material to assure accurate identification. We have pursued this research tenaciously and are satisfied that the probability for error is minimal.

Action Line

After building a log hut in 1719 Christian Wenger (A2) commenced to do battle with the forest and clear a small piece of land for cultivation. As the years went by, he made considerable improvement to the Wenger land located on Mill Creek near Heller's Church in Leacock Township. The records show that he and his sons were quite self-sufficient. To clear the land, strong backs and brawny

Heller's Church, founded in 1725, is a landmark near the Christian Wenger (A2) home.

arms were needed. To cut the trees and underbrush and to dig out grubs, they used the early version of the saw, the axe, the mattock, the spade and the maul. Two splendid yokes of oxen with long log chains snaked the logs where needed. Then the hoe and reaphook found appropriate use. These implements, for the most part, are interpreted from the Christian Wenger (A2) inventory of December 21, 1749.

To cultivate the soil, crude wooden moldboards were used as plows. The wheels of the wagons were cut from wooden blocks, probably the start of the wheelwrights in the coming generations. Harnesses for the horses were made from hickory withes.

As the land was cleared, early versions of the log house came along. The homes and the manner of living were primitive in the extreme. The typical house was a small round log cabin without nails and with little or no glass. Greased paper or thin animal tissues were used to let in light. A short puncheon with pegs fastened to it served as a chair and the bedstead was of rails held up by forked sticks. Plates were generally made of wood and, rarely, of pewter. The wash tub was a trough referred to in the inventory as "belly-tubs." In fair weather the door was left open to let in more light. By night illumination was from the fireplace, a tallow dip, a pork rind or a saucer of lard with a twisted rag for a wick. A substitute for the saucer lamp was a broken teacup, a scooped-out turnip or a frying pan with its handle stuck into a chink between the logs. If pine were convenient, its pitchy knots and "fatted wood" were sometimes used.

Personal Needs and Recrimination

It goes without saying that the men had long beards. They wore long red caps and plain clothes made of coarse material. The women had neither bonnets, hats nor caps, using only a string to keep the hair back. Their petticoats just covered the knee, a habit which attracted the English settlers.

During the winter months the spinning wheel and loom produced linsey and toe linen. Also there was basket weaving, wood turning, and cabinet making. Many long winter days and evenings were spent with all members of the family working at some handicraft. Linen was used for clothing for themselves and they usually had some left over to sell. During the summer all helped in the fields from daylight till dark.

Families were large as was the case in most pioneer communities. Eight children in a family was average, while twelve or more was often the rule. Christian (A2) and Barbara Wenger had four known sons who lived to maturity. At a young age there were tasks and odd jobs that were done by the children. Little time was spent in play. Strict discipline was the order of the day. They were kind to one another without demonstration and the best of relations usually existed among the family and neighbors. Disagreements were settled peacefully, sometimes with the help of the church. Religion played an important part in the family life. It was customary to hold morning worship and ask for guidance and strength for the day's labors. In the evening devotion was held to thank God for his care during the day. God's blessing was always invoked at mealtime. Bible study was stressed and often the children were required to learn selected scripture by heart.

The fireplace not only served to heat the one all-purpose room but served the cooking needs as well. The inventory mentioned three iron kettles, seven spoons, bottles and drinking glasses, a nutcracker and six kitchen utensils.

All was peace and quiet and Christian Wenger (A2) was earnestly engaged in securing a comfortable home. In developing the comforts of the home, the Christian Wenger (A2) inventory does not list complete household furnishings because many of these items automatically went to Barbara, Christian's (A2) widow. However, it should be noted that a large Pennsylvania chest was listed, as well as two deckel beds with bedding and pillows and an "over and under bed" with pillow and bedding. Also two barrels of cider were on hand to augment the warmth of the hearth.

The Christian Wenger (A2) inventory of December 21, 1749, stated his clothes, including neckerchiefs, handkerchiefs, neckties, scarves, and eight pairs of boots had a total value of approximately eight pounds.

Hamlets

Little communities, generally at crossroads, began to spring up. As the white settlements increased in number and extent, they surrounded the old Indian villages. Indian hunting grounds became circumscribed and game was comparatively scarce. This created great dismay among the Indians whose happy hunting grounds were disappearing. They gradually ceased to hunt for game in this region and became persistent beggars among the settlers. They made brooms and willow baskets which they bartered for food and fire water. Christian Wenger (A2) or his sons had a still, but there is no record of them having dealt with the Indians. Moreover, the Indians depended upon the proprietary authorities to furnish them with what little clothing they had or needed. This restlessness among the Indians and settlers, who were constantly pushing the Indians to the west, caused endless trouble. The stories are legion of killings and retribution between the whites and Indians.

Indian Teachings

The Indians taught many useful things to the white man. He had his own house raising and husking bees; he showed the white settler how to clear his land by deadening the trees; how to make deer-skin sieves and how to use medicinal herbs; how to utilize corn husks and how to prepare the corn for food in new ways. The custom of the frontiersman was an approach to the life style of the native and sometimes his cabin was no more tidy.

The white settlers were in constant dread of attacks from wild beasts of the forest which prowled around the log cabins at night and destroyed or carried away fowl and domestic animals.

According to Rupp, the Mennonites feared wolves and panthers the most. These animals committed great depredations, especially among the sheep. The hunters would laugh at the Amish, because the latter would not attempt to destroy wild animals. The Amish said, in justification, that "they considered it a crime to deprive any of God's creatures of life, except those which God gave us for our use; and that to instruct youth in the use of firearms would be to lead them to eternal ruin."

It was the policy of the courts to offer bounties for the scalps of wild animals which disturbed new settlements, in the hope that these inducements would stimulate the hunters. More than half of the bounty payments were made to Indians. After the organization of Lancaster County, the bounties paid for wolves, fox and squirrel scalps increased markedly and, as a result, became quite a burden to the taxpayers.

The Settlements

After the year 1725, the settlements within the present territory of Lancaster County increased and spread much more rapidly than before. While no towns or villages were laid out, the most important and most widely known points for gatherings were the taverns, which were designed to meet the requirements of the ever-increasing volume of immigration and travel along the routes on which they were generally located. One of these was kept by John Postlethwait at a point on Conestoga Creek near Rockville in Conestoga Township. There was a public house kept by Francis Jones at the Gap near where Abraham Wenger (A222) settled years later; another was kept by Wendell Bowman in what is now Strasburg Township where many Wenger and Barr families were to reside; in Beaver Valley in the same township Samuel Taylor had a tavern and a gristmill. Mary Denney had a tavern near Chikis Creek. There were three or four taverns along the Old Peters Road. Jacob Barr lived and kept a tavern near where the Old Peters Road crossed the Horseshoe Road.

The Eby Mills

The grist and sawmills and occasionally a fulling mill and a hemp mill or oil mill were places of note, as widely known as the taverns, and much more useful to life in the community than the latter. Near the Christian Wenger (A2) cabin, Doris Eby had a mill located on Mill Creek. Theodorus (Doris) Eby and his sons were builders of mills. They were skilled and resourceful men. They erected and operated a chain of mills in Leacock, Earl, Warwick, Cocalico, and Elizabeth Townships. It is known that Theodorus Eby had a mill on May 31, 1726, because a road petition of that date refers to the mill in naming the proposed route. This may have been the Eby Mill on Mill Creek near the Christian Wenger (A2) homestead. The Ebys and the Wengers later were to develop family ties of consequence. Peter Eby, prominent son of Theodorus, owned a large acreage adjacent to Christian Wenger (A2). It is known that the Ebys had at least three mills on Mill Creek. Probably the most famous mill established by Theodorus Eby, later known as Rien's Mill, Roland's Mill, Hoover Mill and Old Dutch Mill, was to play a significant role in the Revolutionary War. This mill was located at the junction of Earl, Leacock, and Upper Leacock Townships near the junction of Old Peters Road and Mill Creek.

Food and shelter were the essential ingredients to the life and development of the county. The Eby grist and sawmills played their part; the gristmills for food and the sawmills for timber to supply shelter. Almost the total wealth first consisted of logs. These were taken to the mills and exchanged for flour, meal and cut lumber.

A typical Lancaster County mill.

Long rows of wagons loaded with corn, wheat, oats and rye would line up at the mill site, waiting for their turn at the loading platform. The mills were places where the settlers in the new country met and intermingled more freely and generally than anywhere else except places of public religious worship.

Brotherly Love

Gratz says, "that among the Swiss Mennonites in Pennsylvania, many houses were built with the aid of neighbors. House raisings and barn raisings were big events. For the children, this was frolic, but for the men it meant much hard work. If the frame was not already assembled, the men toiled diligently until it was ready to be raised. After the boards were cut into proper lengths, they were nailed together in the form of a section, then when all was ready, they would put the end logs in the holes made for them at the corner, then raised the beams into place by means of poles with spikes on the ends. Once in place, they were fastened by means of wooden pegs. The men next nailed the first layer of boards on the frame. After the sides were completed, the roof boards were nailed.

These were followed by hand-hewn shingles. It was in this manner that their homes and barns were built. After the work was done, long tables were spread with a sumptuous meal."

Other cooperative enterprises included husking bees, log rollings, and aiding some member of the community who was sick by harvesting a crop for him.

A modern version of a barn raising in Lancaster County.

The Meeting Houses

Few, if any, church edifices or meeting houses had been built in this region at that time. The services of the different denominations, particularly the Mennonites, were held at the dwellings of the settlers most centrally and conveniently located.

Christian Wenger (A2) had left Switzerland, his home country, because he was willing to take a stand for his spiritual convictions. It is believed that his home was amply prepared to hold religious services. As we shall see later, Christian Wenger (A2) was an early minister among the Mennonites. His inventory discloses an old German Bible that probably contained all the family records. In addition he had an Old Testament, a prayer book and psalmbook, all in German. He also had *A Golden Apple in a Silver Basket*. This was a popular devotional book published in German in 1745 at Ephrata, Pennsylvania. Gratz says this book is still sought by the Amish and some Mennonites. Today it is considered a collector's item. Christian (A2) also had a *Question Book Catechism,* which is believed to be a forerunner to a catechism in *Questions and Answers* which was formally published in 1783 by the Mennonites.

The Latter Days

It is evident that Christian Wenger (A2) spent the rest of his life, until the time of his death in 1749, clearing the land and developing his home. By the time his first survey was completed by Isaac Taylor on June 22, 1721, he had cleared 100 acres. The land was warranted in 1735 (C234-255 Harrisburg) and was described as "Christian Wenger, 100 acres on a branch of Mill Creek in Chester County, now Lancaster County." Please note the photocopy of this survey from the files of the Land Office, Bureau of the Department of Public Affairs, Commonwealth of Pennsylvania.

In the Historical Society of Pennsylvania, Manuscript Department, the Taylor Papers, Vol. 5, No. 859, describe the transaction as follows:

> At the request of Christian Wenger of the County of Lancaster that we grant him to take up one hundred and fifty Acres of Land in Leacock Township adjoining to John Lines Land in the said County of Lancaster for which he agrees to pay to our use at the rate of Fifteen pounds ten shillings current money of this Province for one hundred acres and the yearly Quit-rent of an half penny sterling for every Acre thereof; these are to authorize and require thee to survey or cause to be surveyed unto the said Christian Wenger at the Place aforesaid, according to the Method of Township appointed, the said quantity of 150 Acres that hath not been already surveyed or appropriated, and make Return thereof into the Secretary's Office, in order for a further Confirmation; which Survey, in case the said Christian Wenger fulfill the above Agreement within six months from the Date hereof, shall be valid, otherwise to be void.
>
> GIVEN under MY HAND, and the Lesser Seal of our Province, at Philadelphia this 28th Day of November Anno Dom. 1735.
>
> Thomas Penn

Christian Wenger's (A2) hard work set the stage for his son, Henry, Sr. (A22), to farm with fidelity and success. Near his final days Christian Wenger (A2) had acquired all the necessary farm ingredients. He had a mare and filly, nine sheep, seven calves and three swine. He had three wagons, including a conestoga, a plow, a harrow and an assortment of implements and tools. Moreover, the old home place had a windmill and a water system. Perhaps such items as a coach saddle, a wagon saddle, a straw bench, three sieves and a half bushel, a corn screen and fan, and duck equipment had a depth of meaning in 1749; however, in this day it only adds to the wonder of it all. These elements were used to build a homestead that has stood for over 200 years.

Christian Wenger's (A2) Will

In Christian Wenger's (A2) will (J-1-338 Lancaster), dated November 4, 1749, he made provision for his children and widow and decreed that a minister of the church should act as coexecutor. After Christian Wenger's (A2) death, the Christian Wenger (C) of Groffdale in Earle Township, Lancaster County, as a Mennonite minister acted in this capacity. This implies that Christian Wenger (A2), as a preacher and farmer, might have been one of the first ministers in the Lancaster County Mennonite Mill Creek congregation. The *Pennsylvania Dutchman* III, 11 (November 1, 1951, pp. 1, 5, 6) states that the Moravian missionary diary of George Hantsch, Sr., indicates that he visited Christian Wenger, a preacher, on July 16, 1748. Christian Wenger (C), the emigrant of 1727, who resided at Groffdale, was not ordained until 1749. Since the first Christian Wenger (A2) died a year after George Hantsch's visit, it suggests that Christian Wenger (A2) of 1718 was the prior minister and that Christian Wenger (C) of 1727 was his successor. Missionary George Hantsch, Sr., entered the following in his diary: "Then to Christian Wenger's, a preacher, who was quite friendly to us. Our visit at their place went off well for us. We could speak from the heart with him." The Moravian George Hantsch, Sr., was an itinerant minister who carried his message to many places in Lancaster County. This led to the establishment of the Lititz community in Warwick Township. At the direction of Count Zinzendorf, the Moravian leader, the name "Lititz" was given after the Barony of Lititz in Bohemia where the congregation was founded after the martyrdom of John Hus about 1415.

To me, this entry of George Hantsch's indicates much concerning the character of Christian Wenger (A2) and his Mennonite family. They were open-hearted in their reception of Hantsch as a missionary. They apparently were susceptible to "waiting, witnessing and finding," whereas Jacob Summy whom Hantsch had visited earlier in the day was not. The Hantsch visit with Summy was brief due to his preoccupation. As will be seen later, Jacob Summy was named in Christian Wenger's (A2) will as guardian for Barbara Wenger and her children.

It should be noted that the first Mennonite meeting house at Groffdale near the home of Christian Wenger (C) was built of logs in 1755, some five or six years after the death of Christian Wenger (A2). Undoubtedly, prior to 1755 meetings were held in the homes of the members.

In all probability Christian Wenger's (A2) health prompted him to make his will on November 4, 1749. He must have died soon thereafter for his inventory was certified December 21, 1749, and his executors recommended terms of settlement to the Probate Court on May 24, 1750. He died either in November or December 1749. Christian Wenger (C) of 1727 and the other executors dutifully signed the inventory and the recommended terms of settlement.

The will, recorded in Will Book J-1-338 Lancaster County, raises the question as to whether or not Christian Wenger (A2) had unnamed sons and daughters that might have died young or for other reasons were not recorded. The translators, in converting the German to English, had difficulty with the photocopy because folds of the will had obscurred certain words, including a possible "oldest daughter" or "old doctor." If the will refers to "old doctor," the reference could apply to a common name for Dr. Hans Henry Neff who was a large landowner in the county in the early days.

We believe the following quote from the Henry Wenger, Sr., (A22) land patent of 1762 clarifies the problem:

> AND WHEREAS the said Christian Wenger settled and made considerable improvements on the said tract of land before surveyed and died possessed thereof and in and by his last Will and Testament dated the fourth day of November, one thousand seven hundred and forty-nine ordered and directed that his estate should be equally divided among his children Abraham, Christian and Michael providing thereout for Barbara, his wife, in a particular Manor therein mentioned as in and by the said Will duly proved appears AND WHEREAS all the children of the said testator are since dead intestate without issue before any partitioner or

division of the said tract of land or any survey thereof was made except the said Henry, the eldest son, and Abraham, the second son, AND WHEREAS the said Barbara Wenger, the widow, and the said Abraham have by their deed of the second day of January last past bargained, sold and convey all their estate title and interest in the said tract of land unto the said Henry Wenger in fee for the consideration therein mentioned and the said Henry Wenger having paid of our full purchase monies interest and quit rent hath now humbly besought us to grant him our patent of confirmation for the same tract of land which was surveyed at his instance.

From this it can be ascertained that Henry, Sr., (A22) and Abraham (A24) were the only two children alive in 1762. Further, the remainder of the unnamed children, including Christian (A25) and Michael (A26), died without issue. We also conclude that the deacons of the church approved Henry's (A22) acquisition of the farm. We believe, therefore, that the following is a correct translation of the original German will:

IN THE NAME OF GOD, AMEN. I, Christian Wenger, of the Township of Leacock, in the County of Lancaster and Province of Pennsylvania, farmer, being of sound mind, memory and understanding, do make and declare this my last Will and Testament.

IMPRIMIS: It is my will that after my decease that my just debts shall be paid and satisfied and that my wife and children shall keep house together and that the land on which I have made a down payment to the Proprietor shall be paid off as fast as they are able before they receive their inheritance and I appoint Mr. Bennawit of our congregation to act as supervisor. Further, when the commitment to pay for the land is satisfied and a patent is received, the executor and deacons of my church shall decide whether one of my children can hold the land and pay the others their equal inheritance. If they agree that this cannot be done, then they shall sell the land and the Old Doctor shall have the other part.

ITEM: I give to my wife, Barbara Wenger, her third part of all of my possessions, and her living as long as she shall remain a widow, but if she remarries, she shall have only her third part of the aforesaid goods.

ITEM: I appoint Mr. Jacob Summy as my guardian to take care of my wife and children, and to see that they are properly provided for, and the inheritance rightly divided.

ITEM: It is my will that all my children shall have an equal share, the eldest the same as the youngest, the girls the same as the boys. The list of the names of the boys is as follows: The oldest Henry; Abraham, Christian and Michael.

ITEM: I leave to my son, Abraham, 10 pounds in money and two draft horses and to my son, Christian, a colt, because these two sons have been most faithful in helping me to care for them.

94

IN WITNESS WHEREOF, I have subscribed my hand and seal.

4 November 1749   his
Johannes Swoop   Christian (X) Wenger
Christian Sensenig   mark

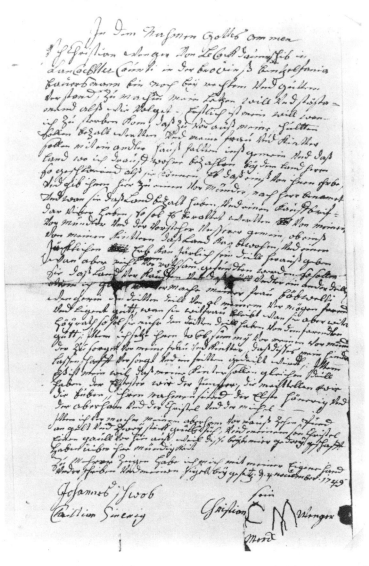

The original Christian Wenger (A2) will in German, dated November 4, 1749.

In Gratitude

With the passing of Christian Wenger (A2) and his brother, Henry (A1), we have covered over 300 years of history that is illustrative of the evolutionary development of our American founding fathers. This trek started in the 14th Century when elementary society decreed that every man should have a surname and thus a "Wenger" was born. His life had to break the bonds of feudalism and earn the right to become a peasant farmer. From the land of Wenger's Hill through the nobility, he became a miller and with it came the battle of conscience.

He became a martyr and bitter persecution caused him to take refuge in the highlands of Switzerland. He moved from the hills to the meadows and then to the streams. He found some status in village civil authority only to keep moving to hamlet, to village, to community, to city and back again to the hills.

He was banished from his country. He returned and a price was put on his head. He worked from sunrise to sunset in a Bernese prison and then was put in a "hole" and attached to iron shackles. He lived on bread and water until the final day of departure. He and scores of others found their way to a new land in the Palatinate of Germany. After years of meager existence as a charge on society, they listened to the voice of William Penn and thus found their way to America.

Here they battled the Indian foe and the wilderness. Daily toil and hardship tried them in the crucible of the right to be free. Freedom to clear the land. Freedom to build a home. Freedom to have a family and freedom to worship according to the tenets of their faith.

This is the story of a lifeline that has left a legacy which helped to develop the American dream. May we all, as Wenger descendants, express our thanks and appreciation to those ancestors that pushed onward and upward that we might have the right to carry on an honorable tradition. While we live, may there be a herculean effort to develop a nation worthy of that great effort. Let us continue with the story of Henry Wenger (A22).

Christian Wenger (A2) Family Tree

1st Hans Wenger (b. About 1430) Blumenstein, Thun

2nd Burkhard Wenger (b. About 1450) Forst, Thun

3rd Peter Wenger (b. About 1470) Wattenwil, Seftigen

4th Peter Wenger (b. About 1490) Wattenwil, Seftigen

5th Rudolfus Wenger (b. About 1510) Wattenwil, Seftigen

6th Hans Wenger (b. About 1530) Wattenwil, Seftigen

7th Rudolfus Wenger (Ch. April 5, 1566) Wattenwil-Thurnen, Seftigen

8th Peter Wenger (Ch. Dec. 13, 1607) Wattenwil-Thurnen, Seftigen

9th Hans Wenger (Ch. May 30, 1633) Wattenwil-Thurnen, Seftigen

    A Christian Wenger (A2) First Generation in America

        b. About 1688, Buchholterberg, Switzerland

        d. 1749, Lancaster County, Pennsylvania

        m. Catharina (Barbara) Bertschy, January 16, 1714, Huberhof, Zweibrücken, Germany

           b. About 1690

           d. About 1765

      B-1 Johannes Jacob Wenger (A21-2nd)

          b. July 29, 1715, Huberhof, Zweibrücken, Germany

          d. Before 1762

      B-2 Johannes Heinrich Wenger (A22-2nd)

          b. July 26, 1716, Huberhof, Zweibrücken, Germany

          d. 1802, Lancaster County, Pennsylvania

          (See following chapter for details)

      B-3 Anna Catharina Wenger (A23-2nd)

          b. August 21, 1718

          d. Before 1762

      B-4 Abraham Wenger (A24-2nd)

          b. About 1721, Lancaster County, Pennsylvania

          d. Before 1762

      B-5 Christian Wenger (A25-2nd)

          b. About 1723, Lancaster County, Pennsylvania

          d. Before 1762

      B-6 Michael Wenger (A26-2nd)

          b. About 1725, Lancaster County, Pennsylvania

          d. Before 1762

CHAPTER FIVE

John Henry Wenger, Sr., of Lancaster County

THE FIFTH day of February, 1762, must have been a proud day for Henry Wenger, Sr. (A22). On that day in the city of Philadelphia James Hamilton, Esquire, in behalf of King George III of Great Britain and Thomas Penn and Richard Penn, the Proprietaries of the Government of Pennsylvania, placed the great Seal of the Province on a much coveted land patent.

That instrument granted Henry Wenger, Sr. (A22), the son of Christian Wenger (A2), 183½ acres in Leacock Township, Lancaster County (Patent Book AA, Vol. 3, p. 70, Philadelphia, 1762). As reported previously, this farm originally had been settled by Henry's father, Christian Wenger (A2), after his arrival in 1718 and surveyed in 1721. Thereafter, it was extended to him through a land warrant under the seal of the land office in Philadelphia in 1735 (C234-255).

In preparation for the land grant in 1762, Henry (A22) at the age of 46 had purchased from his only living brother, Abraham (A23), and his mother, Barbara Wenger, their proprietary interest in the farm. His brothers, Jacob (A21), Christian (A24) and Michael (A25), and his only known sister, Anna (A23), who normally would have inherited an interest in the farm, had already died without issue. Since Henry (A22) had acquired the family homestead, it is apparent that his brother, Abraham (A23), left Lancaster County after 1762. The *Pennsylvania Archives*, Third Series, Vol. 17, p. 625, show Abraham Wenger had 100 acres in Hanover Township in 1779. This was listed as Lancaster County. We believe this Han-

John Henry Wenger, Sr. (A22)

over Township is now in Dauphin County. His father, Christian (A2), may have provided the means of travel by leaving a horse to Abraham (A23) in his last Will and Testament. (H-1-211 Lancaster 1799) (C234-255) We have been unable to trace any pattern which leads to his descendants, if any.

The land survey that Henry, Sr., (A22) had completed that same year revealed that the Wenger farm bordered on the farms of George Lines, Jacob Heller, Peter Eby and Emanuel Carpenter. The tax records of Upper Leacock Township reveal that Henry, Sr., (A22) was getting ahead. He had two horses, three cattle and nine sheep. Land was the precious commodity that enabled a man to marry, raise a family and, if he was successful, accumulate enough material effects to produce an estate for his widow and children. According to an unconfirmed tradition, Henry (A22) had married Barbara Carpenter from the family of his neighbor, Emanuel Carpenter, who was noted for his participation in the affairs of government. This belief was probably based on the fact that Abraham (A222), a son of Henry (A22), had named his first son Emanuel (A2221), a name not often used by this branch of the Wenger family.

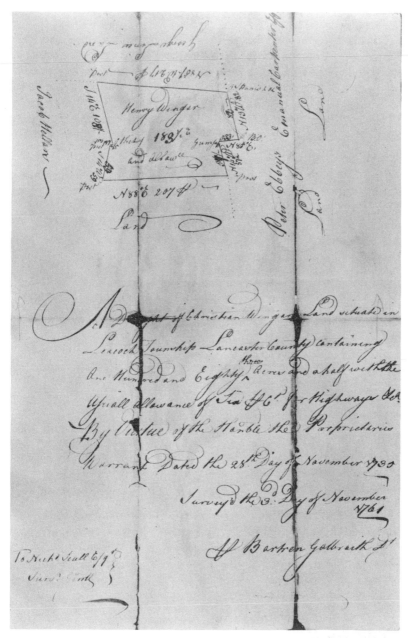

A Henry Wenger, Sr., survey showing 183½ acres joining the land of Jacob Heller, George Lines, Emanuel Carpenter and Peter Eby.

The American Revolution

During the ensuing decade there was trouble in the new land. Many were growing discontented with British rule. It is not our purpose here to review the fundamentals. To chronicle early events, one would have to go back to 1763 when Henry Wenger (A22) was finalizing his land patents through the early efforts of his father, Christian Wenger (A2). One would have to review the Navigation Acts, the Molasses Act and the resentment of taxation without the acquiescence of the Colonies. That, we will not do.

In 1774, under orders from General Washington, a number of military units were organized in Lancaster County and Leacock Township. These units not only had many volunteers but developed several outstanding officers, according to Revolutionary War records. Captain John Roland (sometimes Rowland) together with many prominent citizens organized a militia company in Leacock Township which was to distinguish itself in the war. This association was recruited in 1775, according to Ellis and Evans and the *Pennsylvania Archives,* Series 5, Vol. 3, p. 509, and Vol. 7, p. 970. Its

COMMONWEALTH OF PENNSYLVANIA
PENNSYLVANIA HISTORICAL AND MUSEUM COMMISSION
BUREAU OF ARCHIVES AND HISTORY
WILLIAM PENN MEMORIAL MUSEUM AND ARCHIVES BUILDING
BOX 232
HARRISBURG, PENNSYLVANIA 17108

January 24, 1969

TO WHOM IT MAY CONCERN:

This is to certify that one H E N R Y   W E N G E R was enrolled sometime during the period 1777-1780 as a Private in Fifth Class, Captain John Rowland's Third Company, Seventh Battalion, Lancaster County Militia, according to the evidence of an undated True Account.

WILLIAM H. WORK, Chief
Division of Archives and Manuscripts

Authority: Military Accounts
(Militia), Records of the
Comptroller General, at the
Division of Archives and Manuscripts

Residence ascribed:
Leacock Township

Henry Wenger,
Revolutionary V
Record.

full complement was enrolled from northwest Upper Leacock Township which, among others, included members of the Eby and Wenger families. Henry Wenger, Sr., (A22) and another Christian Wenger, unidentified, as well as Peter Eby, Sr., and his sons, Peter, Jr., Samuel, Henry and John, were members July 5, 1775.

The Commonwealth of Pennsylvania, through the Historical and Museum Commission at the William Penn Memorial Museum and Archives Building in Harrisburg, furnished the writer a certification and a photostatic copy of a True Account of Henry Wenger's (A22) War Service. This certification indicated in part that one Henry Wenger of Leacock Township was enrolled as a Private in the Fifth Class in Captain John Roland's Third Company of the Seventh Battalion in the Lancaster County Militia, according to the evidence of an undated True Account. Since this enrollment was undated, we

e Muster Roll of
ptain John
land. Among the
4 names are those
Wenger, Eby and
rr. Note that
nry Wenger, Sr.
22), is listed in the
nter row, the
venth signature
m the bottom.

believe the period 1775-1780, according to the previous authorities, is correct.

The photocopy of the enrollment contains 124 names, mostly from Upper Leacock and a few from close-by townships. It is interesting to note that several members of the Eby family were members of this unit, including Peter Eby, Sr., the neighbor of Henry Wenger, Sr., (A22).

Captain John Roland's sister, Annie Roland, had married Peter Eby, Sr. The latter was serving under his brother-in-law. The Peter Ebys were the parents of the above mentioned Peter, Jr., Samuel, Henry and John. Thus the Eby boys were serving under their uncle. Anny Eby — a sister of Peter, Jr., and other Eby boys — later married Abraham Wenger (A222), the son of Henry Wenger, Sr. (A22). It follows that Henry's (A22) daughter-in-law, Anna Eby Wenger, was a niece to Captain John Roland. However, Captain Roland's Company was far from being a family affair. This Company suffered the full gamut of deprivations of the Revolutionary War.

The Alarm Companies

According to Christopher Ward's *War of the Revolution*, 1952, the militia were known as Alarm Companies. They were not to be called out on the first alarm. In fact, they were the last resort. They were an ultimate reserve, being composed of boys, old men, magistrates and clergymen. They were considered of little importance in the conflict. This made it easier for those of Mennonite background to join. Such a member of the militia considered that there was little likelihood of a call to arms. It might be considered guard duty at most. However, after these units were organized, the condition of the war changed. As a result, many units were called to arms. There were desertions, but for the most part the membership made the most of it.

In the initial stages the units reported in civilian clothes; there were no uniforms. Their guns were of any sort: Brown Bess muskets from the French and Indian War; muskets issued in King George's War 30 years before; even a few Queen's arms, twice as old, dating from Queen Ann's War; American-made muskets of all dates, fowling pieces, blunderbusses, any kind of gun that would fire. The rifle was largely unknown.

The supplies issued to the militia were few and simple: a powder horn and a bullet pouch, a bullet mold and a bag of extra flints. There might be a haversack and a rolled blanket. Some had bayonets, but not many.

In New York

The Company joined Colonel John Ferree's Battalion in the forepart of July 1776, when the Council of Safety approved the delivery of arms and meals to Captain John Roland's Company because of its association with the Ferree Battalion. This Battalion, which included Henry Wenger, Sr. (A22), joined the "Flying Camp" and was composed of men from Pennsylvania, Maryland and Delaware under General Hugh Mercer. They were under orders to join General Washington in New York. While General Washington employed what troops he had with skill, there were mistakes in strategy and the country was struck with panic. The militia units were engaged in dispirited actions that filled their minds with apprehension and despair. They were dismayed, intractable and impatient to return home — and that they did. Great numbers, almost whole regiments, deserted and their example infected the whole army.

However, many of the battalions and companies, including John Roland's, "served well and honorably with the Army of General Washington in the summer and fall of 1776." According to the Eby brothers, Captain John Roland's militia, which included Henry Wenger, Sr. (A22), was in New York when the British captured the city. (See *Biographical History of Lancaster County*, by Alex Harris, published by Elias Barr and Company, 1872, p. 185.) It is known that Ensign Jacob Weaver, later Captain Jacob Weaver, as a line officer was in New York on June 11, 1776. His battalion started to build Fort Washington which was captured by the British. Weaver escaped and returned to Lancaster. Captain John Roland's battered command also returned home after these two months of action.

In the meantime, General Washington and the Continental Congress had extended all short-term enlistments to two years and later "for the duration of the war."

More Hardships

What influence this action had on Henry Wenger, Sr., (A22) cannot be assessed. There probably was a consolidation of units. The fact remains, as reported in *The History of Lancaster County*, by Ellis and Evans, p. 56, Henry (A22) and a number of his fellow soldiers were serving in Captain Jacob Weaver's Company of the Tenth Pennsylvania Regiment in the fall of 1776. The Tenth was under the command of Colonel Richard Humpton. The Regiment took the field immediately and fought in the Battles of Princeton, Bound Brook, New Jersey, Brandywine, Germantown, Paoli and several of the later battles of the war.

Nevertheless, the Battles of Brandywine and Germantown took their toll. At Brandywine, Paoli and Germantown, the Americans were badly beaten, but an optimistic Captain Anderson wrote, "I saw not a despairing look or word. Instead, I heard 'Come boys, we'll do better another time.'" During the height of the fighting, General Washington sent a call for blankets for his freezing men. Philadelphia and Lancaster had blankets enough, but somehow a lack of general understanding did not bring the "angels of warmth" into being. At Germantown in particular, the whole action was a tragedy of errors. But for misadventure, victory for the Americans was a very near thing. It was not to be.

In the meantime, the victory of General Washington in New Jersey, including Princeton and Bound Brook, which included Captain Weaver's 10th with Henry Wenger (A22) under the command of Colonel Richard Humpton, was a different story. It had an effect on the American cause that heartened the people and strengthened Washington's reputation abroad. Washington had swept the Jerseys clear of the enemy with an army of fewer than 5,000 ragged, shoeless, ill-fed, poorly equipped, often defeated amateur soldiers. They were mostly militia, operating against twice their number of veteran professionals who were abundantly supplied. Within a space of 11 days in the depth of winter, in 1776, Washington won a great victory.

However, the Battle of Germantown increased the problems for Lancaster. Many of the wounded of that engagement were carried back to the city. Between 500 and 600 were placed in hospitals in the Ephrata Cloister where more than 150 of them died. Apparently Henry Wenger, Sr., (A22) was unscathed, although on September 10, 1778, he was listed as "sick at Lancaster." (Pennsylvania Archives, Series 5, p. 509) Later George Washington visited Lancaster and the sick and wounded soldiers at Ephrata.

Tories at Old Dutch Mill

Of prime interest to the hundreds of descendants of Henry Wenger, Sr., (A22) and his son, Abraham (A222), who married Anna

The Old Dutch Mill established by Theodorus Eby and a famous Revolutionary War landmark.

Eby, is the significant part played in the Revolutionary War by the Old Dutch Mill. This mill was built near the present site of New Holland where Mill Creek crosses Old Peters Road. It was originally built in 1717 by Theodorus Eby, founder of the prolific clan, among whom was Anna Eby, who was to become a Wenger. The Eby family pattern will be given later because it contributed so much to the Wenger family. Theodorus Eby, sometimes referred to as Dorst Eby, built the first Dutch Mill of logs. He installed a great water wheel, which lasted from 1717 until 1923 when the mill was destroyed by fire. That wheel was used to grind corn and with special rollers produced flour. Many of the original utensils, along with the original scales, were still used in the mill when it burned down in 1923. Some of the original machinery survived the fire and was later installed in a nearby stonemill.

The mill from Theodorus Eby passed through several owners' hands, including the Roland family. During the Revolutionary War, the proprietors, George and his brother, John Rien, ran the mill. At that time Andrew Snyder, an employee of the mill, discovered that flour from the mill was being sent to the British Army and questioned George Rien concerning the legality of such actions. Moreover, it was discovered that flour being sold for the use of colonial troops was found to contain ground glass. Action was brought against the Rien brothers for selling flour to the British.

At the trial it was developed that the Rien brothers were involved in the theft of horses, running them to Philadelphia where they were sold to the British. It was revealed that the Rien brothers were collaborating with Lieutenant Mansin, an officer of the British Army, Wendel Meyer and Joseph Rode. The testimony disclosed that these conspirators were delivering horses to the British while our own troops were dying from cold and hunger at Valley Forge because of the lack of horses in the Revolutionary Army to deliver supplies. It was disclosed that Rien's Mill was one of the most important stations in an underground system by which flour and supplies were being sent to the British and then to New York. Lieutenant Mansin quite often slept in the mill and used it as a base for operations.

The Trials

History discloses that more fine horses were delivered to the enemy from the area surrounding the Old Dutch Mill than any other area involved in the Revolutionary War. Mansin, Meyer and Joseph Rode were tried and sentenced to the gallows. The Rien brothers were tried in absentia since they had escaped and were with the British in Philadelphia. However, the entire proceedings were set aside by General George Washington when he reviewed the case. Someone evidently had overstepped his authority and had to be placed in his proper station by the Commander in Chief. A second trial followed. Mansin and Meyer were condemned to death. They were hanged in the old jail yard at Prince and Water Streets in Lancaster.

In due course, John Rien, the first of the brothers, returned and hid out among friends and relatives. With the return of peace to the country, prosecutions stopped and George Rien returned and regained possession of the Dutch Mill. Believe it or not, Mr. Snyder, who made the original discovery of these extra-curricular activities, returned to the mill to resume his former employment and to marry a girl, Magdalena Pfieffer, who lived in the Rien household. Incidentally, Snyder died in 1845 at the age of 112 years.

It should be pointed out that the populace in Lancaster County, predominantly of Swiss or German origin, were intensely devoted to the tenets of their religion. After enduring the hardships of Europe, most of them came to Lancaster County between 1727 and 1776. They were asked to take the Oath of Allegiance to the English Crown. In 1776 they were being asked to retract those oaths; and to them oaths were not to be taken lightly. With this as background and by reason of the sheer exhaustion of the local patriots, all persecution of the dissidents was stopped.

The Old Dutch Mill, established by our ancestor, Dorst Eby, bore under the gable end the names of D. and M. Rien, with the date 1793. In 1793 the Rien brothers completely remodeled the mill in the form which lasted until the fire of 1923. In 1968 the writer visited the site of the Dutch Mill of the Eby's, Reins' and Roland's. Parts of the foundation still can be seen on the bank of Mill Creek just off Old Peters Road.

The historical facts concerning the Dutch Mill were reported by R. S. Sprout in the *Lancaster County Historical Society Bulletin,* Vol. LVI-2-1952.

Continental Congress in Lancaster

When the defeat of the American Army at Brandywine took place September 11, 1777, it became evident that General Washington could interpose no successful resistance to the occupation of the City of Philadelphia by the victorious British forces of General Howe.

The Continental Congress and the Executive Council of Philadelphia took measures directed to immediate removal from the city to places of safety. On September 18, the members resolved to repair at once to Lancaster. The Continental records and the Treasury were brought to Lancaster and York where sessions of the Continental Congress were held to plan the further conduct of the war.

On June 18, 1778, the British evacuated Philadelphia and the Continental Congress returned to the city.

In Lancaster the Tenth Pennsylvania Regiment was a skeleton unit out of which the "new Eleventh" was formed under Lt. Col. Commandant Adam Hubley, Jr. That was June 8, 1779. By then Henry Wenger, Sr., (A22) had completed his tour of duty to the cause of the new nation that was being created from man's inhumanity to man.

The historic Zweibrücken Wappen of the Royal Deux Ponts. Note Yorktown, 1781.

The Royal Deux Ponts

An interesting development in this war was that some units of General Lafayette joined Washington's ragged army. Among them was the mercenary regiment known as the Royal-Deux-Ponts which had fought with the French in the Seven Years' War in Europe. This regiment had been recruited in Zweibrücken among the Swiss and German neighbors of the Christian Wenger (A2) family in Huberhof, Zweibrücken. It was where Henry Wenger (A22) had been born. It is hard to imagine the Tenth Pennsylvania Regiment and the Royal Deux Ponts with Zweibrücken recruits fighting in the War of Independence on American soil. Nevertheless, it is a fact that Henry Wenger (A22), American by adoption, with the natives of his own fatherland fought in that conflict.

The regiment Royal-Deux-Ponts was raised by the Duke Deux-Ponts by virtue of a commission in 1757. It was one of four regiments which the Count of Rochambeau commanded in the American Revolutionary War. It embarked at Brest, France, April 4, 1780, for America. Early in July 1780, it disembarked at Newport, Rhode Island. The immaculate white uniforms with multi-colored facings, innumerable bands and banners, including a huge baggage train and a commissary, bugged the eyes of the hungry Colonists.

The Royal-Deux-Ponts saw action in August 1781, when Washington summoned them to join the Continental Army in the siege of Yorktown. On October 14, 400 troops behind Colonel Deux-Ponts charged Redoubt No. 9, anchoring the left of the British line. The action in which Count William Dex Deux-Ponts was wounded cost 114 casualties and Yorktown fell to the Americans. Thus the natives of Henry Wenger's (A22) homeland helped to bring independence to the nation to which so many of their native sons had emigrated. The War for Independence had been won!

General Washington, in the name of Congress, offered to each of the regiments three pieces of cannon which they had taken from the enemy. He stated that he hoped that they would keep them as testimony of the courage with which they took the enemy Redoubt No. 9 on the night of October 14, an action that helped bring the United States into being.

These facts were extracted from reports in the *Biographical History of Lancaster County* by Alexander Harris, published in 1872 by Elias Barr and Company; *The History of Lancaster County* by Ellis and Evans, 1883; *The Biographical History of Lancaster County* by Alex Harris, 1872, and the *Pennsylvania Archives*, Series 5, Vol. 3, p. 509, and Vol. 7, p. 970. Also the True Account of Henry Wenger's (A22) War Service from the Historical and Museum Commission, Harrisburg, and *The Journal of the Siege of Yorktown*, February 17 (calendar day March 3), United States Government Printing Office, Washington, 1931.

Henry Wenger, Sr. (A22), the Wagoner

Henry (A22) was to live another twenty years after his service in the Revolutionary War. The record shows that after the development of his land and as his boys became productive enough to take over the farming, Henry (A22) was developing his skills as a wagoner. His boys, particularly Abraham (A222), followed in his footsteps. Henry's (A22) inventory of his estate, dated July 29, 1802, shows that his wagon business must have been of some importance. Among an exceedingly large inventory of tools, he had 45 chisels, 25 drawing knives, 25 planes, 30 malls and wedges, 38 augers and a dozen hammers. These numbers suggest that more than a handful of people must have been employed. Other items included blacksmith equipment and smithing tools, fire tongs, cedar tubs and a cutting bench in "a large wagon shop." There were miscellaneous items, such as saws of all kinds, two large vises, gauges, hatchets, broad axes, chains, crowbars, spoke shavers and at least 30 compasses. Apparently it was important in those days to furnish a compass with every completed wagon.

Henry Wenger, Sr. (A22), Family Pattern

The Henry Wenger (A22) will has a preamble not unlike most wills of that period. Two reactions may be inferred. First, Henry, Sr. (A22), was 86 years old and the will described him as "very old." Second, strong religious convictions are gleaned from the following quote:

> I commend my soul to God and my body to the earth, to be decently interred as my executors shall direct, in humble hope of a glorious resurrection and a happy admission into the regions of immortal bliss and glory, in and through the merits of my mediator and redeemer, Jesus Christ; and as such worldly estate wherewith God hath blessed me, I do give, devise and bequeath the same in manner following . . . .

The will (H-1-211 Lancaster 1799) discloses that his wife, Barbara, was not mentioned, hence we conclude that she preceded him in death. It does disclose the existence of eight children: Adam (A221), Abraham (A222), Henry (A223), Christian (A224), Salome (A22X), Eve (A22X), Barbara (A22X) and Mary (A22X). Except for Adam Wenger (A221) and Abraham Wenger (A222), the family pattern lacks complete documentation.

Henry's (A22) youngest son, Christian (A224; 1769-1810), was left 12 acres in trust for future generations in the terms of the will. He had a family of seven, Susanna (A2241), Elizabeth (A2242), Barbara (A2243), Leah (A2244), Magdalena (A2245), Jacob (A2246) and George (A2247). It is known that in 1791 he purchased 69½ acres in Derry Township, which is now Dauphin County, Pennsylvania. This land was sold in 1798 to a Henry Shearer.

Christian (A224) died in 1810 leaving two minor boys under the age of 14. At the instance of the widow, Adam Wenger (A221), Christian's (A224) brother, was appointed guardian of Jacob (A2246) and George (A2247). Leah (A2244) and Magdalena (A2245) were under the guardianship of Jacob and Henry Musser, respectively. Elizabeth (A2242) married George Menser. Barbara

(A2243) married Jacob Dietrick, and Susanna (A2241) was a spinster. (See Lancaster County Orphans Court 1808-1813, 196, Recorded August 28, 1810, also Lancaster County Deed Book 4,123,125)

Mary (A22X; b. about 1763) did not marry. Barbara (A22X; b. about 1761) married Peter Bushong. Eve (A22X; b. about 1758) married Joseph Miller. Salome (A22X; b. about 1755) married Peter Reideback. Henry, Jr., (A223; b. about 1768) married Barbara (maiden name unknown).

Henry, Jr. (A223), and Barbara had two children, John (A2231) and Jacob (A2232). Henry (A223) died in February 1823. Apparently his wife, Barbara, preceded him in death. His will dated January 24, 1823, gave his oldest son, John (A2231), seven acres and all buildings thereon located in Manor Township, adjoining the Susquehanna River. He requested that five and one-half acres of woodland on "turkey hill" in Manor Township be sold and the proceeds be divided between his sons, John (A2231) and Jacob (A2232). (See Lancaster County Will Book N-1, 288; 1823) John Wenger (A2231) was a schoolteacher and had a wife, Catherine. He sold his equity in his father's estate to David Herr, April 1, 1818. (Lancaster County Deed Book 1-5,210; 1828). Jacob Wenger (A2232) had previously sold his equity to James Mendenhall, May 15, 1824 (Lancaster County Deed Book A-5,385; 1824).

It should be noted that prior to his death, Henry Wenger, Sr. (A22), gave his son, Abraham Wenger (A222), 18 acres of his land in Upper Leacock Township, July 30, 1787, and 11¾ acres to his son, Henry, Jr. (A223), November 26, 1787. (Lancaster County Deed Book NN222 and Deed Book 1-3. 473). Also on the same date Adam (A221) by indenture agreed to certain obligations to his parents. (Deed Book MM-113-1787) Adam (A221), the elder son, was executor of the estate of Henry Wenger, Sr. (A22). He filed his administration account which was approved by the court, July 25, 1804. (Lancaster County Orphans Court, 1803-1805,180)

Adam (A221) and Abraham (A222) are recorded in separate chapters bearing their names. Separate family trees are included.

Homestead Cemetery

A Wenger family cemetery was originally established on the northeast corner of the Henry Wenger, Sr. (A22), land next to Creek Hill Road. The dividing line between the Wenger property later owned by the two sons of Adam Wenger (A221) bisected this family graveyard. It is believed that all of the early Wengers were buried here with large natural stones as markers. After this land had passed to the descendants of Adam Wenger (A221), a land survey of the tract was completed by Israel Carpenter in 1823. On September 16, 1824, John Wenger (A2211) and Henry Wenger (A2212), the sons of Adam (A221), deeded this cemetery tract to their mother, Juliana Wenger, as a "burial ground for the family and descendants of Adam Wenger of Leacock."

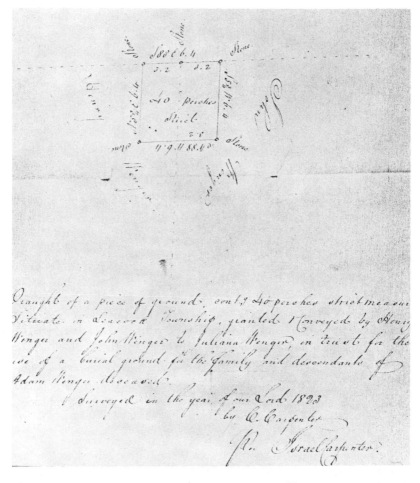

A formalized deed to Juliana Wenger showing the Wenger family burial ground which had been used for the previous 100 years.

However, the deed was not recorded until December 19, 1836. This was the period when Juliana Wenger, the widow of Adam (A221), was left alone, because her son, John (A2211), had gone to Canada and her son, Henry (A2212), had gone to Ohio. She apparently died soon thereafter and was buried in this family cemetery. (See Lancaster County Deed Book F-6, 416). The burial ground was obliterated soon after the death of Juliana and the only legible gravemarkers, those of Adam (A221) and Juliana Wenger and their infant daughter, Elizabeth (A2213), were moved to the Stumpton Mennonite Church Cemetery. This removal probably was prior to 1840.

The original Stumptown Mennonite Church was located on the south side of Stumptown Road next to the Mennonite one-room school, which is still in use. On February 11, 1815, Jacob Wenger (A2214), thought by some to be a son of Adam (A221) and Juliana Wenger, sold the land on the north side of Stumptown Road for the purpose of locating the present church and cemetery.

The Old Homestead

In October 1968, my wife, Rhea Yeager Fetzer, and I visited the old Wenger farm, originally established by Christian Wenger (A2) and developed by his son, Henry Wenger, Sr. (A22). This farm is located in Upper Leacock Township of Lancaster County on Creek Hill Road about midway between Heller's United Church of Christ, which is to the west, and the Village of Monterey to the east.

This beautiful Wenger farm, as this is written, is owned by a very fine Mennonite family, Mr. and Mrs. John Landis. The old section of the farm home is built of brick with unusual walls as "thick as a battleship." The interior reveals the original fireplace, the mantel of which is beautifully hand carved. It is thought to be the handicraft of Henry Wenger, Sr. (A22). The fireplace protrudes from a corner chimney in a first floor dining area and continues through an upstairs bedroom. In the Henry Wenger (A22) inventory of July 29, 1802, two corner cupboards are listed. These could have been designed to fit that angular chimney. This home, when occupied by the Henry Wenger, Sr. (A22), family, had two Bibles and fifteen other books. This was something of an improvement over the status of Christian Wenger (A2), the father. Beyond the Bibles, his library contained only one extra book.

The John Henry Wenger, Sr. (A22), house and barn in 1968.

The John Henry Wenger, Sr. (A22), home it looks today. The gab section on the right is lived to have been b by John Henry Weng Sr. (A22).

The fireplace in the Wenger home is believed to be the handwork of John Henry Wenger, Sr. (A22).

We have covered the first 84 years of this branch of the Wenger family in America, from the time of the arrival of Christian Wenger (A2) in 1718 until the date of the death of Henry Wenger, Sr. (A22), in 1802.

The Henry Wenger, Sr. (A22), Family Tree follows immediately.

Henry Wenger, Sr. (A22), Family Tree

1st Hans Wenger (b. About 1430) Blumenstein, Thun

2nd Burkhard Wenger (b. About 1450) Forst, Thun

3rd Peter Wenger (b. About 1470) Wattenwil, Seftigen

4th Peter Wenger (b. About 1490) Wattenwil, Seftigen

5th Rudolfus Wenger (b. About 1510) Wattenwil, Seftigen

6th Hans Wenger (b. About 1530) Wattenwil, Seftigen

7th Rudolfus Wenger (Ch. April 5, 1566) Wattenwil-Thurnen, Seftigen

8th Peter Wenger (Ch. Dec. 13, 1607) Wattenwil-Thurnen, Seftigen

9th Hans Wenger (Ch. May 30, 1633) Wattenwil-Thurnen, Seftigen

 A Christian Wenger (A2) First Generation (1688-1749)

  B-1 Henry Wenger, Sr. (A22-2nd)
    b. July 26, 1716, Huberhof, Zweibrücken; d. 1802
    m. Barbara Carpenter

    C-X Salome Wenger (A22X-3rd)*
      b. About 1755
      m. Peter Reideback

    C-X Eve Wenger (A22X-3rd)*
      b. About 1758
      m. Joseph Miller

    C-X Barbara Wenger (A22X-3rd)*
      b. About 1761
      m. Peter Bushong

    C-X Mary Wenger (A22X-3rd)*
      b. About 1763

C-1   Adam Wenger (A221-3rd)
         b. Feb. 9, 1766
         d. Jan. 12, 1829
(See Adam Wenger Chapter and Family Tree)

C-2   Abraham Wenger (A222-3rd)
         b. 1767, d. 1845
(See Abraham Wenger Chapter and Family Tree)

C-3   Henry Wenger, Jr. (A223-3rd)
         b. About 1768
         m. Barbara

   D-1   John Wenger (A2231-4th)
            b. About 1790

   D-2   Jacob Wenger (A2232-4th)
            b. About 1793

C-4   Christian Wenger (A224-3rd)
         b. About 1769, d. 1810

   D-1   Susanna (A2241-4th)
            b. About 1788

   D-2   Elizabeth (A2242-4th)
            b. About 1789
            m. George Menser

   D-3   Barbara (A2243-4th)
            b. About 1790
            m. Jacob Dietrick

   D-4   Leah (A2244-4th)
            b. About 1793

   D-5   Magdalena (A2245-4th)
            b. About 1795

   D-6   Jacob (A2246-4th)
            b. About 1797

   D-7   George (A2247-4th)
            b. About 1799

---

*York numbers have been included only in the male lines since the order of birth in the female pattern is speculative.

CHAPTER SIX

Adam Wenger of Lancaster County

ADAM WENGER (A221), born February 9, 1766, in Upper Leacock Township, Lancaster County, was the oldest son of Henry
Wenger, Sr., (A22). He married a woman by the name of Juliana.
They had a family of at least four children and became prominent
land owners in Upper Leacock Township. As the elder son, he inherited land from his father's estate and acquired more Wenger
land through purchases from other members of the family. In Adam's
earlier years as a young man, his father, John Henry Wenger, Sr.
(A22), made numerous cash advances to help Adam (A221). In
the settlement of the John Henry Wenger, Sr. (A22), estate, it was
revealed that he had advanced $482 without interest to Adam
(A221) and that Henry (A22) was holding ten obligation bonds as
guarantee of repayment. On July 31, 1802, Adam Wenger (A221)
appeared at the register's office in Lancaster to acknowledge the
debt, which of course was ultimately retired in the adjustment of
the estate. (See Inventory of Estate of Henry Wenger, Lancaster
County Court House.)

The School Trust

Adam Wenger (A221), together with David Bender and Peter
Eby, on January 31, 1810, entered into a trust arrangement with
John Meixel, Abraham Eby, John Heller, John Hershy and George
Swope. The purpose was to make Upper Leacock land available in
perpetuity for a schoolhouse. Since it is believed that this could
have been for the purpose of establishing the one-room Stumptown
School, rich in early Mennonite history, this entire trust document
is published here (Lancaster County Deed Book 3,226):

The old Stumptown one-room school is still in use.

Whereas the Commonwealth of Pennsylvania by Patent under the hand of John Cochran, Secretary of the Land Office, dated 31 January, 1810, granted to David Bender, Peter Eby and Adam Wenger and their successors forever in trust for the use of a schoolhouse on the hereafter mentioned premises, a tract called "Education" in Leacock Township, Lancaster County, Pennsylvania, adjoining lands of Peter Eby and John Meixel, containing 16 perches and allowance by Patent in the Rolls Office in Patent Book H, Vol. 3, p. 122.

Now know ye that David Bender, Peter Eby and Adam Wenger acknowledge that the purchase money mentioned in the above Patent and other necessary expenses was not intended to be out of their own monies but should be divided in eight equal parts. Three equal eighth parts being of David Bender, Peter Eby and Adam Wenger's own money. Five equal eighth parts being paid this day to David Bender, Peter Eby and Adam Wenger by John Meixel, Abraham Eby, John Heller, John Hershy and George Swope. In consideration of which money being refunded to them, David Bender, Peter Eby and Adam Wenger grant to John Meixel, Abraham Eby, John Heller, John Hershy and George Swope in trust for the use of a schoolhouse and for no other purposes, five equal, undivided eighth parts of the above tract.

It is hereby declared that the true intent of the trust was that the several owners of the several mansion houses on which the parties herein named now live shall forever have the direction and management of the said premises, provided they will contribute toward the repairing and improving of the same as necessary. And a majority of the members shall always govern.

Signed 28 January, 1811   David Bender
                                                       Peter Eby
                                                       Adam Wenger

Witnesses: Joseph Eby, B. Owen
Acknowledged 28 January, 1811
Recorded 6 February, 1811

The former Stumptown Meetinghouse resided on land owned by the several owners of the several mansion houses.

Adam Wenger Family Pattern

Adam (A221) and Juliana Wenger had three known children of the fourth generation: John (A2211), Henry (A2212) and Elizabeth (A2213), who died in infancy, and possibly a fourth child, Jacob (A2214).

It is known that they raised Jacob (A2246) and George (A2247), the minor sons of Adam's (A221) brother, Christian Wenger (A224). They also had a second daughter, Elizabeth (A2213), who married George Metzgar. (Lancaster County Deed Book 4, 123.)

The son, John (A2211), born April 5, 1789, married Susana Eby January 21, 1817, at the Trinity Lutheran Church in Lancaster. She was a daughter of Peter Eby, who was a son of Jacob Eby, third son of Theodorus Eby. Susana Eby Wenger was born November 10, 1792, and died January 3, 1871. John Wenger (A2211) died October 11, 1864. Henry (A2212) married a Mary and Jacob (A2214) married a Susanna. All the Christian (A2) and John Henry (A22) Wenger land eventually passed to Adam (A221) and Juliana Wenger. (Lancaster County Deed Books I-3, 746-1801; B-4, 123-1811; pp. 23-1792) In due course some of the farm passed to their son, John (A2211), and subsequently to their son, Henry (A2212). (Lancaster County Deed Book Y-5, 56) John (A2211) and Henry (A2212), as previously reported, provided a formal deed to their mother, Juliana Wenger, for the family cemetery. (Lancaster County Deed Book F-6, 416)

Grave markers in the foreground of the Stumptown Cemetery showing those of Adam Wenger (A221) and his wife, Juliana, and their two infants.

On April 4, 1835, John Wenger (A2211) sold 97½ acres of the Wenger land to David Landis. The deed provided that Juliana, their mother and widow of Adam Wenger (A221), be granted right by David Landis to live in the original Adam Wenger (A221) home, and have such privileges as the use of the pump, oven, spring house, smokehouse, a one-third use of the garden next to the house and the free use of the walks, paths and gates. She was to have firewood at all times. John Wenger (A2211) agreed to pay her $100 annually the rest of her life. (Lancaster County Deed Book F-6, 73, 76)

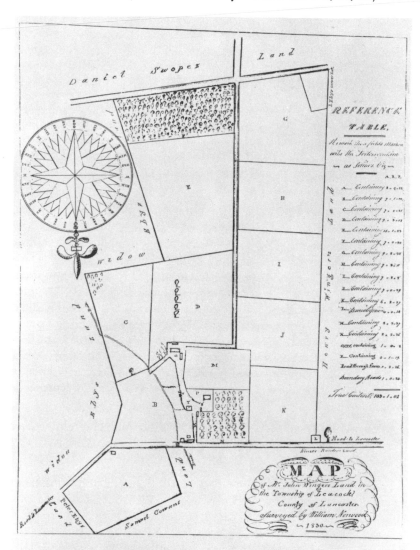

A part of the John Henry Wenger, Sr. (A22), original farm was surveyed in 1830. At that time it belonged to his son, John Wenger (A2211), who later went to Canada.

Events in 1836 and Canada

Juliana Wenger died in 1836 and her will was proved December 19, 1836. (Lancaster County Will Book R-1, 287; 1836) She left her son, John, "my cow, my large copper kettle, my largest iron pot, my dutch oven and my largest cedar wash tub, ten plate stove and pipe, my still yards and two spinning wheels and reel, also my small bureau." The remainder of the estate was to be divided between her sons, Henry (A2212) and John (A2211).

Henry Wenger (A2212), the son of Adam (A221) and Juliana, sold the last 100 acres on March 31, 1837, to Henry Landis. Thus all of the Wenger land after a dozen transactions passed out of the family. Henry (A2212) and his wife, Mary, were reported to have moved first to Canada and then to Ohio. This family never could be located and remains a mystery.

John Wenger (A2211) and his wife, Susana Eby Wenger, sold their Leacock grist, saw and merchant mills to Samuel Ranck and moved to Berlin (Ebytown), Ontario, Canada, about 1836, where both lived the remainder of their lives. (Lancaster County Deed Book E-6-238) The following documentation is from *The Biographical History of Waterloo Township*, by Ezra E. Eby II, 629, 630, article "The Eby Family," 1896, Berlin, Ontario. It should be noted that this book reports that Adam Wenger (A221) was a son of "old Hans Wenger." (See H-6-416; H-8-205; Y-5-56, Lancaster County, Pennsylvania.) He was in fact the son of John Henry Wenger, Sr. (A22), sometimes called Hans, and grandson of Christian Wenger (A2). The latter's father was Hans Wenger as recorded in Switzerland.

John (A2211) and Susana Wenger had the following children of the fifth generation: Peter (A22111), John (A22112), Eli (A22113), Polly (A22114), Rebecca (A22115) and Elizabeth (A22116).

Peter Wenger (A22111) married Marie Bauman. John (A22112) married Elizabeth Masten. Eli Wenger (A22113) died unmarried at age 27. Polly (A22114) married A. Cornell. There is no information concerning her family except that Cornell was from Preston. Rebecca (A22115) married Samuel Roether. Elizabeth (A22116) married Abraham Buehler.

Peter Wenger (A22111) and Maria Bauman Wenger had seven children of the sixth generation: Henry (A221111), Mary (A221112),

William (A221113), Jacob (A221114), Susannah (A221115), Reuben (A221116) and Mariah (A221117), who was unmarried.

John Wenger (A22112) and Elizabeth Masten Wenger resided in Berlin a number of years and then moved to Wooster, Ohio, and had three known children of the sixth generation: Theresa (A221121), Amanda (A221122) and Ella (A221123).

Rebecca (A22115), the wife of Samuel Roether, resided in Walkerton, Bruce County, Ontario, where he was the county jailer. They had a family of six children of the sixth generation. These were Sarah (A221151), Samuel (A221152), Reuben (A221153), Susannah (A221154), Louisa (A221155) and Anna (A221156).

Elizabeth (A22116), who married Abraham Buehler, lived in Waterloo, Ontario. They had the following children of the sixth generation: Susannah (A221161), Hannah (A221162), Lizzie (A221163), Kate (A221164), Abraham (A221165) and Mariah (A221166). It is known that Elizabeth Wenger Buehler (A22116) had a granddaughter, Emma L. Eby, who lived at Burlington, Ontario.

Henry Wenger (A221111) had at least two sons of the seventh generation who lived at Elmira, Ontario. These were Amsa Wenger (A2211111) and Angus Wenger (A2211112).

Mary Wenger (A221112) married Isaac Brock Markle and resided in Windsor, Ontario, and Detroit, Michigan, where he engaged in the implement business. They had three children of the seventh generation. These were Walter (A2211121), William (A2211122) and Ida (A2211123), who married Stanley Gorman. They had a grandson, S. E. Gorman, of the eighth generation who lived in Oakville, Ontario.

William Wenger (A221113) of the sixth generation died in infancy.

Jacob Wenger (A221114) married Mary Weber, daughter of Solomon and Emma E. (Gray) Weber. They resided in Elmira, Ontario, where Mr. Wenger (A221114) engaged in manufacturing woolen goods. They had two sons of the seventh generation, Raymond Morley Wenger (A2211141) and Russell Elmo Wenger (A2211142).

Susannah Wenger (A221115) married Isaac Musselman. They

had a daughter of the seventh generation, Anna Maria (A2211151), who married James Maxwell, a carriage builder. They resided in Bellefountain, Ontario. Anna Marie (A2211151) and James Maxwell had four children of the eighth generation: Zenlda (A22111511), Ida (A22111512), Maude (A22111513) and Orton (A22111514).

Reuben Wenger (A221116) married Martha Armstrong and resided in Elmira, Ontario. He also was in the woolen mill with his two brothers. They had two children of the seventh generation: Melvin Wenger (A2211161) and Dora May Wenger (A2211162).

Mariah Wenger (A221117) was unmarried. She was a bookkeeper in a large manufacturing plant.

Peter Wenger (A22111) of Canada

Peter Wenger (A22111) of the fifth generation, grandson of Adam Wenger (A221), and a son of John Wenger (A2211), was born in Lancaster County, Pennsylvania, April 18, 1818. In 1834 he, in company with George Eby, drove with a horse and buggy from Lancaster County, Pennsylvania, to Waterloo County, Ontario, making the trip in two weeks. In the fall of the same year, he returned to Lancaster County, Pennsylvania, where he remained until May 1835, when he made the second trip to Canada and settled in Berlin, Ontario. He worked the first year in the town of Waterloo in Mr. Jacob Schneider's sawmills receiving a salary of $7 per month. On November 7, 1837, he went to Bridgeport and worked for Jacob S. Shoemaker as a miller for eleven years. In September 1848, he moved to Woolwich Township on the Isaac Hilborn farm. In January 1849, he was appointed assessor for Woolwich Township, then including Pilkington Township. He was one of the early councillors of Woolwich Township and was deputy reeve when Berlin was made the county seat for the newly formed county of Waterloo. Later in life he was engaged in the mercantile, woolen and lumber business. About the year 1867 he received the appointment of postmaster for Elmira, which position he held until his death on July 27, 1889.

The following is from Mr. Wenger's Journal. "A meeting was called by public notice from Peter Wenger, Esq., reeve of the township of Woolwich, and was held at St. Jacobs on the 26th day of March, 1853, for the purpose of forming a township agricultural society. It was unanimously resolved that a society be forthwith formed, to be called the Township of Woolwich Agricultural Society. James Dow was elected president and Charles Hendry vice-president for the current year. James Mirrilees was appointed secretary and treasurer. The following were elected directors for the current year: B. H. Curtic, John Seaton, John Meyers, James Burnett, James Hall, Wm. H. Peterson, Jacob Winkler and Joseph Hardy. Thereupon the meeting adjourned."

Mr. Wenger married Maria Bauman January 24, 1838. She was born January 1, 1817. After her death on April 25, 1886, he married Cathrine Martin, widow of Moses Musselman.

For many years members of the Wenger family have searched for the Christian Wenger (A2) Bibles and other religious books that he was known to have had. Since Adam Wenger (A221) was the oldest son of Henry Wenger (A22), who in turn was the oldest son of Christian Wenger (A2), we can only wonder if these valuable works are hidden away somewhere in Canada. We can only hope that someday these Bibles will be found and preserved for posterity.

The Adam Wenger (A221) Family Tree follows.

Adam Wenger (A221) Family Tree

1st Hans Wenger (b. About 1430) Blumenstein, Thun

2nd Burkhard Wenger (b. About 1450) Forst, Thun

3rd Peter Wenger (b. About 1470) Wattenwil, Seftigen

4th Peter Wenger (b. About 1490) Wattenwil, Seftigen

5th Rudolfus Wenger (b. About 1510) Wattenwil, Seftigen

6th Hans Wenger (b. About 1530) Wattenwil, Seftigen

7th Rudolfus Wenger (Ch. April 5, 1566) Wattenwil-Thurnen, Seftigen

8th Peter Wenger (Ch. Dec. 13, 1607) Wattenwil-Thurnen, Seftigen

9th Hans Wenger (Ch. May 30, 1633) Wattenwil-Thurnen, Seftigen

   A   Christian Wenger (A2), First Generation in America, (1688-1749)

B-1   Henry Wenger (A22), Second Generation in
        America, (1716-1802)

  C-1   Adam Wenger (A221), Third Generation in
          America
          b. Feb. 9, 1766, Lancaster County
          d. Jan. 12, 1829
          m. Juliana
            b. 1765
            d. Nov. 22, 1836

    D-1   John Wenger (A2211-4th)
            b. Apr. 5, 1789
            d. Oct. 11, 1864
            m. Susana Eby Jan. 21, 1817, Lancaster
              b. Nov. 10, 1792
              d. Jan. 3, 1871

      E-1   Peter Wenger (A22111-5th)
              b. Apr. 18, 1818, Lancaster County
              m. Maria Bauman
                b. Jan. 1, 1817
                d. Apr. 25, 1886

        F-1   Henry Wenger (A221111-6th)
                m. Unknown
          G-1   Amsa Wenger (A2211111-7th)
          G-2   Angus Wenger (A2211112-7th)

        F-2   Mary Wenger (A221112-6th)
                m. Isaac Brock Markle
          G-1   Walter Markle (A2211121-7th)
          G-2   William Markle (A2211122-7th)
          G-3   Ida Markle (A2211123-7th)
                  m. Stanley Gorman
            H-1   Unknown (A22111231-8th)
              I-1   S. E. Gorman (A221112311-9th)

        F-3   William Wenger (A221113-6th)
                Died in infancy

        F-4   Jacob Wenger (A221114-6th)
                m. Mary Weber
          G-1   Raymond Morley Wenger (A2211141-7th)
          G-2   Russell Elmo Wenger (A2211142-7th)

F-5 Susannah Wenger (A221115-6th)
      m. Isaac Musselman
  G-1 Anna Maria Musselman (A2211151-7th)
        m. James Maxwell
    H-1 Zenlda Maxwell (A22111511-8th)
    H-2 Ida Maxwell (A22111512-8th)
    H-3 Maude Maxwell (A22111513-8th)
    H-4 Orton Maxwell (A22111514-8th)

F-6 Reuben Wenger (A221116-6th)
      m. Martha Armstrong
  G-1 Melvin Wenger (A2211161-7th)
  G-2 Dora May Wenger (A2211162-7th)

F-7 Mariah Wenger (A221117-6th)
      Unmarried

E-2 John Wenger (A22112-5th)
      m. Elizabeth Masten
  F-1 Theresa Wenger (A221121-6th)
  F-2 Amanda Wenger (A221122-6th)
  F-3 Ella Wenger (A221123-6th)

E-3 Eli Wenger (A22113-5th)
      Died unmarried, age 27.

E-4 Polly Wenger (A22114-5th)
      m. A. Cornell

E-5 Rebecca Wenger (A22115-5th)
      m. Samuel Roether
  F-1 Sarah Roether (A221151-6th)
  F-2 Samuel Roether (A221152-6th)
  F-3 Reuben Roether (A221153-6th)
  F-4 Susannah Roether (A221154-6th)
  F-5 Louisa Roether (A221155-6th)
  F-6 Anna Roether (A221156-6th)

E-6 Elizabeth Wenger (A22116-5th)
      m. Abraham Buehler (Had granddaughter
        Emma L. Eby)
  F-1 Susannah Buehler (A221161-6th)
  F-2 Hannah Buehler (A221162-6th)
  F-3 Lizzie Buehler (A221163-6th)
  F-4 Kate Buehler (A221164-6th)

F-5　Abraham Buehler (A221165-6th)
F-6　Mariah Buehler (A221166-6th)

D-2　Henry Wenger (A2212-4th)
　　　m. Mary (unknown)
　　　(moved to Ohio without trace)*

D-3　Elizabeth Wenger (A2213-4th)
　　　m. George Metzgar

D-4　Jacob Wenger (A2214-4th)
　　　m. Susanna
　　　d. 1820

---

*Note: Henry Wenger (1783-1854) and his wife Myria (1790-1844), buried in Paradise Union Cemetery near Smithville, Wayne County, Ohio, may be Henry Wenger (A2212) and his wife. No verification exists as this is written.

CHAPTER SEVEN

Abraham Wenger of Lancaster County

ABRAHAM WENGER (A222) (1767-1845), next to the oldest son of Henry Wenger, Sr. (A22), and a grandson of Christian Wenger (A2), was born at the John Henry Wenger, Sr. (A22), homestead near Heller's Church, Leacock Township, Lancaster County, about 1767. As a boy he not only learned to farm, but his father taught him many skills in woodworking. As a young man he was to become a wheelwright, following in his father's footsteps. His father granted him 18 acres from the Upper Leacock farm on July 13, 1787. (Lancaster County Deed Book NN, 222) When this land was surveyed in

Abraham Wenger (A222)

This dower chest was made in Lancaster County in 1793, the year Abraham Wenger (A222) and his wife, Anna Eby Wenger, established their home in Salisbury Township. This chest was made for Susana Himelbergin. Another similar chest was made for Sibila Himelbergin in 1792 and is now in the Winterthur Museum, Wilmington, Delaware. This is a photograph of the John E. Fetzer (A2226923) library in Kalamazoo, Michigan.

1787, Abraham's (A222) brothers, Christian (A224) and Adam (A221), had adjoining land. On March 27, 1792, Abraham (A222) sold this 18 acres in Upper Leacock to his brother, Adam Wenger (A221). (Lancaster County Deed Book p. 29)

Abraham (A222) married Anna Eby, the daughter of Peter Eby, Sr., May 22, 1792, at the Trinity Lutheran Church, Lancaster, Pennsylvania. It is believed that Peter Eby, Sr., was opposed to this marriage because, among other reasons, of the disparity of ages. She was 18 years old and he was 25 years of age at the time of their marriage. Peter Eby, Sr., had indicated in his will of June 26, 1793, that the Lancaster and Chester County land, which he had tendered to Anna, should at her death be sold and the proceeds go to the "heirs of her body." (Lancaster County Will Book I-1, 114, 1794)

This will was executed June 26, 1793. The 30 acres in Salisbury Township had been purchased from John and Jane Wilson on April 11, 1793, only a little over two months before. It seems logical to presume that Peter Eby, Sr., had purchased that land in order to give his daughter, Anna Eby, and Abraham Wenger (A222) a start in married life. But in doing so he wanted to protect Anna and her children which was out of necessity good estate planning, a typical characteristic of this pioneer family.

Theodorus Eby Family

It seems appropriate, as stated before, to digress by giving a brief history of the Eby family, since they also are the forebears of our Wenger descendants and contributed so much to the early life of our clan in Lancaster County. The Wengers, along with many other pioneer families, owe a debt of gratitude to the Eby forebears.

The first known ancestor of the Eby family was Theodorus Eby (Aebi), born about 1615, of Trachselwald, Canton of Bern, Switzerland. He had a son of the second generation, Jacob Eby, born about 1640, who was ordained Bishop of the Swiss Mennonites in 1683, Zurich, Switzerland. Of prime concern to us is Theodorus Eby of the third generation, who was born April 25, 1663. He and his family were driven from their home in 1704 during the Reformation. They went to Alsace in France and thence to Holland. There they secured passage and landed in Philadelphia in 1712. Among the family which crossed the Atlantic was a son, Peter Eby, of the fourth generation.

Theodorus Eby of the third generation had a family of eleven children. These children of the fourth generation were Peter, John, George, Christian, Jacob, Barbara Bare (wife of Henry Bare), Barbara, Mary, Ann, David and Elizabeth. The progeny of the Eby family during the last two centuries possessed latent talents distinguishing the descendants as religious leaders, ministers, preachers, missionaries, university professors, teachers, physicians, financiers, lawyers, statesmen, editors and, more generally, as leaders of men.

Theodorus Eby, too, became a leader as one of the first large landowners in Lancaster County. He secured a land patent for 307 acres which was surveyed by Taylor, May 10, 1718. (Harrisburg, Patent Book A., Vol. XI, p. 457) A large part of the City of Lancaster has been built on this land. More than that, Theodorus Eby and his sons led in the solution of the perpetual problem of food and shelter in Lancaster County. These Eby men were skilled in the mechanical arts. They singlehandedly built, owned and operated a chain of sawmills and gristmills at strategic points throughout the country. Among them, as previously reported, was the famous Dutch Mill, variously known as the Eby Mill, the Rein Mill and the Roland Mill. The gristmills supplied the food and the sawmills supplied the shelter that brought Lancaster County into being, helping to convert a wilderness into a garden.

Of the children of Theodorus Eby, Peter, his son of the fourth generation, was best known in the county. His occupations included

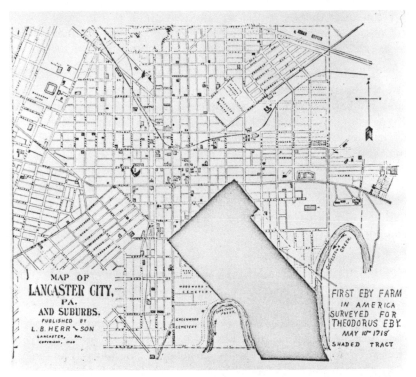

The first Eby farm in America, adjacent to the Christian Wenger (A2) farm. This Eby farm is now within the confines of the City of Lancaster.

that of redemptioner, millwright, miller and constable. In addition, he became a dealer in real estate. He received at least four land patents, including that of his father, and thereafter sold blocks of land to the latecomers from Europe. As constable, his name constantly appeared as a witness and bondsman in the records of the court for the county. He not only served as a juror but found himself under attack as a law enforcement officer. A James Michell on May 6, 1735, was fined for "assaulting and beating Peter Eby, constable." Peter Eby was naturalized October 14, 1729. He was born in 1690 in Canton Zurich and died after 1748 in Earl Township. Many members of the family are buried in the Eby Cemetery near the Eby and Wenger land in Upper Leacock Township, near the Village of Monterey.

Peter of the fourth generation and his wife, Barbara, had a family of eleven of the fifth generation. These were Christian, Jacob, Peter, Henry, Abraham, Isaac, Barbara, Ann, Doorst, Martin and John. The second-born son, who referred to himself as Peter Eby, Sr., is of interest to us.

Peter Eby, Sr., of the fifth generation, married Annie Roland, a sister of Captain John Roland. They had at least eight children of the sixth generation. These were Peter, Jr., Samuel, Henry, Andrew, John, David, Christian and Anna. It is to be noted that of the eight children, seven were boys and their only daughter was Anna, who married our Abraham Wenger (A222). Peter, Jr., Samuel, Henry and John, together with their father, Peter Eby, Sr., served in the Revolutionary War with Henry Wenger, Sr. (A22), as reported in the previous chapter.

Peter Eby, Sr., not only was a large landowner but was considered a man of above average means. In the inventory of his estate dated September 6, 1796, his household effects alone were valued at more than 2,540 pounds, considered a large sum in those days.

All of the Wenger descendants recorded in this chapter and all subsequent chapters are descendants from these well-known Eby ancestors. The summary is as follows: Theodorus Eby (1st), Bishop Jacob Eby (2nd), Theodorus Eby (3rd), Peter Eby (4th), Peter Eby (5th) and Anna Eby Wenger (6th). Most of the Eby story is reported in *The Eby Family Bulletin*, by Franklin Stanton Aby, M.D., Chicago, 1924.

It is interesting to note that David Eby, brother of Anna Eby

Wenger, prior to her marriage to Abraham Wenger (A222) made a conditional sale of 82 acres of the Eby Upper Leacock land to her on February 9, 1791. The land was for half payment of a 500 pound debt of David Eby to his sister, Anna. David was to pay $250 cash by November 1, 1798, or the deal was to become null and void. This transaction (Lancaster County Mortgage Book HH, 487) seems to indicate that Anna Eby had accumulated what would be considered substantial means for a young lady in those early days. This could have been another reason for the documentary planning on behalf of Anna. As a sequel to this instrument, David Eby paid the remaining debt June 6, 1792, at which time it was acknowledged that Anna had intermarried with Abraham Wenger (A222) and that the both of them had acknowledged satisfaction. (Book 00, p. 86) Thus the record shows this couple had at least some substance with which to start married life.

The Abraham Wenger (A222) homestead in Salisbury Township, Lancaster County. Peter Henry Wenger (A2226) was born here.

The Old Abraham Wenger (A222) Home

Abraham (A222) and Anna Eby Wenger in 1793 started their married life in Salisbury Township, Lancaster County, north of the Old Lancaster-Philadelphia Road on the banks of Pequea Creek where the water was "clear, cold and transparent." According to

Smith, this locale had "grapevines and clematis intertwining among the lofty branches of the majestic buttonwood, which formed a pleasant retreat from the noon beams of the summer sun."

This home on the old Abraham Wenger (A222) farm in Salisbury Township is owned by Mr. and Mrs. Harry S. Lapp.

Abraham (A222) built a stone house about 100 feet north of the east-west Lancaster-Philadelphia dirt road which was to be their home for the next 20 years. Mr. Aldus Seldomridge, a lifelong resident of Salisbury Township, lived across the road from the Wenger place and he gave to the writer a graphic description of this original stone house which was destroyed in 1940. As a boy Mr. Seldomridge was in this house and around the Wenger farm a great deal. He described the hillside house, the well in the side yard, the lime kiln on the opposite side of the house and nearby Pequea Creek in such detail that our artist was able to reproduce the picture on this page. Mr. Seldomridge states this reproduction is a near likeness to the original scene. This Wenger farm is now completely modernized and is owned by Mr. and Mrs. Harry S. Lapp.

The Lancaster-Philadelphia Road

This first road to Philadelphia from Lancaster was known as the King's Highway. It was built in 1733. The road followed the old Indian trail all the way to Philadelphia. Later the road was known as the Old Philadelphia Road, the Lancaster-Philadelphia Turnpike, the Provincial Road and, later, the Continental Road, and now is Highway 340. The original old dirt road, particularly in the winter, was made almost impassable by rain and snow. As a result, the public demanded a hard-surfaced road. In 1786 the Lancaster Turnpike Company was chartered to build the first macadamized road in America.

The road was finished in 1794, a year after Abraham Wenger's (A222) stone house was built. The road was 21 feet wide, a great advance over the Old Philadelphia Road. The new road was a great boon to commerce. Numerous stagecoach companies were organized. Traffic was at an all-time high. Over 60 taverns dotted the highway between Lancaster and Philadelphia, not the least of which was the Compassville Hotel or "Sign of the Mariner's Compass." This "well frequented tavern" was owned by Margaret Armor in 1813 and, as late as 1842, was owned by Isaac Eby, both of whom were protagonists, much to the consternation of some members of the Wenger clan.

To the south lay the village of Gap, famous in the early history of the country. It was named after Henry Slaymaker who was a member of the Constitutional Convention in Philadelphia in 1776 and a prominent member of Congress. In 1794, with the completion

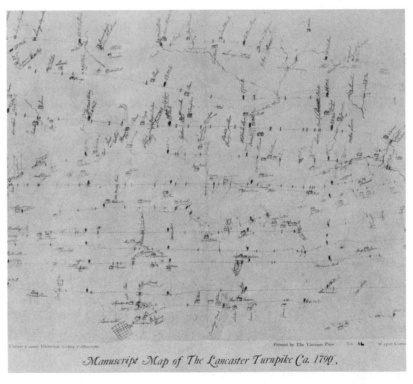

Manuscript Map of The Lancaster Turnpike Ca. 1790.

of the new road, Henry Slaymaker's sons, Amos and his two brothers, established a stage-line and a tavern known as "The Sign of John Adams." In Salisbury Township of Lancaster County and West Caln Township of Chester County, this wayside inn next to the church and school was a most important meeting place.

The Sign of John Adams with the stage travelers, the only post office and the only bank, was a point of community interest and news for miles around.

The Compassville Area

By April 13, 1801, Abraham (A222) had made sufficient progress to purchase in his own name 18 acres in West Caln Township of Chester County located next to the property inherited by his wife. (Chester County Deed Book T-2, 177, 179) He apparently con-

The Compassville hotel and stables as it looks today.

tinued to hold this while living in Lancaster County. The Wenger land of 30 acres in Salisbury Township of Lancaster County was about one and one-half miles west, down the turnpike from the West Caln land in Chester County. The principal community of interest to these two farms was Compassville, although the nearest post office was in the village of Cains.

Some of the nearby communities had blacksmith and wheelwright shops to serve the traffic on the Lancaster-Philadelphia Road. Byerstown had a wheelwright shop owned by James McCachren. Cambridge to the north had a coach, smith and wagon shop. White Horse Village had a combination business consisting of a gristmill, harness manufacturing, a tin shop, a smith shop and cigar manufacturing which was owned by Weiler and Robinson. At Limeville Jacob Barr and his son had a smith and wagon shop. They also owned the lime quarry for which the town was named.

It is altogether within the realm of probability that Abraham (A222) was employed in this neighborhood as wheelwright. Then, too, the demand for lime fertilizer could have sent him to Limeville as it did later when his son, Peter Henry (A2226), not only worked at Limeville but at Quarryville as well.

The one-room school near Lapp.

Near Lapp, one mile southwest of the Wenger Salisbury farm, was the only one-room school to serve the area. Here is where some of the later generation Wenger children may have received a meager education.

Family Pattern

Abraham (A222) and Anna Eby Wenger had eight children of the fourth generation as follows: Emanuel (A2221), Nancy (A2222), Catharine (A2223), Samuel (A2224), Isaac (A2225), Peter Henry (A2226), David (A2227) and John (A2228). The Census of 1800 shows Abraham (A222) and Anna Eby Wenger as residents of Salisbury Township. They had lived there since 1793. In 1800 they had one son and two daughters under ten years of age. These were undoubtedly their son, Emanuel (A2221), and their daughters, Nancy (A2222) and Catharine (A2223). It is thought that the Abraham Wenger (A222) family continued to live in Salisbury Township for at least 17 years and probably longer, since the Census of 1810 showed them living there with four boys under ten and the two girls. The four boys probably were Samuel (A2224), Isaac (A2225), Peter Henry (A2226) and a son who probably died in infancy. The girls were Nancy (A2222) and Catharine (A2223). Emanuel (A2221) may not have been living at home at the time because he was the oldest son. The tax records in Lancaster County show the retention of taxable property in Salisbury by Abraham (A222) until 1846.

West Caln, Chester County

In the Census of 1820, Abraham (A222) and Anna were listed as living in West Caln Township, Chester County. At that time the record shows eight boys and two girls were living with them. Between 1810 and 1820 three more boys were born, one died young. David (A2227) and John (A2228) reached maturity. The total family that survived consisted of six boys and two girls of the fourth generation. However, these records show conclusively that of the eight Wenger children who reached maturity, Emanuel (A2221), Nancy (A2222), Catharine (A2223), Samuel (A2224), Isaac (A2225), Peter (A2226) and possibly David (A2227) were born in Salisbury Township, Lancaster County. John (A2228) was born in 1820, according to the Census of 1870, in West Caln Township, Chester County. According to his will, he died in 1899.

Abraham (A222) and His Sons

Abraham Wenger (A222) was a wheelwright and his son, Emanuel (A2221), followed in the same trade. This probably indicates that Emanuel (A2221), being the oldest son, was trained by his father. Peter Henry Wenger (A2226) was skilled in wood working which suggests that he, too, was trained by his father, but more particularly by his brother, Emanuel (A2221), who was said to be highly skilled. Emanuel (A2221) was ten years older and big brother to Peter Henry (A2226).

If one can judge from hand writing, Abraham Wenger (A222) was above average. From the early land deeds, his signature was written in an exceedingly legible hand, using English letters. This was at a time when most of the Pennsylvania Germans could speak very little English, let alone write the language.

A Chain of Reverses

About that time two events happened. First, Abraham Wenger (A222) and Anna, on August 5, 1819, granted the 30 acres in Salisbury and the 13½ acres in West Caln (willed to Anna by her father) to their son, Emanuel Wenger (A2221), to hold in trust until his mother's death. (Chester County, Deed Book Q-3, 518) Second, on August 31, 1819, the 18 acres containing "a fine good stone house," which Abraham Wenger (A222) bought on April 13, 1801, was seized as a result of legal action instituted by a Margaret Armor, then the owner of the Compassville Tavern and Inn, and a John Hopkins, and "taken in execution as property of Abraham Wenger (A222)." (No. 2, 1806-1823, p. 163)

An analysis of these two acts seems to indicate that since the country was in an economic depression, Abraham Wenger (A222) was in financial difficulty. Knowing this, they protected Anna's property by putting it in the name of their son, Emanuel Wenger (A2221). Secondly, Abraham (A222) lost his land which was seized to satisfy a debt of $456.94.

From 1820 through 1828, Abraham Wenger (A222) was assessed for unseated lands in West Caln Township of Chester County, which means that he was a non-resident landowner. From this we conclude two things. First, he ceased to legally reside in West Caln about 1820 (his land was seized in 1819) and, second, 1828 was the last date of his assessment. This gives rise to further reflection.

This modern home, owned by Mr. and Mrs. James W. Mc-Cowan, stands on the old Wenger farm site in West Caln Township, Chester County. The center portion behind the porch was the original log home in which Anna Eby Wenger lived.

If the "fine good stone house" went with the land in 1819, Abraham (A222) and Anna Eby Wenger had to make alternative provisions for living. It is believed that at about that time they removed to the log house situated on the adjacent land owned by Anna and given to her by her father, Peter Eby, Sr. One tradition, which springs from the distant past and is without verification, suggests that Abraham Wenger (A222), after his financial reverses in Chester County, with family acquiescence, went to Maryland.

In the meantime, his wife, Anna Eby Wenger, continued to live in her log cabin home on the Old Philadelphia Road in West Caln Township in Chester County. Coincidently, this home is still standing, completely modernized and owned by Mr. and Mrs. James W. McCowan. Isaac Wenger (A2228), Anna's son, lived nearly one-half mile south on the Wilmington Road and her sons, John and David, were living nearby. In Maryland, Abraham (A222) was to seek the means by which he could improve the family status. He had planned after success to have the balance of the family follow him there. However, the mission was not sufficiently successful to move the family to that state.

He returned to the family. While he remained with them, he maintained his "official residence" over the line where he held property in Salisbury Township in Lancaster County in order to

This grinding wheel from the nearby Stanton Mill is in the front yard of the McCowan home. The Wengers and the Stantons were neighbors.

avoid further harrassment from his creditors in Chester County. Tax records in Lancaster County show him paying residence taxes on his Salisbury homestead until 1846. It was indicated that he lived to an old age and was buried with his wife, Anna Eby Wenger. If this report is correct, it would account for his absence in Chester County, even though his wife, Anna Eby Wenger, and other members of the family continued to be documented there. At least three of his children named their sons after him. If he was 25 years old when he was married in 1792, it would indicate a birth date about 1767. It seems reasonable to conclude the following vital statistics: Abraham Wenger (A222; 1767-1845), age 78.

Anna Eby Wenger

In the West Caln records, Anna Eby Wenger was listed in the assessment rolls from 1823 to 1846 as head of a household in that township. From this we conclude that she was officially alone after 1823 and that she died in 1846. According to the Census of 1800, we believe she was 18 years old when she married in 1792, which would indicate a birth date of 1774. It seems to be a reasonable assumption that the vital dates would be Anna Eby Wenger (1774-

1846), age 72. Since her estate was settled in her name as Anna Eby Wenger, it seems to give credence to the family report concerning Abraham (A222).

The Inventory

A copy of the appraisal and inventory of the "goods and chattels, rights and credits" of Anna Wenger "late of the Township of West Caln and County of Chester" taken January 31, 1846, is a good barometer of the living arrangements of that day. (Chester County Administration #10909) Among some 50 listed items, we find the following: one horse pistol, one side saddle, one dearborn wagon, one cow, one heifer and one gray mare. The value was a grand total of $254.11.

On February 13, 1846, the household items of Anna Eby Wenger were distributed to those of her children living in Chester County with the exception of brick bands, two hackles and a frying pan valued at 73¢ to Emanuel Wenger (A2221) and a riding bridle valued at 10¢ to Samuel Wenger (A2224). The latter sons lived in Lancaster County. Peter Henry Wenger (A2226), the sixth-born son who lived in Bath Township, Greene County, Ohio, and Isaac Wenger (A2225), the fifth-born son who at that time lived in Lancaster County, were left out entirely. The total value of these items was $151.17.

It is interesting to note the variety of items. David Wenger (A2227) received items listed as follows: One skillet, one tub, a basket of onions, two augers, one bedstead, a drawing knife, steel bars, copper stuff, one lot of boards, four shoats, five chairs, two tablecloths, one quilt, a feather bed, one dresser, dried cherries and one crock of pickles.

John Wenger (A2228) received one smoothing iron, one desk, one pitcher and one sugar bowl. Benjamin Gilbert (A22232) received three plates, cups and saucers, two sauce dishes, a lamp, one waffle iron, a tea set and one crock of pickles. Finally, Isaac Gilbert (A22233) received one churn and one heifer.

Reinforced Evidence

On March 31, 1847, Robert Baldwin purchased the 30-acre Wenger homestead in Salisbury Township, Lancaster County, from the estate of Anna Eby Wenger. This transaction is recorded in Lancaster County (Deed Book D-7, 664). A copy of the Peter Eby, Sr., will (Book I-1, 114-1794) was appended and reiterates all previously indicated facts.

In 1893 this property, with refined description, was conveyed to the heirs of Robert Baldwin, namely A. C. Baldwin et al.

These documents (Deed Book D-7, 644) and the Lancaster County Orphans Court record (Book 1847-March, 1848, p. 315), as well as Lancaster County Deed Book K-14, p. 181, are of such importance that they are abstrated as follows:

Peter Eby, Sr., Administration to Robert Baldwin

Indenture made 31 March 1847 between Joseph Plank of West Caln Township, Chester County, Pennsylvania, administrator de bonis non with the will annexed of Peter Eby Senior, late of Leacock Township, Lancaster County, Pennsylvania, deceased, and Robert Baldwin of Salisbury Township, Lancaster County, Pennsylvania.

Whereas Peter Eby Senior was seized of a tract of land in Salisbury Township.

Beginning at a post on the East side of Pequa Creek thence N 44 deg. E 70 per. to a post, thence N 36 deg. E 20 per. to a post, thence S 72 deg. W 129 per. to a post, a corner of land late of Benjamin Miller, now or late of Archibald Douglas, thence SE 19 per. to a post, thence S 77 deg. E 8 per. to a post by land of Joseph Cookson, S 74 deg. E 40 per. to a post, thence N 8 per. to a post on Pequa Creek, thence up the same on the Several Courses thereof 92 per. to the place of Beginning.

Containing 30¼ Acres 7 perches.

Being the same tract which John Wilson and Jane his wife by Indenture dated 11 April 1793 conveyed to Peter Eby Senior.

Whereas Peter Eby, being so seized, died first having made his will dated 26 June 1793 wherein he devised as follows, viz. Item I give to my daughter Anna, wife of Abraham Wenger, three tracts of land, one in Salisbury Township, Lancaster County, adjoining land of William Boyd, Isaac Attle and others containing 30 Acres more or less, one other in West Caln Township, Chester County, Pennsylvania, adjoining lands of John Boyd and others, containing 10 Acres more or less, and one other in West Caln Township adjoining land of John Boyd, Provincial Road and others, containing 3¼ Acres, more or less. To hold unto my daughter Anna during her natural life, and immediately after the decease of my said daughter Anna, I order my executors and the Survivor or Survivors of them to sell the three tracts to the best advantage they can, and order the proceeds of such sale to be distributed according to the provisions of said will.

Whereas the said Anna the devisee of the land is now deceased and whereas Peter Eby, Senior, in his will, appointed his son Peter Eby and Samuel Eby his sole Executors who are both now deceased and letters of administration de bonis non with will annexed have been granted to Joseph Plank.

Witnesseth that Joseph Plank for $2,855.55 paid by Robert Baldwin hath sold to Robert Baldwin the first described tract containing 30 Acres, more or less.

Signed date above
Witnesses: *John Myers*
          Josiah Lamborn
Acknowledged: 31 March 1847   *Joseph Plank,* Admr.
Recorded: April 1, 1847

Joseph Plank, Administrator of Peter Eby, late of Leacock Township, dec'd, having stated and filed in the Register's Office at Lancaster the administration account on the estate of said dec'd and legal notice thereof being given by said Register, a copy of the same is now produced to the Court for confirmation, whereby it appears that the said account was duly passed by the said Register and that there remains in the hands of said Accountant a balance of $3,091.02. The Court on due examination thereof and advisement had thereon approve of and confirm the same and direct that the said balance be paid and distributed according to law.

(See Chester County F-5, 401; F-11, 168, 171; G-5, 180 and W-12, 567)

Robert Baldwin Heirs to A. C. Baldwin et al.

Indenture made 3 June 1893 Between E. D. Baldwin and Violetta his wife of the Borough of Coatesville, Chester County, Pennsylvania, W. W. Baldwin and Ella M. his wife of the City of Philadelphia, Edith S. Baldwin, Margaret E. Oberholtzer and Christian H. Oberholtzer her husband of Salisbury Township, Lancaster County, Pennsylvania, of the first part and A. C. Baldwin and R. A. Baldwin of Salisbury Township, Lancaster County, Pennsylvania. The said grantors and A. C. and R. A. Baldwin, the grantees, being children of the late Robert Baldwin, dec'd, and legatees under the intestate laws of Pennsylvania.

Witnesseth that E. D. Baldwin and Violetta his wife, W. W. Baldwin and Ella M. his wife, Edith S. Baldwin and Margaret E. Oberholtzer for $1,333.34 paid by A. C. and R. A. Baldwin have sold to A. C. and R. A.

Baldwin all that undivided four sixth interest or part of a tract of meadow and farm land in Salisbury Township, Lancaster County, Pennsylvania.

Beginning at a stone near the South side of the Old Philadelphia and Lancaster Road a corner of land of Isaac B. Sweigert thence by same 11¼ deg. E 7 6/100 chains to a stone and by same N 73½ deg. E 4 92/100 chains to a stone a corner of Jacob Wanner's land, thence by Wanner's land and Reuben Wenger's land respectively N 73¼ deg. E 22 chains to a stone on the West bank of Pequa Creek, thence down the bank of said Creek by land of Abraham Brubaker to a bend in the Creek, thence by land of the Estate of Harriet Skiles S 45½ deg. W 13 4/10 chains to a stone and by said Skiles Estate the next 3 courses and distances S 23 3/4 deg. W 5 8/10 chains to a stone at the edge of a pond S 52½ deg. E 12 63/100 chains crossing Pequa Creek and S 3½ deg. W 3 25/100 chains recrossing Pequa Creek to an Iron pin near the middle of the aforesaid Old Road in line of land of Levi R. Oberholser, thence along near the middle of said Road by land of said Oberholser and John Reeser, respectively, N 70 deg. W 80 59/100 chains to a stone, thence by said Reeser and running toward the South side of s'd Road N 64 3/4 deg. W 18 89/100 chains to place of Beginning.

Containing 20 Acres 25 perches, more or less.

Being the greater part of a tract of 30 Acres 45 perches which Joseph Plank, Administrator de bonus non with Will annexed of Peter Eby, Sr. by Deed dated 31 March 1847 granted to Robert Baldwin (now dec'd). The Indenture recorded in Book D-7, p. 644.

Subject to the sum of $666.66 the interest shall be paid to Harriet Baldwin, widow of Robert Baldwin, dec'd. After the death of Harriet Baldwin, the principal sum of $666.66 shall be paid to the heirs of Robert Baldwin, dec'd.

Signed date above:	*E. D. Baldwin*
Acknowledged: 3 June 1893 and	*Violetta Baldwin*
28 July 1893	*Wm. W. Baldwin*
Recorded: August 7, 1893	*Ella M. Baldwin*
	Edith Baldwin
	Margaret E. Oberholser
	C. H. Oberholser

This finalizes not only our analysis that the 30 acres in Salisbury Township was the locale of the Abraham Wenger (A222) homestead but that all except one of the Wenger children of the fourth generation were born there. It also suggests that this could well be the locale for possible church affiliations and the cemetery of principal Wenger interment.

This document of January 5, 1848, contains some of the original signatures of Emanuel Wenger and other members of the family. The deed is in the possession of Mr. and Mrs. James W. McCowan who consented to the reproduction.

Locale of the Abraham Wenger (A222) Family

Peter Henry Wenger (A2226), the son of Abraham (A222) and Anna Eby Wenger, was listed as a freeman in West Caln in 1827. He was 21 years of age at that time.

It is apparent that the children of Abraham (A222) and Anna Eby Wenger, with the exception of Peter Henry (A2226) and his wife, Anna, (they were living in Greene County, Ohio) were identified as living near their mother at the time of her death. We believe

Abraham Wenger (A222) preceded his wife, Anna, in death, possibly about 1845.

On the 5th of January, 1848, (F-5, 401 Chester County Deed Book) in settling the estate of Anna Eby Wenger, the following children were listed as heirs: Emanuel Wenger (A2221) and his wife, Anna, of Strasburg, Lancaster County, Pennsylvania; Catharine (A2223), (widow of Benjamin Gilbert), of Sadsbury Township, Chester County; Nancy Wenger (A2222) of West Caln, Chester County; Samuel Wenger (A2224) and his wife, Hester, Isaac Wenger (A2225), both of Martic Township, Lancaster County; Peter Henry Wenger (A2226) and his wife, Anna, of Bath Township, Greene County, Ohio; David Wenger (A2227) and his wife, Elizabeth; John Wenger (A2228) and his wife, Jane, both of West Caln Township, Chester County, Pennsylvania.

The importance of this document is such that we reproduce the abstract in its entirety:

Emanuel Wenger et al. to Robert Baldwin

Indenture made 5 January 1848 Between Emanuel Wenger of Strasburg Township, Lancaster County, Pennsylvania, and Ann his wife, Catherine (widow of Benjamin Gilbert deceased) of Sadsbury Township, Chester County, Pennsylvania, Nancy Wenger by her attorney, Samuel B. Thomas, Esquire, of West Chester, Chester County, Pennsylvania, Samuel Wenger of Martic Township, Lancaster County and Hester his wife, Isaac Wenger of same place, Peter Wenger of Bath Township, Greene County, Ohio and Ann his wife by their attorney Joseph Plank of West Caln Township, Chester County, Pennsylvania, David Wenger and Elizabeth his wife, John Wenger and Jane his wife both of West Caln Township, Chester County, Pennsylvania (the said Emanuel, Catherine, Nancy, Samuel, Isaac, Peter, David and John being the only heirs of Nancy Wenger late of West Caln Township, Chester County, Pennsylvania, deceased) and Robert Baldwin of Salisbury Township, Lancaster County, Pennsylvania, merchant.

Witnesseth that Emanuel Wenger and Ann his wife, Catharine Wenger (late Catherine Gilbert) [sic], Nancy Wenger by her attorney, Samuel B. Thomas, Samuel Wenger and Hester his wife, Isaac Wenger, Peter Wenger and Ann his wife, by their attorney Joseph Plank, David Wenger and Elizabeth his wife, John Wenger and Jane his wife for $214.12½ paid to them by Robert Baldwin, have sold to Robert Baldwin, his heirs and assigns, all them two adjoining tracts in West Caln Township bounded as follows:

One beginning at a stone or a post for a corner of other land conveyed to Robert Baldwin thence by same N 52 deg. E 53 per. to a stone in a line of Clement A. & Mathew B. Buckley's land, thence by same N 54 deg. W 13½ per. to a stone thence by said Baldwin's other purchase S 52 deg. W 30½ per. N 62 deg. W 14 9/10 per. to a stone in line of John D. Wilson's land, thence by same, and the other piece of this purchase S 28 deg. W 20 8/10 per. to a post in the Provincial road, thence long same by land of Isaac Eby S 62 deg. E 18 2/10 per. to place of Beginning.

Containing (by a late survey) 5 acres 70 perches. (It being the same premises which Jacob Kurtz by indenture dated 3 September 1820 did grant unto Peter Eby in trust only for the heirs aforesaid [they being then minors] to them their heirs and assigns.)

The other Beginning at a stone for a corner of John D. Wilson's land, thence by same S 79 3/4 deg. E 38 7/10 per. to a stone in a line of the other part of this purchase thence by same S 26¼ deg. W 8 per. to a stone in the Provincial road thence along same by land of Isaac Eby N 74 3/4 deg. W 20½ per. to stone S 82¼ deg. W 14 per. to a stone, thence by land of William Wagoner N 10 6/10 per. to place of beginning.

Containing 1 acre and 112 perches. (It being the same lot that Per. Wagoner and Mary his wife by indenture did grant to said Nancy Wenger (deceased) in trust for her children their heirs and assigns.) Together with the houses, out-houses, buildings, barns, stables, etc., thereunto belonging. And all the estate of each and every one of them, the said Emanuel Wenger and Ann his wife, Catherine Gilbert, late Wenger, Nancy Wenger by her attorney Samuel B. Thomas, Samuel Wenger and Hester his wife, Isaac Wenger, Peter Wenger and Ann his wife by their attorney Joseph Plank, David Wenger and Elizabeth his wife, John Wenger and Jane his wife in the same .

And the said Emanuel Wenger, Catherine Gilbert, Nancy Wenger by her attorney Samuel B. Thomas, Samuel Wenger, Isaac Wenger, Peter Wenger by his attorney Joseph Plank, David Wenger and John Wenger to grant unto Robert Baldwin the said above two described lots.

Signed date above:	*Emanuel Wenger*
Acknowledged: 5 January 1848	*Ann X Wenger*
The said Ann, Hester, Elizabeth	*Catherine X Gilbert*
and Jane being of full age.	*Samuel Wenger*
	Esther Wenger
Recorded: April 1, 1848	*Isaac X Wenger*
	David X Wenger
	Elizabeth X Wenger
	John X Wenger
	Jane Wenger
	Joseph Plank
	(Attorney for
	Peter Henry Wenger
	and Anna Barr Wenger)

Robert Baldwin, the purchaser of the Wenger properties, was a prominent citizen of Salisbury Township in Lancaster County. He came to Salisbury Township from Chester County in 1827. He taught school for three years. In 1843 he erected a large brick building in which he did mercantile business for nearly half a century. This public spirited citizen was a member of the Pennslyvania legislature in 1849 and 1850 and was a member of the Senate in 1857. A. C. Baldwin and his brother and sisters later operated the business as A. C. BALDWIN AND BROTHERS. His descendants are many and are still prominent citizens in this area.

Wenger Family Notes

As for the children of Abraham (A222) and Anna Eby Wenger, five of them of the fourth generation continued to live in Chester County. These were Nancy (A2222), Catharine (A2223), Isaac (A2225), David (A2227), and John (A2228). Emanuel (A2221) and Samuel (A2224) lived in Lancaster County while Peter Henry (A2226) lived in Ohio.

Nancy (A2222) of the fourth generation, born in Salisbury Township, Lancaster County, about 1797, lived in West Chester, Chester County. She did not marry. She died September 7, 1871.

It should be noted that Catharine Wenger Gilbert (A2223) of the fourth generation, who was born in 1800, according to the Census of 1850 resided in Sadsbury Township, Chester County. She married Benjamin Gilbert. They had the following children of the fifth generation: Rachel (A22231), Benjamin (A22232) age 25, Isaac (A22233) age 23, Eliza (A22234) age 18, Edwin (A22235) age 14 and Mifflin (A22236) age 12. Catharine Wenger Gilbert's (A2223) will (U-20, 525; 1856, Chester County) after her death in 1856 divided her estate among her children. She at that time was a resident of Valley Township, formed from Sadsbury in 1852. Isaac Gilbert (A22233) of the above had four children of the sixth generation as follows: Isaac (A222331), Benjamin (A222332), James (A222333) and Kate (A222334).

Isaac Wenger (A2225) of the fourth generation was born in 1805 and died July 23, 1879. Prior to 1850 he lived with his brother Samuel (A2224) in Martic Township, Lancaster County. In 1852 he returned to West Caln Township, Chester County, where on March 25, 1852, he married Isabella Gallagher. On April 3, 1852, he purchased five acres to establish a home. This was located about one-half mile south of his mother's home on the old Wilmington Road. In 1855 Isaac (A2225) and Isabella had a daughter, Sarah A. (Sallie) Wenger (A22251) of the fifth generation. (Administration Book F-6, 376 #19124; 1879)

Bewitchment of Sallie Waddell

Upon reaching maturity, Sallie (A22251) married a man by the name of Waddell. An interesting human interest story concerning Sallie (A22251) appeared in the Daily Local News dated May 19, 1880. It read as follows:

> Bewitched — Mrs. Sallie Waddell, residing in what is known as Frogtown, West Caln Township, has lately become annoyed and alarmed by strange noises about her premises, particularly during the night. All efforts to discover the cause have thus far proved to be of no avail, and she is now laboring under the belief that either one of her relations has bewitched her or her house is haunted by evil spirits. Sallie had better put a few rat traps about her house, and perhaps she may be able to capture a few of those "evil spirits."

After the death of Isaac Wenger (A2225) in 1879, Robert Baldwin, administrator of his estate, petitioned the judge of the Orphans Court to sell the Wenger property for the payment of the debts of the decedent (F-6,376 #19124; 1879). The Judge granted the request October 6, 1879, and on November 22, 1879, Robert Baldwin sold the property for $179 to A. C. Baldwin! (Chester County Orphans Court Docket 30, 159, and Deed Book L-11, 41, 91)

David Wenger (A2227)

It is believed that David Wenger (A2227) of the fourth generation was born about 1815 and died in Chester County prior to 1866. He probably lived elsewhere for a time, returning to Chester County prior to 1866. (Ad. BK 8, 43, #26495; 1899) In the newspaper called the Village Record dated December 22, 1866, we find the following item:

"By writ of Vend. Exp. will be sold on Friday the 15 January next at 12 noon at Compass Tavern, West Caln, all the interest of David Winger in a tenement and tract bounded by lands of John Wilson, George Buckley and others containing about 25 acres, 3 log houses, frame stable and timberland. Seized and taken in execution as

property of David Winger, and to be sold by J. B. Wood, Sheriff."
At that time the Compassville Tavern was owned by Isaac Eby who
was the litigant against David Wenger.

David (A2227) was married twice. His first wife's name was
Elizabeth and his second wife had the name of Susan. On November 2, 1866, Letters of Administration (15458) on the estate of David
Wenger (A2227) of West Caln Township, Chester County, contained the renunciation of his widow, Susan Wenger. (Ad. Bk. 6, 27,
#15458; 1866) There is no record of children from either wife.

John Wenger (A2228)

John Wenger's (A2228) will (32,95; 1899 West Caln, Chester
County) appointed his wife as executrix. Her name was Mary
Margaret Rebecca Wenger. John (A2228) of the fourth generation
was born in West Caln Township, Chester County, and died in the
same place in 1899. The Census of 1870 in West Caln, Chester
County, lists John Wenger (A2228) age 50, Mary age 31, Abraham
(A22281) age 10, Emanuel (A22282) age 6 and Emma (A22283)
age 4, the latter three of the fifth generation. John's (A2228) first
wife was named Jane.

Little Emanuel (A22282) came to a very sad ending. In the newspaper *American Republican* in the issue of January 14, 1873, the
following item appeared:

> Bled to death — About two years ago, Emanuel Wenger, a son of John
> Wenger of West Caln, while playing with one of the neighbor's children,
> was struck in the stomach with a stone, which caused him to bleed
> profusely; since that time, whenever hurt, he would bleed profusely
> from the mouth. On Thursday evening the wound was opened again,
> and he bled to death. He was about 8 years old.

There is no further record concerning these children of John
Wenger (A2228).

Samuel Wenger (A2224) of Lancaster County

Samuel (A2224) and his first wife, Hester, lived near Smithville
in Martic, later Providence Township, Lancaster County. They had
five known children of the fifth generation. Susanna (A22241),
Isaac (A22242), Elizabeth (A22243), Jacob (A22244) and John
(A22245). All are believed to be buried in the Providence Mennonite Cemetery, Providence Township, Lancaster County. John

The Samuel Wenger (A2224) farm house in Providence Township, Lancaster County, as it looks today. This is now the Ray Deiter farm near Hessdale.

(A22245) was in the Civil War. President Lincoln called for 75,000 volunteers from the State of Pennsylvania in July 1862. The Governor of the State authorized a camp east of the City of Lancaster where volunteers were inducted into the army. Regiment 122 of the Pennsylvania Volunteers was formed on August 11, 1862. John Wenger (A22245) joined Company D. The Regiment was rushed into action in the Washington, D.C., area. John Wenger (A22245) was killed in action, October 7, 1862.

Susanna (A22241) married John Miller. They had a daughter Mary Ann (A222411) of the sixth generation who died in 1867 at the age of 20. She is buried in the Providence Mennonite Cemetery. It is believed that both Samuel (A2224) and his wife Hester (she died prior to 1860) are buried in the same cemetery, but there are no grave markers. Samuel (A2224) married his second wife, Barbara, prior to 1870.

Isaac (A22242) married Ann Kreider. In the Census records of 1860, 1870 and 1880, Isaac (A22242) was indicated a farmer in Providence Township (formerly Martic), where he resided on a farm near his father, Samuel (A2224), and had the following children of the sixth generation: Hettie Ann (A222421), born in 1857; Mary Elizabeth (A222422), born in 1859; Emma (A222423), born in 1866; Ann (A222424) born in 1867; Susan (A222425) born in 1869 and John (A222426) born in 1872. The grandfather, John Kreider, was living with Isaac (A22242) and Ann Wenger in 1880.

For the record of the first-born son of Abraham Wenger (A222) and Anna Eby Wenger, namely Emanuel Wenger (A2221) and the sixth-born son, Peter Henry Wenger (A2226), see the chapters bearing their names.

Providence Mennonite Meetinghouse and Cemetery.

The Abraham Wenger (A222) Family Tree follows.

Abraham Wenger (A222) Family Tree

1st Hans Wenger (b. About 1430) Blumenstein, Thun
2nd Burkhard Wenger (b. About 1450) Forst, Thun
3rd Peter Wenger (b. About 1470) Wattenwil, Seftigen
4th Peter Wenger (b. About 1490) Wattenwil, Seftigen
5th Rudolfus Wenger (b. About 1510) Wattenwil, Seftigen
6th Hans Wenger (b. About 1530) Wattenwil, Seftigen

7th Rudolfus Wenger (Ch. April 5, 1566) Wattenwil-Thurnen, Seftigen

8th Peter Wenger (Ch. Dec. 13, 1607) Wattenwil-Thurnen, Seftigen

9th Hans Wenger (Ch. May 30, 1633) Wattenwil-Thurnen, Seftigen

    A Christian Wenger (A2) First Generation in America (1688-1749)

        B-1 Henry Wenger, Sr. (A22) Second Generation in America (1716-1802)

            C-1 Abraham Wenger (A222) Third Generation in America
b. 1767, d. 1845, Pennsylvania
m. Anna Eby May 22, 1792, Lancaster
b. 1774, d. 1846

                D-1 Emanuel Wenger (A2221-4th)
(See Emanuel Wenger Chapter and Family Tree, following)

                D-2 Nancy Wenger (A2222-4th)
b. 1797, d. Sept. 7, 1871

                D-3 Catharine Wenger (A2223-4th)
b. 1800, d. 1856
m. Benjamin Gilbert
d. before Jan. 5, 1848

                    E-1 Rachel Gilbert (A22231-5th)
m. Stevenson

                    E-2 Benjamin Gilbert (A22232-5th)
b. 1825

                    E-3 Isaac Gilbert (A22233-5th)
b. 1827, d. Dec. 3, 1902

                        F-1 Isaac Gilbert (A222331-6th)
m. Sarah A.

                        F-2 Benjamin Gilbert (A222332-6th)
m. Annie M.

                        F-3 James Gilbert (A222333-6th)

                        F-4 Kate Gilbert (A222334-6th)

                    E-4 Eliza Gilbert (A22234-5th)
b. 1832

                    E-5 Edwin Gilbert (A22235-5th)
b. 1836, d. Oct. 13, 1881
m. Bell

E-6 Mifflin Gilbert (A22236-5th)
    b. 1838, d. 1919
    m. Bell, Sept. 11, 1885

D-4 Samuel Wenger (A2224-4th)
    b. 1803
    m. Hester before 1825 (1st)
    d. prior to 1860
    m. Barbara before 1870 (2nd)

E-1 Susanna Wenger (A22241-5th)
    m. John Miller

  F-1 Mary Ann Miller (A222411-6th)
      b. 1847, d. 1867

E-2 Isaac Wenger (A22242-5th)
    b. 1830, d. after 1880
    m. Ann Kreider
    b. 1833

  F-1 Hettie Ann Wenger (A222421-6th)
      b. 1857

  F-2 Mary Elizabeth Wenger (A222422-6th)
      b. 1859

  F-3 Emma Wenger (A222423-6th)
      b. 1866

  F-4 Ann Wenger (A222424-6th)
      b. 1867

  F-5 Susan Wenger (A222425-6th)
      b. 1869

  F-6 John Wenger (A222426-6th)
      b. 1872

E-3 Elizabeth Wenger (A22243-5th)
    b. 1832

E-4 Jacob Wenger (A22244-5th)

E-5 John Wenger (A22245-5th)
    b. 1839, d. Oct. 7, 1862

D-5 Isaac Wenger (A2225-4th)
    b. 1805, d. July 23, 1879
    m. Isabella Gallagher, March 25, 1852

E-1 Sarah A. (Sallie) Wenger (A22251-5th)
    b. 1855
    m. Waddell

D-6 Peter Henry Wenger (A2226-4th)
     (See Peter Henry Wenger Chapter and
     Family Tree, following)

D-7 David Wenger (A2227-4th)
     m. Elizabeth (1st)
     m. Susan (2nd)

D-8 John Wenger (A2228-4th)
     b. 1820, d. July 20, 1899
     m. Jane (1st)
     m. Mary Margaret Rebecca (2nd)
       b. 1839

  E-1 Abraham Wenger (A22281-5th)
      b. 1860

  E-2 Emanuel Wenger (A22282-5th)
      b. 1864, d. 1873

  E-3 Emma Jane Wenger (A22283-5th)
      b. 1866
      m. Gilbert

  E-4 Catharine Wenger (A22284-5th)
      m. Allen

  E-5 Rachel Wenger (A22285-5th)
      m. Siverd

Chapter Eight

Emanuel Wenger of Lancaster County

EMANUEL WENGER (A2221) was born in Salisbury Township, Lancaster County, Pennsylvania, November 6, 1795. He was the oldest son of Abraham Wenger (A222) and Anna Eby Wenger, the grandson of Henry Wenger, Sr. (A22), and the great-grandson of Christian Wenger (A2). As the oldest son, he played the role of big brother to the other seven brothers and sisters in his family.

A traditional story in Lancaster County indicated that Emanuel (A221) was an immigrant and was shipwrecked off the coast of Ireland. As a result, he stayed in that country for seven years. He was supposed to have married an Irish lass after which they came to Lancaster County, Pennsylvania. It was indicated that this family had no relationship whatsoever to the other Wenger families residing in that county. This story proved to be completely erroneous. Emanuel Wenger (A2221) not only was born in Salisbury Township, Lancaster County, but he was the brother of the writer's great-grandfather, Peter Henry Winger (A2226). It is true that Emanuel Wenger (A2221) married an Irish girl, Anna Griffith, but he married her in Lancaster County. Anna was the daughter of Thomas Griffith and was born in Lancaster County, April 14, 1798.

Through Maud Yuninger (A2221433), a descendant of Emanuel Wenger (A2221), we learn of a tradition that Emanuel (A2221) and his father Abraham (A222) were extremely skilled as wheelwrights and wood craftsmen. They made complete wheels and parts for Conestoga wagons which hauled freight to Philadelphia over the old Lancaster-Philadelphia turnpike. They also were renowned for fine cabinetwork and wood finishing.

The inventory of the Emanuel Wenger (A2221) estate dated September 10, 1864 (Book-1, 424, Lancaster County), shows evidence of him as a wagoner. It indicates he had many wheelwright tools, spokes, and dressed felloes, lines, ropes, a crosscut saw and gauges, a jack screw, chains, perch poles and small spokes, wagon bows, an anvil, trussels, a grindstone, a wagon bed, wagon tongs, wagon tires, a large assortment of lumber, ash, oak and pine planks, an assortment of axles, a shaving and turning lathe and 54 finished spokes.

Emanuel Wenger (A2221) Farm

Emanuel and his wife, Anna, spent most of their adult life on a three-acre tract of land one and one-half miles south of the Village of Strasburg in south central Lancaster County. The abstracts from Deed Book A, Mis, p. 216, March 26, 1859, in Lancaster County explain the transfer of this property. "HENRY AND BARBARA NEFF, of Strasburg Township, sold to Emanuel Wenger, wagon-maker, property for $500, on the road from Strasburg to White Oak Tavern, by lands of Henry Musselman, David Steiner, Frederick Fitzmayer, Christian Hoover, by other land of Henry Neff, containing three acres (being part of larger estate which Senator John Strohm, assignee of Jacob H. Hoover and wife Ann by date of March 29, 1858, sold to Neff)."

Emanuel Wenger (A2221) farm house south of Strasburg.

The writer and his wife visited this old homestead in the summer of 1968. A part of the old house built by Emanuel Wenger (A2221) is still standing and is occupied by the present owner, Mr. Clarence R. Hess.

Undoubtedly some of the cabinetwork of Emanuel Wenger (A2221) is not only in this old home, but in the hands of some of his multitudinous descendants. His inventory included a cherry table, two chests, numerous chairs and a spinning wheel.

Emanuel Wenger (A2221) living on a three-acre tract and trying to raise a family of eight was in a situation that was scarcely conducive to prosperity. Even skilled artisans of that time were fortunate to earn a dollar a day. Practically all the Wenger families that succeeded in acquiring leftover small parcels of land were in a similar predicament. In most cases, aside from the oldest children who inherited the old home farm of the early generations, it was the families that went west which found a better life. At the time of Emanuel's (A2221) death, he had 35 chickens, a hog, 5 bushels of corn, 8 barrels of flour, a cider barrel, two meat strands, potatoes and fodder. He had a vegetable garden and assorted garden tools and a plow.

Emanuel (A2221) and Peter Henry Wenger (A2226)

Judging from the material presented in the chapter on Peter Henry Wenger (A2226), it can be surmised that he and his brother Emanuel (A2221) maintained the closest relationship of any of the brothers and sisters. After Peter Henry Wenger (A2226) went to Ohio, he had visiting relatives from Lancaster County which we construe to be the families, not only of Emanuel (A2221), but their brother Samuel (A2224) who lived near Hessdale in what is now Paradise Township, Lancaster County. This seems a safe assumption since all other brothers and sisters lived in Chester County, Pennsylvania. The Ohio visitors were always referred to as being from Lancaster County. The traditional stories about Peter Henry Wenger (A2226) returning to Lancaster County from time to time in order to secure work and the funds necessary to purchase seed for planting seem to agree with this thought. Since Peter Henry Wenger (A2226) was skilled as a wheelwright and blacksmith and since both Emanuel (A2221) and Samuel (A2224) were trained in the same profession, it seems logical that these three brothers worked together in Lancaster County.

The grave site of Emanuel Wenger (A2221) and his wife, Anna Griffith, in the Mennonite Cemetery of Strasburg.

Emanuel Wenger (A2221; November 6, 1795-August 15, 1863) and his wife, Anna Griffith (April 14, 1798-June 26, 1878), are buried in the Mennonite Cemetery in Strasburg.

Peter Wenger (A22214), the son of Emanuel Wenger (A2221), was the administrator of the estate. On August 3, 1867, Peter sold this three acres to Christian Huber of West Lampeter Township for $676.50. There was a division of the proceeds to Rebecca Carr (A22217), Mary Kurtz (A22215), John Wenger (A22213), Peter Wenger (A22214), Amaziah Wenger (A222121) — the only heir of George W. Wenger (A22212) — and Lydia A. Singer (A222112) and Aldus J. Wenger (A222111) — the only heirs of Samuel Wenger (A22211).

Family Pattern

Emanuel (A2221) and his wife, Anna Griffith Wenger, had a family of eight children in the fifth generation, four boys and four girls. These are as follows: Samuel Wenger (A22211), George W. Wenger (A22212), John Wenger (A22213), Peter Wenger (A22214), Mary Ann Wenger (A22215), Anna Wenger (A22216), Rebecca Wenger (A22217) and Lydia Wenger (A22218).

Samuel Wenger (A22211) was born in 1815. He married Elizabeth Fry at the Strasburg Methodist Episcopal Church, January 18, 1849. They had two children of the sixth generation. These were: Aldus J. Wenger (A222111) born April 5, 1850, and Lydia Ann Wenger (A222112) who was born April 10, 1853, and married William Singer. Samuel (A22211) enlisted as a private in Company F-50 Pennsylvania Infantry, August 23, 1863. During the Civil War his company was sent to Virginia. Samuel (A22211) was on picket duty at the Weldon Railroad Station in Petersburg, Dinwiddie County, Virginia, where he was shot in the head. He died August 19, 1864. Samuel's son, Aldus J. Wenger (A222111), after his father's death was raised by Emanuel (A2221) and his wife, Anna. Samuel (A22211) in his earlier life was a farmer near Refton and Hessdale.

George W. Wenger (A22212) also was reported killed as a soldier in the Civil War. No facts seem to be available although he appeared in court on September 10, 1864, in connection with his father's estate. He was born October 22, 1824, and died in 1867, according to the estate papers. According to the Census of 1860, George Wenger's (A22212) wife was Rachael, who was 24 years of age at that time. They had one son of the sixth generation, Amaziah Wenger (A222121).

John Wenger (A22213) of the fifth generation was born October 28, 1828, and died September 24, 1907. He married Martha Wirt. He too was a cabinetmaker. John (A22213) and Martha Wirt Wenger had two sons of the sixth generation: John Wenger (A222131) and Wilmer Wenger (A222132).

John Wenger (A222131) of the sixth generation married Emma Weaver. He was a storekeeper and cigar maker. He also served as a councilman in Lancaster. He died in 1939. John (A222131) and Emma Weaver Wenger had a son of the seventh generation. He was Ralph Wenger (A2221311) who was born May 15, 1890. He married Regina Rote and died December 11, 1929. The Ralph Wengers (A2221311) had a son, John A. Wenger (A22213111), of the eighth generation, who was born May 2, 1917, and married Jane Lampeter. He is an account executive in the Andes Advertising Agency of Neffsville, Pennsylvania. John A. (A22213111) and Jane Lampeter Wenger have one son, David L. Wenger (A222131111), of the ninth generation who was born December 9, 1948. He is a student at Miami University.

Wilmer Wenger (A222132) of the sixth generation was born

February 4, 1875, and married Anna Mary Bauman Weaver. He died June 1, 1946. Anna Mary Bauman Weaver was born March 4, 1882, and died April 15, 1955. They are buried in the Millersville Mennonite Cemetery. The Wilmer Wengers (A222132) had two children of the seventh generation. The first is Grace W. Wenger

Peter Wenger (A22214), son of Emanuel (A2221) and Anna Wenger.

(A2221321) who was born April 1, 1906. She rendered distinguished service to the country in the Navy Nurse Corps during World War II and, prior to retirement, served on the Lancaster County Board of Assistance, Department of Public Welfare. She resides in Landisville. The second child was Gladys B. Wenger (A2221322) who was born December 12, 1907, and died in August 1908.

Peter Wenger (A22214)

The fourth son of Emanuel (A2221) and Anna Wenger was Peter Wenger (A22214) of the fifth generation. He was a venerable and lifelong resident of Lancaster County. His home was in Strasburg. He was a skilled wood craftsman and mechanic. As an avocation, he was devoted to horses. He helped to build many homes in the Strasburg area, some of which are now over 100 years old. He learned his cabinetmaking under Christian Bachman at a location just off the Strasburg Square, now the site of the Strasburg Bank. Many of his fine pieces of furniture and cabinets found their way into the homes of Strasburg and vicinity. He also helped to build many buildings in Philadelphia at the time of the Centennial there in 1876. At that time Peter Wenger (A22214) took his three youngest children to see his handiwork at the exhibition.

Peter Wenger (A22214) and his brother, John (A22213), narrowly escaped death when working on a scaffolding with the Hull brothers. The rig broke and two of the Hull brothers were killed. Peter managed to hang on to a ladder and was saved.

In the last ten years of his life, Peter (A22214) lived with his daughter and son-in-law, Mr. and Mrs. Jacob Yuninger, of Paradise Township near Mt. Pleasant Church. Peter Wenger (A22214) was born October 1, 1830, and married Martha Ann Eshleman. He died August 21, 1918. Martha Ann Eshleman Wenger was born November 11, 1832, and died June 25, 1892. They are buried at the Longenecker's Reformed Mennonite Cemetery near Strasburg. The Peter Wengers (A22214) had three children as follows: Frank Eshleman Wenger (A222141), Salome Wenger (A222142) and Ella Wenger (A222143).

Frank Wenger (A222141) Family

Frank Eshleman Wenger (A222141) of the sixth generation was born in Strasburg July 21, 1870, and married Luella Mae Glouner July 11, 1891. He died May 20, 1942. Luella Mae Glouner Wenger was born July 15, 1872, and died February 13, 1938. They are buried in Longenecker's Cemetery. They had thirteen children of the seventh generation. These are as follows: Clarence Roy Wenger (A2221411), Luella Blanche Wenger (A2221412), Frank Peter Wenger (A2221-413), Bessie Delilah Wenger (A2221414), Herbert Elim Wenger (A2221415), Estella Mae Wenger (A2221416), Lillian Marie Wenger (A2221417), Harry Glouner Wenger (A2221418), Lena Gertrude Wenger (A2221419), Cora Ethel Wenger (A2221410), John Edgar Wenger (A222141A), Martha Ann Wenger (A222141B) and George James Wenger (A222141C).

Luella Blanche Wenger (A2221412) stated that her father was a baker by trade in his early years and later in life he turned successfully to the profession of cigar making. She also related that her mother, Luella Mae Glouner Wenger, took all the children to Lancaster over the Old Philadelphia Road by stage coach. The purpose of the trip was to have their pictures taken. To the Wenger children, it was a great event. Later in life she watched with great interest when the interurban lines were developed.

This family was prolific in its development. There are over one hundred descendants which are indicated on the Frank Eshleman Wenger Family Tree. This is the issue of the fifth generation as indicated on the chart following that of Emanuel Wenger (A2221).

Salome Wenger (A222142) of the sixth generation and the second-born child of Peter Wenger (A22214) of the fifth generation married Levi Mellinger. The Mellingers (A222142) lived in Lancaster and had a child, Florence Mellinger (A2221421). They are buried in the Greenwood Cemetery in Lancaster.

Ella Wenger (A222143) of the sixth generation, the third daughter of the Peter Wengers (A22214), married Jacob Yuninger. They had ten children of the seventh generation. These are as follows: W. Ross Yuninger (A2221431), Edith Yuninger Hassel (A2221432), Maud Yuninger (A2221433), Jacob T. Yuninger (A2221434), Edgar K. Yuninger (A2221435), Anna Yuninger (A2221436), Ada B. Yuninger (A2221437), Jennie Yuninger (A2221438), Emily Yuninger (A2221439), and Clayton W. Yuninger (A2221430).

The fifth-born child of Emanuel (A2221) and Anna Wenger was Mary Ann Wenger (A22215) who married Samuel Kurtz. This family lived in Ohio and in Waldron, Hillsdale County, Michigan.

Anna Wenger (A22216) of the fifth generation married Jacob Hersh and had two children of the sixth generation. The first was Jones Hersh (A222161). He lived at Nickel Mines, South Lancaster County. The second child was William Hersh (A222162). Anna (A22216) and Jacob Hersh are buried in the Strasburg Mennonite Cemetery.

Rebecca Wenger (A22217), a daughter of Emanuel Wenger (A2221), married Henry Carr.

Lydia Wenger (A22218) of the fifth generation, the last-born child of Emanuel Wenger (A2221), married Samuel Myers and had a son, Aldus Myers (A222181).

Emanuel Wenger (A2221) and his son, Peter Wenger (A22214), and Frank Eshleman Wenger (A222141), the son of Peter (A22214), all had fine reputations as good men. However, none of them were too affirmative about religious matters. Their Family Tree follows.

Emanuel Wenger (A2221) Family Tree

1st Hans Wenger (b. About 1430) Blumenstein, Thun

2nd Burkhard Wenger (b. About 1450) Forst, Thun

3rd Peter Wenger (b. About 1470) Wattenwil, Seftigen

4th Peter Wenger (b. About 1490) Wattenwil, Seftigen

5th Rudolfus Wenger (b. About 1510) Wattenwil, Seftigen

6th Hans Wenger (b. About 1530) Wattenwil, Seftigen

7th Rudolfus Wenger (Ch. April 5, 1566) Wattenwil-Thurnen, Seftigen

8th Peter Wenger (Ch. Dec. 13, 1607) Wattenwil-Thurnen, Seftigen

9th Hans Wenger (Ch. May 30, 1633) Wattenwil-Thurnen, Seftigen

    A   Christian Wenger (A2) First Generation in America (1688-1749)

        B-1   Henry Wenger, Sr. (A22) Second Generation in America (1716-1802)

            C-1   Abraham Wenger (A222) Third Generation in America (1767-1845)

                D-1   Emanuel Wenger (A2221) Fourth Generation in America
b. Nov. 6, 1795, d. Aug. 15. 1863
m. Anna Griffith
b. Apr. 14, 1798, d. June 26, 1878

                    E-1   Samuel Wenger (A22211-5th)
b. 1815, d. Aug. 19, 1864
m. Elizabeth Fry Jan. 18, 1849

                        F-1   Aldus J. Wenger (A222111-6th)
b. Apr. 5, 1850

                        F-2   Lydia Ann Wenger (A222112-6th)
b. Apr. 10, 1853
m. William Singer

                    E-2   George W. Wenger (A22212-5th)
b. Oct. 22, 1824, d. 1867

                        F-1   Amaziah Wenger (A222121-6th)

E-3   John Wenger (A22213-5th)
      b. Oct. 28, 1828, d. Sept. 24, 1907
      m. Martha Wirt

  F-1   John Wenger (A222131-6th)
      b. Unknown, d. 1939
      m. Emma Weaver

    G-1   Ralph Wenger (A2221311-7th)
      b. May 15, 1890, d. Dec. 11, 1929
      m. Regina Rote

      H-1   John Andrew Wenger (A22213111-8th)
        b. May 2, 1917
        m. Jane Lampeter

        I-1   David L. Wenger (A222131111-9th)
          b. Dec. 9, 1948

  F-2   Wilmer Wenger (A222132-6th)
      b. Feb. 4, 1875, d. June 1, 1946
      m. Mary Weaver
      b. Mar. 4, 1882, d. Apr. 15, 1955

    G-1   Grace W. Wenger (A2221321-7th)
      b. Apr. 1, 1906

    G-2   Gladys B. Wenger (A2221322-7th)
      b. Dec. 12, 1907, d. Aug. 1908

E-4   Peter Wenger (A22214-5th)
      b. Oct. 1, 1830, d. Aug. 21, 1918
      m. Martha Ann Eshleman
      b. Nov. 11, 1832, d. June 25, 1892,
      Strasburg, bur. Longenecker's
      Cemetery

  F-1   Frank Eshleman Wenger (A222141-6th)
      (See separate Family Tree.)

  F-2   Salome Wenger (A222142-6th)
      m. Levi Mellinger

    G-1   Florence Mellinger (A2221421-7th)

  F-3   Ella Wenger (A222143-6th)
      b. Apr. 17, 1857, d. Feb. 21, 1951
      m. Jacob Yuninger
      b. Aug. 19, 1859, d. Apr. 12, 1946

    G-1   W. Ross Yuninger (A2221431-7th)

    G-2   Edith Yuninger (A2221432-7th)
      m. Harry Hassel

G-3 Maud Yuninger (A2221433-7th)

G-4 Jacob T. Yuninger (A2221434-7th)

G-5 Edgar K. Yuninger (A2221435-7th)

G-6 Anna Yuninger (A2221436-7th)

G-7 Ada B. Yuninger (A2221437-7th)

G-8 Jennie Yuninger (A2221438-7th)

G-9 Emily Yuninger (A2221439-7th)

G-10 Clayton W. Yuninger (A2221430-7th)

E-5 Mary Ann Wenger (A22215-5th)
      m. Samuel Kurtz

E-6 Anna Wenger (A22216-5th)
      m. Jacob Hersh

  F-1 Jones Hersh (A222161-6th)

  F-2 William Hersh (A222162-6th)

E-7 Rebecca Wenger (A22217-5th)
      m. Henry Carr

E-8 Lydia Wenger (A22218-5th)
      m. Samuel Myers

  F-1 Aldus Myers (A222181-6th)

Frank Eshleman Wenger (A222141) Family Tree

1st Hans Wenger (b. About 1430) Blumenstein, Thun

2nd Burkhard Wenger (b. About 1450) Forst, Thun

3rd Peter Wenger (b. About 1470) Wattenwil, Seftigen

4th Peter Wenger (b. About 1490) Wattenwil, Seftigen

5th Rudolfus Wenger (b. About 1510) Wattenwil, Seftigen

6th Hans Wenger (b. About 1530) Wattenwil, Seftigen

7th Rudolfus Wenger (Ch. April 5, 1566) Wattenwil-Thurnen, Seftigen

8th Peter Wenger (Ch. Dec. 13, 1607) Wattenwil-Thurnen, Seftigen

9th Hans Wenger (Ch. May 30, 1633) Wattenwil-Thurnen, Seftigen

  A Christian Wenger (A2) First Generation in America (1688-1749)

    B-1 Henry Wenger, Sr. (A22) Second Generation in America (1716-1802)

      C-1 Abraham Wenger (A222) Third Generation in America (1767-1845)

D-1 Emanuel Wenger (A2221) Fourth Generation
in America (1795-1863)

E-1 Peter Wenger (A22214) Fifth Generation
b. Oct. 1, 1830, d. Aug. 21, 1918
m. Martha Ann Eshleman
b. Nov. 11, 1832
d. June 25, 1892,
Strasburg, bur. Longenecker's

F-1 Frank Eshleman Wenger (A222141-6th)
b. July 21, 1870, Strasburg
d. May 20, 1942, Soudersburg
m. Luella Mae Glouner, July 11, 1891,
Lancaster
b. July 15, 1872, Ringtown
d. Feb. 13, 1938, bur. Longenecker's

G-1 Clarence Roy Wenger (A2221411-7th)
b. Apr. 22, 1892, Strasburg
m. Mable Wiker, Mar. 23, 1916,
Soudersburg
b. June 3, 1897, Paradise

H-1 Raymond Wiker Wenger
(A22214111-8th)
b. Dec. 1, 1916, Paradise
m. Jenny Harner, Aug. 26, 1939
b. Dec. 13, 1920, Quarryville

I-1 Thomas Roy Wenger
(A222141111-9th)
b. July 28, 1940, Soudersburg
m. Marian Bowman, Sept. 1, 1963,
Leola
b. June 1, 1943, Leola

J-1 Barbara Susan Wenger
(A2221411111-10th)
b. Dec. 11, 1964, Lancaster

J-2 Adrienne Marie Wenger
(A2221411112-10th)
b. June 6, 1968, Lancaster

I-2 Raymond Neil Wenger
(A222141112-9th)
b. June 28, 1954, Lancaster

I-3 Kathy Ann Wenger (A222141113-9th)
    b. Apr. 20, 1958
    d. Jan. 9, 1959, Lancaster
    bur. Mellingers

H-2 Jay Wiker Wenger (A22214112-8th)
    b. Mar. 11, 1920, Soudersburg
    m. Lillian Helm, Jan. 6, 1946
    b. Apr. 29, 1921, Lancaster

I-1 Dennis Jay Wenger (A222141121-9th)
    b. Nov. 28, 1951, Soudersburg

H-3 Donald Wiker Wenger
    (A22214113-8th)
    b. July 10, 1924, Soudersburg
    m. Erna Kraft, Feb. 5, 1966,
    Maryland
    b. Nov. 12, 1922, Reading

G-2 Luella Blanche Wenger (A2221412-7th)
    b. Jan. 9, 1894, Paradise
    Unmarried

G-3 Frank Peter Wenger (A2221413-7th)
    b. Apr. 20, 1896, Paradise
    m. Sally Katie Heinly, July 8, 1922,
    Ephrata
    b. May 14, 1901, Ephrata

H-1 Charles Edward Wenger
    (A22214131-8th)
    b. Nov. 9, 1923, Ephrata
    m. Betty Miller, June 16, 1946
    b. July 19, 1926, Leacock

I-1 Bruce Allen Wenger
    (A222141311-9th)
    b. June 8, 1948, Paradise
    m. Joyce Sinclair, July 2, 1966
    b. Aug. 4, 1945

J-1 Suezette Lynn Wenger
    (A2221413111-10th)
    b. Dec. 7, 1966, Ephrata

I-2 Barry Charles Wenger
    (A222141312-9th)
    b. May 20, 1950, Paradise

I-3   Florence Ethel Wenger
(A222141313-9th)
b. July 17, 1925, Clay
m. Marvin M. Schmeck,
Feb. 11, 1950
b. Aug. 4, 1931, Reinholds

J-1   Donna Jean Schmeck
(A2221413131-10th)
b. May 26, 1955, Lancaster

H-2   Paul Lawrence Wenger
(A22214132-8th)
b. Jan. 28, 1927, Clay
m. Geraldine Sipe, Apr. 5, 1947,
Lancaster
b. Aug. 15, 1927, Lancaster

I-1   Sharon Louise Wenger
(A222141321-9th)
b. Feb. 7, 1953, Paradise

G-4   Bessie Delilah Wenger (A2221414-7th)
b. May 7, 1897, Paradise, Pa.
m. Robert Sanford Sterling, Mar. 14,
1920, Lancaster
b. Mar. 21, 1901, Gap
d. Nov. 26, 1946, Gettysburg
bur. Evergreen
m. Joseph Bennet Boggs, Mar. 24,
1952, Pittsburgh
b. Mar. 8, 1904, Pittsburgh
d. Dec. 26, 1959, Pittsburgh
bur. Monroeville Presbyterian

H-1   Emma Mae Sterling (A22214141-8th)
b. June 20, 1922, Kinzer
m. Leonard Conrad Whitecar,
Aug. 24, 1942, Pittsburgh
b. Jan. 14, 1924, New Jersey

I-1   Leonard Robert Whitecar
(A222141411-9th)
b. Sept. 29, 1946, Pittsburgh

H-2   Betty Jane Sterling (A22214142-8th)
      b. July 15, 1926, Soudersburg
      m. Lawrence Richard Rice,
        Jan. 23, 1947, Biglerville
      b. Jan. 21, 1926, Biglerville

  I-1   Barry Eugene Rice (A222141421-9th)
      b. Apr. 8, 1948, Biglerville

G-5   Herbert Elim Wenger (A2221415-7th)
      b. May 13, 1899, Paradise
      m. Margaret Carpenter, Sept. 25,
        1925, Paradise
      b. Jan. 19, 1904, Leaman Place

H-1   Rose Marie Wenger (A22214151-8th)
      b. Aug. 26, 1926, d. Aug. 26, 1926,
      Soudersburg, bur. United
      Brethern, Paradise, Pa.

H-2   Ruth Arlene Wenger (A22214152-8th)
      b. Sept. 30, 1928, Soudersburg
      m. Gordon Benard Ressler,
      Mar. 28, 1948, Paradise
      b. Apr. 7, 1925, Paradise

  I-1   Debra Jean Ressler
      (A222141521-9th)
      b. Apr. 7, 1954, Paradise

  I-2   Gordon Kent Ressler
      (A222141522-9th)
      b. June 6, 1957, Paradise

G-6   Estella Mae Wenger (A2221416-7th)
      b. Aug. 27, 1901, Paradise
      m. Richard Kenneth Reinfried,
      Dec. 21, 1926, Lebanon
      b. June 21, 1900, Lititz

H-1   June May Reinfried (A22214161-8th)
      b. Apr. 1, 1928, Lancaster
      m. Kenneth Clay Gochnauer,
      May 21, 1949, Valley Forge
      b. Nov. 8, 1926, Manheim

  I-1   Richard Kenneth Gochnauer
      (A222141611-9th)
      b. Apr. 6, 1952, Millersville

I-2   Timothy Ross Gochnauer
      (A222141612-9th)
      b. May 23, 1954, Lancaster

H-2   Joyce Elaine Reinfried
      (A22214162-8th)
      b. Sept. 4, 1932, Leaman Place
      m. Clayton Lester Frackman,
      Apr. 5, 1953, Strasburg
      b. Aug. 17, 1933, Strasburg

    I-1   Karen Susanne Frackman
         (A222141621-9th)
         b. Oct. 12, 1955, Strasburg

    I-2   Lisa Lorene Frackman
         (A222141622-9th)
         b. Jan. 27, 1958, Strasburg

    I-3   Denise Renee Frackman
         (A222141623-9th)
         b. Feb. 14, 1960, Strasburg

G-7   Lillian Marie Wenger (A2221417-7th)
      b. Oct. 19, 1903, Paradise
      m. John Frank LeFevre, Dec. 24, 1930
      Lancaster
      b. June 14, 1902, Strasburg

    H-1   Carl John LeFevre (A22214171-8th)
         b. Nov. 25, 1933, d. Nov. 25, 1933,
         Strasburg, bur. Longenecker's
         Reformed Mennonite Cemetery

    H-2   Pauline LeFevre (A22214172-8th)
         b. May 20, 1935, Ronks, R.D.
         m. Leon Chandler Gilgore, Jan. 26,
         1957, Maryland
         b. Dec. 7, 1930, Shillington

G-8   Harry Glouner Wenger (A2221418-7th)
      b. June 6, 1905, Paradise
      m. Bernice Knosh, May 5, 1934,
      Upper Leacock
      b. May 4, 1912, Upper Leacock

G-9 Lena Gertrude Wenger (A2221419-7th)
  b. Aug. 3, 1908, Paradise
  m. Jay Samuel Benard, Apr. 16, 1927,
  Paradise
  b. July 12, 1906, Quarryville

H-1 Betty Jane Benard (A22214191-8th)
  b. Jan. 24, 1928, Bird-in-hand
  m. Paul Elmer Coble, Dec. 19,
  1947, Paradise
  b. June 22, 1927, Lititz

  I-1 Paul Michael Coble (A222141911-9th)
    b. June 7, 1949, Lititz

  I-2 Beth Ann Coble (A222141912-9th)
    b. Nov. 27, 1951, Lititz

  I-3 Jo Lynn Coble (A222141913-9th)
    b. Mar. 11, 1955, Lancaster

H-2 Jay Robert Benard (A22214192-8th)
  b. Oct. 19, 1930, Soudersburg
  m. Mary Ann Poloni, Oct. 4, 1952,
  Bird-in-hand
  b. July 29, 1932, Lancaster

  I-1 Bonnie Lynn Benard
    (A222141921-9th)
    b. Aug. 19, 1953, Lancaster

  I-2 Jay Douglas Benard
    (A222141922-9th)
    b. Aug. 1, 1955, Lancaster

G-10 Cora Ethel Wenger (A2221410-7th)
  b. Feb. 5, 1910, Soudersburg
  m. Clarence Edgar Theis, Dec. 24,
  1931, Lancaster
  b. Jan. 10, 1911, Virginia

H-1 Lorraine Ethel Theis (A22214101-8th)
  b. June 7, 1932, Lancaster R.D.
  m. John Murry Silknetter,
  Apr. 18, 1957, Lancaster
  b. Oct. 14, 1930, Lancaster

  I-1 Jennifer Ellen Silknetter
    (A222141011-9th)
    b. June 24, 1957, Lancaster

I-2   Daniel Warren Silknetter
(A222141012-9th)
b. Mar. 13, 1957, Lancaster

H-2   Gloria Ann Theis (A22214102-8th)
b. May 17, 1934, Lancaster R.D.
m. Kenneth George Ernst,
July 12, 1952, Lancaster

I-1   Robert Kent Ernst (A222141021-9th)
b. Dec. 13, 1952, Coatesville

H-3   Nancy Jane Theis (A22214103-8th)
b. July 11, 1936, Lancaster R.D.
m. Arthur Gore, Nov. 29, 1968,
Lancaster

H-4   Luella Mae Theis (A22214104-8th)
b. May 6, 1938, Soudersburg
m. Peter Lane Zook, Dec. 23, 1955,
Lancaster
b. Nov. 29, 1937, Lancaster

I-1   Lucinda Lane Zook (A222141041-9th)
b. Sept. 3, 1956, Lancaster

I-2   Rebecca Lane Zook
(A222141042-9th)
b. Oct. 4, 1958, Lancaster

I-3   Peter Lane Zook, Jr.
(A222141043-9th)
b. July 11, 1961, Lansdale

H-5   Clarence Edgar Theis, Jr.
(A22214105-8th)
b. Mar. 19, 1940, Soudersburg
m. (1st) no details
m. (2nd) Donna Mae Kinsey,
Feb. 20, 1967, Lancaster
b. May 5, 1943, Hawaii

I-1   Thomas Edward Theis
(A222141051-9th)
b. Apr. 21, 1961, Lancaster

I-2   Victoria Elizabeth Theis
(A222141052-9th)
b. Nov. 20, 1962, Lancaster

I-3 Stephen Anthony Theis
(A222141053-9th)
b. Oct. 22, 1964, Lancaster

I-4 Susan Michelle Theis
(A222141054-9th)
b. Dec. 28, 1967, Utah

H-6 John William Theis (A22214106-8th)
b. Sept. 5, 1944, Lancaster R.D.
m. Barbara Jean Sweigart,
May 7, 1966, Lancaster
b. Oct. 11, 1943, Elizabethtown

I-1 Kelly Jean Theis (A222141061-9th)
b. July 21, 1967, Lancaster

I-2 Lucinda Jean Theis (A222141062-9th)
b. Sept. 3, 1968, Lancaster

H-7 Mary Ann Theis (A22214107-8th)
b. May 8, 1951, Lancaster
d. Aug. 25, 1960, Minnesota
bur. Conestoga Memorial Park

G-11 John Edgar Wenger (A222141A-7th)
b. Oct. 10, 1912, Soudersburg
m. Blanche Louise Fisher,
Mar. 26, 1938, Paradise
b. Oct. 29, 1913, S. Hermitage

H-1 Shirley Ann Wenger (A222141A1-8th)
b. June 26, 1939, Ronks
m. Arthur Miller, Apr. 26, 1958,
Paradise
b. July 31, 1939, Lancaster

I-1 Jeffrey Arthur Miller
(A222141A11-9th)
b. Sept. 26, 1958, Lancaster

H-2 John Edgar Wenger, Jr.
(A222141A2-8th)
b. July 13, 1942, Ronks
m. Shirley Ann Rineer,
Jan. 4, 1964, Paradise
b. Mar. 2, 1941, Paradise

I-1   Kimberly Ann Wenger
(A222141A21-9th)
b. Apr. 4, 1966, Paradise

H-3   Susan Luella Wenger (A222141A3-8th)
b. July 23, 1945, Ronks
m. John William Mitchell,
July 23, 1966, Paradise
b. Dec. 22, 1944, Manheim

I-1   Stephen John Mitchell
(A222141A31-9th)
b. Jan. 8, 1967, Lancaster

H-4   Robert Frank Wenger
(A222141A4-8th)
b. Nov. 15, 1946, Ronks
m. Eva Geraldine Good,
Dec. 5, 1964, Brownstown
b. Sept. 13, 1947, Lancaster

I-1   Michelle Marie Wenger
(A222141A41-9th)
b. June 16, 1965, Lancaster

G-12 Martha Ann Wenger (A222141B-7th)
b. Oct. 14, 1913, Soudersburg
m. Dr. Everett Edwin Denlinger,
Apr. 25, 1937, Maryland
b. Dec. 17, 1915, Kinzer

H-1   Linda Lee Denlinger (A222141B1-8th)
b. Feb. 16, 1939, Paradise
m. Dr. Garry Housel Carson,
Dec. 17, 1960, Paradise
b. Nov. 18, 1935, Colorado

I-1   Gill Renee Carson (A222141B11-9th)
b. Nov. 8, 1961, Brooklyn, N.Y.

I-2   Janice Kay Carson (A222141B12-9th)
b. Nov. 21, 1962, Bermuda

I-3   Craig Allen Carson (A222141B13-9th)
b. Dec. 20, 1963, Bermuda (twin)

I-4   Gregg Everett Carson
(A222141B14-9th)
b. Dec. 20, 1963, Bermuda (twin)

I-5 Mathew Jon Carson
(A222141B15-9th)
b. Nov. 1, 1968, Colorado

G-13 George James Wenger (A222141C-7th)
b. May 7, 1918, Soudersburg
m. Dorothy Weaver, Oct. 11, 1947,
Strasburg
b. Aug. 10, 1925, Strasburg

H-1 Sandra Kay Wenger (A222141C1-8th)
b. July 2, 1949, Lancaster

H-2 Barbara Ann Wenger
(A222141C2-8th)
b. Sept. 13, 1952, Lancaster

Peter Henry Winger (A2226) (1806-1889)

CHAPTER NINE

Peter Henry Winger
of Pennsylvania and Ohio

PETER HENRY WINGER (A2226) was born in Salisbury Township, Lancaster County, Pennsylvania, February 26, 1806. He was the son of Abraham (A222) (1767-1845) and Anna Eby Wenger (1774-1846), the grandson of John Henry Wenger, Sr. (A22), and the great-grandson of Christian Wenger (A2). He lived the first 30 years of his life in Lancaster County or nearby, where the family homestead was established. He lived for at least a year in West Caln Township in Chester County, Pennsylvania, where his mother was living at the time. In 1827, at the age of 21, he appeared as a freeman on the tax assessment list in that county. Peter Winger's (A2226) father, Abraham Wenger (A222), was a farmer and skilled wheelright and Peter Winger (A2226) followed in his steps. He, too, was a farmer

Anna Barr Winger (1806-1896)

and wheelwright, as well as following the blacksmith trade as a young man.

Many years later Charles Winger (A222671), a grandson of Peter Henry Winger (A2226), told the writer that as a teen-aged boy Peter Winger (A2226) ran away and joined the armed forces in an expedition to Florida to help clear out the Seminole Indians. The rigors of that adventure soon proved to be more than a boy could handle, so he returned to Lancaster County. It also was stated that Peter Henry Winger (A2226) "knew Jeff Davis." This story probably sprang from the fact that a sister of Jefferson Davis married John Wenger of a residual family in Lancaster County.

Marriage to Anna Barr

At the age of 23 Peter Henry Winger (A2226) lived in Lancaster Township across the line from Strasburg. In the latter community, he met Anna Barr, the daughter of John Barr, one of the early pioneer families of Lancaster County.

John Barr (1771-1843) had an uncle, Martin Barr who developed the limestone fertilizer business. Near Quarryville, he established

Barr's Quarries at Quarryville

Barr's Quarries, largely a deep surface, lime mining operation. Farmers in Lancaster and adjacent counties worked the quarries for limestone in the winter and then hauled it to their own farms. There they built lime kilns to burn the limestone into fertilizer. Subsequently, it was applied to the worn-out fields of that region. The results of the Quarryville lime brought about a three-to-fourfold crop improvement. For a time the industry thrived, bringing employment, attracting capital and miscellaneous trade. In the early stages, lumber to fire the kilns was abundant, but as the supply of wood diminished, it became necessary to use coal which was too expensive. By 1835 lime quarrying was on the decline.

In the meantime Peter Henry Winger (A2226) as a young man had learned to surface mine from a small lime pit on his father's farm. He worked in the lime quarry at Limeville owned by Jacob Barr and his son and in Quarryville near the Barr's great stone dwelling house, the Ark. At the latter quarry he worked night and day to supply limestone for the kiln on his father Abraham's (A222) 30-acre farm in Salisbury Township.

The Winger and Barr families had had a long relationship and it was through this that Peter (A2226) met, courted and married Anna Barr, the daughter of John Barr (1771-1843). In 1829 Peter (A2226) gave a valentine to Anna Barr to commemorate their engagement. Peter Henry Winger (A2226) had made it himself. The upper right-hand panel of this penknife valentine had to be restored, together with the sentiment therein. The verses, sentiment and historical information on the valentine, pictured here, read as follows:

> Round is the ring, it has no end
> So is my love to you my friend
> If you love me as I love you
> No knife will cut our love in two
> So read on round and then you will see
> That I love Anny and Anny loves me.
>
> For as the grape grows on the vine
> I chose you out for to be mine
> Mine now and mine forever
> Oh may we live in love together
> And when this life on Earth is done
> Oh may we dwell above the Sun.

On the fourteenth day of February
It was my lot for to be merry
Lots were cast and lots were drew
Kind fortune says it must be you
And so this valentine I cut
And with my pen I in it wrote
And ever grateful may I be
For the apt care my parents took of me.

Anny Barr of Strasburg was born
on the 28th day of February, A.D.,
1806 and was engaged February 14th,
the year of 1829, to Peter Winger,
who was 23 years of age.

The above valentine, the work of Peter Henry Winger (A2226), was presented to Anna Barr in 1829 at the time of their engagement.

Peter Henry Winger (A2226) married Anna Barr in the German Lutheran and Reformed Church, East Main Street, Strasburg, Pennsylvania, by the Reverend J. J. Strine September 23, 1830. The Reverend John Jacob Strine was one of the popular "marrying parsons." The number of couples joined together by him was 4,532 which he recorded in three books of the church. The entries are beautifully written in bold, clear characters, making research in them a delight.

The Barr Family

The story of the Barr (Bâr, Bear, Bare, Bahr, etc.) family takes its place with equal importance to that of the Eby family, the Herr family and several others that significantly contributed to the Winger saga. Its treatment, therefore, is included in the main text along with the beginning contributions of Rev. Hans Herr and his family, much of which is recorded in the Genealogical Record of Rev. Hans Herr and his Lineal Descendants by Theodore W. Herr, 1908. In addition to being the progenitor of the Herr clan, Rev. Hans Herr is also the ancestor of all descendants of Peter Henry (A2226) and Anna Barr Winger.

The fact that (1) Rev. John Barr (Est. 1650-1735) is the first known ancestor of not only the line of Barrs incident hereto, but many other lines, leads us to Switzerland and the Palatinate of Germany as well as adjacent territories. Researchers in Lancaster County, Pennsylvania, all agree that the early records indicate that (1) Rev. John Barr (Est. 1650-1735) came from one or more of the above-indicated places.

The writer has spent much time and effort in the archives of Europe. Starting in the Zurich area of Switzerland, where our ancestor purportedly was born, we bring multitudinous records to light. The emigrations of different members of the Barr family are widespread, particularly from the district of Kronau (Ottenbach, Lunnern, Uerzlikon, Kappel am Albis, Rifferswil, Affoltern am Albis) to Pennsylvania, Carolina, the Palatinate (Zweibrücken, Nunchweiler, Maudach, Michelfeld), the Alsace, Wurttemberg, Baden (Mannheim) Bayern and in the Dutch military services.

It becomes apparent, therefore, that much additional time and effort through intelligent research will have to be forthcoming before definitive answers can be found.

Ottenbach, Switzerland

To use one example, the village of Ottenbach, widely reputed to be the center of the Barr family, reveals in the archives in Zurich that the first-known Barr ancestor was John (Hans) Barr, who was born about 1610. He married Klianna Hufschmid, August 3, 1630. She was born November 25, 1610.

John and Klianna Barr had four known children. The first known was John (Hans) Barr who was born at Ottenbach, February 21, 1641. He married Elizabeth Brenner.

The second known descendant of John and Klianna Barr was Melchior Barr who was born at Ottenbach, May 23, 1643. He married Anna Grob on November 28, 1671. They had a son, John (Hans) Barr, who was born September 2, 1694, at Ottenbach.

The third known son of John and Klianna Barr was Jacob (Joss) Barr who was born at Ottenbach, August 8, 1647. He married first Margaret Grob, October 11, 1674. His second marriage was to Margaret Good, February 23, 1686.

The final known son of John and Klianna Barr was Hans Jacob Barr, born August 11, 1650, in the same village.

This family remained in Ottenbach until about 1696 when John Barr (b. 1641), Melchior Barr (b. 1643) and his two-year-old son, John (Hans) Barr, and the third brother, John Jacob Barr (b. 1650), went to Zwei-brücken in the Palatinate, now West Germany.

The family of Jacob (Joss) Barr (b. 1647) remained in Ottenbach. A long line of descendants are recorded there and elsewhere in Switzerland. Of these, Jacob (Joss) Barr's two grandsons, Heinrich Barr and John Heinrich Barr, came to Pennsylvania on the Ship Lydia, arriving December 11, 1739. (The Genealogy of Henry Baer by Willis N. Baer, Allentown, Pennsylvania, 1955.)

In Zweibrücken

From the three brothers who went to Zweibrücken about 1696, there are literally scores of descendants living today in the city of Zweibrücken, as well as a number of villages including Nünchweiler, Dusenbrücken, Windserg and Huberhof. Throughout the area these Barr families trace their ancestry starting as early as 1669, when the first Barr arrived, back to the District of Kronau, particularly Ottenbach, Londern and other hamlets in Switzerland.

Of interest is the fact that the line of John Barr (b. about 1610), Melchior Barr (b. 1643), John Barr (b. 1694) and John Cristophel Barr (b. Oct. 27, 1719), finds a long line of descendants in America. The latter two, father and son, emigrated from Zweibrücken to Pennsylvania in 1743 on the Ship Phoenix. Frank Lewis Baer, husband of Mable VanDyke Baer, Washington genealogist, is a descendant of this line. There is a rare book,

Genealogy of Johannes Baer, 1749-1910, by Daniel M. Baer and Robert Bruce Baer, that covers this line of the family.

The above examples serve to show the immensity of the problem in tracing the families of the many Barrs that emigrated from Switzerland.

In Lancaster County

In Lancaster County, Pennsylvania, several researchers have tried to identify fully (1) Rev. John Barr (Est. 1650-1735) with varying degrees of success. Considerable data is available in the genealogical record of Rev. Hans Herr by Theodore W. Herr, 1908. This is generally accurate with some notable exceptions. A second Rev. John Barr, who may have been a son or grandson of (1) Rev. John Barr (Est. 1650-1735), complicates research. Wills, tax and court records have been meticulously examined. As a result, we speculate that the following were the children of (1) Rev. John Barr (Est. 1650-1735): Barbara, Madalene, Henry, Martin, Elizabeth, John and Jacob. We know of no authentic single source that shows his family pattern. Numerous isolated indications, such as those in Herr's book, the record of the Miller and Pursel families by Vida Miller Pursel, the compilation by G. Walter Barr of Keokuk, Iowa, records presented by Ira Landis and several others, turn up data that leads to the above approximate family pattern.

Mary S. Streeter of New York City, whose ancestor was Jacob Barr (b. January 8, 1723), believes that her line stems from (1) John Barr (Est. 1650-1735). She states, as does the writer, that the (1) Rev. John Barr (Est. 1650-1735) family pattern will have to come out of the process of elimination of conflicting data by the cause and effect method.

We have concluded that the line of Barrs incident hereto are descendants from (1) Rev. John Barr (Est. 1650-1735) based upon the following documentary evidence:

From a Lancaster County Will dated February 2, 1776, (3) Martin Barr, Jr. (Est. 1710-1784), of Strasburg indicates that his father, (2) Martin Barr, Sr. (Est. 1680-1760), conveyed 80 acres near Strasburg to him. This acreage was adjoining 150 acres which was originally owned by John Herr, the father-in-law of (3) Martin Barr, Jr. (Est. 1710-1784). This total of 230 acres was a part of the 10,000 acres originally acquired by Rev. Hans Herr, (1) Rev. John Barr (Est. 1650-1735) and a host of other Mennonites who fled to Lancaster County from the Palatinate and Switzerland. From this it is apparent that Rev. Hans Herr conveyed this parcel of land to his son, John Herr, and he in turn conveyed the land to his son-in-law, (3) Martin Barr, Jr. (Est. 1710-1784), the husband of his daughter, Elizabeth Herr. Originally (1) Rev. John Barr (Est. 1650-1735) had purchased 500 acres from the Rev. Hans Herr parcel. This warrant was granted May 14, 1718, and it was surveyed May 30, 1718. The land patent was granted June 20, 1718. The property was located southwest of Strasburg covering an extensive area north of Quarryville (Barrville) and was bisected by Beaver Creek.

(3) Martin Barr, Jr. (Est. 1710-1784), the maker of the 1776 Will, represented that his father, (2) Martin Barr, Sr. (Est. 1680-1760), conveyed 80 acres to him. The records show this transfer was land residing within the confines of the original 10,000 acres owned by Rev. John Herr, and more precisely from within the 500 acres owned by (1) Rev. John Barr (Est. 1650-1735). Thus it becomes the strongest sort of evidence that (2) Martin Barr, Sr. (Est. 1680-1760) received

The Hans Herr house erected in 1719 still stands on the original site in Lancaster County, Pennsylvania. This picture was taken in 1969 by the writer just before restoration was started. Eventually, complete restoration will be effectuated. All descendants of Peter Henry (A2226) and Anna Barr Winger are offsprings from this most honored ancestor, Rev. Hans Herr, 1639-1725.

his land from his father, who could have been none other than the (1) Rev. John Barr (Est. 1650-1735). Moreover, the land descriptions largely substantiate this.

A Will of 1757

There is further evidence in a Will dated August 2, 1757, by Martin Barr of Lampeter Township. The Barr properties of our reference overlapped Beaver Creek into a part of Lampeter Township. We believe the maker of this Will was (2) Martin Barr, Sr. (Est. 1680-1760). This Will divides his estate among his wife, Elizabeth, and *all* his children, including Christian, Jacob and Martin Barr. The latter was named Executor. From the context of this Will and land descriptions in deeds, we believe that our (3) Martin Barr, Jr. (Est. 1710-1784), was the third brother of the trio of Christian, Jacob and Martin Barr. Here we have additional evidence to that outlined above of a father-to-son transfer out of the original (1) John Barr (Est. 1650-1735) tract.

In a Jacob Eshleman Will dated 1758 (Deed 1-219), he refers to John Herr, the son of Rev. Hans Herr (1639-1725), as an "Elder" in the church. Likewise, the same Will refers to John Herr's contemporary, (2) Martin Barr (Est. 1680-1760), as an "Elder." Thus the evidence compounds that (2) "Elder" Martin Barr (Est. 1680-1760) was the son of the Mennonite Churchman, (1) Rev. John Barr (Est. 1650-1735). Moreover, the (3) Martin Barr, Jr. (Est. 1710-1784), Will of 1776 refers to his adjacent land purchased from Jacob Eshleman. This, again, is significantly evidential.

John Barr (1749-1813)

In the Will of 1776, (3) Martin Barr, Jr. (Est. 1710-1784), conveys this 230 acres, together with the merchant mill, grist and sawmill in Strasburg Township on Beaver Creek to his son, (4) John Barr (1749-1813). This made him the most prominent miller in the area. In the same Will, (3) Martin Barr, Jr. (Est. 1710-1784), also conveys 300 acres, together with a mansion house to his other son, (4) Martin Barr (1756-1844).

The Will also conveys considerable property from the (3) Martin Barr, Jr. (Est. 1710-1784), estate to his daughters, Magdalena (Martha) who later married Samuel Miller, Elizabeth Barr (single girl), Mary Barr who married Christian Martin, Anna Barr who married Christian

Hare and Feronica (Fannie) Barr who married Francis Hare. (3) Martin Barr, Jr. (Est. 1710-1784), actually owned nearly 800 acres of fine farm land. This family was of well-known heritage in Strasburg Township and Lancaster County. It was (4) Martin Barr (1756-1844) who built the famous Barr Ark and operated the adjacent Barr lime quarries. He married Fanny Neff, a descendant of a prominent pioneer family.

(4) John Barr (1749-1813), the son, was named executor of (3) Martin Barr, Jr's. (1710-1784) estate. Thereafter, (4) John Barr (1749-1813), in drafting his Will dated September 13, 1811, significantly signed it as John Barr, *miller*. The latter designation is confirmatory in that he is one and the same as the (4) John Barr (1749-1813) who

This Barr-Neff barn is the site of many family traditions as related by Ira R. Barr of Yellow Springs, Ohio.

received the "merchant mill, grist and sawmill" from his father, (3) Martin Barr, Jr. (Est. 1710-1784), as a result of the Will dated February 2, 1776. The mill properties are thus identified through three estates, namely (1) Rev. John Barr, (2) Martin Barr, Sr., and (3) Martin Barr, Jr. Moreover, the land description pinpoints the exact location of the Barr homes and farms that were later owned by those Barrs who went to Ohio and Delaware.

The Union of Families

Meantime, (4) John Barr (1749-1813) married Elizabeth Robinson and had a son, (5) John Barr (1771-1843). After the death of Elizabeth

Robinson Barr, (4) John Barr (1749-1813) married a widow, believed to be Elizabeth Stehman Brown. They had a son (5) Martin Barr (1793-1874) who was a half-brother to (5) John Barr (1771-1843). This second son, (5) Martin Barr (1793-1874), was to become a physician and the progenitor of an extraordinary family. (4) John Barr's (1749-1813) second wife, Elizabeth Brown, had a daughter by her previous marriage designated as Susanna, the wife of Abner Eshleman.

The Herr book, in reporting the whereabouts of (5) Dr. Martin Barr (1793-1874) and his half-brother, (5) John Barr (1771-1843), stated they both had gone to Baltimore. This was wrong on two counts. Even though both might have originally gone to Baltimore, the fact is that (5) Dr. Martin Barr (1793-1874) went to Middletown, Delaware, and (5) John Barr (1771-1843), together with the Wingers, went to Ohio in 1836.

Anna Barr Winger, the daughter of (5) John Barr (1771-1843), named her youngest son, Joseph Levi *Robinson* Winger (A22269). There is a presumption that Anna Barr Winger named her son *Robinson* after the family name of her grandmother. Moreover, Anna Winger's sister, Elizabeth Barr Keeler, named one of her sons *Robinson* Keeler. The Robinson family was often referred to by the Barr and Winger families in Ohio. Anna Barr Winger, as reported previously, often spoke of "Uncle" (4) Martin Barr (1756-1844) who built the

The Barr's "Ark"

"Ark." In fact, "Uncle" (4) Martin Barr (1756-1844) was a brother to Anna Barr Winger's grandfather, (4) John Barr (1749-1813). In both the Barr and Winger families in later years there were extended discussions about "Uncle" (4) Martin's (1756-1844) Ark, where Peter Henry Winger (A2226) worked in the nearby quarries. The same holds true for "Lame" Jacob Barr (1778-1874) who later owned the "Ark." Peter Winger (A2226) repeatedly told of the exploits of "Lame" Jacob Barr who was a well-known teamster on the Old Philadelphia Road. "Lame" Jacob was a second cousin to (5) John Barr (1771-1843).

The Breckbill-Neff Cemetery

It is thought that most of the early Barrs are buried in the Breckbill-Neff Cemetery about one mile southwest of Strasburg. Many stones are no longer legible. (1) Rev. John Barr (1650-1735) and his wife, as well as their son, (2) Martin Barr, Sr. (Est. 1680-1760) and his wife are undoubtedly interred there. No physical record remains. The same holds true for (3) Martin Barr, Jr. (Est. 1710-1784). However, his wife, Elizabeth Herr Barr, has a marker. She was born in 1719 and died August 9, 1807. (4) John Barr (1749-1813) was buried in the Breckbill-Neff Cemetery but there is no evidence that his first wife, Elizabeth Robinson Barr, was there. (4) John Barr was born November 22, 1749, and died March 25, 1813. His second wife, Elizabeth Brown Barr, after his death went in 1817 to Middletown, Delaware, to live with her son, (5) Dr. Martin Barr (1793-1874). She is buried in the Presbyterian Cemetery there with her son. She was born in 1749 and died March 20, 1837. Martin Barr (1756-1844), the brother of (4) John Barr (1749-1813), is buried at Breckbill-Neff together with his wife, Fanny Neff. He was born August 20, 1756, and died June 20, 1844. Fanny Neff Barr was born October 3, 1763, and died July 3, 1840. (4) John Barr's (1749-1813) daughter, Lucinda, born August 24, 1783, and died September 24, 1789, is also buried at Breckbill-Neff.

(4) John Barr (1749-1813) and his brother, Martin Barr (1756-1884), may have had a first cousin who was buried nearby. This references the grave of Jacob Barr who was born January 1, 1749, and died May 11, 1834. His date of birth is sufficiently separated to make him a contemporary. He had a wife, Mary, who married a Maxwell after his death. She is buried next to Jacob (1749-1834) and their two sons, John (1780-1828) and Isaac Barr (1807-1812). This Jacob Barr (1749-1834) could be one and the same as Jacob Barr who was discharged in 1783 as an Ensign in the Revolutionary War. The family has an heirloom sword said to have belonged to such a soldier.

Middletown, Delaware

In the History of Delaware by Runk and Company, 1899, furnished me by R. Thomas Mayhill, Publisher in Knightstown, Indiana, the sketch of (5) Dr. Martin Barr (1793-1874) shows him to be the father of a family of 12. This family was of some distinction in the Delaware environment.

This history mistakenly refers to (5) Dr. Martin Barr's (1793-1874) grandfather as John Barr when in reality he was (3) Martin Barr (Est. 1710-1784). We have definitely shown from the Will of February 2, 1776, that the grandfather was (3) Martin Barr, Jr. (Est. 1710-1784), de facto. On May 6, 1817, (5) John Barr (1771-1843) and his half-brother, (5) Dr. Martin Barr (1793-1874), as executors of their father (4) John Barr's (1749-1813) estate, sold the mill and surrounding land to their uncle, Benjamin Barr, the son of (4) Martin Barr (1756-1844), for $21,000. The deed D5-316 dated May 6, 1817, definitely states that (3) Martin Barr (Est. 1710-1784) was the father of (4) John Barr (1749-1813). It also shows that the mill property was deeded from (3) Martin Barr (Est. 1710-1784) to his son, (4) John Barr (1749-1813), on December 13, 1784. The above error in referring to the grandfather as John instead of Martin not only has led to a timely correction but has completely identified the authentic family line of our branch of the Barrs.

In any event, the history states that the grandfather, whom we have shown to be (3) Martin Barr (Est. 1710-1784), was a patriot during the Revolutionary War, having supplied wheat to Washington's army at Valley Forge.

(5) Dr. Martin Barr (1793-1874) married Jane Adams of Mt. Pleasant, Pennsylvania, in 1817 and was educated at the University of Pennsylvania. He graduated in 1813. He was born October 27, 1793, at Strasburg and died September 16, 1874, at Middletown, Delaware. He is interred in the Middletown Presbyterian Cemetery with many members of his family, including his mother.

The Barr Family Line

Even though much more confirmatory evidence would be salutary, we are satisfied that our documentation is wholly accurate with the following family line dated from about 1650: (1) Rev. John Barr (Est. 1650-1735), (Switzerland-Zweibrücken-Pennsylvania), (2) Martin Barr, Sr. (Est. 1680-1760), (Strasburg), (3) Martin Barr, Jr. (Est. 1710-

1784), (Strasburg), (4) John Barr (1749-1813) (Strasburg), (5) John Barr (1771-1843) (Strasburg and Ohio) and (5) Dr. Martin Barr (1793-1874) (Strasburg and Middletown, Delaware).

(5) John Barr (1771-1843) had a family of seven. These were Martha Barr Barge, Henry Barr, John Barr, Hetty Barr Finfrock, David Barr, Elizabeth Barr Keeler and Anna Barr who married our Peter Henry Winger (A2226). John Barr (1771-1843) died November 13, 1843. He was buried in the Folck Cemetery near Fairborn, Ohio. In recent years this cemetery was all but obliterated. In 1967, at the instance of Ira R. Barr and the writer, his grave and monument were moved to the Fairfield Cemetery at Fairborn, Ohio.

For details concerning the Ohio Barr families, see Barr Genealogy, 1963, by Ira R. Barr, Yellow Springs, Ohio.

> The facts in Switzerland, Zweibrücken and Lancaster County, Pennsylvania, were taken from the official records of the constituted custodians of official sources in secular, church and parish files by the writer. Three trips to Europe and many visits to Lancaster County finally have resulted in working out this hypothesis. (2) Martin Barr's (Est. 1680-1760) Will, dated August 7, 1757, (3) Martin Barr's (Est. 1710-1784) Will, dated February 2, 1776, and (4) John Barr's (1749-1813) Will (K-1-423) of 1811 are of particular interest. Deeds 10-538, D5-316 and 15.145 are completely confirmatory. These instruments have many items of evidential quality. We believe this report can be the basis of an exhaustive Barr family history for those who really care.

Peter (A2226) and Anna Winger Family

Peter (A2226) and Anna Winger had a family of nine children. Hester Ann (A22261), Susan Ann (A22262) and Elizabeth Ann (A22263) were all born in Lancaster County, Pennsylvania, between the years 1831 and 1834. The other six children were born in Ohio. Abraham Winger (A22264), Mary Ann (A22265), Catherine Ann (A22266), John (A22267) and Eliza (A22268) were born in Bath Township, Greene County, Ohio, between 1838 and 1846. The youngest son, Joseph (A22269), was born in Darke County, Ohio, in 1848. Abraham (A22264), being the first-born son, was named after Peter Henry's (A2226) father, Abraham (A222).

To Greene County, Ohio

Peter (A2226) and Anna Winger came from Lancaster County, Pennsylvania, to Greene County, Ohio, in 1836. No doubt the de-

PUBLIC SALE.

ON THURSDAY, THE 18TH DAY OF AUGUST NEXT,

Will be offered at public sale, at the public house of Jesse Tweed, (sorrel horse)

A TRACT OF FIRSTRATE

Limestone Land,

situate in Strasburg township, Lancaster county, seven miles east of the city of Lancaster, one mile from Withers's mill on the public road leading from Lancaster to New Providence; adjoining lands of Henry Diffenbaugh, Jacob Barge and others, containing 8 acres, in a high state of cultivation, under good fence, and divided into four convenient fields; 1200 bushels of lime has been put on this land. The improvements are a good one and a half story frame

HOUSE,

with two rooms and a kitchen on the lower floor, the front room is large and convenient it having been kept as a tavern for two years and known as a good stand for that business; a large frame barn with a thrashing floor and good stables, a large grain shed;

A SMITH'S SHOP

and shed; also, a one story dwelling house on said premises in good repair, and other necessary outbuildings; a well of water near the door which was never known to fail, and a good bearing

ORCHARD

of choice fruit. There are few properties known to excel this in point of beauty and location, either as a place for public busines or a private residence. Any person wishing to view the property previous to the day of sale, will please to call on Simon Groff, living on the same. Possession will be given on the first day of April next.

Sale to commence at 1 o'clock, P. M. of said day, when attendance will be given and terms of sale made known by

JOHN BARR.

July 29, 1836.

HENRY MILLER, JR. PRINTER, LAMPETER SQUARE.

The John Barr handbill, July 29, 1836.

cision of Peter (A2226) and Anna to move their family from Pennsylvania to Ohio was influenced by Anna's father, John Barr, (1771-1843), who had decided that he would take his entire family to Ohio where he believed they would have better fortunes. In preparation for the move, John Barr, Anna's brother, held a public sale of all of his household effects on the premises of Jacob Neff, February 7, 1835. A record of the sale indicates that over 100 friends and neighbors purchased articles from the John Barr household that date. (See Appendix.)

On July 29, 1836, John Barr posted handbills, shown here, advertising the fact that he would have a public sale on August 18, 1836, at the public house (the Sorrel Horse) of Jesse Tweed. At this sale he sold his limestone land in Strasburg Township which was located one mile from Wither's Mill on the public road leading from Lancaster to New Providence. With the sale went a smith's shop and two dwelling houses. This was the preparation for the Winger and Barr expedition to Ohio.

They left by covered wagon in August 1836. There were so many members of both families that there was not room enough in the wagon for everyone, so some of the more able members had to take turns walking. John Barr (1771-1843) started a new life by purchasing a farm near Fairfield and Osborn, now known as Fairborn, Ohio. In the early stages Peter (A2226) and Anna Barr Winger lived on the same farm with Anna's father, John Barr (1771-1843). After the death of John Barr in 1843, his account book revealed that he had, between April 1831, and October 1836, given to Peter (A2226) and Anna Barr Winger one bed and bedding, one bureau, one spinning wheel and cash to a total of $87. This illustrates the meagerness with which life was frought in those early days.

To Darke County

In 1848 Peter (A2226) and Anna Barr Winger, having inherited meager capital from the estate of Peter's mother, Anna Eby Winger, bought 66 acres from Samuel Wise who resided in Miami County, Ohio. This land was located in Richland Township on Ohio State Route 121, about one-half mile east of the cemetery, reasonably

Since the Wingers and the Barrs left for Ohio in August 1836, this reproduction of Barr's Ark and the Conestoga Wagon seems to depict the event. The original water color was done by C. X. Carlson from the book Old Lancaster.

near Harris Creek in the vicinity of Versailles and Bradford in Darke County. (V-1-166)

Members of the family stated that the first home Peter (A2226) and Anna had in Darke County was built on a tract of wild timberland on which not a stick had been cut or an improvement made. Peter (A2226) built a crude cabin of rough logs without nails, fastening the shack on poles and pegs. This log cabin was erected in the center of Indian territory. Anna baked bread and always had an abundant supply on hand. This was held for the purpose of feeding the Indians. Often they stalked into the cabin unannounced, picked up her bread and left at once. By following this strategy, she was able to keep the Indians from doing any harm to the family. They were so poor that in the winter Peter (A2226) would walk all the way back to Lancaster County, Pennsylvania, fording Ohio streams and rivers, so that he could be with people he knew, probably his brothers, Emanuel Wenger (A2221) and Samuel Wenger (A2224).

Here he worked in the limestone mine at Quarryville or in the smith or wagon shops, following his trade of wheelwright to get enough money to sustain the family. By spring he would come back to Ohio with the seed money needed to put in the crop for the next season. They were so poor that they could not afford dishes. For the most part, Peter (A2226) carved wooden plates from logs.

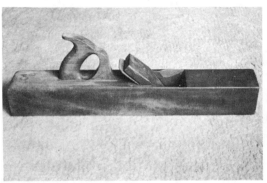

An early wooden plane, the only remaining evidence of the wagon production engaged in by Peter Henry Winger (A2226), now in the possession of John E. Fetzer (A2226923).

On the Move

On October 3, 1851, they sold their 66 acres to Amy Routzong (V-1-167) and bought 40 acres in Wayne Township located on the south side of Burns Road, about one and a quarter miles west of French Town. This was sold to Henry Burns May 29, 1855, and they moved to Versailles, Ohio (D-2-178).

In the late fall of 1860, the entire family went to Marshall County, Iowa, where 80 acres was acquired. The story is told that when Peter (A2226) and his family arrived in Iowa, Peter (A2226), as a result of their hardships, wanted to turn around and go home. Anna, his wife, would have no part of it. She said, "After coming this distance, we have to make the best of it." They had passed through windstorms, snow and cold, and about every other kind of misfortune had overtaken them. When they crossed the Mississippi River, an accident with the ferry not only dumped the horses into the river, but they lost nearly all of their personal belongings as well. In any event, they gave Iowa a trial for two years, after which they sold out and returned to Ohio.

They returned to Patterson Township in Darke County where

in 1862 they purchased 20 acres of land on the east side of Conover Road, about one and three-quarter miles south of State Route 705,

To Iowa and return.

where they stayed for eight years. On May 28, 1870, they bought 80 acres from William Miller (R3-T12-S1) in Patterson Township on the north side of State Route 705 and bordering Mendenhall Road on the east. On this tract of land Peter Winger (A2226) built a log house similar to most of that day. It was located near the Winger-Magato Creek about 15 rods north of Route 705 and about 10 rods west of Mendenhall Road. The entrance to the house was from Mendenhall Road. In 1969 Mr. Joseph R. Frey, who has lived all his life in this neighborhood, described the Winger log home and the nearby house and barn of Joseph Winger (A22269) as he saw them in his early life. From this description the artist has drawn these homesteads shown here.

The land records in Darke County of those early times were ill kept. Peter (A2226) remained on this 80-acre farm the balance of his life. Anna remained on the farm until the approximate time of her terminal illness.

Their decision to move to Patterson Township proved to be good. After years of struggle Peter (A2226) cleared and cultivated land, principally in fine crops of tobacco, which turned out to be some of the best in the Midwest.

William Limes (A222631), a grandson of Peter (A2226) and Anna Winger, reported that in later years they had many Winger and Barr relatives as visitors from Lancaster County. He learned from some of the conversations exchanged between these visitors and Anna Winger of the falling of the stars in 1833.

Peter Winger (A2226), having been born into a Mennonite family, continued to wear the plain clothes and broadbrimmed hat characteristic of that faith. The vicissitudes of pioneer life in Ohio out of necessity presented a confused picture of church affiliations. Peter

On the upper left, the log cabin in which Peter Henry Winger (A2226) first lived. On the right side was the home of Joseph Winger (A22269), the youngest son of Peter Henry (A2226). The Winger-Magato Creek runs between the two houses.

Henry (A2226) and his wife, Anna, were known as devoutly religious people. Since churches were few and far between (for the most part services were held in schoolhouses), they attended religious services without regard to church affiliation.

About 1875 Peter Winger (A2226) became seriously ill with "lung fever." All hope had been abandoned for his recovery. Preacher Peck of the New Light Church (now Christian Church) came to hold the last rites and convinced Peter (A2226) that he should be baptized by immersion. Peter (A2226) consented. In the dead of winter, the party went to nearby Winger-Magato Creek which ran across the farm. It was necessary to break about ten feet of ice and dam up the water in order to hold the service. Peter was taken into the freezing water and was baptized. After returning the "remains" to his sick bed, Peter Winger (A2226) made a complete recovery, much to the amazement of family and neighbors.

The Human Side

Members of the family have reported that Peter Winger (A2226) was of even temperament and loved by everybody. He was considered the peacemaker and would go to great lengths to avoid trouble. He loved his family and children and was always ready to extend a helping hand.

Anna, Peter's wife, was a small woman. She was a little over four feet tall and weighed not more than 85 to 90 pounds. She made up for her stature with a fiery temper. She was described as easy to wrath and at times was subject to being misunderstood. She was religious and had a "tender undercover" which for the most part was reluctant to manifest itself.

The story is told that time and again, when the boys went to the barn in the morning to feed the horses, they would find the manes of the horses completely braided. It, of course, involved considerable work to comb out the manes so that the horses would have the neat appearance which Peter required. As a result, the neighbors charged that this phenomenon was due to Anna Winger (she being addicted to witchcraft). Some members of the family took a dim view of these charges. Probably some of the boys were playing pranks and knew considerably more about braiding manes than they admitted.

The Winger-Magato Creek where the "final rights" of baptism were held.

One day Peter Winger (A2226) hitched his horse, Lucy, (she was so fat she could hardly walk) to his spring wagon, which was loaded with four sacks of raw wheat and corn, to go to the grist mill. He started to the village of Minster. As he entered the village, he came to the Erie Canal. As he neared the drawbridge, a horse-drawn boat approached the bridge. A bystander yelled at Peter (A2226) not to cross. He was a little deaf and did not hear. The keeper immediately opened the bridge to accommodate the boat. Lucy, already on the bridge landing, was unable to stop. The horse, the spring wagon, and all the grain were dumped into the Canal. Peter (A2226) fell in, head over heels. A rescue mission followed. Later his son, Joseph Winger (A22269), reprimanded his father for being careless. Peter (A2226) retorted, "Never hurt me a bit."

Another incident related by family members was about Peter's (A2226) well-known dislike of turtle soup. One day Anna gave him "chicken soup" which he liked very much. Afterwards she told him that it was turtle soup. Peter (A2226) was convinced. He said, "I could eat that any time."

Fifth Generation Winger Sisters

Peter (A2226) and Anna Winger's first-born child, Hester Ann (A22261), of the fifth generation, was born in Lancaster County, Pennsylvania, December 15, 1831. She was named after Hester Ann, the wife of Samuel (A2224), Peter's (A2226) brother. She married Joseph H. Sipes on October 8, 1852, in Darke County, Ohio. By 1860 Hester Ann (A22261) was a widow, residing in Wayne Township, Darke County. At that time she had three children. Mary Elizabeth (A222611) was born in 1853, Anna (A222612) in 1854 and Orlandus (A222613) was born in 1860. Orlandus was known to have lived in Mercer County near Celina, since the Joseph Winger (A22269) children remembered him as a cousin who frequently came to visit.

Susan Ann Winger (A22262) of the fifth generation was born in Lancaster County, August 2, 1833. She was reported to have married Robert Keeler and is thought to have lived for a time in Marshall County, Iowa, having gone there with her parents in 1860. However, a Susan Ann Winger on August 25, 1852, married David Patterson near Versailles by R. Brandon, M.G. Due to these conflicting data, the family history is somewhat in limbo. In any event, this family could never be located and is unknown at this writing.

The Limes Family

Elizabeth Ann Winger (A22263) of the fifth generation was born in Lancaster County, July 3, 1834. She married Michael Limes February 20, 1862, in Darke County. She had a reputation for being "too good to her family." They lived in Darke County from 1864 to 1877. From 1877 to 1890 they resided in Mercer County, post office Stetke, Ohio. From 1890 to 1898 they lived in Melrose, Paulding County, Ohio. Michael Limes died December 30, 1898. After the death of her husband, Elizabeth Winger Limes (A22263) lived with her daughter and son-in-law, Margarette Ellen (A222634) and Robert Keeling, at Melrose, Ohio. Michael Limes, Elizabeth Ann's (A22263) husband, was a member of Company F, 152 Ohio Volunteer Infantry, in the Civil War.

The Limes had a family of five children. William H. (A222631) was born in 1862 and died in 1948. Rose Ann (A222632) was born in 1864. She married Warren Brown and had a family of six children. A third child, Lucy (A222633), died in infancy. The fourth child, Margarette Ellen (A222634), who was born in 1867, married Robert Keeling and had a family of seven. August Limes (A222635) was the fifth child of the sixth generation. Michael and Elizabeth Winger Limes (A22263), along with Rose Ann (A222632) and Margarette Ellen (A222634), are buried in Celina, Ohio.

The August Limes (A222635) of the sixth generation had six children of the seventh generation. Their first-born child was Hurless Franklin Lime (A2226351), who was born January 16, 1895, in Celina and died December 27, 1952. He is buried in the North Grove Cemetery in Celina. He married first Bertha Baker who was born in October 1895, in Celina and died in Celina in 1929. She, too, is buried in the North Grove Cemetery. Hurless Lime (A2226351) married Marie Cain as his second wife on July 28, 1947.

The second child of the seventh generation was Clarence August Lime (A2226352), who was born June 19, 1898, in Celina. He married Esther Hoenie Deitrick (A222691) as recorded in the chapter entitled The Winger Sisters in Ohio.

The third child of the August Limes (A222635) was Alie Deloss Lime (A2226353) of the seventh generation. She was born March 31, 1901, in Celina. She married Hern Eblen on July 6, 1927, in Celina. He was born in Celina on July 8, 1905.

The August Limes (A222635) had a fourth child, Leona Opal Lime (A2226354), born September 11, 1903, in Celina. She married Clifford Hay November 12, 1924, in Celina. He was born December 6, 1896, in Celina.

The fifth child was Edith Lime (A2226355), who was born October 22, 1906, and died April 11, 1908. She is buried in Swamp College, Celina.

The last child of the seventh generation was Rolland Charles Lime (A2226356), born August 10, 1909, in Celina. He married Edith Lawrina Schaadt who was born January 10, 1917, in Celina.

Geaubaux-Marker Families

Mary Ann Winger (A22265) of the fifth generation was born in Bath Township, Greene County, Ohio, February 11, 1840. She married Samuel Marker about 1868 in Darke County. For a time they lived in Michigan on a farm that had very poor land. The only thing they could raise on the land was potatoes. Mary Ann (A22265) contracted tuberculosis, and her husband, Sam, made a bed for her in the hay on the wagon and drove her all the way from Michigan to Ohio. He came to the home of Peter (A2226) and Anna Winger, but Anna was unable to take care of her, so Grandmother Woods Winger, who happened to be there at the time, took them to her home. They had an infant daughter, who was born and died May 22, 1871. Mary Ann (A22265) died in Darke County, September 1, 1872. She is buried in Tea Cup Cemetery near Osgood and York.

Catherine Ann Winger (A22266) of the fifth generation was born in Bath Township, Greene County, Ohio, January 30, 1842. She married August Geaubaux in Darke County on January 21, 1862. She died February 4, 1872, and is buried in Tea Cup Cemetery near Osgood and York. They had two children, Calvin (A222661) and Josephine (A222662). Calvin (A222661) became a Dunkard preacher and Josephine (A222662) became a Catholic sister. She died before reaching the age of 20.

Eliza Winger Barnhart (A22268)

Eliza Winger (A22268) of the fifth generation was born April 13, 1846, in Bath Township, Greene County, Ohio. She married Charles Barnhart (1825-1912) in Darke County and died in 1923. The Barnharts are buried in the Mendenhall Cemetery near Yorkshire. They lived on a farm near the Joseph Winger (A22269) farm one mile north of the Village of Osgood. The writer remembers visiting their home when he was a child. He recalls how impressed he was that Aunt Liza (A22268) had all the pots and pans highly polished, and that everything in the house was immaculate and clean to the nth degree.

The Barnharts had eight sets of twins. They were all girls except the last, which was a boy and a girl. All of them died as infants except the last boy and girl. The boy died at the age of 19 and the girl lived to be 21 years old. She married a man from the South. They had an infant son and, a month after delivery, she died. The father took his baby to the South where the boy's paternal grandparents raised him.

The boy grew up, married a Chippewa Indian girl, and returned to Ohio on a visit. He and his wife visited Eliza (A22268), who was living north of Osgood, at a time when she had fallen and broken her hip. There was nobody to take care of her so this couple stayed for two years, nursing her through her terminal illness. This grandson inherited the Barnhart farm. The present whereabouts of this unusual couple is not known.

Eliza Winger Barnhart (A22268) with her nephew, Charles E. Winger (A222671), and their favorite watch dog.

The particulars concerning the three sons of Peter (A2226) and Anna, namely Abraham (A22264), John (A22267) and Joseph (A222-69) follow in separate chapters.

The Later Years

In the later years of their lives, Peter (A2226) and Anna Winger decided to convey their 80-acre farm to their children. After an equitable settlement had been reached with Abraham (A22264), John Winger (A22267) retained 60 acres and Joseph Winger (A222-69) retained 20 acres. Joseph (A22269) had the north 20 acres and Peter (A2226) and Anna continued to occupy their log home which was near the north end of the remaining 60 acres .(The exact location was about 15 rods north of Route 705 and about 10 rods west of Mendenhall Road.) They could look out the window and see their son, Joseph (A22269), plowing in his fields.

As long as Joseph (A22269) lived on this 20-acre farm, until the fall of 1880, he and his family looked after Peter (A2226) and Anna. There was a close family relationship. This continued after the Joseph Winger (A22269) family moved to Mercer County. Peter (A2226) would drive his horse, Lucy, to Mercer County and on occasion would take his wife, Anna, with him.

Peter Winger (A2226) died on his Patterson Township farm in Darke County, November 15, 1889. He was buried in the Mendenhall Cemetery near Yorkshire within three miles of his home.

The log cabin home stood for many years after Peter's (A2226) death. To this day there is a living memorial to Peter Winger (A2226). As one walks across the fields of this farm and comes to the site where the cabin once stood, there grow the tall mustard grass and weeds that more often than not commemorate a building that once stood upon that spot.

Some time after the death of Peter Winger (A2226), Joseph (A222-69) and Abraham (A22264) went to the Peter Winger (A2226) farm, got their mother, Anna Barr Winger, and brought her to Mercer County. Grandmother Nancy Jane Woods Winger wanted to take care of her, but Calvin Geaubaux (A222661), who became an orphan at the age of seven and was raised by Joseph (A22269) and Nancy Jane Woods Winger, insisted that "Granny" come to live with him and his wife, Mary. They lived on the Frahm Pike at Five Points about a mile and a half toward Celina from the Joseph Winger (A22269) farm. Joseph (A22269) and his brother, Abraham (A22264), paid Calvin Geaubaux (A222661) to take care of their mother. When Anna Bárr Winger died March 10, 1896, her remains were taken from Celina on the old CH&D Railroad to Versailles and then to Yorkshire where she was buried in the Mendenhall Cemetery next to Peter (A2226).

Anna Barr Winger (1806-1896) at the age of 90 years.

In 1944 the writer and Charles Winger (A222671) jointly furnished and installed a monument to Peter Henry Winger (A2226) and his wife, Anna Barr Winger.

See the Peter Henry Winger (A2226) Family Tree which follows.

Peter Henry Winger (A2226) Family Tree

1st Hans Wenger (b. About 1430) Blumenstein, Thun
2nd Burkhard Wenger (b. About 1450) Forst, Thun
3rd Peter Wenger (b. About 1470) Wattenwil, Seftigen
4th Peter Wenger (b. About 1490) Wattenwil, Seftigen
5th Rudolfus Wenger (b. About 1510) Wattenwil, Seftigen
6th Hans Wenger (b. About 1530) Wattenwil, Seftigen
7th Rudolfus Wenger (Ch. April 5, 1566) Wattenwil-Thurnen, Seftigen

8th Peter Wenger (Ch. Dec. 13, 1607) Wattenwil-Thurnen, Seftigen

9th Hans Wenger (Ch. May 30, 1633) Wattenwil-Thurnen, Seftigen

    A   Christian Wenger (A2) First Generation in America (1688-1749)

        B-1   Henry Wenger, Sr. (A22) Second Generation in America (1716-1802)

            C-1   Abraham Wenger (A222) Third Generation in America (1767-1845)

                D-1   Peter Henry Winger (A2226) Fourth Generation in America

                        b. Feb. 26, 1806, Lancaster County

                        d. Nov. 15, 1889, Darke County

                        m. Anna Barr, Sept. 23, 1830, Strasburg, Pa.

                            b. Feb. 28, 1806, Strasburg

                            d. Mar. 10, 1896, Mercer County

                    E-1   Hester Ann Winger (A22261-5th)

                            b. Dec. 15, 1831, Lancaster County

                            m. Joseph H. Sipes, Oct. 8, 1852, Darke County

                      F-1   Mary Elizabeth Sipes (A222611-6th)

                            b. 1853, Darke County

                      F-2   Anna Sipes (A222612-6th)

                            b. 1854, Darke County

                      F-3   Orlandus Sipes (A222613-6th)

                            b. 1860, Darke County

                    E-2   Susan Ann Winger (A22262-5th)

                            b. Aug. 2, 1833, Lancaster County

                            m. Robert Keeler or David Patterson, Aug. 25, 1852, Versailles

                    E-3   Elizabeth Ann Winger (A22263-5th)

                            b. July 3, 1834, Lancaster County

                            d. Unknown

                            m. Michael Limes, Feb. 20, 1862, Darke County

                    F-1   William H. Limes (A222631-6th)

                            b. 1862, Darke County

                            d. 1848, Celina

                    F-2   Rose Ann Limes (A222632-6th)

                            b. 1864, Darke County

                            m. Warren Brown

F-3 Lucy Limes (A222633-6th)
  Died in infancy

F-4 Margarette Ellen Limes (A222634-6th)
  b. 1867, Darke County
  m. Robert Keeling

F-5 August Limes (A222635-6th)
  b. Aug. 12, 1870, Darke County
  d. Oct. 9, 1952, bur. Swamp College,
  Celina
  m. Cecil Shinn, Dec. 6, 1894

  G-1 Hurless Franklin Lime (A2226351-7th)
    b. Jan. 16, 1895, Celina
    d. Dec. 27, 1952, Celina,
      bur. North Grove
    m. Bertha Baker (1st)
      b. Oct., 1895, Celina
      d. 1929, Celina, bur. North Grove
    m. Marie Cain (2nd) July 28, 1947

  G-2 Clarence August Lime (A2226352-7th)
    b. June 19, 1898, Celina
    m. Esther Hoenie Deitrick
      (A222691-7th)
      b. June 8, 1901, Celina, Ohio

  G-3 Alie Deloss Lime (A2226353-7th)
    b. Mar. 31, 1901, Celina
    m. Hern Eblen, July 6, 1927, Celina
      b. July 8, 1905, Celina

  G-4 Leona Opal Lime (A2226354-7th)
    b. Sept. 11, 1903, Celina
    m. Clifford Hay, Nov. 12, 1924, Celina
      b. Dec. 6, 1896, Celina

  G-5 Edith Lime (A2226355-7th)
    b. Oct. 22, 1906, Celina
    d. Apr. 11, 1908, Celina,
      bur. Swamp College

  G-6 Rolland Charles Lime (A2226356-7th)
    b. Aug. 10, 1909, Celina
    m. Edith Lawrina Schaadt
      b. Jan. 10, 1917, Celina

E-4 Abraham Winger (A22264-5th)
  (See separate chapter)

E-5 Mary Ann Winger (A22265-5th)
     b. Feb. 11, 1840, Greene County
     d. Sept. 1, 1872, Darke County
     m. Samuel Marker about 1868,
     Darke County
  F-1 Infant daughter (A222651-6th)
     b. and d. May 22, 1871
E-6 Catherine Ann Winger (A22266-5th)
     b. Jan. 30, 1842, Greene County
     d. Feb. 4, 1872, Darke County
     m. August Geaubaux, Jan. 21, 1862,
     Darke County
  F-1 Calvin Geaubaux (A222661-6th)
     m. Mary Shipman
    G-1 Daisy Geaubaux (A2226611-7th)
    G-2 Jessie Geaubaux (A2226612-7th)
  F-2 Josephine Geaubaux (A222662-6th)
E-7 John Henry Winger (A22267-5th)
     (See separate chapter)
E-8 Eliza Winger (A22268-5th)
     b. Apr. 13, 1846, Greene County
     d. 1923, Darke County
     m. Charles Barnhart
      b. 1825
      d. 1912, Darke County
E-9 Joseph Levi Winger (A22269-5th)
     (See separate chapter)

The Winger grave marker.

CHAPTER TEN

Abraham Winger of Ohio

ABRAHAM WINGER (A22264) was born in Bath Township, Greene County, Ohio, October 17, 1838. The Winger family came from Lancaster County, Pennsylvania, to Greene County in 1836. The first three children, all girls, were born in Lancaster County. Abraham (A22264), the oldest and first-born boy in the family, was born in Ohio after the arrival of the family two years earlier. Following the early custom, Abraham (A22264) was named after his grandfather, Abraham Winger (A222).

Abraham (A22264) was brought by his parents from Greene County to Darke County, Ohio, when he was ten. That was in 1848.

Abraham Winger (A22264)

He was trained as a farmer as were his brothers who were to follow. He attended a nearby one-room school as his good friend and neighbor, John B. Hole, attested many years later. As a boy he worked on the farm of his father, Peter Henry Winger (A2226), first in Richland Township, then Wayne Township and finally in Patterson Township, all in Darke County.

Abraham (A22264) met a neighbor girl, Margaret Ellen Carlock. They were married in the Methodist Episcopal Church in Versailles, Ohio, September 3, 1860, the Reverend Henry J. Burns presiding.

Blanche Lucinda Passwater (A2226410), a granddaughter of Abraham Winger (A22264), said that, when her grandparents were first married, they lived in Darke County near the home of Peter Henry Winger (A2226). Abraham (A22264) started to build a log house. In the meantime, due to their poor circumstances, they went to the groves where there were small trees, pulled them to the ground and piled sod on the branches. The boughs were tied to striplings. The result was a shelter much like a thatched hut. This was used as temporary quarters until the log cabin was completed. It was here that Margaret Winger established the reputation as one of the best cooks "found anywhere." A start was made to raise a large family.

Margaret Ellen Carlock, wife of Abraham Winger (A22264).

Their first-born child was Martha Ann Winger (A222641) of the sixth generation. She was born August 17, 1861. In spite of a desire to build a family life, Abraham (A22264) and his wife, Margaret Ellen, were aware that the nation was in desperate peril. The war between the states had begun.

The Civil War and the 94th

Abraham Winger (A22264) had a keen sense of duty and felt that he should do his part to preserve the nation. He enrolled August 13, 1862, in Company K, Regiment 94 of the Ohio Infantry Volunteers. Margaret Ellen Winger and her daughter, Martha Ann Winger (A222641), were to be without husband and father for three long years. They were cared for by the parents on both sides of the family.

Abraham was mustered into the army August 23, 1862. The records of the army of that day describe Abraham Winger (A22264) as being five feet, four inches tall, fair complected, with light hair and blue eyes. During his tour of duty with the "Gallant 94th" he fought in many battles.

On the 28th of August 1862, without uniforms or camp equipment, and never having been drilled as a regiment, the 94th was ordered to Kentucky. Upon arriving in Lexington, Colonel J. W. Frizell, the commanding officer, succeeded in obtaining three rounds of cartridges per man. The regiment proceeded to Yates Ford, 15 miles east of Lexington on the Richmond Road. They ran into a rebel ambush which resulted in the death of two men and the wounding of six. After regrouping their forces, the Gallant 94th engaged the enemy in full-fledged action.

During the course of the fighting, an order was received for the 94th to return to Lexington with all dispatch. A successful retreat was effectuated, but the men were tired and footsore and in bad condition for further marching. The season was very dry and little water was available. The suffering was grave and many soldiers gave as much as $5 for a canteen full of muddy water, a dollar for a drink, and many drank the water from standing pools that the horses refused to touch. The roads were almost ankle-deep in dust and there were scarcely any provisions for the troops. In due course, the 94th reached Louisville where the men were utterly exhausted, having been deprived of sleep, water or food for seven days, marching night and day with feet and limbs swollen almost to bursting, and every sense dulled by the suffering. In this action 218 men were lost.

Their Second Wind

In time the regiment regained strength, vigor and spirit and were ready for duty again. The regiment engaged in the battle of Perryville where they drove the rebel army from Kentucky. The regiment broke camp near Nashville on Christmas Day, 1862, and was in advance of the army marching on Murfreesboro. Later they engaged in the battle of Stone River.

The 94th again was in the advance on Tullahoma, participating in the fight at Hoover's Gap in June 1863. It had a skirmish at Dug Gap, and was engaged in the hard-fought battle of Chickamauga. At Lookout Mountain and Mission Ridge the regiment again took a prominent part, participating in the grand charge upon the ridge. It was with Sherman on the march to Atlanta, taking part in the battles at Buzzard's Roost, Resaca, Kingston, Pumpkin-Vine Creek, Kenesaw Mountain, Chattahoochie River, Peachtree Creek, Atlanta, and Jonesboro.

After pursuing Hood, the 94th participated in Sherman's grand march to the sea, arriving in Savannah before Christmas. On the 20th of January, 1865, it was again on the march through South and North Carolina, and, after participating in the battle of Bentonville, North Carolina, arrived at Goldsboro on the 23rd of March, 1865.

The 94th was the first regiment of infantry to enter Raleigh, North Carolina. Soon after the surrender of Johnston, the regiment marched to Washington, via Richmond and Alexandria, participated in the grand review before President Lincoln, General Grant and others, and in June 1865 had an aggregate of 381 men — all that was left of the original 1010!

The Aftermath

In later years Abraham (A22264) was reticent to talk about his experiences, but he mentioned the Battle of Chickamauga more than any other. He had a high opinion of his commander, Captain Charles Reffle, but his sergeant was something less than attractive. In fact the unit men called him names that would be inappropriate to repeat. Abraham (A22264) told the story that the troops, who were hungry most of the time, would catch wild game, such as turkeys, geese, etc. They cooked them over the fire. The sergeant, seeing this, always commandeered the cooked meat, leaving the men empty-handed. Abraham Winger (A22264) concocted a plot to fix this "petty officer." The "rank and file" caught a dog, killed and cleaned it. After the "barbecue" started, the sergeant made his usual demand. They gave the "delicacy" to the "high command" and he seemed to have had a very satisfying meal. The soldiers had a good time over the episode, barking whenever they passed the sergeant. No further explanation was given to the sergeant.

On another occasion, Abraham (A22264) entered a southern home and found some cornmeal. Abraham told a companion to go into the milk house and get some milk so they could make mush. He tried, but the woman of the house ran out and beat him over the head with a broom. The soldier managed to get away with the milk while Abraham (A22264) went out the other door. Abraham (A22264) built a fire and a few starved soldiers had a feast on cooked cornmeal mush and milk.

During the course of the war, Abraham (A22264) served as a foot soldier in combat and later in the Ambulance Corps. Near the end of the war he was a fifer, leading the troops into battle. Finally, he was transferred to the Veterans Reserve Corps. The hardships of the war brought him a series of health impairments. He contracted rheumatism from exposure and was sickened with malaria near Covington, Kentucky. Later he was treated for lung, liver and kidney complications by regimental physicians in Louisville, Nashville and Chattanooga. He remained more or less in poor health for the rest of his life.

According to his pension applications, which were filed after the war and from which most of his war record and family statistics have been gleaned, he was mustered out and honorably discharged from the Army on June 5, 1865, in Columbus, Ohio.

Abraham Winger (A22264) Returns Home

Abraham Winger (A22264) returned to his log cabin home east of Versailles and south of Frenchtown, in Wayne Township, Darke County, to join his wife, Margaret Ellen, and his baby daughter, Martha Ann (A222641), who was now nearly four years old. The next three children of the sixth generation were born in Darke County. They were Rachel Jane Winger (A222642), James Henry Winger (A222643), and John Calvin Winger (A222644). Viola Minerva Winger (A222645) and Charles Otto Winger (A222646) were to be born in Mercer County. It is known that Abraham (A22264) owned town property in Versailles, which he sold in 1867. He sold his log cabin home and farm in Wayne Township in 1868.

Some time after the birth of his son, John Calvin Winger (A222-644) in 1871, Abraham (A22264) moved his entire family from Darke County to Mercer County about 20 miles north. He established a log house and farm near St. Marys, the closest town being Durbin, Ohio. During the next few years he developed this farm and acquired other interests in Mercer County and Celina, the county seat. In the Census of 1880, he and his family of four children at that time were living in Liberty Township, Mercer County, Ohio. The record shows him to have retained connections in St. Marys, Durbin, Mendon, Wabash, Celina, Hopewell Township in Mercer County and Versailles in Darke County.

He made many friends and acquaintances. Some of these were B. M. Clendening, G. H. Hanson, John B. Hole, Dr. John C. Williams, Grandville Fifer, John Smeltzer, W. C. Snyder, G. H. Hauser, B. F. Shiner, Lorenzo D. Karr, Emory Louderback, John Gephart, Leroy Swatz, Edwin Sheels and Theodore Kiser. Needless to say, the many ties with his brothers, Joseph L. Winger (A22269) and John H. Winger (A22267), and their families were maintained through the years.

A Fast Deal

One of the first lessons Abraham (A22264) and his brother, Joseph Winger (A22269), learned about human nature was the result of an incident with a smooth-talking stranger. As young men, Abraham (A22264) and his brother, Joseph (A22269), jointly owned a fine team of horses and a spring wagon. They drove to Celina one day and there they met a man from Kosciusko County, Indiana. This man commented that the beautiful spring wagon and the team of horses owned by Abraham (A22264) and Joseph (A22269) were among the finest he had ever seen. In fact he was so complimentary that both Abraham (A22264) and Joseph (A22269) were much taken with the stranger.

Finally the topic of conversation led to the stranger's disclosure that he owned one of the finest farms in Kosciusko County, Indiana. He went to great lengths to describe the property. Both Abraham (A22264) and Joseph (A22269) expressed the wish to see this fine farm. The man apparently was a master strategist for he whet the appetites of the Winger brothers to the point that they expressed the desire to someday own a nice farm like it. The magnanimous gentleman, after due consideration, made an offer to trade his farm for the spring wagon and the team of horses. Abraham (A22264) and Joseph (A22269) thought the proposal so good that they made a sight-unseen trade before the gracious gentleman could change his mind.

A quitclaim deed was given to Abraham (A22264) and Joseph (A22269) and just before the man drove away with the wagon and the horses he complimented the brothers for their sagacity in talking him into such a one-sided deal.

In due course the Winger brothers went to Kosciusko County to claim the manor mansion and farm only to find a gigantic drainage canal went through the middle of the acreage and the balance of the land was practically worthless. The Winger brothers sat down and cried at their misfortune but, of course, were much wiser as a result.

Grand Lake

Between Celina and St. Marys lies one of the largest artificial lakes in the world. Grand Lake contains 17,550 acres of land under water. It was started in 1837 and completed in 1845. Many years before the turn of the century, speculators started to drill for oil between the two communities of Celina and St. Marys. The area contained some of the finest farm land in Ohio. There was much drilling for oil and the land was overrun with oil derricks and mobs of speculative people.

Some farmers smelled riches in the oil and favored it, while others preferred not to mar the land. Most of the farmers in the lowland, where the soil was most fertile, were against the formation of the lake and the intrusion of the oil men. When the lake was formed, valuable crops were destroyed. The farmers got together and decided that by removing certain dams along Old Beaver Channel they could divert the water and drain much of the lake. They took action and considerable damage resulted. Many arrests were made. Abraham Winger (A22264) joined the cause, but escaped arrest.

The irony of the episode was that it stopped neither the drilling for oil nor the completing of the lake. The writer well remembers visiting Grand Lake many times as a boy. As far as the eye could see, the tall wooden oil derricks dotted the lake and the pumps were going day and night. Today the derricks are gone and the lake is a beautiful recreation attraction.

Abraham (A22264) Loses his Wife

On January 11, 1901, Abraham (A22264) went outside his farm home near Durbin to bring in wood for the fireplace. When he returned he found his wife, Margaret Ellen Winger, on the floor, dead. She was reported as having passed away as a result of a longstanding disease, in that day called dropsy. Abraham (A22264) and Margaret had just returned from Frankfort, Indiana, where they had intended to spend the winter with their son. It had been due to Margaret's poor health that they came home. Funeral services were held the following Sunday at Mt. Carmel by the Reverend Meyer. Interment was at Swamp College, Celina, Ohio.

After the death of his wife, Abraham (A22264) gave up his home. His principal home thereafter was in Celina. He lived variously with his daughters, Martha Ann Dittmore (A222641), Rachel Jane Hager (A222642) and Viola Minerva Watters (A222645). From time to time, he visited his brothers and sisters in Darke and Mercer Counties, and on one occasion visited Frankfort, Indiana, where the writer lived for a short time as a boy. I recall Uncle Abraham (A22264) visiting my mother, Della Winger Fetzer (A222692), in our home. At that time his hair was white as snow and he was delighted beyond words at the sight of my mother. They had a happy time together discussing the Winger family and the events of the past. That was the one and only time that the writer saw Abraham Winger (A22264).

As mentioned earlier, Abraham (A22264) made numerous applications for pensions as the result of his Civil War service. His grandchildren were always happy to see Grandpa receive his monthly pension check. Each month he would buy something for them, particularly if he happened to be staying in their home at the time. Blanche Passwater (A2226410) states that she remembers that Abraham (A22264) bought a huge band ring for her mother and presented a beautiful rug to her parents, Martha Ann (A222641) and George Dittmore. She also has in her possession Abraham's (A22264) powder horn and a pair of dice that he used in the Civil War.

Abraham Winger (A22264) Passes

For a number of years Abraham's (A22264) health had not been good. In 1910 he progressively became worse and was bedridden. He had a lingering illness that lasted several weeks. He first became ill at the home of his daughter, Viola Minerva Winger Watters (A222645), 635 Heirholzen Street, Celina, Ohio. After a number of weeks he was taken to the home of his daughter, Rachel Jane Winger Hager (A222642), four and one-half miles northwest of St. Marys near the village of Mendon, Ohio, where in recent years he had been making his home. He died May 8, 1910. The remains were returned to the home of Viola Minerva Winger Watters (A222645) in Celina the following Monday. Services were held on Tuesday at the Swamp College Chapel by the Reverend Charles Bennett. Burial was in the Swamp College Cemetery beside his wife, Margaret Ellen Carlock Winger.

The Family Pattern

As stated previously, Abraham (A22264) and Margaret Ellen Winger had six children of the sixth generation. These were as follows: Martha Ann (A222641), Rachel Jane (A222642), James Henry (A222-643), John Calvin (A222644), Viola Minerva (A222645) and Charles Otto Winger (A222646).

Martha Ann Winger (A222641)

It is the purpose of this section to indicate all known descendants and residual information concerning Martha Ann Winger (A222641), the first-born child of Abraham (A22264) and Margaret Ellen Winger. Martha Ann Winger (A222641) was born in Darke County, Ohio, August 17, 1861. She moved with her parents from Darke County to Mercer County where she was raised on the farm. Abraham (A22264) prospered and employed farm hands, both old and young. Among the younger men was George Dittmore whom Abraham (A22264) had known as a member of the militia. Abraham (A22264) felt that this young man fell far short of his own high standards as to what a young man should be. The inevitable happened in 1879. Martha Ann Winger (A222641), who was 18, fell in love with George Dittmore, age 20. Abraham (A22264) took a dim view of this development. As a result, Martha Ann and George Dittmore decided to elope. While Abraham Winger (A22264) was in the field shocking wheat, the young couple ran away, expropriating a horse and spring wagon. They went to the court house, got a license and were married by the justice of the peace. Martha Ann (A222641) was barefooted and had on her sunbonnet, an appropriate setting for marriage. When Abraham Winger (A22264), the father, heard of the elopement he was furious. Martha Ann (A222641) and George had three children before Abraham (A22264) and his wife, Margaret Ellen Winger, were reconciled to the marriage.

Martha Ann (A222641) and George Dittmore had eleven children of the seventh generation. Hannah Ellen Dittmore (A2226411) was born near Celina, Ohio, April 29, 1880. She married George Hayes, March 19, 1898. The Hayes lived in Cleveland Heights and Dayton, where they both died. She died about 1950. They had no children.

The second-born child of Martha Ann (A222641) and George Dittmore was Mary Emeline Dittmore (A2226412) of the seventh generation. She was born April 2, 1882, and died August 29, 1884.

The Winger-Dittmore Line

Eliza Jane Dittmore (A2226413) was born March 3, 1884. She married Frank Tyndall, August 18, 1901, and married her second husband, Edward Makley, June 13, 1912. She had two children by Frank Tyndall, Bernice Bertha Tyndall (A22264131) and Gladys Tyndall (A22264132). Eliza Jane Dittmore (A2226413) lived in St. Marys and died in 1962.

The fourth child of Martha Ann Dittmore (A222641) was George Edward Dittmore (A2226414) of the seventh generation, born March 6, 1886. He married first Cora King, May 30, 1913, and second Esther Weaver in 1926. He had two children by his first wife, namely Mary Dittmore (A22264141), born about 1926, (who married Paul Suchland), and Lucille Dittmore (A22264142), born about 1930, both of the eighth generation. They lived in Ohio and Indiana. He died December 8, 1931.

Bertha Elmira Dittmore (A2226415) of the seventh generation was born August 1, 1888. She did not marry. She died May 1, 1955, in Ft. Wayne.

Lottie May Dittmore (A2226416) of the seventh generation was born May 15, 1893, and presently lives in New York. She has been married three times. Her first husband was Lee Todd, the second Charles Keller and the third was John Divato.

William Henry Dittmore (A2226417), the seventh child of Martha Ann (A222641) and George Dittmore, was born September 10, 1890. He married first Estelle Linton in August 1913 and second, Carrie Floy, January 9, 1922. He lives in Ft. Wayne, Indiana.

The next child of Martha Ann (A222641) and George Dittmore was Sarah Jane Dittmore (A2226418) of the seventh generation, born March 8, 1896. She married first, William Scherer in December 1913, and second, Charles Schuman in 1919 with whom she now lives in California. She had two girls by William Scherer. These are Agnes Scherer (A22264181), who married Joseph Mosley, and Loretta Rosemary Scherer, who married John Knabenshue. Both girls are of the eighth generation.

John Calvin Dittmore (A2226419) of the seventh generation was born October 15, 1898, and died March 19, 1920. He died as the result of an accident in a paper mill in Wabash, Indiana. He was to have been married in two weeks. He was a veteran of World War I and is buried in Swamp College.

The Winger-Dittmore-Passwater Line

Blanche Lucinda Dittmore (A2226410) was the tenth-born child of Martha Ann Winger (A222641) and George Dittmore. She was of the seventh generation and was born July 2, 1901. She was married December 3, 1920, to Howard Stanley Passwater in Ft. Wayne where they continue to make their home. The Passwaters had six children of the eighth generation.

The first child was Richard (A22264101), who was born March 20, 1921. He served in World War II. His first marriage was with Arlene Hilliard from Albion, Indiana, and his second was with Helen Myers, January 7, 1948. He has two children by his second wife, Helen Myers. The first was a daughter, Linda Passwater (A222641011), of the ninth generation who married an unrelated Myers. They had a son, Danny Myers (A2226410111), of the tenth generation who was born in October 1967. The second was a son, John Passwater (A222641012).

Blanche Lucinda Dittmore (A2226410) and Howard Stanley Passwater then had Juanita Eilen (A22264102) of the eighth generation, born February 28, 1926. She married Elmer Moening in April 1946. They have a son, Lynn Moening (A222641021), of the ninth generation who is serving in Vietnam. The youngest son, Michael Moening (A222641022), was born in 1952.

The third child was Howard Stanley Passwater II (A22264103) of the eighth generation. He was born September 6, 1929. He married Joan Stringer of Fall River, Massachusetts, in 1950 and they have three children of the ninth generation. Howard Stanley Passwater III (A222641031) was born in 1954, Russell Passwater (A222-641032) was born in 1956 and Nancy Passwater (A222641033) was born in 1958.

Blanche Lucinda Dittmore (A22-26410), daughter of Martha Ann Winger Dittmore (A222641). She was the wife of Howard Stanley Dittmore.

John Sanford Passwater (A22264104) of the eighth generation was born June 23, 1866, and died January 18, 1935, near St. Marys, a girl by the name of Margy, he made his home in Keystone, Florida. They have a son, Michael Passwater (A222641041) of the ninth generation, who was born in 1954.

Blanche Lucinda Dittmore (A2226410) and Howard Stanley Passwater I then had Kathlynn Passwater (A22264105), their fifth-born child who was born September 7, 1935. She was married first in Angola, Indiana, to Russell Oberley in June 1953, and then to Robert Heinold in January 1962. She has three children of the ninth generation with her first husband. They are Valerie Lucinda Oberley (A222641051), born December 27, 1953; Jeffery Alan Oberley (A222-641052), born December 14, 1955, and Nikki Denise Oberley (A222-641053), born in Florida in 1958. The last-born child was by her second husband, Robert Heinold. Rae Ann Heinold (A222641054) was born in 1963.

The last-born child of Blanche (A2226410) and Howard Passwater was Keith Edward Passwater (A22264106) of the eighth generation. He was born in Ft. Wayne, June 21, 1945. After a tour of duty in the navy, he married Barbara Lengacher, June 28, 1966. This couple had one unidentified son (A222641061).

The eleventh child of Martha Ann Winger (A222641) and George Dittmore was Myrtle Lula Dittmore (A222641A) of the seventh generation, born August 6, 1905. She married Harold Clinton Fisher, September 15, 1924. They had two girls of the eighth generation. These are Virginia Fisher (A222641A1), who was born in September 1926, and Phyllis Fisher (A222641A2), who was born in September 1929. After the death of George Dittmore (1859-1910), Martha Ann Winger (A222641) married Frank Kantner, August 15, 1913, and John Bitner, June 13, 1921.

The Winger-Hager Line

The second child of Abraham (A22264) and Margaret Ellen Winger was Rachel Jane Winger (A222642) of the sixth generation. She was born June 23, 1866, and died January 18, 1935, near St. Marys, Auglaize County, Ohio. She married James Hager who was born

James Hager and his wife, Rachel Jane Winger Hager (A222642).

July 4, 1861, and died November 1, 1924. The Hagers had four children of the seventh generation. The first was Charles Hager (A2226421), who was born January 26, 1888, and died February 24,

1925. The second was Cora Hager (A2226422), born August 5, 1890, and died October 18, 1967. She married Henry Shelby. Emma Hager (A2226423), the third child, was born February 24, 1892. She lives in St. Marys. The fourth and last child of Rachel Jane Winger (A222642) and James Hager was Forrest Hager (A2226424), who was born August 8, 1896, and lives in Kokomo, Indiana.

The third child of Abraham (A22264) and Margaret Ellen Winger was James Henry Winger (A222643) of the sixth generation, who was born August 18, 1867, in Darke County, Ohio. He died in Oklahoma in 1930. He married Mary Walker and was without issue. He was a blacksmith by trade and lived in Okmulgee, Oklahoma. Two of the Hager girls were reported to have visited the James (Jim) Wingers (A222643) in Oklahoma. Cora Hager (A2226422) and Emma Hager (A2226423) visited them about 1920.

The fourth child of Abraham (A22264) and Margaret Winger was John Calvin Winger (A222644). He was born in Darke County, Ohio, June 23, 1871, and died March 12, 1949. He married Emaline Hullinger and was without issue. He and his wife are buried in Memorial Park, Kokomo, Indiana. The writer briefly visited John Calvin Winger (A222644) on July 6, 1948. At that time he was living with his niece, Forrest Hager (A2226424), near the village of McGrawsville, Indiana. He was most helpful, giving me several leads to valuable historical material concerning the Winger family.

The Winger-Watters Family

The fifth child of Abraham (A22264) and Margaret Ellen Winger was Viola Minerva Winger (A222645) of the sixth generation. She was born December 29, 1877, in Mercer County, Ohio, and died in her home, 1017 West Taylor Street, Kokomo, Indiana, January 14, 1928. She married Henry Eliza Watters July 9, 1898, in Celina, Ohio. Henry Watters was born September 19, 1868, in Celina and died in Kokomo December 9, 1934. He was the son of Eliza Washington Watters, born July 8, 1840, and died September 28, 1913. His mother was Frances Caroline Large Watters, born December 8, 1846, and died in November 1913. The Watters moved from Mendon, Ohio, to Kokomo, Indiana in 1916.

Viola Winger Watters (A222645) joined the Friends Church when she was a young woman. She was a member of the Union Street Friends Church and of the Security Benefit Association in Kokomo.

She was a sensitive and Christian woman in the best Winger tradition. During the funeral service, conducted by Reverend E. Howard Brown and Reverend Lewis E. Stout, it was said that she had suffered greatly during her terminal illness and that she had born it all

Viola Minerva Winger (A222-645). She was the wife of Henry Eliza Watters.

patiently and courageously. Her eulogy included the following quotation from Appleby:

> There is no prison for the soul
> That dwells within God's boundless peace;
> And sickness builds no dungeon walls
> For one who knoweth sin's surcease;
> He soars on tireless pinions high,
> And lives beneath the open sky.

Viola Minerva Winger Watters (A222645) and her husband, Henry Eliza Watters, are buried in the Crown Point Cemetery near Kokomo.

Herman Clifford Watters (A2226451)

Viola Minerva (A222645) and Henry Watters had a family of five, two of whom died in infancy. Herman Clifford Watters (A2226451) of the seventh generation was born February 7, 1902, in Celina, Ohio, and died in Ft. Wayne, Indiana, April 4, 1957. He married

Agnes Bagley February 1, 1923, in Kokomo, Indiana. She was born October 8, 1905. After starting married life in Kokomo, Mr. and Mrs. Herman Watters moved to Ft. Wayne, Indiana, where the Watters Photographic Studios were established. Mrs. Agnes Watters has continued the operation of this business with her son, Paul Edward Watters (A22264514), since the death of her husband, Herman Watters (A2226451), in 1957.

Herman (A2226451) and Agnes Watters had a family of five, all born in or near Ft. Wayne. The first child was Helen Louise Watters (A22264511) of the eighth generation. She was born February 23, 1924, and first married Donald Buchtel in 1940 after which she married George Johnstone in 1953. Helen Watters (A22264511) by her first husband had a daughter, Agnes Rosemary Buchtel (A222645111), of the ninth generation. She was born June 9, 1943, and married James Stephens. Agnes (A222645111) and James Stephens had two children of the tenth generation. These are Brenda Ann Stephens (A2226451111) born in 1961 and Barbara Ann Stephens (A222645-1112) born in 1963.

The second child of Herman (A2226451) and Agnes Watters was Henry Eugene Watters (A22264512) of the eighth generation. He was born August 8, 1925, in Ft. Wayne and married Anna Laura Algaier in Germany after World War II in 1947. Anna Laura Algaier was born near Heidelberg. They have no children but have adopted a boy and a girl, Deborah Sue (A222645121-By assignment) and Kevin Eugene Watters (A222645122-By assignment). This family lives outside Ft. Wayne in New Haven, Indiana.

The third child of Herman (A2226451) and Agnes Watters was Rex Francis Watters (A22264513) of the eighth generation, born July 20, 1927. He married Patricia Barr in 1948. They had a family of seven of the ninth generation. These are as follows: Francis Watters (A222645131), born July 10, 1950; Randy Guy Watters (A222-645132), born November 27, 1951; Reneé Watters (A222645133), born January 27, 1953; Roseanne Watters (A222645134), born May 5, 1955; Roxanne Watters (A222645135), born May 5, 1955 (twins); Rickey Watters (A222645136), born September 27, 1956, and Robin Watters (A222645137), born in 1958.

Herman (A2226451) and Agnes Watters then had Paul Edward Watters (A22264514) of the eighth generation who was born January 18, 1929, in Ft. Wayne. He married Sondre L. Brown. They have three children of the ninth generation. These are Beth Ann Watters (A222645141), born in 1957; Elizabeth Ann Watters (A222-645142), born in 1959, and Stephen Watters (A222645143), born in 1960.

The fifth and last child of Herman (A2226451) and Agnes Watters was Walter LeRoy Watters (A22264515) of the eighth generation. He was born February 6, 1934, in Ft. Wayne. He married Connie Syndram and had a family of three. The children of the ninth generation are as follows: Karen Sue Watters (A222645151), born in 1959; Judy K. Watters (A222645152), born in 1964, and Sarah Watters (A222645153), born in 1966.

Dallas Oren Watters (A2226452)

Dallas Oren Watters (A2226452) was the second child of Viola Minerva Winger (A222645) and Henry Eliza Watters. He was born July 26, 1905, in Mercer County. He married Mary Frances Merrell December 12, 1925. She was born in Kokomo, Indiana, December 28, 1906. Dallas O. Watters (A2226452) has lived in Ft. Wayne, Indiana, all his business life and has been with the International Harvester Company since 1925.

Dallas O. Watters (A2226452), Fort Wayne, Indiana.

The Watters have three children of the eighth generation. The first was Shirley Ann Watters (A22264521) who was born in Ft. Wayne, December 23, 1927. First she married William Rhonemus, April 3, 1948, in Ft. Wayne. Her second marriage was with Donald Parker, March 1, 1952, also in Ft. Wayne. Donald Parker was born

December 6, 1927, in Ft. Wayne. William Rhonemus and Shirley Ann (A22264521) were the parents of Sherry Lee (A222645211), who was born February 2, 1949, in Raleigh, North Carolina. Donald Parker adopted her so she assumed the name of Parker. The Parkers had six children of the ninth generation as follows: Gary Allen Parker (A222645212) was born February 13, 1952; Linda Kay Parker (A222645213) was born October 29, 1953; Michael Eugene Parker (A222645214) was born February 18, 1955, and died March 15, 1955; David Wayne Parker (A222645215) was born February 5, 1956; Janet Frances Parker (A222645216) was born June 30, 1957, and, finally, Vickie Jane Parker (A222645217) was born November 27, 1960. All were born in Ft. Wayne.

Martha Jane Watters (A22264522) was the second child of Dallas O. (A2226452) and Mary Frances Watters. She was of the eighth generation and was born May 23, 1929, in Ft. Wayne. She married Max Hume, September 16, 1950, in Peru, Indiana. He was born December 31, 1927, in Ft. Wayne. There are no children. Martha Jane (A22264522) now lives with her parents and has resumed the name of Watters.

The last child of Dallas O. (A2226452) and Mary Frances Watters was Mona Lou Watters (A22264523) of the eighth generation. She was born January 8, 1933, and married Donald L. Mettert, September 19, 1953. He was born May 15, 1933, in Ft. Wayne. They have two children of the ninth generation. These are Ronda Dee Mettert (A222645231), born January 9, 1957, and Randall Dean Mettert (A222645232), born June 12, 1962.

Edith G. Watters (A2226453)

The third and last child of Viola Minerva Winger (A222645) and Henry E. Watters was Edith G. Watters (A2226453), who was born at Rockford, Ohio, November 24, 1908. She married Ralph J. Smith in Vincennes, Indiana, September 21, 1929. He was born in Kokomo, Indiana, June 3, 1902. They have two children of the eighth generation. The first was Jack Richard Smith (A22264531), born July 18, 1930, in Kokomo, Indiana. First he married Thelma Coy, October 25, 1954, in Kokomo and then Doris Louise Miller, March 24, 1960, in the same city. She was born March 24, 1930, in Kokomo. Jack Richard (A22264531) and Doris Smith have two children of the ninth generation. These are Jacqueline Reneé Smith (A222654311), born in Phoenix, Arizona, December 25, 1961, and Kimberly Kay Smith (A222645312), born August 7, 1963, in the same city.

The second child of Edith (A2226453) and Ralph Smith was Annetta Lee Smith (A22264532), born June 23, 1932, in Kokomo. First Annetta Lee (A22264532) married James Turner in 1951 and second John Paul Karabin, January 29, 1960. He was born October

Left to right: Jack Richard Smith (A22264531), his wife Doris Louis Miller Smith, Edith G. Watters Smith (A2226453) and her husband, Ralph J. Smith.

11, 1929, in Kokomo. Annetta Lee (A22264532) and James Turner have two children of the ninth generation. These are James L. (A222645321), born in Kokomo, June 11, 1951, and Teresa Elaine (A222645322), born July 14, 1953. After the marriage of Annetta Lee (A22264532) to John Paul Karabin, the two girls were adopted by him. Thereafter Annetta Lee (A22264532) and John Paul Karabin had a son of the ninth generation, namely Robert Paul Karabin (A222645323). He was born in Kokomo, December 10, 1963.

The Finale

The sixth and last child of Abraham (A22264) and Margaret Ellen Winger was Charles Otto Winger (A222646). He was born in Mercer County, Ohio, January 29, 1882. He died in Dayton, Ohio, March 28, 1948. He is buried in the Elerton Cemetery of that city. First he married Justina Brunswick in Celina, Ohio, with whom he had two daughters. After the death of Justina Brunswick in St. Marys, Ohio, in 1920, he married Edna Doss, April 13, 1926. She was born November 15, 1905, in Miamisburg, Ohio. The two children mentioned above were of the seventh generation. These were Lucille Winger (A2226461), born February 19, 1914, and Eileen Winger (A2226462), born May 23, 1916. Lucille Winger (A2226461) was reported to have married a man by the name of Ruggeman. Charles Otto Winger (A222646) was a barber by trade. He lost a leg due to an injury on a barber chair. This ultimately led to his death. He lived in Celina, Kokomo and Dayton during the course of his life.

Left to right: John Calvin Winger (A222644), Charles Otto Winger (A222646) and James Henry Winger (A222643).

This chapter, covering 95 descendants of Abraham Winger (A222-64), is unusual in that all of the descendants are in the maternal line. There is not a single male to survive with the name of Winger. Thus Abraham Winger (A22264), the great-great-grandson of Christian Wenger (A2), will have no progeny to carry on the name of Winger in his branch of the family. For the family tree of Abraham Winger (A22264), please see the following details of the family issue in the fifth generation.

Abraham Winger (A22264) Family Tree

1st Hans Wenger (b. About 1430) Blumenstein, Thun

2nd Burkhard Wenger (b. About 1450) Forst, Thun

3rd Peter Wenger (b. About 1470) Wattenwil, Seftigen

4th Peter Wenger (b. About 1490) Wattenwil, Seftigen

5th Rudolfus Wenger (b. About 1510) Wattenwil, Seftigen

6th Hans Wenger (b. About 1530) Wattenwil, Seftigen

7th Rudolfus Wenger (Ch. April 5, 1566) Wattenwil-Thurnen, Seftigen

8th Peter Wenger (Ch. Dec. 13, 1607) Wattenwil-Thurnen, Seftigen

9th Hans Wenger (Ch. May 30, 1633) Wattenwil-Thurnen, Seftigen

  A   Christian Wenger (A2) First Generation in America (1688-1749)

    B-1   Henry Wenger, Sr. (A22) Second Generation in America (1716-1802)

      C-1   Abraham Wenger (A222) Third Generation in America (1767-1845)

        D-1   Peter Henry Winger (A2226) Fourth Generation in America (1806-1889)

          E-1   Abraham Winger (A22264) Fifth Generation

            b. Oct. 17, 1838, d. May 8, 1910,

              bur. Swamp College

              m. Margaret Ellen Carlock, Sept. 3, 1860, Versailles, Ohio

                b. 1841, d. Jan. 11, 1901,

                bur. Swamp College

            F-1   Martha Ann Winger (A222641-6th)

                b. Aug. 17, 1861, Darke Co., d. After 1921, bur. Swamp College

                m. George Dittmore (1st) 1879

                  b. 1859, d. 1910

                m. Frank Kantner, Aug. 15, 1913

                m. John Bitner, June 13, 1921

              G-1   Hannah Ellen Dittmore (A2226411-7th)

                  b. Apr. 29, 1880, d. 1950, Dayton

                  m. George Hayes, Mar. 19, 1898

                  (No Issue)

G-2   Mary Emeline Dittmore (A2226412-7th)
      b. Apr. 2, 1882, d. Aug. 29, 1884

G-3   Eliza Jane Dittmore (A2226413-7th)
      b. Mar. 3, 1884, d. 1962
      m. Frank Tyndall, Aug. 18, 1901 (1st)
      m. Ed Markley, June 13, 1912

   H-1   Bernice Bertha Tyndall
        (A22264131-8th)

   H-2   Gladys Tyndall (A22264132-8th)

G-4   George Edward Dittmore (A2226414-7th)
      b. Mar. 6, 1886, d. Dec. 8, 1931
      m. Cora King, May 30, 1913 (1st)
      m. Esther Weaver, 1926 (2nd)

   H-1   Mary Dittmore (A22264141-8th)
        b. about 1926
        m. Paul Suchland

   H-2   Lucille Dittmore (A22264142-8th)
        b. about 1930

G-5   Bertha Elmira Dittmore (A2226415-7th)
      b. Aug. 1, 1888, d. May 1, 1955,
      in Ft. Wayne

G-6   Lottie May Dittmore (A2226416-7th)
      b. May 15, 1893
      m. Lee Todd, About 1911 (1st)
      m. Charles Keller (2nd)
      m. John Divato (3rd)

G-7   William Henry Dittmore (A2226417-7th)
      b. Sept. 10, 1890
      m. Estelle Linton, Aug. 1913
      m. Carrie Floy, Jan. 9, 1922

G-8   Sarah Jane Dittmore (A2226418-7th)
      b. Mar. 8, 1896, d. 1940
      m. William Scherer, Dec. 1913 (1st)
      m. Charles Schuman, 1919

   H-1   Agnes Scherer (A22264181-8th)
        m. Joseph Mosley

   H-2   Loretta Rosemary Scherer
        (A22264182-8th)
        m. John Knabenshue

G-9 John Calvin Dittmore (A2226419-7th)
     b. Oct. 15, 1898, d. Mar. 19, 1920,
     bur. Swamp College

G-10 Blanche Lucinda Dittmore
     (A2226410-7th)
     b. July 2, 1901
     m. Howard Stanley Passwater,
     Dec. 3, 1920, Ft. Wayne, Ind.

  H-1 Richard Passwater (A22264101-8th)
      b. Mar. 20, 1921
      m. Arlene Hilliard (1st)
      m. Helen Myers, Jan. 7, 1948 (2nd)

    I-1 Linda Passwater (A222641011-9th)
       m. John Myers

      J-1 Danny Myers (A2226410111-10th)
        b. Oct. 1967

    I-2 John Passwater (A222641012-9th)

  H-2 Juanita Eilen Passwater
      (A22264102-8th)
      b. Feb. 28, 1926
      m. Elmer Moening, 1946

    I-1 Lynn Moening (A222641021-9th)

    I-2 Michael Moening (A222641022-9th)
       b. 1952

  H-3 Howard Stanley Passwater II
      (A22264103-8th)
      b. Sept. 6, 1929
      m. Joan Stringer, 1950

    I-1 Howard Stanley Passwater III
       (A222641031-9th)
       b. 1954

    I-2 Russell Passwater (A222641032-9th)
       b. 1956

    I-3 Nancy Passwater (A222641033-9th)
       b. 1958

  H-4 John Sanford Passwater
      (A22264104-8th)
      b. Sept. 10, 1931
      m. Margy (Unknown)

    I-1 Michael Passwater (A222641041-9th)
       b. 1954

H-5 Kathlynn Passwater (A22264105-8th)
    b. Sept. 7, 1935
    m. Russell Oberley, 1953 (1st)
    m. Robert Heinold, 1962 (2nd)
  I-1 Valerie Lucinda Oberley
    (A222641051-9th)
    b. Dec. 27, 1953
  I-2 Jeffery Alan Oberley
    (A222641052-9th)
    b. Dec. 14, 1955
  I-3 Nikki Denise Oberley
    (A222641053-9th)
    b. 1958
  I-4 Rae Ann Heinold (A222641054-9th)
    b. 1963
H-6 Keith Edward Passwater
    (A22264106-8th)
    b. June 21, 1945
    m. Barbara Lengacher, June 28,
    1966, Ft. Wayne
  I-1 (One son) (A222641061-9th)
G-11 Myrtle Lula Dittmore (A222641A-7th)
    b. Aug. 6, 1905
    m. Harold Clinton Fisher,
    Sept. 15, 1924
  H-1 Virginia Fisher (A222641A1-8th)
    b. July 1926
  H-2 Phyllis Fisher (A222641A2-8th)
    b. Sept. 1929
F-2 Rachel Jane Winger (A222642-6th)
    b. June 23, 1866, Darke County
    d. Jan. 18, 1935, bur. Elm Grove
    Cemetery, St. Marys
    m. James Hager
      b. July 4, 1861
      d. Nov. 1, 1924, bur. Elm Grove
      Cemetery, St. Marys
  G-1 Charles Hager (A2226421-7th)
    b. Jan. 26, 1888, d. Feb. 24, 1925
  G-2 Cora Hager (A2226422-7th)
    b. Aug. 5, 1890, d. Oct. 18, 1967
    m. Henry Shelby

G-3 Emma Hager (A2226423-7th)
    b. Feb. 24, 1892

G-4 Forrest Hager (A2226424-7th)
    b. Aug. 8, 1896

F-3 James Henry Winger (A222643-6th)
    b. Aug. 18, 1867, Darke Co., d. 1930
    m. Mary Walker
    (No Issue)

F-4 John Calvin Winger (A222644-6th)
    b. June 23, 1871, Darke Co.
    d. Mar. 12, 1949, bur. Memorial Park,
    Kokomo, Ind.
    m. Emaline Hullinger
    (No Issue)

F-5 Viola Minerva Winger (A222645-6th)
    b. Dec. 29, 1877, Mercer Co.
    d. Jan. 14, 1928, bur. Crown Point
    Cemetery, Kokomo, Ind.
    m. Henry Eliza Watters, July 9, 1898,
    Celina, Ohio
    b. Sept. 19, 1868
    d. Dec. 9, 1934, bur. Crown Point
    Cemetery, Kokomo, Ind.

  G-1 Herman Clifford Watters
    (A2226451-7th)
    b. Feb. 7, 1902, Celina, Ohio
    d. Apr. 4, 1957, Ft. Wayne
    m. Agnes Bagley, Feb. 1, 1923,
    Kokomo, Ind.
    b. Oct. 8, 1905

    H-1 Helen Louise Watters
      (A22264511-8th)
      b. Feb. 23, 1924
      m. Donald Buchtel, 1940 (1st)
      m. George Johnstone, 1953 (2nd)

      I-1 Agnes Rosemary Buchtel
        (A222645111-9th)
        b. June 9, 1943
        m. James Stephens

J-1 Brenda Ann Stephens
       (A2226451111-10th)
       b. 1961
J-2 Barbara Ann Stephens
       (A2226451112-10th)
       b. 1963
H-2 Henry Eugene Watters
       (A22264512-8th)
       b. Aug. 8, 1925, Ft. Wayne
       m. Anna Laura Algaier, 1947
   I-1 Deborah Sue Watters
          (A222645121-By assignment)
   I-2 Kevin Eugene Watters
          (A222645122-By assignment)
H-3 Rex Francis Watters (A22264513-8th)
       b. July 20, 1927
       m. Patricia Barr, 1948
   I-1 Francis Watters (A222645131-9th)
          b. July 10, 1950
   I-2 Randy Guy Watters
          (A222645132-9th)
          b. Nov. 27, 1951
   I-3 Reneé Watters (A222645133-9th)
          b. Jan. 27, 1953
   I-4 Roseanne Watters (A222645134-9th)
          b. May 5, 1955
   I-5 Roxanne Watters (A222645135-9th)
          b. May 5, 1955
   I-6 Rickey Watters (A222645136-9th)
          b. Sept. 27, 1956
   I-7 Robin Watters (A222645137-9th)
          b. 1958
H-4 Paul Edward Watters (A22264514-8th)
       b. Jan. 18, 1929, Ft. Wayne
       m. Sondre L. Brown
   I-1 Beth Ann Watters (A222645141-9th)
          b. 1957
   I-2 Elizabeth Ann Watters
          (A222645142-9th)
          b. 1959

I-3 Stephen Watters (A222645143-9th)
b. 1960

H-5 Walter LeRoy Watters
(A22264515-8th)
b. Feb. 6, 1934, Ft. Wayne
m. Connie Syndram

I-1 Karen Sue Watters (A222645151-9th)
b. 1959

I-2 Judy Kay Watters (A222645152-9th)
b. 1964

I-3 Sarah Watters (A222645153-9th)
b. 1966

G-2 Dallas Oren Watters (A2226452-7th)
b. July 26, 1905, Mercer Co., Ohio
m. Mary Frances Merrell, Dec. 12, 1925
b. Dec. 28, 1906, Kokomo, Ind.

H-1 Shirley Ann Watters (A22264521-8th)
b. Dec. 23, 1927, Ft. Wayne
m. William Rhonemus, Apr. 3, 1948,
Ft. Wayne (1st)
m. Donald Parker, Mar. 1, 1952,
Ft. Wayne (2nd)
b. Dec. 6, 1927, Ft. Wayne

I-1 Sherry Lee Parker (A222645211-9th)
b. Feb. 2, 1949, Raleigh, N.C.

I-2 Gary Allen Parker (A222645212-9th)
b. Feb. 13, 1952, Ft. Wayne

I-3 Linda Kay Parker (A222645213-9th)
b. Oct. 29, 1953, Ft. Wayne

I-4 Michael Eugene Parker
(A222645214-9th)
b. Feb. 18, 1955, Ft. Wayne
d. Mar. 15, 1955, Ft. Wayne

I-5 David Wayne Parker
(A222645215-9th)
b. Feb. 5, 1956, Ft. Wayne

I-6 Janet Frances Parker
(A222645216-9th)
b. June 30, 1957, Ft. Wayne

I-7   Vickie Jane Parker
(A222645217-9th)
b. Nov. 27, 1960, Ft. Wayne

H-2   Martha Jane Watters (A22264522-8th)
b. May 23, 1929, Ft. Wayne
m. Max Hume, Sept. 16, 1950,
Peru, Ind.
b. Dec. 31, 1927, Ft. Wayne

H-3   Mona Lou Watters (A22264523-8th)
b. Jan. 8, 1933, Kokomo, Ind.
m. Donald L. Mettert, Sept. 19,
1953, Ft. Wayne
b. May 15, 1933, Ft. Wayne

I-1   Ronda Dee Mettert (A222645231-9th)
b. Jan. 9, 1957, Ft. Wayne

I-2   Randall Dean Mettert
(A222645232-9th)
b. June 12, 1962

G-3   Edith G. Watters (A2226453-7th)
b. Nov. 24, 1908, Rockford, Ohio
m. Ralph J. Smith, Sept. 21, 1929,
Vincennes, Ind.
b. June 3, 1902, Kokomo, Ind.

H-1   Jack Richard Smith (A22264531-8th)
b. July 18, 1930, Kokomo, Ind.
m. Thelma Coy, Oct. 25, 1954,
Kokomo, Ind.
m. Doris Louise Miller, Mar. 24,
1960, Kokomo, Ind.
b. Mar. 24, 1930, Kokomo, Ind.

I-1   Jacqueline Reneé Smith
(A222645311-9th)
b. Dec. 25, 1961, Phoenix, Ariz.

I-2   Kimberly Kay Smith
(A222645312-9th)
b. Aug. 7, 1963

H-2   Annetta Lee Smith (A22264532-8th)
b. June 23, 1932, Kokomo, Ind.
m. James Turner, 1951
m. John Paul Karabin, Jan. 20, 1960
b. Oct. 11, 1929, Kokomo

I-1 James L. Turner Karabin
        (A222645321-9th)
        b. June 11, 1951, Kokomo

I-2 Teresa Elaine Turner Karabin
        (A222645322-9th)
        b. July 14, 1953

I-3 Robert Paul Karabin
        (A222645323-9th)
        b. Dec. 10, 1963

F-6 Charles Otto Winger (A222646-6th)
        b. Jan. 29, 1882, Mercer County, Ohio
        d. Mar. 28, 1948, Dayton, O.,
           bur. Elerton Cem., Dayton, Ohio
        m. Justina Brunswick, Celina, Ohio
           d. 1920, St. Marys
        m. Edna Doss, Apr. 13, 1926
           b. Nov. 15, 1905, Miamisburg, Ohio

G-1 Lucille Winger (A2226461-7th)
        b. Feb. 19, 1914
        m. Ruggeman

G-2 Eileen Winger (A2226462-7th)
        b. May 23, 1916

CHAPTER ELEVEN

John Henry Winger
of Darke County, Ohio

JOHN HENRY WINGER (A22267) was born in Bath Township, Greene County, Ohio, February 27, 1844. He was brought by his parents to Darke County, Ohio, at the age of four years. He was raised a farmer and was exposed to a life of hard work. He became known as a thorough and systematic farmer. He acquired his father's farm and ultimately purchased adjacent land to bring the total to

John Henry Winger (A22267)

100 acres. He was described as being 5 feet, 7 inches tall, having light hair and complexion, and gray eyes.

During the Civil War he enlisted at Versailles, May 1, 1864, in Company E, 152nd Ohio Volunteer Infantry. Colonel David Putman was the commanding officer. This Company was employed on skirmish line in Virginia guarding wagon trains. They were in Hunter's raid down Shenandoah Valley and had charge of 214 wagons. They marched from Martinsburg to Lynchburg on the old Cumberland Pike. Its main engagement was over the Blue Ridge Mountains to White Sulphur Springs, then to Webster, Virginia, a march of 535 miles on foot. After six months, upon the expiration of his term of enlistment, John Winger (A22267) was honorably discharged at Camp Dennison, Ohio. While in the service he developed a disease of the eyes and was hospitalized at Cumberland, Maryland.

Civil War Experiences

The story is told that Company E came upon a beautiful southern mansion and fruit farm. The apple trees were in blossom. The Union Army Command ordered all the trees cut down. The regiment complied with the order. Afterwards, many of the soldiers went into the house and found the kitchen table covered with freshly baked pies. The troops devoured the pies. However, John arrived too late and so missed out. He was so hungry that he sat down and cried. This turned out to be his good fortune for the pies were poisoned, and many soldiers had long periods of illness, and some died.

John often repeated the story that on one occasion he entered a home and saw a watch and chain on a dressing table. He was about to expropriate it when a young girl came into the room crying, and said that her father had given her the watch and chain when she graduated from school, and she wanted to keep it. John put the chain around her neck and told her to keep it under her clothing because if somebody else saw it, they would take it.

Return Home

After his discharge September 2, 1864, John returned to his father's farm in Darke County. He was to remain there for 15 years. Prior to going into the Army, John was engaged to Nancy Jane Woods. In the meantime she fell in love with John's brother, Joseph (A22269), and married him. John (A22267) continued to live on his father's farm and ultimately met Rachel Ann Coble. John and Rachel Ann joined an excursion to Jackson, Michigan, where they were married October 10, 1881, by a justice of the peace. Rachel Ann Coble was born in Osborn, Ohio, May 4, 1847. Her father was Anthony Coble and her mother was Susanna Swallows Coble. John and Rachel Ann Winger had four children of the sixth generation. These were Charles E. Winger (A222671), born August 28, 1882, Susie Winger (A222672), born September 17, 1884, Alva John Winger (A222673), born January 27, 1886, and Maude Mae Winger (A222674), born April 6, 1889.

Life Story

In the records of the National Archives in Washington is a complete record of the pension application of John Winger (A22267). In one report Special Examiner H. T. Cathcart said, "Claimant has a good reputation for truthfulness and apparently is stout and hardy." Samuel McCartney said September 20, 1902, that "John Winger was a very religious and conscientious man." In 1914 John Winger (A22267) sent his mother's German Bible to the Bureau of Pensions as proof of certain vital statistics. Fred J. Braendale, translator, stated on May 8, 1914 as follows: "The New Testament, printed in Germantown in 1819, after the translation by Martin Luther, has 537 pages and is bound. It contains no entry of the soldier's birth." The Bureau returned this Bible to John Winger some time later and thereafter it fell into the hands of Charles Winger (A222671). Charles Winger presented this Bible to the writer about 1945. At that time he stated that as a child his grandmother, Anna Barr Winger, would read to him by the hour from this Bible.

About 1870 John Winger (A22267) went to Versailles to visit with William Brown about the possible purchase of a horse. Since he intended to go squirrel hunting later in the day, he took his gun with him. John was climbing a fence and accidentally fired the gun. The bullet pierced the palm of his right hand. William Brown described his hand as in awful condition.

John Winger used to love to go fishing in Harris Creek with his uncle, Joseph Keeler, whose wife was Anna Barr Winger's sister. The Keelers had moved from Greene County to Darke County at the same time the Wingers came. Both families lived near Harris Creek. John Winger used to like to reminisce about Preacher John Barr, who was Anna Barr Winger's brother. He had six boys who would go around the neighborhood visiting the needy, giving provisions and help.

Affluence and Friends

Through the years John Winger prospered as a farmer and at the same time developed affluence and friends. It is said that "he had a large rich farm and had several thousand dollars and bonds in the Osgood State Bank." The records indicate that Finley R. Reed on a nearby farm and John Winger "worked together chopping and making rails." Also, S. H. English said that he and John Winger had "worked together in the harvest fields and at threshing time."

Some of his close friends were David Fulkerth, Simon Swank, Dr. J. P. Gordon, Dr. E. A. Fuller, John Guckel, Philip Gardner, Henry Baker, Congressman Asa S. Bushnell, James H. Cooper, Cooper Ludlow, W. T. Fitzgerald, John C. Hoover, A. M. Pearson, Thomas Dustin, James W. Goodall, George Sweigert, Jacob Shappey, Robert McGinnes, J. W. Kechler, Charles Pearson and F. J. Alexander.

John Winger (A22267) was an honored member of the Grand Army Post and served as Vice Commander. For six years he served the office of road supervisor for Patterson Township, Darke County.

The writer remembers visiting, as a young boy, the John Winger (A22267) family. I well remember the family home on the edge of Osgood. The milk house with running cold water, and storage provisions for food were most intriguing. It seemed to be a happy family with close family relationships.

Family Pattern

John Henry Winger (A22267) was born in Bath Township, Greene County, Ohio, February 27, 1844, and died in Patterson Township, Darke County, March 4, 1931. His wife, Rachel Ann Coble Winger, was born May 4, 1847, and died in 1914. They are buried in the Mendenhall Cemetery near Yorkshire.

John H. Winger (A22267) and Rachel Ann Coble Winger's family in the sixth generation developed as follows: Charles Edwin Winger (A222671) was born in Osgood, August 28, 1882, and lived in the village of Brock, Ohio. He died November 12, 1964, in Greenville and is buried near the village of York in Mendenhall Cemetery

The John Henry Winger (A22267) home near Osgood. Left to right: Rachel Ann Coble Winger, John Henry Winger (A2226732), John Henry Winger (A22267), Maude Mae Winger (A222674), Charles E. Winger (A222671), Josephine B. Burns Winger and Alva John Winger (A222673).

next to his father, John Winger (A22267), and his mother. He never married but raised, along with his parents, the two children of Alva John Winger (A222673).

Winger-Hess-Detrick Families

Susie Ellen Winger (A222672) was born in Osgood, September 17, 1884, and died one month and five days later, October 22, 1884.

Alva John Winger (A222673) was born in Osgood, January 27, 1886, and died in Osgood of tuberculosis at the age of 28, March 12, 1914. He married Josephine B. Burns, January 8, 1910. She was born October 14, 1893.

Maude Mae Winger (A222674) was born in Osgood, April 6, 1889, and died at Coldwater, Ohio, January 19, 1964. She is buried in the Brock Cemetery. She married Jonas Alva Hess of Passburg, Ohio, at the Methodist Church in Greenville, December 24, 1913. He was born March 18, 1889, and died October 13, 1950, and is buried in the Brock Cemetery.

Alva John Winger (A222673) and Josephine Burns Winger had

two children of the seventh generation. The first was Odyne Beulah Winger (A2226731) who was born near Osgood, January 19, 1911. She married Floyd Robert Detrick in Winchester, Indiana, June 2, 1932. He was born November 5, 1910. They live at West Milton, Ohio. The second was John Henry Winger (A2226732) who was born near Osgood, August 5, 1913. He lives in Dayton, Ohio. He married Beatrice Folkerth in Richmond, Indiana, August 1, 1936.

Odyne Beulah Winger Detrick (A2226731) and her husband, Floyd Robert Detrick, had two children of the eighth generation. These are Myrna Mae Detrick (A22267311) and Stephen Douglas Detrick (A22267312).

Myrna Mae Detrick (A22267311) was born in West Milton, Ohio, July 30, 1936. She married Donald L. Roberts at the Center Friends Parsonage, June 19, 1954. He was born November 15, 1936. The Roberts had three children of the ninth generation. These are Randy Craig Roberts (A222673111) who was born in West Milton, November 14, 1954. Scott Jeff Roberts (A222673112) was born in West Milton, January 15, 1957. The third child, Robin Mathew Roberts (A222673113), was born in West Milton, December 23, 1966.

Stephen Douglas Detrick (A22267312) of the eighth generation was born in West Milton, October 16, 1940. He married Sherryl Hart at Laura, Ohio, November 25, 1961. She was born at Laura, May 19, 1942. They had three children of the ninth generation as follows: Ty Kerry Detrick (A222673121) who was born at West Milton, March 17, 1963; Ky Barry Detrick (A222673122) who was born at Troy, May 21, 1964, and Kelly D. Detrick (A222673123) who was born at Troy, September 7, 1968.

John Henry Winger (A2226732) Family

John Henry Winger (A2226732) and his wife, Beatrice Folkerth Winger, had four children of the eighth generation. These are Bruce A. Winger (A22267321), John R. Winger (A22267322), Gloria Ann Winger (A22267323) and Dawn R. Winger (A22267324). John H. Winger (A2226732) is a foreman at the Frigidaire plant in Dayton.

Bruce A. Winger (A22267321) was born April 17, 1937, in Dayton, Ohio. He married Evelyn Biller, April 30, 1961, in Dayton. Evelyn Biller Winger was born May 20, 1940, in Harrisonburg, Virginia. They have two children of the ninth generation. These are

Susan Lynette Winger (A222673211), born November 7, 1961, and Douglass Scott Winger (A222673212), born January 7, 1964. Both were born near Laura, Ohio. Bruce A. Winger (A22267321) is a group leader at Globe Industries in Dayton.

John R. Winger (A22267322), who now lives near Greenville, Ohio, was born May 31, 1940, in Dayton, Ohio. He married Shirley Squires, July 31, 1960, in Dayton. Shirley Winger was born June 4, 1941, in Dayton. They have four children of the ninth generation. These are Doreen Kay Winger (A222673221), born September 7, 1961; John Raymond Winger (A222673222), born July 22, 1965; Mark Kenneth Winger (A222673223), born September 29, 1967, and Kathleen Lynn Winger (A222673224), born November 26, 1968. John R. Winger (A22267322) is a sheet metal worker.

Gloria Ann Winger (A22267323) was born May 28, 1943, in Dayton. She married David P. Martin, January 25, 1964, in Dayton. David Martin was born in Dayton, August 15, 1938. He is a dealer in Pepperidge Farm Products. They have no children.

Dawn Rae Winger (A22267324) was born June 8, 1947, in Dayton and married Wayne Clinton Smith, August 25, 1968, in Dayton. He was born July 15, 1947, in Darke County, Ohio, and is a school teacher in Monroe, Indiana. They are without issue.

Maude Mae Winger Hess (A222674) and Jonas Alva Hess of the sixth generation had two children. These are Gerald A. Hess (A222-6741) and Alice Irene Hess (A2226742) of the seventh generation.

Gerald A. Hess Family

Gerald A. Hess (A2226741) of the seventh generation was born November 1, 1915, in Darke County, Ohio. He married Elizabeth Ann Steinke, November 23, 1938, at the Guadaloupe Catholic Church, Mercer County, by the Reverend Charles Heaber C.P.P.S. Gerald A. Hess (A2226741) joined the Catholic Church, March 24, 1956, at the Holy Family Church, Frenchtown, Darke County, Ohio. Elizabeth Ann Steinke, wife of Gerald (A2226741), was born July 11, 1919, in Darke County to William H. Steinke and Rosa E. (Rutschilling) Steinke.

The Hesses had four children of the eighth generation. Gary Allen Hess (A22267411) was born at the Gibbons Hospital, Celina, Ohio, October 10, 1939. His attending physician was Dr. B. J.

Sawyer. Michael John Hess (A22267412) was born January 15, 1944, at the Wayne Hospital, Greenville, Ohio. His attending physician was Dr. Guthermuth. Nicholas Bryan Hess (A22267413) was born July 27, 1947, at Brock, Ohio, in Darke County. His attending

Back row (standing): Rachel Ann Coble (wife of John H. Winger, A22267), Charles E. Winger (A222671), Helen Brown, Odyne Beulah Winger Detrick (A2226731), Josephine B. Burns Winger (wife of Alva John Winger, (A222673), Myrtle Gardner and Maude Mae Winger Hess (A222674).

Center row (sitting): John Henry Winger (A22267), Jane Hess (mother of Jonas Hess), Jonas Hess (husband of Maude Mae Winger, A222-674).

Bottom row (sitting): John H. Winger (A2226732), Alice Irene Hess (A2226742) and Gerald A. Hess (A2226741).

physician was Dr. John S. Meyers. Lisa Rose Hess (A22267414) was born March 3, 1960, at Our Lady of Mercy Hospital, Coldwater, Ohio. The attending physician was Dr. D. J. Schweiterman.

Michael John Hess (A22267412) married Linda Adelle Holtman May 24, 1969, at the Immaculate Conception Catholic Church, Celina, Ohio. She was born April 2, 1948, the daughter of Jerome and Mildred (Dorsten) Holtman. Nicholas Bryan Hess (A22267413) married Janice Mary Droesch, April 23, 1969, at the St. Henry's Catholic Church, St. Henry, Mercer County, Ohio.

Alice Hess McKee Family

Alice Irene Hess (A2226742) of the seventh generation was born February 23, 1920, near North Star, Ohio. She graduated from Miami University of Ohio and is now a school teacher at Ansonia, Ohio. She married Jay C. McKee, June 21, 1941, at North Star, Ohio. He was born April 5, 1920, in Greenville, Ohio. He served in World War II in the 37th Division of Ohio. He was killed in an automobile accident May 13, 1952, and is buried in Ft. Jefferson ,Ohio.

Alice Hess (A2226742) and J. C. McKee had two children (identical twins) of the eighth generation. Sharon K. McKee (A22267421) was born October 31, 1942, in Greenville, Ohio. Sharon (A22267421) is a graduate of the Springfield School of Nursing, Springfield, Ohio. She is a registered nurse and served at the Wayne Hospital, Greenville, Ohio, for six years. She now is a private nurse. She married Michael Wright, March 1, 1964, at the United Church of Christ at North Star, Ohio. He was born July 13, 1942, in Dayton, Ohio.

Karen J. McKee (A22267422) was born October 31, 1942, in Greenville, Ohio. She is a graduate of the University of Miami of Ohio. She married Douglas A. Shellhaas at the United Church of Christ at North Star, December 25, 1953. He was born January 6, 1942, in Greenville, Ohio.

Karen J. McKee (A22267422) and Douglas Shellhaas have one son of the ninth generation. He is David Douglas Shellhaas (A222-674221), born November 21, 1965, in Greenville, Ohio.

See the John P. Henry Winger Family Tree which follows.

John Henry Winger (A22267) Family Tree

1st Hans Wenger (b. About 1430) Blumenstein, Thun
2nd Burkhard Wenger (b. About 1450) Forst, Thun
3rd Peter Wenger (b. About 1470) Wattenwil, Seftigen
4th Peter Wenger (b. About 1490) Wattenwil, Seftigen
5th Rudolfus Wenger (b. About 1510) Wattenwil, Seftigen
6th Hans Wenger (b. About 1530) Wattenwil, Seftigen
7th Rudolfus Wenger (Ch. April 5, 1566) Wattenwil-Thurnen, Seftigen
8th Peter Wenger (Ch. Dec. 13, 1607) Wattenwil-Thurnen, Seftigen

9th Hans Wenger (Ch. May 30, 1633) Wattenwil-Thurnen, Seftigen

A   Christian Wenger (A2) First Generation in America (1688-1749)

B-1   Henry Wenger, Sr. (A22) Second Generation in America (1716-1802)

C-1   Abraham Wenger (A222) Third Generation in America (1767-1845)

D-1   Peter Henry Wenger (A2226) Fourth Generation in America (1806-1889)

E-1   John Henry Winger (A22267) Fifth Generation
b. Feb. 27, 1844, Greene County, Ohio
d. Mar. 4, 1931, Darke County, Ohio
m. Rachel Ann Coble, Oct. 10, 1881
b. May 4, 1847, d. 1914
Both buried Mendenhall Cemetery

F-1   Charles Edwin Winger (A222671-6th)
b. Aug. 28, 1882, Osgood, Ohio
d. Nov. 12, 1964,
bur. Mendenhall Cemetery
(No Issue)

F-2   Susie Ellen Winger (A222672-6th)
b. Sept. 17, 1884, Osgood, Ohio
d. Oct. 22, 1884,
bur. Mendenhall Cemetery

F-3   Alva John Winger (A222673-6th)
b. Jan. 27, 1886, Osgood, Ohio
d. Mar. 12, 1914, Osgood, Ohio
bur. Mendenhall Cemetery
m. Josephine Burns, Jan. 8, 1910
b. Oct. 14, 1893

G-1   Odyne Beulah Winger (A2226731-7th)
b. Jan. 19, 1911, living
m. Floyd Robert Detrick June 2, 1932
b. Nov. 5, 1910

H-1   Myrna Mae Detrick (A22267311-8th)
b. July 30, 1936, living
m. Donald L. Roberts
June 19, 1954
b. Nov. 15, 1936

I-1   Randy Craig Roberts
(A222673111-9th)
b. Nov. 14, 1954

I-2   Scott Jeff Roberts (A222673112-9th)
b. Jan. 15, 1957

I-3   Robin Mathew Roberts
(A222673113-9th)
b. Dec. 23, 1966

H-2   Stephen Douglas Detrick
(A22267312-8th)
b. Oct. 16, 1940
m. Sherryl Hart Nov. 25, 1961
b. May 19, 1942

I-1   Ty Kerry Detrick (A222673121-9th)
b. Mar. 17, 1963
d. Mar. 17, 1963

I-2   Ky Barry Detrick (A222673122-9th)
b. May 21, 1964

I-3   Kelly D. Detrick (A222673123-9th)
b. Sept. 7, 1968

G-2   John Henry Winger (A2226732-7th)
b. Aug. 5, 1913
m. Beatrice M. Folkerth Aug. 1, 1936,
Richmond
b. Sept. 19, 1913

H-1   Bruce A. Winger (A22267321-8th)
b. Apr. 17, 1937
m. Evelyn Biller Apr. 30, 1961,
Dayton
b. May 20, 1940

I-1   Susan Lynette Winger
(A222673211-9th)
b. Nov. 7, 1961, Laura, Ohio

I-2   Douglass Scott Winger
(A222673212-9th)
b. Jan. 7, 1964, Laura, Ohio

H-2   John R. Winger (A22267322-8th)
b. May 31, 1940, Dayton, Ohio
m. Shirley Squires
July 31, 1960, Dayton
b. June 4, 1941, Dayton

I-1 Doreen Kay Winger
(A222673221-9th)
b. Sept. 7, 1961, near Dayton

I-2 John Raymond Winger
(A222673222-9th)
b. July 22, 1965, near Dayton

I-3 Mark Kenneth Winger
(A222673223-9th)
b. Sept. 29, 1967, near Greenville

I-4 Kathleen Lynn Winger
(A222673224-9th)
b. Nov. 26, 1968

H-3 Gloria Ann Winger (A22267323-8th)
b. May 28, 1943, Dayton, O.
m. David P. Martin,
Jan. 25, 1964, Dayton
b. Aug. 15, 1938, Dayton

H-4 Dawn Rae Winger (A22267324-8th)
b. June 8, 1947, Dayton, O.
m. Wayne Clinton Smith,
Aug. 25, 1968, Dayton
b. July 15, 1947, Darke Co.

F-4 Maude Mae Winger (A222674-6th)
b. Apr. 6, 1889, Osgood, Ohio
d. Jan. 19, 1964, Coldwater, Ohio
m. Jonas Alva Hess, Dec. 24, 1913,
Greenville
b. Mar. 18, 1889, Passburg, O.
d. Oct. 13, 1950, North Star

G-1 Gerald A. Hess (A2226741-7th)
b. Nov. 1, 1915, Darke County
m. Elizabeth Ann Steinke, Nov. 23,
1938, Mercer County
b. July 11, 1919, Darke County

H-1 Gary Allen Hess (A22267411-8th)
b. Oct. 10, 1939, Celina, Ohio

H-2 Michael John Hess (A22267412-8th)
b. Jan. 15, 1944, Greenville, Ohio
m. Linda Adelle Holtman, May 24,
1969, Mercer County
b. Apr. 2, 1948, Mercer County

H-3   Nicholas Bryan Hess (A22267413-8th)
      b. July 27, 1947, Brock, Darke Co.
      m. Janice Mary Droesch,
        Apr. 23, 1969
      b. Jan. 6, 1949, Mercer County
H-4   Lisa Rose Hess (A22267414-8th)
      b. Mar. 3, 1960, Coldwater, Ohio
G-2   Alice Irene Hess (A2226742-7th)
      b. Feb. 23, 1920, near North Star
      m. Jay C. McKee, June 21, 1941,
      North Star
      b. Apr. 5, 1920, d. May 13, 1952
      bur. Ft. Jefferson, Ohio
H-1   Sharon K. McKee (A22267421-8th)
      b. Oct. 31, 1942, Greenville, Ohio
      m. Michael Wright, Mar. 1, 1964,
      North Star
      b. July 13, 1942, Dayton, Ohio
H-2   Karen J. McKee (A22267422-8th)
      b. Oct. 31, 1942, Greenville, Ohio
      m. Douglas A. Shellhaas,
        Dec. 25, 1963, North Star
      b. Jan. 6, 1942, Greenville, Ohio
  I-1   David Douglas Shellhaas
      (A222674221-9th)
      b. Nov. 21, 1965, Greenville, Ohio

CHAPTER TWELVE

Joseph Levi Winger
of Darke County, Ohio

JOSEPH LEVI ROBINSON WINGER (A22269), a son of Peter Henry Winger (A2226), a grandson of Abraham Wenger (A222), a great-grandson of Henry Wenger, Sr. (A22), and a great-great-grandson of Christian Wenger (A2), was born in Richland Township, Darke County, Ohio, July 17, 1848. The names of Joseph and Levi were commonly used in the Winger family. The name of Robinson was chosen from an uncle by the name of Robinson Keeler. Joseph Winger's (A22269) older sister, Susan Ann Winger (A22262), had married Joseph Keeler. Joseph's father, Peter Henry Winger (A2226), and Anna Barr Winger, his mother, had purchased 66 acres on March 17, 1848, a farm site near Bradford. The Keeler family had also moved from Greene County, Ohio, to the same neighborhood in Darke County. It was on this land that his father, Peter (A2226), built a crude cabin to house a large family. Moreover, from March to June was little enough time not only to build a roof to cover the family, but to prepare for the arrival of the ninth child, who was to be Joseph (A22269). The first three children of Peter (A2226) had been born in Lancaster County, Pennsylvania, and the next five were born in Bath Township, Greene County, Ohio. So Joseph (A22269), the ninth child, was the only member of the family to be born in Darke County.

On the Move

Just as most Wingers in this branch kept on the move, Joseph (A22269) was no exception. In 1851, when Joseph (A22269) was three years old, his father moved to Wayne Township in Darke

County. In 1855 they moved again. This time to Versailles when Joseph (A22269) was eight years of age.

In 1860, when Joseph (A22269) was 12 years old, the entire family moved to Marshall County, Iowa. After two years they returned to Patterson Township in Darke County as Joseph reached the age of 14. The father, Peter Henry Winger (A2226), had purchased 20 acres and was to settle there for eight years.

The Civil War and Courtship

During this time Joseph learned to farm under the tutelage of his father. In 1865, when Joseph (A22269) was 17, his two older brothers, Abraham (A22264) and John (A22267), who were 27 and 21 years of age, respectively, joined the Army. This left Joseph (A22269) alone to help his father with the farming. Since his father was 60 years of age at the time, Joseph (A22269) had to do most of the heavy work himself.

In the meantime, Joseph (A22269) had met Nancy Jane Woods, the daughter of Henry Josephus Woods, who was also serving in the Civil War. John Winger (A22267) had been courting Nancy Jane Woods, but before the courtship had bloomed into marriage (they were engaged) John (A22267) had to leave for the Army. While John was in the war, Joseph (A22269) joined the winter sleigh bell brigade and started to take Nancy Jane to church. She was of the Dunkard faith, but they attended the New Light (Christian) Church whose minister was the Reverend Peck. They fell in love and soon sleigh bells turned into wedding bells.

Joseph Winger (A22269) Marries

Joseph Winger (A22269) and Nancy Jane Woods were united in marriage at Versailles, April 5, 1868. Joseph and Nancy Jane had their first-born child, John William Winger (A222691), September 1, 1869. At that time it is thought they were living in the village of Gettysberg in Van Buren Township in Darke County. We know they were living there in 1870. The fact that members of the Keeler family, relatives of Anna Barr Winger, also lived in this neighborhood probably was an attraction. Joseph (A22269) in the Census of 1870 was listed as a woodchopper. This Census also indicated a monetary value on his land. Therefore, it is surmised that he was clearing a small acreage where he would fell the trees and cord the wood for the city market. He certainly needed to secure funds.

Since this Census was taken August 10, 1870, he must have sold out immediately following, because by December 21, 1870, he was living in Patterson Township of Darke County. He probably was

Joseph Levi Winger (A22269) and his bride, Nancy Jane Woods Winger.

attracted to this locality because his parents, on May 28, 1870, had purchased 80 acres in this township. Then, too, Phillip Geaubaux, father of August Geaubaux, a brother-in-law of Joseph's (A22269), had a log cabin in a wooded section immediately west of the village of Osgood. He offered the cabin to the young couple for their use. This log house was on the south side of State Road 705 in the center of an 80-acre farm now owned by Herbert and Marie Liening.

Cabin in the Woods

It was in this log cabin that a start was made to establish their own home. During the day Joseph (A22269) spent his time cutting trees and hauling logs. This left Nancy Jane alone with her second-born child, Della Frances (A222692). Sadness had entered their new home because John William (A222691) had contracted pneumonia and died January 7, 1871. This death had occurred less than one month after Della Frances (A222692) was born December 21, 1870. Franklin Josephus (A222693) was born April 20, 1872.

There were still Indian raids from time to time. As a result, Nancy Jane was deathly afraid during the day, since her husband Joseph

(A22269) was in the woods at work. She apparently was afraid of every sound. At times she would put the clock in the feather bed (a gift from the parents) and cover it up to silence the ticking, so that she could hear sounds outside the house.

Della Frances Winger (A222692) was the mother of the writer. He well recalls a visit in 1910 to Osgood when a child. The log house in which she was born was still standing in the center of a corn field. It was dilapidated, almost ready to fall down. It was over 40 years old at that time. The cabin was located on the south side of Ohio State Route 705, west of Mendenhall Road, on the west side of the village of Osgood.

Della Frances Winger (A222692) remembered her grandparents very well. In fact, most of the family data and stories contained herein were related by her to the writer. She recalled that the Peter Winger (A2226) farm of 80 acres was located immediately north of her home on Ohio State Route 705 and was bordered on the east by Mendenhall Road. This is on the west side of the village of Osgood. It is now owned by the Bohman family. The Winger-Magato Creek, which was dammed up for the winter baptism of Peter Winger (A2226), runs across the northeast corner of the old Winger farm.

The source of the Winger-Magato Creek is near the Conover Road on a farm now owned by Verena Grillot. This is just south of Route 705. From there the creek runs north through the Bohman land and back southeast through the Peter Winger farm, where it crosses Mendenhall Road and runs south through the western edge of Osgood. The Winger-Magato Creek was named after the families of Peter Winger (A2226) and Joseph Magato who were neighborhood landowners. In fact the original maps called it the Winger-Magato Creek. The Magato farm was located across Mendenhall Road, northeast of the Winger farm.

Joseph (A22269) Acquires a Farm

By 1874 Peter Winger (A2226) had sold his 80-acre farm to his son John (A22267) and he in turn sold 20 acres off the north end to Joseph (A22269). Another hewed log house was built on this land by Joseph (A22269) which the family lived in until the clearing of most of the woods was completed. After that he built his first frame and plank house, facing Mendenhall Road. Since the Joseph Winger (A22269) farm was adjacent to the Peter Henry Winger (A2226) farm, there was constant visiting back and forth. Peter Henry Winger (A2226) loved to talk to the family and occasionally related stories about Lancaster County, Pennsylvania.

Della Frances Winger (A222692) stated that all the children had to work on the farm, and hard work it was. She said when she was six years old she worked in the fields. She would trail along after the plow. If young corn stalks were plowed up she would put each stalk back in the ground and pack the dirt around it. On one occasion her nose started to bleed because of the dust. The bleeding was so severe that she bent over to keep the blood from her clothes. Just at that time, her Aunt Liz (Eliza) Winger Barnhart (A22268), who lived on a nearby farm, came along, saw the situation and had a straight talk with her brother Joseph (A22269). Mother stated that her father was so sorry that she was never again required to work in the field.

In those days when the rains were about to come at harvest time, the women went to the fields and helped put up hay and stack the wheat and oats in shocks.

The story of another accident was related by Della (A222692). When she was five years of age, she was in the barnyard when her father was bringing in the horses from the field. Della (A222692) thought she could help and started to open the barn doors. Her father called to her to get back to the house before she got hurt. Mother Della (A222692) started for the house, but in doing so she went behind Old Nance, her father's favorite horse. As quick as a flash, the horse kicked the child, the hoof catching just below the left eye. Her face was cut open and the nose was broken. When she regained consciousness after the doctor had sewed up the cut, she found two sticks up her nose to hold it in place. As usual the whole family participated in first aid and care for her. She carried the half-moon scar on her face the rest of her life.

School Days

Mother Della (A222692) remembered her school days in Darke County very well, in spite of the fact that she attended school there only two winters before leaving the county. The school was about three-quarters of a mile from her home. Of the brothers and sisters, only Frank (A222693) was old enough to attend school with her. In discussing her school, she related the following:

> Yes, I remember about my first days of school and my teachers. I remember my first teacher's name was John Schilling. The last teacher I had was Henry Burns. I had summer school teachers. The only one I remember was Theodore Snyder. I had two, one of them taught for a while and something went wrong and he went away and didn't ever come back. His replacement went to sleep one day and someone suggested that we take a walk, so we all did. I don't know how many there were but I suppose there were a dozen children. There was a little creek up the road and a bridge across it. So we all went up there, got on the bridge and were walking over the bannisters and here we saw the teacher coming down with a big stick. We all assembled in a hurry. He threatened to use the stick, but didn't. We were all nearly frightened to death!

Family Item

Another story she loved to tell was that, while the family lived in Darke County, there was a neighbor by the name of Nan Clegg. She was a prophet of doom and was always saying that the world would soon come to an end. She said that when the fatal day arrived, Gabriel would come on a white horse, blowing his horn. One day Grandpa Winger (A22269) and Grandma had gone to town. Frank (A222693) and Della (A222692), who at that time were about six and eight years old, were left alone. They saw a man drive into the farmyard on a white horse and they were frightened. He blew a cowhorn several times to announce his presence. By this time the children came out of hiding from an upstairs room and asked the man from the window if he was Gabriel and whether or not the world was coming to an end. The man replied laughingly, "No, the world is not coming to an end, although I am the tax collector."

One final item on life in Darke County is the fact that Mother often stated that when she was a child the winters were so severe in Darke County that she and other members of the family would ride a bobsled all the way to Versailles, going as the crow flies. The snow was so deep and encrusted by ice that they would ride over the roads, ditches and fences without detouring.

Final Days in Darke County

Of the eight Joseph Winger (A22269) children, six were born in Darke County. Della Frances (A222692) and Franklin Josephus (A222693) were previously recorded. Ida Mae (A222694) was born

December 21, 1873, and died July 25, 1875. She is buried in Tea Cup Cemetery near Osgood and Yorkshire. Charles Elwood Winger (A222695) was born July 4, 1875. Amanda Ellen (A222696) was born August 9, 1878. Henrietta Hannah (Attie) Winger (A222697) was born May 20, 1880. Two more were to come, but they are a part of the Mercer County, Ohio, story which follows.

In the fall of 1880 the whole Joseph Winger family moved to Mercer County. Joseph's older brother Abraham (A22264) had settled on a farm in Mercer County and that led to the quest of Joseph (A22269) for a large farm to support a large family. An assist from Abraham (A22264) helped Joseph (A22269) to find an ideal farm which was acquired the fall of 1880.

Peter (A2226) and Anna Winger, having now reached an advanced age, were to remain in Darke County. Their son John (A22267) and daughter Eliza (A22268) remained close by.

Thus we come to an end of the Joseph Winger (A22269) Darke County story.

CHAPTER THIRTEEN

Joseph Levi Winger
of Mercer County, Ohio

IN OCTOBER 1880, Joseph (A22269) and Nancy Jane Woods Winger, his wife, together with five children moved from Patterson Township, Darke County, to an 80-acre farm in Hopewell Township, Mercer County, on Frahm Road about three miles northwest of Celina, Ohio. At that time Della Frances (A222692) was ten years old. Franklin Josephus Winger (A222693) was eight years of age. Charles Elwood Winger (A222695) was five years of age. Amanda Ellen Winger (A222696) was two years old and Henrietta (Attie) Winger (A222697) was only five months old. For the most part, these children in chronological order were known as Della (Dellie), Frank, Charlie (Bud), Amanda (Mandy) and Attie. Two more children were born in Mercer County; Luallen (Allen) Winger (A222-698) was born January 1, 1882, and Carey Edmond (Ed) Winger (A222699) was born September 19, 1884.

Joseph Winger (A22269), prior to his departure from Darke County, had sold his 20-acre farm to his brother, John Winger (A222-67). This gave him sufficient funds to move the family and make a substantial payment toward the purchase of a new 80-acre farm. This farm was all green woods and in the initial stages four acres of ground were cleared. Here a log house was built. This house was made from mortised logs and rough planks of timber and had three rooms downstairs and one large room upstairs. Even though substantial progress was made, Joseph (A22269) needed working capital. In 1881 he sold ten acres of his farm which today is owned by Walter H. Shively, Route 3, Box 130, Celina. This left 70 acres to be developed. The latter acreage is owned today by Mood T. Fetters, Route 3, Box 130, Celina.

Clearing the Land

Joseph Winger (A22269) almost singlehandedly cleared four acres of ground and built the log cabin. As time went on, he built another smaller cabin, on Frahm Road, across from the original house. He hired a single man to live in this cabin and made an arrangement for him to help with the clearing. With his help ten acres of land were cleared the first winter. In 1881 Joseph (A22269) built another log house up Frahm Road which bisected the farm. This house was about a quarter of a mile from the main house. After securing a family to live there, he made an arrangement with them to clear ten acres at a time. They were permitted to use the timber for

Left to right: Henrietta (Attie) Winger (A222697), Della Frances Winger (A222692), Joseph Levi Winger (A22269), Harriett Cecelia Evans (A2226921), Nancy Jane Woods Winger, Luallen (Allen) Winger (A222698), Carey Edmond Winger (A222699), Charlie (Bud) Winger (A222695), Franklin Joseph Winger (A222693) and Amanda Ellen Winger (A222696).

personal use or to sell it. By using this method to clear the land, eventually the entire 70 acres was cleared and ultimately turned into one of the finest farms in Mercer County. In fact, they did such a good job clearing the land that years later they had to plant shade trees around the house. As time went on, Joseph (A22269), with an assist by the neighbors, built a seven-room house with rough plank siding. In the early days the neighbors helped each other with the bigger back-breaking jobs. Ultimately, a fine barn and cribs and other out buildings necessary to house farm implements were built.

They had a boarded-up windmill, which pumped water through a trough in the milk house to keep the milk and butter cold. The residue ran out through a trough into a big tank where the horses and cattle came to drink. Another trough ran to the big barn where a supplementary tank was used for other animals. Joseph (A22269) also piped water to the roadside so that anyone with horses could stop there for a free drink. Installing this tank near the roadside prevented other farmers from coming into his farmyard with their horses or diseased animals. He wanted to protect his own.

The Earlier Years

In the earlier years, along with clearing the land, Joseph (A22269) planted a fine orchard. As the land was cleared, the logs were split and made into rail fences around the fields, including the perimeter of the farm. In those days much of the timber was burned in order to dispose of it. You could go in any direction in the country and see gangs of men at work burning down trees. Timber was considered an awful nuisance. It was so thick that cattle and hogs would get lost for days at a time. However, even in those days there was minority opposition to the destruction of so much good timber. In retrospect, it seems that more should have listened to Russell's song, "Woodman, spare that tree."

This section of Ohio had great flocks of wild turkeys, wild geese and ducks. Herds of deer and fox were much in evidence. As a result, there was always plenty of meat available for the family. After the farm was in full production, a granary was always full, the smokehouses were full of all kinds of meat and a big cellar was full of apples, potatoes and a variety of other fruits and vegetables. Social security was the smokehouse and the milk house, together with all of the other foods in storage. The Huggins huckster wagon would stop to trade coffee, tea, sugar, thread, pepper, salt, calico, etc., for eggs, tallow, beeswax, calamus root, coon skins, deer hides and sassafras bark.

The settlers had what they called butchering rings. The men did all the hard work and the wives did the cooking. They also had cornhusking bees. When it came time to make apple butter, around October 15, the neighbors had what they called an apple pealing. Even the young folks participated and usually the event lasted well into the night. They used large copper kettles that hung on strong poles over the fire. Under them the settlers had mounted big iron kettles that were used to enhance the production.

Hard work was the order of the day. This was particularly true at planting time. All of the youngsters participated. Amanda (A222-696) used to tell of the time when they were planting beans. The youngsters got so tired of planting row after row that they decided to end it by digging a hole and dumping in all the remaining beans. The hole was neatly covered and apparently Grandfather Winger (A22269) was none the wiser. However, the next spring there was the largest concentration of bean stalks around that hole that one could imagine. It did not take Grandfather long to diagnose the problem. The truth came out and, of course, appropriate disciplinary action followed.

The Peter Henry Winger (A2226) Visits

Della F. Winger (A222692), granddaughter of Peter Henry Winger (A2226), recounts the visits of Peter (A2226) to her father's farm. As a child, she remembers that at least once every summer, Peter Winger (A2226) would drive his horse and buggy into the barnyard after a long trip from Patterson Township in Darke County. All the Winger children would see Grandfather coming and would rush to meet him, the carriage and his faithful horse Lucy. She said that Grandfather Peter Winger (A2226) would say, "Now that I have seen you all from the buggy, I guess I'll turn right around and go home," whereupon the children would push and beg him to stay. Of course, in the end, he would always reluctantly agree. He greatly enjoyed the children pleading him to stay.

On one such visit, he brought a tomcat which had been left behind in Darke County when Joseph Winger (A22269), Peter's (A2226) son, moved to Mercer County. The children went into ecstasy to see their playful kitty Tom. The report indicates the cat was equally happy.

Peter (A2226) loved the children and would spend hours with them before starting the long trek back to Darke County. The children described him as a man about five feet, eight or nine inches tall, a little on the heavy side, with gray-green eyes and a white flowing beard.

The School

A one-room schoolhouse was located about a mile and a half northwest of the Winger farm. Today it is a private home and is located on the southeast corner of the junction of Hellworth and Morrow Roads. Della (A222692) and all of the other Winger children attended this school. Her daughter, Harriett (A2226921), was to attend this same school years later. It was known as School No. 3 and continued in use until 1920. Mother Della (A222692) said that she remembered all her teachers in that school. She remembered

The one-room School No. 3 still stands as a private home. Two generations of Wingers attended this school.

Daniel Klinger the best. Others were Messrs. Morrow, Wilson, Beehammer and Kimball. She also remembered Blanche Andrew. She went on to say that she got all of the country education available. She studied geography, history, grammar and arithmetic. She had exhausted the entire curriculum by the time she was 16 years old. Considering the trials and tribulations of early education, she said that when she finished she was considered pretty well educated.

She went on to say that she could have passed the examination for a teacher's certificate; however, a turn of events prevented her from doing so.

The 1886 Cyclone

Mother Della (A222692) described the great cyclone:

It was one mile wide and 30 miles long. It came at 9 at night. Father Joseph (A22269) was building a new barn and there were seven carpenters there. I was 16 years old at this time. The carpenters had gone to bed upstairs; the family was downstairs. First it rained and stormed. The cyclone followed. All of the family's clothes were upstairs. The wind blew the roof off. Everything on the second floor went. The carpenters all got out alive but no one knows how. All the windows flew out. Father tried to open the doors and couldn't. The last thing I remembered was going through a window with Ed under one arm and Allen under the other. Ed was two and Allen was four. I lost them but found out later that my father had them. What was left of the house was lifted up and moved off the foundation and before it landed the floor fell out. All our household goods, bedding, clothes, everything was gone.

We had a big hewn-log barn. That is the logs were made square. All the horses were in the barn. The logs had fallen all around them. The barn was full of hay and a lot of farm implements. Lightning struck what was left standing. Father went in the barn and got the halters, as each horse was in a stall and had to be tied. Usually a horse becomes panicky in a fire and will not try to get out, but these horses jumped over the logs and every one was saved. Father didn't lose any stock, not even chickens. However, the feathers were blown off most of them. The barn they were building went with the wind.

When I came to my senses, all I had on was my nightgown and I was lying in a ditch, holding on to a currant bush. On the other side was one of the carpenters holding on to the same bush. All he had on was his shirt. I never saw him again. It was raining hard and still blowing. The farm was a mass of debris everywhere. Everything was gone but the log house on the other end of the farm. The only thing saved was a big hogshead barrel of hams and someone had stolen that.

At the break of day Grandpa and Grandma Woods (the parents of Nancy Jane Woods Winger) came driving in. They had a wagon loaded with feather beds, pillows, bed clothes of all kinds and wearing apparel. They brought groceries and Grandma Woods had boiled beef in big kettles and made soup. We were never so glad to see anyone in our lives as we were when we saw Grandpa and Grandma Woods drive in. The soup was still warm. They brought beds, tables, chairs and stoves. I don't know what we would have done without them.

My brothers and sisters, Frank, Charley, Amanda and Attie, looked the farm over for new shingles. The carpenters had taken the bundles of shingles up on the top of the barn to begin the roof the next morning.

They found only a few of them with the help of neighbors who had escaped the storm and had come in to help clear the farm. In the years following the storm, the family prospered immensely. A nice new home was built. I heard father say, if a calamity befell you, through no fault of your own, the Lord would bless you.

As a sequel to the storm, the State of Ohio set aside a large sum of money for the storm victims. Joseph Winger (A22269) never made application for help. He always said that "the honorable thing to do is to work for what you get, and not ever be a charge on society."

After the storm of 1886, Joseph Winger (A22269) and his sons rebuilt their home. This is how it looks today.

Spelling Bees

The schoolhouse was considered a social center in those days. There were spelling bees all year around which created excitement in the nearby farming communities. In the winter people would come for miles in bobsleds and sleighs to attend these functions. Della (A222692) described these bobsled transports as pretty large affairs filled with straw. The boys and girls would climb into the piles of straw underneath buffalo robes and horse blankets. In fact, they used any kind of a blanket to keep warm. They also brought along heated soapstones, bricks and irons or hot water bottles to help keep their feet farm. The participants were instructed to bring *McGuffey Readers, Webster's Elementary Speller* and *Payson Copy Book*. In the summer, girls were expected to wear sunbonnets, gingham aprons, short dresses (ladies of course) and pantalettes with ruffles at the bottom. Those that had coppertoe shoes were asked to wear them. Mohair garters were in style, so those who did not have coppertoe shoes were told to wear garters with rubber stretchers on each side. The boys were told to come barefooted, if possible, but in any case, if they should have bunions, they should wear red top boots!

There were so many good spellers in those days that the spelling bees would last for several hours. Mother Della (A222692) described how the spelling bees were conducted. She said the boys and girls would stand up around the four sides of the room while the audience occupied the desks in the center. She said at that time she was a pretty good speller. She recalled that she had spelled the school down on many occasions.

Other Social Activities

The social functions in the schoolhouse were not confined to spelling bees. There were also what were called singing schools. The singing teachers would bring everybody who were not only taught to sing in the schools but had experience in singing in the church choirs. Whole families would gather and sing all evening long to their hearts' desire. During intermission there would be plenty of apples and popcorn balls to go around. At home on the farm every winter night either Attie (A222697) or Amanda (A222696) would play the organ and the family would sing hymns. Joseph Winger's (A22269) favorite hymns in those days were "There is a Fountain Filled with Blood" and "At the Cross."

Albright Church

The Albright Lutheran Church was located about one and one-half miles from the Winger homestead on Hellworth Road, about one-half mile south of Frahm Road. Its congregation was a mixture of a wide variety of protestant religions. As this is written in 1969, the church is known as the Hope Evangelical United Brethren Church. In earlier days, it was the habit of people in the neighborhood to attend whatever church was available. Joseph Winger (A22-

269) was raised a Mennonite but he attended the Albright Lutheran Church. There were no Mennonite churches in that vicinity. Nancy Jane Woods Winger, his wife, was a Dunkard but, because there were no churches of that denomination near by, she too attended the Albright Lutheran Church.

Mother Della (A222692) remembered some of her girl friends in the social activities surrounding the Albright Church. She remembered Ida Miller, Marian Carrie, Callie Crouch and even some of her first boy friends. She and her sisters, Mandy and Attie, did all of their courting during that period. She said that she could remember the sleighs coming with bells ringing, driven by the boys who came to pick up the girls and take them to church. In those days, there was hardly any other place to go. She related a story about a boy in the neighborhood by the name of Walley Landon who was a sewing machine agent. He had a spring wagon to take his sewing machines to potential customers. One day he came to the Winger farm while Della was entertaining a group of girls from her Sunday school class. The group had just finished dinner when this charming young man came. He offered to take the girls for a ride, so they put a number of chairs in the spring wagon and the girls sat down. They left for church, but the horses bolted and ran off. The chairs tipped over backwards and the girls fell out. Luckily none was hurt, though they did acquire a number of well-assorted bruises.

Courting Days

Mother Della (A222692) said her first beau was a boy named George Stevenson who lived on the next farm. Another beau was John Hameline who had come to that vicinity from Kalamazoo, Michigan. She said that he was probably a relative of one of their neighbors by the name of Johnson. Mother said that after her first date with him, she developed a wholesome dislike for his singing a song about Kalamazoo. She said she always remembered one phrase of the song which ended "old pipe in Kalamazoo, Michigan." She said, "I can just hear him yet." She said that every time they would go to church he would sing that song all the way. Like big sisters, Della (A222692) would take her younger sister, Mandy (A222696), to stand between her and this aggressive young man.

The three Winger girls, Della (A222692), Amanda (A222696) and Attie (A222697), were courted by neighborhood boys during this period. Grandfather Joseph Winger (A22269) was very strict with the girls and would always set a time when the girls were to return home. In order to enforce his curfew, he would sleep on the floor next to the front door so that the girls would awaken him upon their return. However, he was such a sound sleeper that more often than not the girls would quietly open the door and step over him so deftly that he would not awaken. Come morning, Grandfather (A22269) could not understand how the girls got to their bedrooms without his knowing. No amount of explanation ever succeeded in straightening out the dilemma.

The neighborhood families, such as the Pierstorffs, Hoenies, Fetters, Morrows, Fasts and Stevensons, had many eligible boys. The girls were not at a loss for companionship.

Amanda (A222696) was the first of the Winger girls to marry. She married Frank J. Pierstorff, the son of a prosperous neighborhood farmer. They were married in Celina, September 6, 1894. The first few years of their married life were spent in the log house on the Joseph Winger (A22269) place. It was here that their first-born son, Rolland (A2226961), arrived.

We now turn to the story of Della Frances Winger (A222692) who was to start life in the state of Indiana.

CHAPTER FOURTEEN

Joseph Levi Winger and the Middle Years

DELLA FRANCES (A222692) at the age of 18 moved to Decatur, Indiana, at the invitation of neighbors near the Celina farm who had moved there previously. She referred to these neighbors as Uncle Ben Graham and Aunt Hulda Grant. They asked Mother Della (A222692) to come to Decatur and live with them in their home. This she did. It was here that she met David E. Evans and married him June 27, 1889. Della Winger (A222692) and David Edward Evans had two children of the fifth generation. Harriett Cecelia Evans (A2226921) was born September 2, 1890, and Joseph Lawrence Evans (A2226922) was born February 15, 1892.

The Evans Family

David Edward Evans, born May 6, 1870, near Monmouth, Indiana, was the great-grandson of Robert and Elizabeth Evans. The original ancestor of this line of Evans was of Scotch-Irish descent. Robert Evans of the first known generation was born in Massachusetts in 1768. He and his wife, Elizabeth, went briefly to New Hampshire and then to New York State. They first lived in St. Lawrence County, later moving to Montgomery County.

It was here that their son, John K. Evans, of the second generation was born on November 16, 1795. He received a fine education, having graduated from law school in that state in 1816 at the young age of 21. That same year he came west, settling in Columbus, Ohio, seeking to practice law. He soon left Columbus for Dayton since he had a good prospect there. The prospect turned out to be a Margaret Wise with whom he fell in love. She was the daughter of John and Sarah (Sowders) Wise, a prosperous German family.

They were married in 1817 in Wapakoneta, Ohio. In 1822 they moved from Dayton to near Rockford, Ohio (then Shane's Crossing), Mercer County, where he acquired 80 acres of land. After a few years as a farmer and country lawyer, it was decided, in 1832, that the vicinity of Decatur, Indiana, had better prospects.

John K. Evans left the family in Mercer County while he went to the vicinity of Monmouth in Root Township, Adams County, Indiana. With hired help, he cut away and cleared nine acres of land. He then returned to Mercer County for his family. They made a comfortable place for camping while their cabin was being built. The cabin was made of round logs, scotched down on the outside. A bed quilt was used to cover the entrance because there was no door. There was no floor, just the bare ground. John K. Evans then hired Ebenezer Goddard from Ohio to build a two-story hewed-log house. The family then moved into it and the first house was converted to a stable.

John K. Evans as a farmer ultimately acquired 225 acres of fine farm land and at the same time became an outstanding member of the bar in Decatur. He was considered to have amassed quite a fortune for that day. He became Associate Judge where he presided for 12 years, the only judge to preside in that post. John K. and Margaret Wise Evans had four children of the third generation. These were Harriett, Elizabeth, John K. and Robert.

In the meantime, the parents of John K. Evans, Robert and Elizabeth Evans of the first generation, moved from New York State to live with John K. and his wife, Margaret. Robert Evans died in 1845 at the age of 77. He and his wife are buried in the Evans Cemetery on the family farm in Root Township of Adams County.

To Fort Wayne

In 1850 Judge John K. and Margaret Evans left their farm with their sons, Robert and John K. Evans, and moved to Ft. Wayne where he was to practice law. Shortly thereafter Margaret Wise Evans passed away. In due course Judge Evans remarried and had a long and distinguished career. He died February 22, 1874. He and his wife, Barbara, are buried in the Beery Cemetery in Ft. Wayne.

Concerning the third generation children of Judge John K. Evans and his wife, Margaret Wise Evans, of prime interest is Harriett, who married David Studebaker of the famous automobile family in South Bend, Indiana. Harriett Evans Thomas (A2226921), the daughter of David Edward Evans, was named after Harriett, the wife of David Studebaker. Also of interest is their son, John K. Evans, who married Barbara Cecelia Iyanson. She was the daughter of Joseph Iyanson, a manufacturer of tile and brick. He built many buildings in Decatur. The Judge's son, Robert, married Elizabeth Sparks, a daughter of a Methodist minister. He inherited large acreage from his father.

John K. Evans, the brother, also inherited a large farm from his parents. He and his wife, Barbara Cecelia Iyanson Evans, successfully ran the farm and developed a family of four of the fourth generation. Harriett Evans married David Rice; John K. and Samuel Evans never married. David Edward Evans married Della Frances Winger (A222692).

In summary, Harriett (A2226921) and Joseph Evans (A2226922) are descendants in the fifth generation of the Evans family as follows: Robert Evans (1st), John K. Evans (2nd), John K. Evans (3rd), David Edward Evans (4th) and Harriett (A2226921) and Joseph Evans (A2226922) (5th).

The Mystery of David Edward Evans

David Edward Evans, soon after Joseph Lawrence Evans (A2226922) was born, went to the western part of the United States on a business venture and mysteriously disappeared. A maze of conflicting reports followed. At one time, he was reported killed in an accident with a runaway horse. Other reports from western states were in direct conflict. The name of Evans was sufficiently common to complicate identification. In due course, the court declared him legally dead. Della Frances Evans (A222692), after the loss of her husband, sent little Joe (A2226922) to live with her parents, Joseph (A22269) and Nancy Jane Winger. Joseph (A2226922) was named after his Grandfather Joseph Winger (A22269). He arrived at the Winger homestead in 1892. They had him for almost five years. They loved him as a child of their own. Harriett (A2226921) remained with her mother in Decatur, Indiana.

It was during this period that Grandfather Winger (A22269) gave Della (A222692) a dapple gray horse. Della (A222692) named her Floria. It was a beautiful young mare, just nicely broken in. Della

(A222692) would put a blanket on Floria and take Harriett (A222-6921), who was four years old at the time, for long rides over the countryside. When Floria was put to pasture, she would come up the lane and snicker several times a day. Floria wanted affection, so Della (A222692) would go out and pet her on each of these summons. Della (A222692) talked about Floria the rest of her life.

Harriett's Visits to the Winger Farm

Mother Della (A222692) traveled between her parents' farm and Decatur as the opportunity afforded. Harriett (A2226921) visited the farm and stayed for extended periods. Through her, much of the remaining history of the Winger family has been brought to light. She made the comment:

> I think a lot about things that happened back then. You know they were always a close family. I went there when I was four years old, and Joe (A2226922) was already there. My, they just loved us to death! I don't have one unpleasant thought about the time that I was there. To look back on it, it was the most pleasant time of my life.
>
> On one of my visits, I caught the whooping cough from my Great-grandmother Woods. I then gave it to Grandpa Winger (A22269). Grandpa promptly announced that all other members of the family were quarantined upstairs while he and Harriett (Hattie-A2226921) stayed downstairs. The program worked. None of the rest of the family got it.
>
> I always spent every summer with Grandpa (A22269) and Grandma Winger whom I loved with all my heart. When I was a child, I would go down the lane to the woods, roam through the woods, go down to the log house, first over the fence. At the edge of one corner of the woods was about one-half an acre that had been cleared. It was sandy loam. That may be why the woods was left standing. The rest of the farm was rich black loam like prairie loam. Anyway, it was the melon patch — cantaloupe, big ones, and they were good.
>
> One day Grandpa said, "There is a little girl visiting my melon patch." Someone said, "How do you know it is a little girl." Grandpa (A22269) said, "I see her footprints." Ed (A222699) and Allen (A222698) taught me how to detect a ripe melon. I would get two of them, that was all I could carry, and Ed (A222699) and Allen (A222698) would help me over the fence. I would go down the edge of the woods. They would be working in the fields and, since they knew where I was, they would leave the field, cut the melons and, of course, we would eat them on the spot.

You see, to begin with, we were eating the first melons, the family wasn't getting any. I never confessed my crime. It would implicate others.

Ed (A222699) was 12, Allen (A222698) was 14, and I was six. I was always devoted to Allen (A222698). When he grew older, he was probably the most loved of the younger boys. He was the peacemaker in

Harriett Evans (A2226921) and Rolland Pierstorff (A2226961), a pair of cousins that enlivened the Winger homestead.

the family. There never was any hard feelings created between him and the other six children. If a problem did develop, he would always step in to iron it out between the brothers and sisters. Allen (A222698) was devoted to his nephew, Rolland Pierstorff (A2226961). When Rolland (A2226961) was at home, he and Allen (A222698) were always together.

Rolland (A2226961) related later that when he lived on the Winger farm as a child, he fell off a load of wheat. He landed on his head. Allen (A222698) thought Rolland (A2226961) was seriously injured or killed. He carried Rolland (A2226961) to the house in tears, only to find that it was just a bump on the head. Thereafter, Rolland (A2226961) and Allen (A222698) were closer than ever.

An Eye Witness Account

My sister Harriett C. Thomas (A2226921) tells the following as an eye witness account:

On Saturday the girls baked all day. You see, there was a big family. As you went up the stairs into a room (the stairway just divided that room), Grandma used one side of the room for cooling purposes and as the pies were baked she would take them up there and let them cool. There was one window there and beside that window was an apple tree. I went up there just in time to see Uncle Charlie (A222695) take the screen out; he had climbed up the apple tree, took out the window screen and he took one pie and handed it out the window, then another one and another one — three pies — one for Uncle Ed (A222699), one for Uncle Allen (A222698), and one for himself. I said, "Oh, Grandma, come here," and she came just in time to see Uncle Charlie's (A222695) foot go out the window. She held her hand on my mouth and took me on downstairs. "Now," she said, "I don't want you to say one word about this, not one word; if you do, the girls will stop baking." She said, "Those boys, if they want a pie, that's all right, it's coming to them," so I didn't dare to tell it.

Nance, 28-Year-Old Horse

Harriett (A2226921) continued:

I must tell you about Nance, their 28-year-old horse. Grandpa Winger (A22269) kept her because she had such nice colts. Nance was a pacer and could she cause damage! When Mother Della (A222692) was 15 years old, a cousin was coming to visit. Grandpa (A22269) hitched Old Nance to a brand-new buggy and Mother (A222692) drove into town to meet the cousin. She arrived on the train. Driving home, Nance ran away, threw Mother (A222692) and the cousin on a pile of fence rails, skinned them all up, and broke the new buggy to pieces. I would have thought Grandpa (A22269) would have known better.

Old Nance wasn't through yet. When I was a child, Mother (A222692) went home to show me to the folks. Grandpa (A22269) sent Uncle Charley (A222695) in a buggy with Old Nance to town to meet Mother (A222692) and me. Fortunately, they had had a heavy snow the middle of October. Old Nance ran away and I was thrown in a snow bank.

Grandma Winger was so indignant. She told Grandpa (A22269) he could never hitch Old Nance to another rig. He never did. She was older than Mother (A222692). They had to work her alone in the field. She would kick and bite the other horses. She was an ornery critter!

Calvin Geaubaux (A222661)

Calvin Geaubaux (A222661), son of Catherine Winger Geaubaux (A22266) and nephew of Joseph Winger (A22269), was raised as a son by Joseph (A22269) and Nancy Jane Winger. He became a Dunkard minister, probably because his foster mother, Nancy Jane, whom he loved, was a Dunkard. It was he and his wife, Mary Shipman Geaubaux, that attended Anna Barr Winger, his grandmother, through her terminal illness.

Calvin Geaubaux (A222661) has been described as an eloquent speaker and a great influence for good. Harriett Thomas (A2226921) states that he was over six feet tall and had a large flowing red beard. He lived at a spot called Five Points, a junction of Frahm, Miller and Hoenie Roads, which was about midway between Celina and the Winger place. Near his home he installed a sorghum

Calvin Geaubaux (A222661) and his wife, Mary Shipman Geaubaux.

mill and a Dunkard church. (Both have long since disappeared.) Through the week he worked in the mill and on Sunday he preached in his church. Occasionally, he would go to Lima to preach to the inmates in the state prison. He believed in baptism by immersion and regularly used the reservoir (now Grand Lake) in Celina for this purpose.

The sorghum mill had big tanks of sorghum which were brought to boiling. When the syrup was properly attended, residue would drain off into smaller tanks. Allen (A222698), Edward (A222699) and Harriett (A2226921) would drive to the mill with horse and buggy to "lick the skimmins," a phrase coined by the boys. The youngsters had paddles to scoop up the "skimmins." Cal Geaubaux (A222661) would solemnly point a finger at Harriett (Hattie) (A2226921) and say, "That will make you sick." Sometimes a little discipline was required to terminate the "lickin' the skimmins."

Calvin (A222661) had a sister, Josephine (A222662), who lived with an aunt. (Both children had become orphans at a young age.)

Josephine (A222662) became a Catholic Sister. Calvin (A222661) and Mary Shipman Geaubaux had two children, a daughter, Daisy (A2226611), and a son, Jessie (A2226612).

Threshing Stories

The story is told that during threshing season, Calvin (A222661) came to Grandpa Winger's (A22269) and wanted Mother Della (A222692) and her two sisters, Amanda (A222695) and Attie (A222-697), to come to his house and get the threshers' dinner and supper. This, they did. His living room was quite large and there were chairs right up against each other all around the room. In the evening, after they got through threshing, the men cleaned up and came in the living room, and sat down to hold a religious service. Calvin (A222661) would preach. They were all Dunkard men, so when they got ready to leave, the first one nearest the door went around to his right and kissed each man on the cheek, a custom of Dunkards when they departed. They called it a holy kiss. So the first one started around and when he got next to Mother Della (A222692), who was sitting on the last chair next to the kitchen door, Harriett (A2226921) thought that he was going to kiss her mother. She was about six years old and she screamed, "Don't you kiss my mother." Cal (A222661) came in a hurry and explained, "No Hattie, they are not going to kiss your mother." Hattie (A2226921) was still a little unconvinced and retorted, "Well, he'd better not."

Rolland Pierstorff (A222691) tells another story of threshing:

This was a great and wonderful event. All of the crew stayed and ate with the family. They were joined by the neighbors. Sometimes the neighbors would stay all night or, if they lived close by, they would come in for the day. In any event, they were always there at meal time. How they did eat! Mother Winger and the girls worked like trojans to feed the hungry workers.

I was born in the log house on Grandpa Joseph Winger's (A22269) place and, as a young boy, I would look forward to the arrival of the threshing crew. They would come in with a steam engine pulling a separator and a water tank behind it. They had an engineer, an oiler and fireman to operate the front end. When they needed water, they would hitch horses to the wagon tank and go to the nearest stream. The tank man would use a special hand pump to pull the water to the tank. Since I was permitted to accompany the water man, he always was my hero among all the crewmen.

On one occasion I followed the threshing crew (they were not Dunkards) to another nearby farm. After a hard day's work, the home farmer rewarded the men by passing a jug of whiskey around the standing circle of crewmen. I managed to get into the circle and took my manly turn at the jug. When Grandfather Winger (A22269) learned of my misdemeanor, he let me know in no uncertain terms that he took a dim view of such liberties. Needless to say, there were new ground rules applied at once.

A Visit to Aunt Eliza (A22268)

On one occasion Henrietta (Attie) Winger (A222697) made the long trip to Darke County to visit members of the Winger family. She stopped to see her Aunt Eliza Winger Barnhart (A22268) who was still living on the farm north of Osgood. Eliza (A22268) persuaded Attie (A222697) to stay all night. She slept in the large feather bed with her aunt. Attie (A222697) saw that Aunt Eliza's (A22268) pillow seemed to be unusually high and that her aunt seemed to have some difficulty adjusting it. Curiosity got the best of Attie (A222697) and finally she asked her aunt what was the problem with the pillow. Aunt Eliza (A22268) lifted up the pillow, and there was a 25-pound sugar sack filled with money. Attie (A222-697) asked how much money was there and Aunt Eliza (A22268) promptly said $800. Aunt Eliza (A22268) explained that this was her "chicken and egg money" from selling them on the market. She went on to explain, "This is only the middle of the summer, by fall I will have $1,600 and then I will go to the bank." She believed in going to the bank only once a year!

Back to John Henry Wenger, Sr. (A22)

Grandfather Joseph Winger (A22269) on occasion would call one of the younger children "you little Hessian" when they would do something of which he did not approve. Joseph Winger (A22269) said the expression was handed down from father to son in his branch of the Winger family dating back to the time of the American Revolution. He said the family tradition indicated that during the course of the Revolutionary War the English hired thousands of German soldiers who were called Hessians. The Hessians, of course, fought with the English in the American Revolution against Henry Wenger, Sr. (A22), who was "the ancestor way back who fought in the Revolutionary War." He said that back in Pennsylvania the Wenger families were afraid that Hessian soldiers would molest them. After the war was over, the grownups referred to the Hessians as very terrible soldiers. It probably was Joseph Winger's (A22269) great-grandfather, Henry Wenger, Sr. (A22), who was in much of the fighting, that promulgated the phrase "a little Hessian" to the succeeding Winger generations.

Pranks of Little Joe

Grandma Woods Winger used to bake bread. She would put her covered bread to rise on the floor behind the heating stove. Always one loaf would be mashed down and always at the same place. She could not understand why. One day Grandpa Winger (A22269) caught Joe (A2226922), who was a little boy, putting his foot in it, so he called Grandma and he said, "Now, you spank him." Grandma said, "Joe, you spank him," so neither one of them spanked him. Neither one of them had the heart.

Of course, in those days country people went to all the funerals. There had been a revival meeting and Joe (A2226922) had learned all the songs. One song started, *Tis Low, Tis Low* and Joe (A222-6922) would sing, *Tid Low, Tid Low.* Grandma was missing some chickens. They caught Joe (A2226922); he had wrung the necks of the chickens and he had a funeral every day. He would bury the chickens and then he sang his song to them.

One day Joe (A2226922) came in the house crying as hard as he could. Grandpa said, "What in the world is wrong with you?" Joe (A2226922) said, "Grandma spanked me." Grandpa said, "What did you do?" He knew that Joe must have done something terrible. Joe (A2226922) said, "All I did was throw the old cat in the lye." Grandma was getting ready to make soap when little Joe (A2226922) had thrown the cat in the lye. The boys had to kill the cat to end its misery. That was all he had done and he was heartbroken because he got a spanking.

Harriett Thomas (A2226921) tells the following story:

One time when I was out there, one of the boys did some misdemeanor and then he said that I did it, so Grandma penned me up in the corncrib. I thought I'll get out of here when Grandpa (A22269) comes. Grandpa (A22269) had gone to town and I knew that when he went to town, upon his return he always put the horse up, then he would come to the corncrib and get a measure of corn for the horse. Grandpa (A222-69) opened the door and saw me standing there. He said, "What are you doing here?" I said, "Well, Grandma put me here." He didn't ask why or anything; he got his corn, shut the corncrib and locked it. So the boys, Ed (A222699), Allen (A222698) and Charlie (A222695), came in from the field, they came to the corncrib to get corn and, oh, were they mad that I was locked in. I got sympathy from some quarter — from the boys (my uncles).

The family was growing up.

Back row: Attie Winger Hoenie (A222697), Della Frances Winger Evans (A222692), Charles (Bud) Winger (A222695) and Amanda Winger Pierstorff (A222696).

Middle row: Joseph Levi Winger (A22269) with Harriett Evans (A22-26921), Nancy Jane Woods Winger with Joseph Evans (A2226922) and Edmond Winger (A222699).

Sitting on floor, center: Allen Winger (A222698).

Chapter Fifteen

Joseph Levi Wenger of Celina, Ohio

JOSEPH (A22269) and Nancy Jane Winger had crowded a lot of history into a limited lifetime. They decided, after the death of little Joe Evans (A2226922) on September 15, 1897, that they would quit the farm. Little Joe (A2226922), at the age of five, had been returned to his Mother Della (A222692) in Decatur. He contracted diphtheria which caused his death. Both Grandfather Joseph (A222-69) and Grandmother Nancy Jane took his death very hard. They had accumulated sufficient means to live life with less hard labor and more leisure time. They had raised a large family and each was now either on his own or ready for marriage. They knew that the farm would be a drab place after all the children were gone. Also Joseph (A22269) wanted to join his cronies in the afternoon games of checkers that were an Ohio pastime. With the proposed sale of the farm in 1898, they were to become town dwellers.

Move to Celina

Joseph (A22269) and Nancy Jane Winger decided they would retire from farm life at a comparatively young age. Just before the turn of the century, Joseph (A22269), at the age of 50, and Nancy Jane, who was 49 years of age, decided to move to Celina. Their first home was on Wayne Street in a fairly large house. For a time their sons, Charles (A222695), Allen (A222698) and Ed (A222-699), as well as their daughter, Attie (A222697), continued to live with their parents as town dwellers.

Joseph (A22269) had sold his farm for enough to let him invest in town property (and other farm property, too) and to provide for both him and his family in retirement. After a few years, Joseph (A22269) and Nancy Jane moved to a moderately large white house located on the northwest corner of the junction of Brandon and

Joseph Levi Robinson Winger (A22269)

Lisle Streets, within two blocks of the Wayne Street house. In the meantime, the family was shocked and saddened by the death of Allen (A222698), who died of typhoid fever November 5, 1900. He was buried in the Winger lot in Swamp College Cemetery. Franklin Joseph (A222693) had moved to Decatur, Indiana (his sister Della was there), where he married Alice Belle Baxter, October 27, 1898.

The farm Joseph (A22269) and Nancy Winger left at the turn of the century; today a modern farm owned by Mood T. Fetters.

Amanda Ellen (A222696) had married Frank J. Pierstorff, September 6, 1894, and continued to live for a time in the log house on her parents' farm. Charles Elwood (A222695) married Emma Richeson in November 1902, and resided first in Celina and then in Dayton, Ohio. Henrietta (A222697), sometimes Hannah but always known as Attie, had been courting a fine neighbor boy from the Hoenie family. She married G. Nelson Hoenie, September 5, 1900. The latter established a home on Wayne Street near the original Winger homestead. Carey Edmond (A222699) married Anna Reigelsperger, November 5, 1919, and resided in Dayton.

Joseph Winger (A22269) Letter

The following letter addressed to his daughter, Della Frances (A222692), and his son, Franklin Joseph (A222693), in Decatur gives insight to the life of that day:

Celina, Ohio
September 21, 1902

Dear Children:

I take the pleasure of writing you a few lines to let you know how we are getting along. We are all up and around at present but Ma (Nancy Jane) is just getting around after a spell of erysipelas and rheumatism. She has not been able to do her housework for two weeks, although she struggles to do the little things. Ed (Carey Edmond A222699) has also been sick, so I have been doing the work of all three of us the best I can. You can't get a girl to do household work here, but I manage the best I can.

Don't look for us to pay you a visit just now as Ma isn't able to travel, but if everything goes alright maybe we can come over this fall. I would like to come as I am getting homesick to see you all.

Bud (Charles Elwood A222695) and his intended wife (Emma Richeson) have gone to Lima today to see the folks over there (The Pierstorffs). After that they may come to see you in Decatur. I can't say. I think they will get tied up by all counts before very long and I will be happy for them. Ed (A222699) will be the only one left and of course with all of you married, Mom can breathe easier. I want her to be able to take things easy the rest of her life. That is why I left the farm.

Hattie (Harriett A2226921), you don't need to look for Uncle Ed (A222-699) to come over. He isn't well enough to come and he is not up to writing either. I am sorry to say, since he is the last of the boys, we have spoiled him. He acts like a baby doing things contrary to our advice. I will close by saying goodbye to you all and hope you have a good time at the Fair. Please answer this letter from your father.

Joseph Winger

Nancy Jane Woods Winger Dies

Nancy Jane Winger, born June 29, 1849, was a deeply religious woman. During her years in Celina, she and Joseph (A22269) attended the Church of God. In those days, Nancy Jane, who liked everybody, was known far and wide for her warm heart and willingness to give a helping hand when other families were in need. She was always on hand in periods of sickness, whether it was an ordinary cold or a baby about to be born.

She always kept her family problems to herself. It did not make any difference how many troubles arose, she believed that discussion never contributed much to the solution of her problems. She would talk to the children personally about their problems and always told them that religious beliefs and prayers to the Divine Creator would ultimately bring solutions.

Rolland Pierstorff (A2226961), in expressing his deep regard and love for his Grandmother Nancy Jane Winger, said, "I well remember her holding me in her lap and rocking me to sleep. She would then put me in the large feather bed with warm bricks wrapped in wool. These would keep me warm the whole night through."

The writer, as a young boy, visited Grandpa (A22269) and Grandma Winger where he had opportunity to sleep on that large feather bed. It was a memorable experience. When Grandmother Winger was undergoing her terminal illness, he stood at the bedside. She had a broken arm and hip as a result of a fall from a chair and, of course, she was in great pain. Her arm was in a cast. In spite of that, she, with extreme difficulty, extended the arm to him in love and encircled him with the other arm. That was the last time he saw her before she died. At the time of her death, scores of neighbors attended her funeral, lamenting their loss of a loved and dear friend.

Grandpa Joseph Winger (A22269) took the death of his wife, Nancy Jane, very hard and the rest of his life expressed sorrow that he might not always have treated her as well as he should have. Undoubtedly, this was a reaction to his extreme sorrow at having lost the dear companion of a lifetime and the mother of his large Winger family. You will recall that in his letter to his children, dated September 21, 1902, Joseph (A22269) said his reason for leaving the farm was to relieve Nancy Jane of the hard work, and that he wanted her to have an easier life. She died March 16, 1911, and was buried in Swamp College Cemetery.

The Woods Family

Nancy Woods Winger was the great-granddaughter of Robert Woods of Scotch-Irish extraction. The Woods family came to Pennsylvania early in the 18th Century. It is believed three families of this pre-revolution era, all from North Ireland, found their way to Cumberland County where they were to live a half century. The

McGrews, the Brandons and the Woods families were to find an association that was to last for another hundred years.

Just as the Woods family, who were originally French Huguenots, migrated to England, Scotland, Ireland and then to America, so the Robert Woods family came from their home near the Blarney Stone in Ireland to Cumberland County, Pennsylvania, to Virginia, to Ohio, Indiana and across the nation. Wherever the Woods were found, there you would find the McGrews and Brandons. The families intermarried and produced farmers, clergymen, educators, businessmen, engineers, scientists, lawyers and legislators.

In Pennsylvania the Woods and Brandons were members of the Big Springs Presbyterian Church. The McGrews were Quakers. Robert Woods was a member of Captain John Carothers' Company, sixth class of the Pennsylvania Militia, September 20, 1780, and Patrick McGrew was a member August 1, 1780. Richard Woods, the brother of Robert Woods, was a member of the same company with Robert, September 11, 1781.

The Onward Move

In 1786 the McGrews and Brandons followed by the Woods moved to Monongalia County, Virginia, in what is now Preston County, West Virginia. They established farms in Grant District about four miles south of the Pennsylvania line. The village of Brandonville was established and named after Alexander and Jonathan Brandon. That same year the first Quaker meeting house in the area was established by Patrick McGrew.

Patrick McGrew, whose wife was Martha Welsh, had a family of nine. His oldest son, named James after Patrick's father, was a colonel of the 104th Regiment of the Virginia Militia. He married Isabella Clark, a native of Ireland, and had a family of nine. Of this family, James C. McGrew was a banker in Kingwood and became a member of the House of Representatives for two terms in Washington. He was a trustee for many years of the Ohio Wesleyan University.

Patrick and Martha Welsh McGrew had a daughter, Jane, born in 1790, who was to marry Henry Woods, the first-born son of Robert Woods.

Robert Woods and his wife, Catherine, had a family of eight. Of particular interest to us are the sons, Henry Woods, born April 3, 1789, and Moses Woods, born June 26, 1793, both in Virginia. Both served in the War of 1812. Henry Woods was a private in Captain Leonard Cupp's Company, 2nd Regiment (Evans), Monongalia County, Virginia Militia, and Moses Woods, his brother, served in Lieutenant Christian Core's Detachment of the 104th Regiment commanded by his brother-in-law, Colonel James McGrew.

To Ohio

In 1814 the two Woods brothers, Henry and Moses, together with their parents, Robert and Catherine Woods, and a number of family members representing the Woods, Brandons and McGrews left Monongalia County, Virginia, bound for Ohio. They went overland to the Ohio River and thence by boat to Cincinnati. They first settled on a small farm near Springdale in Hamilton County, Ohio. They stayed there for three years when Robert Woods met with a falling-tree accident in the woods and was instantly killed. Henry, Moses and their mother, Catherine, then went to Preble County, Ohio, where they stayed but a short time. The McGrews and Brandons had begun to settle in Preble and Darke Counties to the north. The Woods family then settled in Harrison Township of Darke County where after eight years Henry, his wife Jane, and his mother Catherine, now the wife of Richard Brandon, moved to Wayne Township in the same county.

Moses Woods stayed on in Harrison Township. He taught school in Yankeetown in a one-room log schoolhouse in the winter and farmed in the summer. He ultimately took part in politics and in 1839 was elected Commissioner of Darke County. He was active in the establishment of the Erie Canal and was identified with many pioneer activities in the county. For more than 20 years he ran a successful farm and retired in 1858. He spent the rest of his life in Palestine where he died at the age of 83, April 15, 1876.

The Henry Woods Family

Meantime Henry Woods built a log house over a spring near the Stillwater Creek in Wayne Township. The land was a wilderness of dense forest and hard work was the order of the day. The village of Versailles was nearby, a settlement of only a few houses, and the families were few and far between. That was in 1833, 14 years before Peter Henry Winger (A2226) arrived in the same general vicinity. Henry Woods was born April 3, 1789, in Virginia and Jane McGrew Woods was born in 1790 in the same state. He died December 3, 1853, and she died May 13, 1841. Both are buried in the Versailles cemetery.

Henry and Jane McGrew Woods had a family of six of the third generation. These were Samuel, Martha Jane, Henry Josephus, Catherine, Caroline and William. Of these Samuel and Henry Josephus Woods are of particular interest.

The Henry Woods log house over a spring near Stillwater Creek outside Versailles, Ohio, still stands to commemorate a pioneer Ohio family.

Samuel M. Woods was born in Hamilton County, Ohio, June 9, 1817. He was a self-educated man, there being few schools to attend. He was a successful farmer, businessman and educator. He was a trustee and supervisor in the township for more than 15 years, a school director and supervisor and was a director of the county infirmary. He married Harriet Harrison, October 10, 1844, and they had a family of twelve.

Henry Josephus Woods, Samuel Woods' brother, was born in

Darke County, June 7, 1827, and died in Celina, Ohio, June 7, 1899. He was in the Civil War, enlisting October 1, 1862, Private, Company D, 88th Ohio Infantry, Captain F. S. Parker, and was discharged July 3, 1865. He married Hannah Rock, July 4, 1847. After her death, May 15, 1880, he married Eliza Jane Bushman, February 7, 1886. Henry Josephus and Hannah Rock Woods had a family of six in the fourth generation. These were Joseph Woods, who married Josephine Brandon; John Woods, who married Mary Keefer; Mary Ellen Woods, who married Henry Hole; Margaret Woods, who married Martin Burris; Malinda Woods, who married a Miller, and Nancy Jane Woods, who married Joseph Levi Winger (A22269).

In summary, Nancy Jane Woods Winger was a descendant in the fourth generation as follows: Robert Woods (1st), Henry Woods (2nd), Henry Josephus Woods (3rd) and Nancy Jane Woods Winger (4th).

A Family of Love

My sister, Harriett (A2226921), speaks about the relationship between Nancy Jane Woods and her brothers and sisters as well as of her parents. She said that when her Aunt Margaret and Uncle Martin Burris came to visit Joseph (A22269) and Nancy Jane from St. Marys, that Aunt Margaret would always be wearing her bonnet and shawl and Uncle Martin his broadbrimmed hat. They, of course, were all members of the Dunkard church as were the parents. Josephus Woods also wore a wide hat and had a long flowing beard. He was a veteran of the Civil War and had a hip injury as a result of a wound sustained while in action in the South. He always limped and had to use a cane. Grandfather Josephus Woods ran a small hotel in Celina. When my sister, Harriett (A2226921), and my mother, Della Frances (A222692), visited in Celina, the Woods would reserve a nice room for them at the end of the upstairs hall. Grandmother Nancy Jane Winger used to warn her father, Josephus, not to give candy to the children because it was bad for their teeth. Harriett (A2226921) said that she remembered when she was a child that there was quite a space under the door to their room. She said that she could hear Grandpa coming because he would make a noise with his cane. He would always come by the door, stoop down and a sack of candy would slide under the door. Harriett (A2226921) said that she kept this a state secret and Grandmother Nancy Jane Winger never knew that this side play was going on.

Josephus Woods' second wife, Eliza Jane Bushman (May 31, 1831-May 12, 1928), outlived him by many years. She was in her 90's when Grandfather Joseph Winger (A22269) was in his 70's. In the meantime Joseph (A22269) had moved to a home at 218 West Warren Street. Eliza always wanted to be near Grandfather Winger

The Henry Josephus Woods home near Versailles, Ohio. Nancy Jane Woods, the wife of Joseph Levi Winger (A22269), was born here.

(A22269) in order to take care of him. He had already engaged the Mazenbrink family to live in the other side of the double house to look after his needs. However, during Eliza's waning years, Joseph Winger (A22269) would go to her house to take care of the things that needed to be done. He would shovel the coal, build the fires, get her groceries for her and, when necessary, would shovel the snow.

Harriett (A2226921) Visits

Harriett C. Thomas (A2226921), my sister, reports many of her visits to the home of her grandparents in Celina. She describes Grandpa Joseph Winger (A22269) as one who was a proud man. He insisted that the family look well and prosperous. After Harriett

(A2226921) had visited the boys who were living in Dayton, Ohio, she would stop in Celina to visit Grandpa Joseph Winger (A22269). He would frequently ask her if the boys were keeping up a fine appearance. He wanted to know whether they were well dressed, whether their shoes were good and whether they were keeping their hair trimmed. He was particular to make an inquiry as to whether or not they were clean shaven. He was, of course, from the old school; he believed in hard work and a thrifty application in the making of proper investments in order to make residue available to support the church of his choice. Harriett (A2226921) remembered that Grandpa Joseph (A22269) one day called her to one side and said that her underskirt was showing. He said, "That looks tacky, don't let that happen again." Harriett (A2226921) said that she took particular pains to see that it did not.

Reminiscences

The writer remembers visiting Grandpa Joseph Winger (A22269) with his sister, Harriett (A2226921). She said, "You know, I'm afraid John (A2226923) is going to be a preacher." Grandpa Winger (A22-269) retorted, "My goodness, girl, what's wrong with you. Don't you know that when one is a minister of the gospel, it is the highest calling that one can have." At that particular time, Uncle Frank Winger (A222693) was visiting Celina from Dayton. He and his father, Joseph Winger (A22269), both pinned the ministerial label on him and indicated that they were going to visit his church and urged that he should also hold "tent meetings."

As it turned out, they were poor prognosticators, since he did not follow their predictions. Later, however, the writer developed an extensive interest in comparative religions. In August and September of 1921, he exchanged a series of letters with Grandfather Winger (A22269). Only two of those communications have survived. These two letters, dated July 30, 1921, and August 31, 1921, from him express his delight that the writer had such an interest. He went on to say that the Law of God should be obeyed and quoted scripture and verse upon verse from the Bible. He finalized his admonition by saying, "You are young yet and will receive influences which could lead you astray. Be careful and stay out of bad company and take good advice. If you do, you will come out all right."

On one occasion the writer attended church with Grandfather Joseph Winger (A22269) who loved to sing hymns and participated with great vigor, coming through loud and clear. As a matter of fact, his voice could be heard above almost everybody else in the congregation. He always believed that singing was a fundamental and foremost part of religious worship.

On one occasion, when the writer was visiting his Aunt Attie (A222697) and Uncle Nelson Hoenie in Celina, he discovered that Uncle Nelson had a bicycle. The writer was so small at the time that he could not sit on the seat of the bicycle but could peddle by standing up and oscillating over the crossbar. He tried several times to ride the bicycle without success. However, one day he finally learned to balance himself and keep the bicycle going. He went down the street, turned to the right, and rode for another block toward Grandpa Winger's (A22269) home. His balance was sufficiently poor that he tracked all over the street. Nevertheless, he stayed right side up. As he pulled into Grandpa Joseph Winger's (A22269) yard, Grandpa, who was sitting on the porch, said, "My goodness, young man, when I saw you coming down the street, I thought to myself, what in the world is going on. What kind of a freak of nature is that?" He said, "Don't you know that a horse and buggy could run right over you?"

Another occasion he recalls is Joseph (A22269) taking him to the Mercer County Fair and to the horse races. He loved horses and would always go to the races every afternoon when the fair was on. He did not enjoy sitting in the grandstand, but he would always hang on the rail so he could be closer to the horses when they went by.

Other Stories

Another incident in Celina concerned my Uncle Nelson Hoenie — his wife was Attie (A222697). Uncle Nelson liked to fill a big pail with his favorite beverage and lower it on a rope into a deep well to keep it cool in the cold spring water. My cousins, Esther (A222-6971) and Ruth Hoenie (A2226972), and the writer on occasions would help ourselves to the contents. He recalls on one occasion when Grandpa Joseph Winger (A22269) found this out, he severely reprimanded us for performing at the wrong time in the wrong place. Another activity was fishing in the old reservoir (Grand Lake or Lake Mercer). Grandpa Joseph Winger (A22269) from time to time would take the writer to the docks to fish, never enjoying too much success.

One time the writer was about to pass through Celina on an excursion train for Cedarpoint. Knowing that the train was not scheduled to stop in Celina, he wanted to send Grandfather (A222-69) a message, so he stuffed a note into a pop bottle and threw it out of the train as it went through Celina. He asked the finder of the message to deliver it to Grandfather Joseph Winger (A22269). Later, when he asked Grandfather (A22269) if he ever got the mes-

Beaver Chapel at Swamp College Cemetery west of Celina, Ohio. The last rites of all the Winger people buried in Swamp College were held here. Joseph Winger's (A22269) favorite hymns were heard here as a part of his final service.

sage, he said, "Nobody ever delivered such a thing to him and, besides, what a way to send a message. For two cents you could send me a letter in the mail."

Esther Hoenie Limes (A2226971) reports that a few years prior to the death of Joseph Winger (A22269) she lived close to the Joseph Winger (A22269) home. She called on her Grandfather Joseph Winger (A22269) every day. She said that Grandfather (A22269) still had his pump organ which he had brought to Celina from the farm. Every day he insisted that she play the organ while he sang the hymns. In his later life, he sang "Nearer My God to Thee" and "Jesus, Lover of my Soul," every day.

A letter dated March 28, 1928, from Franklin Winger (A222693) to his sister, Della Frances (A222692), stated that Dad (A22269) had sold his house at 218 West Warren Street and had gone to stay with their sister, Attie Hoenie (A222697). Undoubtedly it was a foreboding of things to come.

Joseph Winger (A22269) Dies

It was my good fortune to see Grandmother Nancy Jane Winger during the time of her terminal illness. I was not so fortunate when Grandfather Joseph Winger (A22269) died December 31, 1928. Just before his death, he called for me. I did not arrive in Celina in time, and he passed away before my arrival. He was laid to rest in the Swamp College Cemetery. Final rights were held in the Beaver Chapel next to the cemetery. This Congregational Church was built in 1887 and is located at the junction of Karch and Swamp Roads, a few miles west of Celina.

A fitting memorial.

After his death, Della Winger Fetzer Pyle (A222692), as the senior member of the family, was named coexecutor of his estate. The Articles of Agreement on the disposition of the estate of Joseph Winger (A22269), dated January 2, 1929, contain the original signatures of all of the heirs. These were as follows: Frank Winger

Joseph Levi Winger (22269) and Nancy Jane Woods Winger in front of their home at the corner of Brandon and Lisle Streets, Celina, Ohio.

(A222693), Della Frances Fetzer Pyle (A222692), Amanda Pierstorff (A222696), Attie Hoenie (A222697), Ed Winger (A222699), Emma Winger (Mrs. Charles Winger A222695), J. A. Winger, Mildred Foster, Charles E. Winger, Frank Winger by Emma Winger and Russell B. Winger.

The Joseph (A22269) and Nancy Jane Winger Bible, at the time this is written, is in the hands of Ruth Hoenie Mendenhall (A222-6972) in Celina, Ohio. Grandfather Joseph Winger (A22269) kept meticulous family records in this Bible. All of these records were copied and sent to the writer February 1, 1969, by Esther Hoenie Limes (A2226971). These records were used in the preparation of the vital statistics contained herein.

See the Joseph Levi R. Winger (A22269) Family Tree which follows.

Joseph Levi Winger (A22269) Family Tree

1st Hans Wenger (b. About 1430) Blumenstein, Thun

2nd Burkhard Wenger (b. About 1450) Forst, Thun

3rd Peter Wenger (b. About 1470) Wattenwil, Seftigen

4th Peter Wenger (b. About 1490) Wattenwil, Seftigen

5th Rudolfus Wenger (b. About 1510) Wattenwil, Seftigen

6th Hans Wenger (b. About 1530) Wattenwil, Seftigen

7th Rudolfus Wenger (Ch. April 5, 1566) Wattenwil-Thurnen, Seftigen

8th Peter Wenger (Ch. Dec. 13, 1607) Wattenwil-Thurnen, Seftigen

9th Hans Wenger (Ch. May 30, 1633) Wattenwil-Thurnen, Seftigen

    A   Christian Wenger (A2) First Generation in America (1688-1749)

        B-1   Henry Wenger (A22) Second Generation in America (1716-1802)

            C-1   Abraham Wenger (A222) Third Generation in America (1767-1845)

                D-1   Peter Henry Winger (A2226) Fourth Generation in America (1806-1889)

                    E-1   Joseph Levi Robinson Winger (A22269) Fifth Generation
    b. July 17, 1848, d. Dec. 31, 1928
    m. Nancy Jane Woods, Apr. 5, 1868, Versailles, Ohio
    b. June 29, 1849, d. Mar. 16, 1911

                        F-1   John William Winger (A222691-6th)
    b. Sept. 1, 1869, d. Jan. 7, 1871
    (No issue)

                        F-2   Della Frances Winger (A222692-6th)
    b. Dec. 21, 1870, d. Feb. 12, 1958
    (See chapter - Della Frances Winger of Indiana)

                        F-3   Franklin Josephus Winger (A222693-6th)
    b. Apr. 20, 1872, d. July 1, 1929
    (See chapter - Winger Brothers in Ohio)

F-4 Ida Mae Winger (A222694-6th)
    b. Dec. 21, 1873, d. July 25, 1875
    (No issue)

F-5 Charles Elwood Winger (A222695-6th)
    b. July 4, 1875, d. Sept. 19, 1922
    (See chapter - Winger Brothers
    in Ohio)

F-6 Amanda Ellen Winger (A222696-6th)
    b. Aug. 9, 1878, d. Aug. 8, 1959
    (See chapter - Winger Sisters in Ohio)

F-7 Henrietta (Attie) Winger (A222697-6th)
    b. May 20, 1880, d. Feb. 10, 1969
    (See chapter - Winger Sisters in Ohio)

F-8 Luallen (Allen) Winger (A222698-6th)
    b. Jan. 1, 1882, d. Nov. 5, 1900
    (No issue)

F-9 Carey Edmond Winger (A222699-6th)
    b. Sept. 19, 1884, d. Aug. 5, 1946
    (See chapter - Winger Brothers
    in Ohio)

CHAPTER SIXTEEN

The Winger Brothers of Ohio

THE FIRST of the Winger brothers in Ohio was John William Winger (A222691) of the sixth generation, who was born September 1, 1869, on the Joseph Winger (A22269) farm in Darke County. He died January 7, 1871, and is buried in Tea Cup Cemetery near Osgood, Ohio.

Franklin J. Winger Family

Franklin J. Winger (A222693) was born on his father's farm in Patterson Township, Darke County, April 20, 1872. Most of his early life is recorded in the chapter on Joseph Levi Winger (A22269), his father. Franklin (A222693) was very close to Della Frances Winger (A222692), his sister, who had gone to live at Decatur, Indiana. Due to force of circumstances, she lived alone with her two children.

Franklin J. Winger (A222693) and his wife, Alice Belle Baxter Winger.

Franklin (A222693), in his first trip away from home, went to Decatur to look after his sister, Della (A222692). Harriett Evans Thomas

(A2226921), the daughter of Della (A222692), reports that Uncle Frank (A222693) really took the place of her father. She said, "When I was a youngster, I used to have the croup. In the middle of the night, when Uncle Frank (A222693) would hear me cough, he always got out of bed to give me his favorite cough medicine. He was one of the kindest men I ever knew."

It was in Decatur, Indiana, that Franklin Winger (A222693) met Alice Belle Baxter, his wife to be. Franklin (A222693) and Alice Belle Baxter were married October 27, 1898. Della Frances (A222-692), his sister, and Harriett Evans (A2226921), Franklin's niece, along with James Ball, another friend of the family, were witnesses. James (Jim) Ball was the second husband of Barbara Cecelia Iyanson Evans, who was the grandmother of Harriett Evans (A2226921).

Franklin (A222693) and his bride, Alice Belle, who was born March 7, 1875, in Monmouth near Decatur, moved to Celina and later to Dayton where they spent the remainder of their lives. Franklin (A222693) and Alice Belle Winger had four children of the seventh generation. These were Lawrence Franklin Winger (A222-6931), Mable Esther Winger (A2226932), Raymond Edgar Winger (A2226933) and Ralph Jennings Winger (A2226934).

As this was written, a communication from Lawrence Winger (A2226931) stated that his father, Franklin (A222693), was "a good father and provider." Most of his working life, Franklin Winger (A222693) spent with the National Cash Register Company in Dayton.

Apparently the last communication Franklin Winger (A222693) had with his sister, Della Frances (A222692), was March 31, 1928. This climaxed a correspondence that had endured for more than 40 years. He was most pleased to report a trip he had taken with his sons, Lawrence (A2226931) and Ralph (A2226934). They drove their car on a two-day trip of 180 miles to Kadova, West Virginia, and to Gatters Burgh and Ashland, Kentucky, and return. He described the mountains and the Ohio and Big Sandy Rivers, the ferry boats, et al. He talked of visits with all his brothers and sisters, and expressed the hope that 1928 would not bring the trouble that 1927 had presented. He had lost his wife, Belle, that year. As was his habit, he wrote to Della Frances (A222692) April 18, 1926, describing the illness of his wife, Belle, which proved to be terminal June 20, 1927.

Franklin Winger (A222693) closed his letter of March 31, 1928, by saying, "My love and good luck to you all — God bless us all is my prayer tonight. Your brother, Frank." Little did he know that he was soon to join those who had already passed on. They all had

Above: Mable Esther Winger (A2226932), Lawrence Franklin Winger (A2226931).
Below: Raymond Edgar Winger (A2226933) and Ralph Jennings Winger (A2226934).

either written or called for Della Frances (A222692) just before the end — Della Frances (A222692), the undisputed leader of the family.

Franklin Winger (A222693) died July 1, 1929, and is buried along with his wife, Belle Baxter Winger, in the Willow View Cemetery, Dayton.

The Seventh Generation

Lawrence Franklin Winger (A2226931) of the seventh generation was born in Celina, Ohio, February 3, 1900. He attended the public schools after which he joined the army during World War II. He developed bronchial trouble and was given honorable discharge. Later, he attended a trade school in Chicago after which he specialized in refrigeration and air conditioning. He has spent his productive years at the Wright Patterson Air Force Base near Dayton where he installed refrigeration and air conditioning equipment in all types of airplanes. He was under Civil Service. Harriett Thomas (A2226921) describes him as a man given to silent charity. "He does a lot of things to help people that no one knows about." Lawrence Franklin Winger (A2226931), who is unmarried, is spending his retirement years at his home, 980 Wilmington Avenue, Dayton, Ohio. He travels over the country every year which adds a great deal of zest to his living.

Mable Esther Winger (A2226932) of the seventh generation was born in Celina, Ohio, August 23, 1901. Mable Winger (A2226932) never married. She attended the public schools in Celina after which she became matron of the Montgomery County Hospital in Dayton, serving the needs of those around her. She died January 14, 1946, and is buried in Willow View Cemetery near Dayton.

On October 16, 1945, Mable Winger (A2226932) had written to her aunt, Della Frances (A222692), that she had been ill for more than a year and that her doctor had advised her to go to Arizona to live. She said that she had often thought of her Aunt Della and felt compelled to write. It was her last letter.

Raymond Edgar Winger (A2226933) was the third child of Franklin (A222693) and Belle Winger. He was born in Celina, Ohio, May 20, 1904, and died in Dayton, May 16, 1918. There was no issue. He is buried in the Willow View Cemetery in Dayton.

Ralph Jennings Winger (A2226934) of the seventh generation was the youngest son of Franklin (A222693) and Belle Winger, having been born October 21, 1908. He attended the public schools in Dayton where he graduated from Stivers High School. He married a widow, Alberta Louise McGrath, on April 10, 1939, in Lafayette, Indiana, and adopted her son, William Ralph Winger.

Ralph Winger (A2226934) is a machinist by trade, having been connected with the Delco Company all of his working years. He is a member of the Central Christian Church of Kettering (Disciples of Christ), where he has presided as an elder. He has been a Mason since 1953 and during this time has been a member of all Masonic bodies. He has served in every office in the line and is now Past Master of his lodge. He is highly respected and admired by the many friends he has made while serving in his Masonic work. Ralph Winger (A2226934) and his wife, Alberta, have retired and now live in Ft. Myers, Florida.

Another Winger

William Ralph Winger (A22269341), the only child of Ralph (A2226934) and Alberta Winger, was born December 27, 1933, in Burville, Tennessee. He attended Fairview High School, Patterson Cooperative High School, Miami University of Ohio, University of Dayton and the United States Navy Electronics School at Great Lakes, Illinois. As an electronics technician on the *U.S.S. Johnston,* he had complete charge of radar and sonar equipment. As an engineer and electronics technician, William Ralph Winger (A222-69341) has performed in a wide spectrum of services with distinction with such companies as the Delco Products Division of General Motors, the National Cash Register Company, Daytronic Corporation, Westgate Laboratory, Inc., and WacLine, Inc. At the present time, he is an active partner and founder of Hyde Park Electronics,

From left to right: William Ralph Winger, Jr. (A222693411), William Ralph Winger, Sr. (A22269341), Alberta Louise McGrath Winger (seated), Ralph Jennings Winger (A2226934) standing, Wendolyn Ann Winger (A222693412), the little girl standing in front of her mother, Caroline Beth Tonini Winger, the wife of William Ralph Winger, Sr. (A22269341).

Inc., a company specializing in electronic controls. He has been active in many business, professional and civic organizations.

William Ralph Winger (A22269341) married Carolyn Beth Tonini, January 26, 1957, in Dayton. She was born June 20, 1934, in Burlington, Iowa. She is National Vice President of the Sigma Beta sorority and has been named Outstanding Young Woman in America. The Wingers have two children of the ninth generation. They are William Ralph Winger, Jr. (A222693411), who was born October 1, 1960, and Wendolyn Ann Winger (A222693412), born March 24, 1963. Both were born in Dayton, Ohio.

Charles E. Winger Family

Charles Elwood Winger (A222695) of the sixth generation and a son of Joseph (A22269) and Nancy Jane Winger was born in Patterson Township, Darke County, Ohio, July 4, 1875. His early life is fully documented in the chapter on the Joseph Levi R. Winger (A22269) family. Charles E. Winger (A222695) as a young man

Emma Adaline Oyler Richeson Winger, the wife of Charles Elwood Winger (A222695).

joined his brother, Frank (A222693), in standing by in Decatur, Indiana, to help his sister, Della Frances (A222692), who was in need of family solicitude. After a solution had been reached in

Charles E. Winger (A22-2695) memorial at Swamp College Cemetery near Celina, Ohio.

Decatur, Charles (A222695) returned to his Celina home with his parents. There he met Emma Adaline Oyler Richeson, an extraordinary widow from a fine pioneer family. They were married November 4, 1902, in Celina.

Emma Richeson's first husband was Henry Howard Richeson. The Richesons had three children. The first was Harold Lawrence Richeson, who prior to retirement was Vice President of the Pfeiffer Brewing Company in Detroit, Michigan. The second was Claude Andrew Richeson who performed administrative work for the City of Dayton, Ohio, prior to retirement. The third child was Mary M. Richeson, whose husband is Judge Joseph J. Takacs of Middlesex County District Court, New Brunswick, New Jersey. Mary Richeson Takacs was Director of Health in the public school system of New Brunswick prior to her marriage.

Years later Mildred Foster (A2226952) described her father, Charles Elwood Winger (A222695), as a gentle man, a hard worker and a stern disciplinarian when required. Harriett Thomas (A222-6921) states that he could not tolerate hypocrisy in any form. He never hesitated to expose it. She said that he and her Uncle Frank Winger (A222693) in their lighter moments used to sing duets together. The family greatly enjoyed their musical improvising.

Charles (A222695) and Emma Winger had a family of five. The first three were born in Celina and the last two in Dayton. Charles (A222695) and Emma were to move to Dayton in 1910 where Charles (A222695) was to become a successful restauranteur. Charles (A222-695) died September 19, 1922, in Dayton, Ohio, and is buried with his parents at the Swamp College Cemetery near Celina, Ohio. Emma Richeson Winger was born December 25, 1867, at Stockwell, Indiana, and died October 15, 1947, in Dayton, Ohio. She is buried in the North Grove Cemetery, Celina, Ohio.

A Mark of Distinction

Joseph Allen Winger (A2226951) was named Joseph for his grandfather, Joseph Winger (A22269), and Allen for his uncle, Allen Winger (A222698). He was born in Celina, August 12, 1903. Joseph (A2226951) attended the public schools in Dayton, Ohio, and in due course met and married Lillian McCarty, September 30, 1925, in her native community of Lawrenceville, Illinois. Joseph (A2226951) had joined the Indian Refining Company in Lawrenceville as a draftsman, later becoming an engineer in charge of station properties. In 1930 the Indian Refining Company was merged with the Texaco Company, Inc. With Texaco, Joseph (A2226951) progressed through a number of assignments in sales and operations. During

Joseph Allen Winger (A22269-51) and his wife, Lillian McCarty Winger.

the years in the petroleum industry, he served in Chicago with the Petroleum Administration as Assistant Manager and during the course of events lived, among other places, in Northville, Indianapolis, Houston, and New York. In New York he was Vice President and Manager of Operations. This executive position at Texaco covered Domestic Sales Operations in all 50 states. He lived in Greenwich, Connecticut.

After 42 years of service with Texaco, Joseph Winger (A2226951) decided to retire. In 1965, after a full recovery from major surgery, Joseph (A2226951) and his wife, Lillian, moved to a beautiful new home at 635 North Owl Drive, Bird Key, Sarasota, Florida. In Sarasota he was Chairman of the Board of Trustees of the First Congregational Church and a member of the Y.M.C.A. Board. He was a Blue Lodge Mason and a Scottish Rite Member of Egypt Temple. He was a member of the Sarasota Yacht Club and the Bird Key Yacht Club, as well as the Long Beach Boat Club. Here the Wingers enjoyed a quiet life in semi-retirement. Joseph (A222-6951) kept himself fully occupied by operating his own company known as Winger Enterprises. This operation was engaged in the development and marketing of patents. Joseph (A2226951) had been in apparently good health when suddenly on August 8, 1970, he died of a heart seizure. He is interred in the Sarasota Memorial Park.

A Family of Three

Joseph (A2226951) and Lillian Winger had a family of three children of the eighth generation. These are Richard Allen Winger (A22269511), David Paul Winger (A22269512) and JoAnn Lee Winger (A22269513).

Richard Allen Winger (A22269511) of the eighth generation was born August 22, 1926, in Lawrenceville, Illinois. He married Marjorie Mills in July 1945, in Indianapolis, Indiana. His second marriage was with Ruth Louise White, June 18, 1955, in Tyler, Texas. Richard Winger (A22269511) is a manufacturer's representative in Dallas, Texas. The Wingers live in Garland, Texas, and have two children. Thomas Allen Winger (A222695111) of the ninth generation was born December 9, 1947, at Lawrenceville, Illinois. His mother was Marjorie Mills Winger. The second-born son was Allen Monroe Winger (A2226951112) whose mother is Ruth Louise White Winger. He was born September 12, 1956, in Garland, Texas.

The second-born child of Joseph (A2226951) and Lillian Winger is David Paul Winger (A22269512) of the eighth generation. He was born November 16, 1930, at Lawrenceville, Illinois. He married Dorine Smoke, August 1, 1959, in Little Rock, Arkansas. David Winger (A22269512) is an Industrial Engineer with the U.S. F. & G. Company in Houston, Texas. He and his wife, Dorine, live in Houston.

Douglas Christopher Winger (A222695121) of the ninth generation was born May 5, 1960. Daniel Paul Winger (A222695122) was born May 17, 1962. Donna Louise Winger (A222695123) was born May 9, 1964, and Teresa Diana Winger (A222695124) was born November 15, 1965. All were born in Tulsa, Oklahoma.

JoAnn Lee Winger (A22269513), the daughter of Joseph (A222-6951) and Lillian Winger, was born September 5, 1933, in Indianapolis, Indiana. She married Robert Everett Willis, Jr., August 20, 1957. JoAnn (A22269513) and Robert Willis, Jr., each had a child by a former marriage. Alexandra Willis (A222695131-By assignment),

Left to right: David Paul Winger (A22269512), Joseph Allen Winger (A2226951) with Thomas Allen Winger (A222695111) in front and Richard Allen Winger (A22269511).

the daughter of Robert Willis, Jr., was born September 8, 1950, in Greenwich, Connecticut. She was legally adopted by JoAnn (A222-69513). Bruce Willis (A222695132), a son of JoAnn (A22269513), was born June 24, 1956, in Greenwich, Connecticut. He was legally adopted by Robert Everett Willis, Jr. JoAnn (A22269513) and Robert Everett Willis, Jr., had two children of the ninth generation. These

Left to right: Bruce Willis (A222695132), Lillian McCarty Winger, Robert Everett Willis III (A222695134) in front, Alissa Ann Willis (A222695133) and Jo Ann Lee Winger Willis (A22269513).

are Alissa Ann (A222695133), who was born September 11, 1958, and Robert Everett Willis III (A222695134), who was born June 28, 1960. Robert E. Willis, Jr., is a maintenance engineer in Greenwich, Connecticut.

The Lone Sister

Mildred Lela Winger (A2226952) of the seventh generation, the daughter of Charles (A222695) and Emma Winger, was born December 22, 1905, in Celina, Ohio. She lived her younger life with her parents in Dayton, Ohio, and married Clyde Ernest Foster, June 21, 1923, in the same city. Clyde Ernest Foster was born November 24, 1903, in Huntsville, Tennessee. He died April 24, 1949, in Miami, Florida. He is buried in the Flagler Memorial Cemetery in Miami.

Clyde Foster was Secretary-Treasurer of the Hotel and Restaurant Employees International Union which was affiliated with the

American Federation of Labor. The Fosters had four children of the eighth generation, the last three of which were born in Florida, since they moved from Dayton to Miami in 1925.

Clyde Ernest Foster, Jr. (A22269521), was born September 4, 1924, in Dayton. He attended the public schools in Miami and graduated in law at the University of Miami. Clyde (A22269521) married Jeanne Lee Griffin, January 17, 1946, in Miami. She was born November 4, 1925, in Miami. She was the daughter of Currie Lee Griffin, born in Mississippi, and Raynette Barnes Griffin, born in Cleveland, Ohio. They had three children of the ninth generation. James Ernest Foster (A222695211) was born September 16, 1946, in Miami. He married Annette Marie Ritchie, November 26, 1966, in Tiajuana, Mexico. She was born April 12, 1948, at Breckinridge, Minnesota. They have a daughter of the tenth generation, Susanne Marie Foster (A2226952111), who was born July 4, 1967, in Los Angeles. James Ernest Foster (A222695211) is a machinist in Los Angeles.

The second child of Clyde (A22269521) and Jeanne Foster was Thomas Currie Foster (A222695212) of the ninth generation. He was born February 9, 1952, in Miami, Florida. The last child of the Fosters was Jeannette Lee Foster (A22269213) of the ninth generation. She was born September 21, 1955, in Miami. The latter two girls are students.

Subsequently Clyde Ernest Foster, Jr. (A22269521), after a divorce February 14, 1964, married Delores May Singer. She was born February 17, 1924. Her parents were Martin Luther and Martha Nella Anderson Singer. Delores Singer had five children by her first marriage with Eugene Joseph Galipeau of Lake Linden, Michigan. These are as follows: Kathleen Louise Galipeau was born September 30, 1945, in Racine, Wisconsin. She married Michael Richard Miller on November 7, 1964, in Racine, Wisconsin. He was born March 12, 1943, in Kent, England, and is a member of the Racine Police Department. They have two children: Michele Kathleen Miller, born June 18, 1965, and Tracy Lynn Miller, born July 14, 1966, both in Racine, Wisconsin. Rodger Allen Galipeau was born October 3, 1947, at Racine, Wisconsin. He is single and a machinist by trade. He presently is in the military service in Vietnam. Martha Mae Galipeau, born May 15, 1951, at Racine, Wisconsin, is married to Alroy Frank Cacciotti. They were married June 6, 1968, at Clinton,

Iowa, and have a daughter, Jody Lynn Cacciotti, who was born July 21, 1968, at Racine, Wisconsin. Her husband is a machinist and was born September 28, 1950, in Racine, Wisconsin. Jeffrey Gene Galipeau, born September 18, 1952, at Racine, Wisconsin, is single and a student. David John Galipeau, born February 15, 1957, at Miami, Florida, is single and a student.

Clyde Ernest Foster, Jr. (A22269521), is in the brokerage business in Racine.

Left to right: Clyde Ernest Foster, Jr. (A22269521), in front James Ernest Foster (A222695211), Jeanne Lee Griffin Foster, with baby Thomas Currie Foster (A222695212), Martha Lou Foster Butt (A22269522), with baby Donna Louise Butt (A222695221), Mildred Lela Winger Foster (A2226952), in front a child friend, Robert David Butt, Charles Sanders Foster (A22269523) with baby Paul Foster (A222695231), Sheila Maureen Murphy Foster, with baby Timothy Foster (A222695232).

The second child of Mildred (A2226952) and Clyde Foster was Martha Lou Foster (A22269522) of the eighth generation. She was born in Miami, February 24, 1926. She was educated in Miami and became a member of the school system in that city. She married Robert David Butt, June 2, 1945, in Knoxville, Tennessee. He was born September 12, 1927, in Knoxville. They have an adopted daughter, Donna Louise Butt (A222695221-By Assignment), who was born December 23, 1951, in Miami.

The third child of Mildred (A2226952) and Clyde Foster was Charles Sanders Foster (A22269523) of the eighth generation. He was born July 8, 1927, in Dayton, Ohio, and died November 8, 1968, in Miami, Florida. He was educated in the public schools of Miami and was a graduate of Miami University. He entered the teaching profession and became Principal of the Miami Carol City High School, a fine institution of over 3,000 students. Charles S. Foster (A22269-523) was named after his grandfather, Charles Winger (A222695). He married Sheila Maureen Murphy, August 14, 1949, in Miami. She was born September 28, 1929, in Westport, Conn. The Fosters (A22269523) had three children of the ninth generation. Charles Paul Foster (A222695231) was born March 3, 1951, in Miami. Timothy Foster (A222695232) was born January 27, 1952, in Miami. The last child, Stephen Andrew Foster (A222695233), was born January 30, 1955.

The fourth child of Mildred (A2226952) and Clyde Foster was Paul Norman Foster (A22269524). He was born May 25, 1932, in Dayton, Ohio. He is an electronic engineer with the United Fruit Company. He married Maria Carmel DiManbro, April 5, 1956, in Miami. She was born June 4, 1929, in New York. The Fosters (A222-69524) have no children.

The Final Three

Charles (A222695) and Emma Winger's third child was Charles Edmond Winger (A2226953) of the seventh generation. He was born February 26, 1908, in Celina, Ohio. He attended the public schools in Dayton and has continued his residency there throughout his life. He married Ruth Naomi Holsattle, October 5, 1939, in Dayton. She was born in 1907. The Wingers (A2226953) have two sons of the eighth generation. Charles Edmond Winger, Jr. (A22269531), was born June 19, 1941, in Dayton. He attended preparatory college in the military and is unmarried. The second son is Thomas Allen Winger (A22269532). He was born March 9, 1944, in Dayton. He attended the University of Dayton. He is unmarried and is a draftsman by profession. Charles Edmond Winger, Sr. (A2226953), is a buyer for the Concord Provision Company in Dayton.

Howard Franklin Winger (A2226954) of the seventh generation and the fourth-born child of Charles (A222695) and Emma Winger was born August 2, 1910, in Dayton. During World War II he was a utility man as a Merchant Seaman. He was a member of the crew of the S.S. *Walter R. Gresham,* operated by the Standard Fruit and Steamship Company. The ship was hit by a German submarine off the Virginia coast and sank. All on board including Howard Franklin Winger (A2226954) went down in a devastating disaster. That was reported March 18, 1943. Howard Franklin Winger (A2226954) was issued seaman's documents May 10, 1937. He had six years service when his ship went down.

Charles (A222695) and Emma Winger's last-born child was Russell Beck Winger (A2226955) of the seventh generation. He was born January 21, 1913, in Dayton. He married Emma Lou Stevenson of Bellfountain, Ohio. She was born July 20, 1919, at Bellfountain. Russell Winger (A2226955) has been in sales work for the Independent Grocers Alliance (I.G.A.) stores, working the midwest territory. The Wingers (A2226955) had one daughter, Susan Lynne (A22269551), of the eighth generation. She was born August 4, 1944, in Bellfountain. She married Wayne Eldon Chapman, February 23, 1963, in Bellfountain. They have two children of the ninth generation. Steven Russell Chapman (A222695511) was born December 9, 1964, and Wayne Joseph Chapman (A22269512) was born January 2, 1966, both in Bellfountain.

The Last Two Ohio Brothers

The last two sons of Joseph (A22269) and Nancy Jane Winger follow. Luallen (Allen) Winger (A222698) of the sixth generation was born January 1, 1882, on the Mercer County, Ohio, farm of his parents. His life story is recorded in the Joseph Levi R. Winger (A22269) chapter. He was the family peacemaker. He loved his brothers and sisters. His premature passing was a severe blow to the family. As a young man of 18 years, he died November 5, 1900, in Celina, Ohio. He is buried in the Swamp College Cemetery near Celina, Ohio.

Carey Edmond Winger (A2226999) of the sixth generation, also born in Mercer County, September 19, 1884, lived most of his adult life in Dayton. "Uncle Ed," says Harriett Thomas (A2226921), "after a little unsteadiness as a youngster, was most lovable. He became even-tempered and always did his work without fanfare. He was modest to the extreme, a warmhearted soul." He was an interior

At Swamp College Cemetery.

decorator. He married Anna Reigelsperger, November 5, 1919, in Ft. Recovery, Ohio. He died August 5, 1946, in Dayton and is buried at Swamp College near Celina. There is no descending family.

Left to right: Franklin J. Winger (A222693), Carey Edmond Winger (A222699) and Charles Elwood Winger (A222695).

The Winger Brothers Family Tree

1st Hans Wenger (b. About 1430) Blumenstein, Thun
2nd Burkhard Wenger (b. About 1450) Forst, Thun
3rd Peter Wenger (b. About 1470) Wattenwil, Seftigen
4th Peter Wenger (b. About 1490) Wattenwil, Seftigen
5th Rudolfus Wenger (b. About 1510) Wattenwil, Seftigen
6th Hans Wenger (b. About 1530) Wattenwil, Seftigen
7th Rudolfus Wenger (Ch. April 5, 1566) Wattenwil-Thurnen, Seftigen
8th Peter Wenger (Ch. Dec. 13, 1607) Wattenwil-Thurnen, Seftigen
9th Hans Wenger (Ch. May 30, 1633) Wattenwil-Thurnen, Seftigen
    A   Christian Wenger (A2) First Generation in America (1688-1749)
        B-1   Henry Wenger, Sr. (A22) Second Generation in America (1716-1802)
            C-1   Abraham Wenger (A222) Third Generation in America (1767-1845)
                D-1   Peter Henry Winger (A2226) Fourth Generation in America (1806-1889)
                    E-1   Joseph Levi R. Winger (A22269)
Fifth Generation
b. July 17, 1848, Darke County, Ohio
d. Dec. 31, 1928, Mercer County, Ohio
m. Nancy Jane Woods, Apr. 5, 1868, Versailles, Ohio
b. June 29, 1849, Darke County
d. Mar. 16, 1911, Mercer Co.,
bur. Swamp College
      F-1 John William Winger (A222691-6th)
b. Sept. 1, 1869, Darke County
d. Jan. 7, 1871, Darke County
bur. Tea Cup Cemetery, Darke County
(No issue)
      F-2 Franklin Josephus Winger (A222693-6th)
b. Apr. 20, 1872, Darke County
d. July 1, 1929, Dayton,
bur. Willow View Cemetery
m. Alice Belle Baxter, Oct. 27, 1898, Decatur, Ind.
b. Mar. 7, 1875, Monmouth, Indiana

d. June 20, 1927, Dayton,
bur. Willow View Cemetery

G-1 Lawrence Franklin Winger
(A2226931-7th)
b. Feb. 3, 1900, Celina, Ohio
m. Unmarried   (No issue)

G-2 Mable Esther Winger (A2226932-7th)
b. Aug. 23, 1901, Celina, Ohio
d. Jan. 14, 1946, Dayton, Ohio
(No issue)

G-3 Raymond Edgar Winger (A2226933-7th)
b. May 20, 1904, Celina, Ohio
d. May 16, 1918, Dayton, Ohio
m. Unmarried   (No issue)

G-4 Ralph Jennings Winger (A2226934-7th)
b. Oct. 21, 1908, Celina, Ohio
m. Alberta Louise McGrath, Apr. 10,
1939, Lafayette, Indiana
b. Feb. 11, 1913, Burville, Tenn.

H-1 William Ralph Winger
(A22269341-8th)
b. Dec. 27, 1933, Burville, Tenn.
m. Carolyn Beth Tonini, Jan. 26,
1957, Dayton
b. June 20, 1934, Burlington, Iowa

I-1 Wm. Ralph Winger, Jr.
(A222693411-9th)
b. Oct. 1, 1960, Dayton, Ohio

I-2 Wendolyn Ann Winger
(A222693412-9th)
b. Mar. 24, 1963, Dayton, Ohio

F-3 Charles Elwood Winger (A222695-6th)
b. July 4, 1875, Darke County
d. Sept. 19, 1922, Dayton, Ohio,
bur. Swamp College
m. Emma Adaline Richeson, Nov. 4,
1902, Celina, Ohio
b. Dec. 25, 1867, Stockwell, Indiana
d. Oct. 15, 1947, Dayton, Ohio,
bur. North Grove Cemetery,
Celina, Ohio

G-1 Joseph Allen Winger (A2226951-7th)
 b. Aug. 12, 1903, Celina, Ohio
 d. Aug. 8, 1970, Sarasota
 m. Lillian McCarty, Sept. 30, 1925,
 Lawrenceville, Illinois
 b. Jan. 13, 1903

 H-1 Richard Allen Winger
  (A22269511-8th)
  b. Aug. 22, 1926,
  Lawrenceville, Illinois
  m. Marjorie Mills, July, 1945,
  Indianapolis
  m. Ruth Louise White, June 18,
  1955, Tyler, Texas (2nd)

  I-1 Thomas Allen Winger
   (A222695111-9th)
   b. Dec. 9, 1947 (1st)
   Lawrenceville, Illinois

  I-2 Allen Monroe Winger
   (A222695112-9th)
   b. Sept. 12, 1956 (2nd)
   Garland, Texas

 H-2 David Paul Winger (A22269512-8th)
  b. Nov. 16, 1930, Lawrenceville, Ill.
  m. Dorine Smoke, Aug. 1, 1959,
  Little Rock, Ark.

  I-1 Douglas Christopher Winger
   (A222695121-9th)
   b. May 5, 1960, Tulsa, Okla.

  I-2 Daniel Paul Winger
   (A222695122-9th)
   b. May 17, 1962, Tulsa, Okla.

  I-3 Donna Louise Winger
   (A222695123-9th)
   b. May 9, 1964, Tulsa, Okla.

  I-4 Teresa Diana Winger
   (A222695124-9th)
   b. Nov. 15, 1965, Tulsa, Okla.

 H-3 JoAnn Lee Winger (A22269513-8th)
  b. Sept. 5, 1933, Indianapolis, Ind.
  m. Robert Everett Willis, Jr.,
  Aug. 20, 1957, Greenwich, Conn.

I-1 Alexandra Willis (A222695131-By
Assignment)
b. Sept. 8, 1950, Greenwich, Conn.

I-2 Bruce Willis (A222695132-9th)
b. June 24, 1956, Greenwich Conn.

I-3 Alissa Ann Willis (A222695133-9th)
b. Sept. 11, 1958,
Greenwich, Conn.

I-4 Robert Everett Willis III
(A222695134-9th)
b. June 28, 1960,
Greenwich, Conn.

G-2 Mildred Lela Winger (A2226952-7th)
b. Dec. 22, 1905, Celina, Ohio
m. Clyde Ernest Foster, June 21, 1923,
Dayton, Ohio
b. Nov. 24, 1903, Huntsville, Tenn.
d. Apr. 24, 1949, bur. Flagler
Memorial Cemetery, Miami, Fla.

H-1 Clyde Ernest Foster, Jr.
(A22269521-8th)
b. Sept. 4, 1924, Dayton, Ohio
m. Jeanne Lee Griffin,
Jan. 17, 1946 (1st)
b. Nov. 4, 1925
m. Delores Singer, June 4, 1966,
Racine, Wis. (2nd)

I-1 James Ernest Foster
(A222695211-9th)
b. Sept. 16, 1946, Miami, Florida
m. Annette Marie Ritchie, Nov.
26, 1966, Tiajuana, Mexico
b. Apr. 12, 1948,
Breckinridge, Minn.

J-1 Susanne Marie Foster
(A2226952111-10th)
b. July 4, 1967,
Los Angeles, Calif.

I-2 Thomas Currie Foster
(A222695212-9th)
b. Feb. 9, 1952, Miami, Fla.

I-3 Jeannette Lee Foster
(A22269213-9th)
b. Sept. 21, 1955, Miami, Fla.

H-2 Martha Lou Foster (A22269522-8th)
b. Feb. 24, 1926, Miami, Fla.
m. Robert David Butt, June 2, 1945,
Knoxville, Tenn.
b. Sept. 12, 1927, Knoxville, Tenn.

I-1 Donna Louise Butt (A222695221-
By Assignment)
b. Dec. 23, 1951, Miami, Fla.

H-3 Charles Sanders Foster
(A22269523-8th)
b. July 8, 1927, Dayton, Ohio
d. Nov. 8, 1968, Miami, Fla.
m. Sheila Maureen Murphy, Aug.
14, 1949, Miami, Fla.
b. Sept. 28, 1929, Westport, Conn.

I-1 Charles Paul Foster (A222695231-9th)
b. Mar. 3, 1951, Miami, Fla.

I-2 Timothy Sanders Foster
(A222695232-9th)
b. Jan. 27, 1952, Miami, Fla.

I-3 Stephen Andrew Foster
(A222695233-9th)
b. Jan. 30, 1955, Miami, Fla.

H-4 Paul Norman Foster (A22269524-8th)
b. May 25, 1932, Dayton, Ohio
m. Maria Carmel DiManbro, Apr. 5,
1956, Miami, Fla.
b. June 4, 1929, New York
(No issue)

G-3 Charles Edmond Winger (A2226953-7th)
b. Feb. 26, 1908, Celina, Ohio
m. Ruth Naomi Holsattle, Oct. 5, 1939,
Dayton, Ohio
b. 1907

H-1 Charles Edmond Winger, Jr.
(A22269531-8th)
b. June 19, 1941, Dayton, Ohio
m. Unmarried

H-2   Thomas Allen Winger (A22269532-8th)
b. Mar. 9, 1944, Dayton, Ohio
m. Unmarried

G-4   Howard Franklin Winger (A2226954-7th)
b. Aug. 2, 1910, Dayton, Ohio
d. Mar. 18, 1943 at sea
(No issue)

G-5   Russell Beck Winger (A2226955-7th)
b. Jan. 21, 1913, Dayton, Ohio
m. Emma Lou Stevenson
b. July 20, 1919, Bellfountain, Ohio

H-1   Susan Lynne Winger (A22269551-8th)
b. Aug. 4, 1944, Bellfountain, Ohio
m. Wayne Eldon Chapman, Feb. 23,
1963, Bellfountain, Ohio

I-1   Steven Russell Chapman
(A222695511-9th)
b. Dec. 9, 1964, Bellfountain, O.

I-2   Wayne Joseph Chapman
(A222695512-9th)
b. Jan. 2, 1966, Bellfountain, O.

F-4   Luallen (Allen) Winger (A222698-6th)
b. Jan. 1, 1882, Mercer County, Ohio
d. Nov. 5, 1900, Celina, Ohio
(No issue)

F-5   Carey Edmond Winger (A222699-6th)
b. Sept. 19, 1884, Mercer County, Ohio
d. Aug. 5, 1946, Dayton, Ohio
m. Anna Reigelsperger, Nov. 5, 1919,
Ft. Recovery, Ohio
(No issue)

CHAPTER SEVENTEEN

The Winger Sisters of Ohio

IDA MAE WINGER (A222694) of the sixth generation was born December 21, 1873, in Darke County and died July 25, 1875, in the same county. She is buried in Tea Cup Cemetery near Osgood and York.

Left to right: Amanda Ellen Winger Pierstorff (A222696), Henrietta (Attie) Winger Hoenie (A222697) and Della Frances Winger Evans Fetzer (A222692).

Amanda Ellen Winger (A222696)

Amanda Ellen Winger (A222696) of the sixth generation was born August 9, 1878, on the Joseph Winger (A22269) farm near Osgood in Patterson Township, Darke County, Ohio. The full account of her earlier life is recorded with that of her parents and brothers and sisters in the Joseph Winger (A22269) story. As reported earlier, she married Franklin John Pierstorff, September 6, 1894.

Both Amanda (A222696) and her husband, Franklin Pierstorff, were interested in family history. Amanda, years ago, corresponded with the writer and others in an effort to secure the early history of the Winger family. Franklin Pierstorff, who was a schoolteacher, farmer and businessman, was born December 23, 1871, on a farm near Celina. During the course of his career, he and his family lived in Celina, Lima and Lebanon, Ohio. Amanda Ellen (A222696) died August 8, 1959, in Dayton, Ohio. Franklin, her husband, died October 27, 1954, near Lebanon, Ohio. Both are buried in Swamp College Cemetery near Celina.

At Swamp College Cemetery.

The Two Sons

Amanda (A222696) and Frank Pierstorff had two sons of the seventh generation. Rolland Franklin Pierstorff (A2226961) was born near Celina, April 13, 1896. He attended the public schools in Celina and later became a telegraph operator for the Western Union Telegraph Company, a position which he held until 1917. At that time he enlisted in the United States Army Signal Corps, July 2, 1917, and was sent to the European Theater during World War I on June 12, 1918. He was in three major offensives, Oise-Aisne,

Aisne-Marne and Meuse Argonne. At the end of the war he served in the Army of Occupation for seven months on the Rhine River. He returned to the United States August 1, 1919, and was honorably discharged August 7, 1919.

Rolland Pierstorff (A2226961) returned to the Western Union Telegraph Company upon resumption of civilian life. Thereafter he joined the American Telephone and Telegraph Company as a tech-

Left to right: Rolland Franklin Pierstorff (A2226961), Amanda Ellen Winger Pierstorff (A222696), Robert John Pierstorff (A2226962) and Frank J. Pierstorff.

nician. There he had a long and distinguished career of 37 years. He retired in 1957 to his country home near Lebanon, Ohio. Rolland Pierstorff (A2226961) married Edna Cecilia Watson in Lima, Ohio, April 22, 1922. She was born January 24, 1899. The Pierstorffs had no children.

In their retirement years the Pierstorffs became world travelers. They have traveled around the world and have frequently joined trailer caravans to remote sectors of the North and South American

Continents. They usually spent winters in Acapulco, Mexico. The rest of the year they lived a rural and restful life in their Ohio farm near Lebanon and Mason, Ohio.

Rolland Franklin Pierstorff (A2-226961) as a member of the United States Signal Corps during World War I.

While this history was in preparation, Rolland and his wife, Edna, visited our home in Tucson, Arizona, early in December 1969. Rolland, who had always been like a brother to the writer, enjoyed himself to the fullest. It was a happy parting as the Pierstorffs left for Acapulco, not knowing that was the last time we were to see each other. Less than a month later we received the sad news that Rolland Pierstorff had died suddenly of a heart attack. He died in Acapulco, his winter home, December 28, 1969. After considerable difficulty in Mexico, his body was brought to his home near Lebanon, Ohio, where final rights were held Friday, January 2, 1970. He was buried in the Rose Hill Cemetery, Mason, Ohio.

The second son of Amanda (A222696) and Frank Pierstorff was Robert John Pierstorff (A2226962) of the seventh generation. He was born in Celina, August 29, 1900. He attended the public schools in Celina and Lima. As a young man he had an active mind and always was alert to his environment. He was athletically minded and as a youngster loved to swim in the old reservoir, now Grand Lake. He resided in Dayton, Ohio, for many years, where he was a machinist for General Motors. He married Ursula Carey of Detroit,

Michigan. They had one child, Ellen Ursula Pierstorff (A22269621), who lives in California. Robert John Pierstorff (A2226962) died February 4, 1966, and is buried in Dayton.

Attie Winger (A222697)

Henrietta (Attie) Winger (A222697) of the sixth generation, often referred to as Hannah, was born in Darke County, Patterson Township, near the village of Osgood, May 20, 1880. The history of her early life is recorded in the previous chapter. She led an exemplary life which was devoted fully to her family. She remained close to the side of her father and mother, always there to lend a helping

Henrietta (Attie) Winger Hoenie (A222697), Esther Mary Hoenie Deitrick Lymes (A2226971), Ruth Helen Hoenie Mendenhall (A2-226972) in front, and George Nelson Hoenie.

hand. Her father, Joseph Winger (A22269), spent his declining days in her shadow where he always felt safe and secure.

Henrietta (A222697) married George Nelson Hoenie of a thrifty and devoted family in Celina, September 5, 1900. They set up housekeeping on Wayne Street in Celina where the writer often visited as a boy. It was a cheerful home, always to be remembered for a sense of humor with religious overtones. Uncle Nelson, who was a painter and decorator by trade, set the family pattern with a prayer of thanks at meal time. Aunt Attie would set a table of deliciously cooked foods that had the Pennsylvania Dutch influence, a tradition handed down from generation to generation for more than 200 years.

Attie Winger (A222697) and Nelson Hoenie had a family of three of the seventh generation, Esther Mary Hoenie (A2226971), Ruth Helen Hoenie (A2226972) and Russel Edward Hoenie (A2226973).

Esther Mary Hoenie (A2226971) and Family

Esther Mary Hoenie (A2226971) of the seventh generation was born in Celina, June 8, 1901. She has lived in Celina since childhood and attended the public schools of that city. Esther (A2226971) was devoted to her mother and was in constant attendance to Attie Hoenie (A222697) through her terminal illness. Esther married Homer Everet Deitrick in Celina, February 4, 1924. He was born in Celina, May 15, 1902, and died in the same city, December 16, 1945. After the death of Homer Deitrick, who was a barber by trade, Esther Hoenie (A2226971) married Clarence August Lymes, October 18, 1948. They were married in Lexington, Kentucky. Clarence Lymes was born June 19, 1898. He has retired from the Frigidaire Company, Dayton.

Esther (A2226971) and Homer Deitrick had one son of the eighth generation, Kenneth Eugene Deitrick (A22269711). He was born in Celina, March 7, 1925. After finishing high school in Celina, he joined the armed forces in 1943. He served overseas and was injured September 10, 1944 in Brest, France. He was discharged January 29, 1946, and was awarded the Purple Heart. The day before he was wounded, he came under machine gun fire. The man on his right and the man on his left were hit, but Kenneth Deitrick was unscathed. The strange coincidence was that the man on his left, a total stranger, also was named Kenneth Deitrick. Kenneth Deitrick (A22269711) is a barber by trade.

Kenneth Deitrick (A22269711) married Mary Elizabeth Schulte, May 18, 1948, in Celina. She was born in Osgood, April 23, 1924. They have four children of the ninth generation, all born in Celina. Nancy Kay Deitrick (A222697111) was born January 14, 1949. Susan Elaine Deitrick (A222697112) was born January 12, 1951. Linda Lee Deitrick (A22269113) was born April 12, 1955. The final child, Karen Luedna Deitrick (A222697114) was born June 23, 1956. Nancy Kay Deitrick (A222697111), the oldest, graduated from the Immaculate Conception High School in Celina in 1967 and attends Ohio State University's School of Cosmetology.

Ruth Helen Hoenie (A2226972) and Family

The second daughter of Attie (A222697) and Nelson Hoenie is Ruth Helen Hoenie (A2226972) of the seventh generation. She was born in Celina, October 3, 1903. She was devoted to her husband and family. She, too, attended the public schools in Celina and married Belva Thomas Mendenhall in Pioneer, Ohio, August 24, 1926. He was born in Osgood, Ohio, October 15, 1904, and died in Celina, June 10, 1964. He was a restauranteur in Celina. The Mendenhalls had three sons of the eighth generation. William Thomas Mendenhall (A22269721) was born in Celina, July 20, 1927. He

Ruth Helen Hoenie Mendenhall (A2226972) and her sister, Esther Mary Hoenie Deitrick Lymes (A2226971).

attended the public schools in Celina after which he joined the Navy. After finishing his tour of duty, he returned to Celina and joined his father in the restaurant business. Later he entered the insurance profession and has been eminently successful. He is a partner in the Stauffer-Andrews-Mendenhall Insurance Agency in Defiance, Ohio. He married Phyllis Jane Guyer in Greenville, Ohio,

June 7, 1954. She was born in Findlay, Ohio, December 30, 1932. The Mendenhalls are active in the Lutheran Church.

William (Bill) Mendenhall (A22269721) and Phyllis, his wife, have three children of the ninth generation. The first son is Thomas William Mendenhall (A222697211) born at Cambridge, Ohio, January 1, 1956. The second son is Donald Edward Mendenhall (A222697-212), who was born in Findlay, Ohio, October 21, 1957. The last child, Julie Ann Mendenhall (A222697213), was born in Findlay, Ohio, November 28, 1959.

The second son of Ruth (A2226972) and Belva Mendenhall is Donald Homer Mendenhall (A22269722) of the eighth generation, born at Wapakoneta, Ohio, May 23, 1930. He served in the United States Air Force for four years. As this is written he is a partner in The Dairy Cone in Celina. He is unmarried.

The third son of Ruth (A2226972) and Belva Mendenhall is Jerry Edward Mendenhall (A22269723) of the eighth generation. He was born in Celina, April 21, 1932. He is a graduate from the Ohio Northern Law School. He spent four years in the United States Air Force, three years in Japan in the Judge Advocate's Office. He held the rank of Captain when he retired from the Air Force. He is now an attorney for the Central Life Insurance Company in Dallas, Texas. He is unmarried.

The Last Rites

The last-born child to Attie (A222697) and Nelson Hoenie was Russel Edward Hoenie (A2226973). He was born in Celina, February 6, 1909, and died April 9, 1911. He is buried in the North Grove Cemetery in Celina.

During her terminal illness, Aunt Attie (A222697), told her daughter, Esther Hoenie Lymes (A2226971), "Esther, I love both you and Ruth, you are all I have, but I don't want to live longer, I want to go home." She said that her loved ones were gathering. In addition to her mother, Nancy Jane Woods Winger, Attie spoke of Della Frances Winger Fetzer (A222692) and her living daughter, Harriett C. Thomas (A2226921), and with love and affection Attie held her long-gone son, Russel (A2226973), on her lap. She could not understand why those standing at her bedside could not see the ones that came from the Other Side.

The writer well remembers Russel (A2226973). As a child, he thought Russel (A2226973) to be the most beautiful baby in the world.

On July 24, 1947, Aunt Attie (A222697) wrote the writer as follows: "John, you are very special to us, even though we don't get to see you as much as we would like. We always enjoy hearing you, Esther (A2226971) and Ruth (A2226972) reminisce about your special performances as youngsters."

In 1960 we sent Aunt Attie (A222697) a special arrangement of roses to celebrate her eightieth birthday. Her loving response was a heartwarming experience.

Henrietta (Attie) Winger died in Celina, February 10, 1969. George Nelson Hoenie died in Celina, July 16, 1965. Both are buried in the North Grove Cemetery, Celina.

For the complete Family Tree starting with the issue in the sixth generation covering the families of the Winger Sisters in Ohio, please see the following tabulation.

At North Grove Cemetery, Celina, Ohio.

The Winger Sisters Family Tree

1st Hans Wenger (b. About 1430) Blumenstein, Thun
2nd Burkhard Wenger (b. About 1450) Forst, Thun
3rd Peter Wenger (b. About 1470) Wattenwil, Seftigen
4th Peter Wenger (b. About 1490) Wattenwil, Seftigen
5th Rudolfus Wenger (b. About 1510) Wattenwil, Seftigen

6th Hans Wenger (b. About 1530) Wattenwil, Seftigen

7th Rudolfus Wenger (Ch. April 5, 1566) Wattenwil-Thurnen, Seftigen

8th Peter Wenger (Ch. Dec. 13, 1607) Wattenwil-Thurnen, Seftigen

9th Hans Wenger (Ch. May 30, 1633) Wattenwil-Thurnen, Seftigen

    A Christian Wenger (A2) First Generation in America (1688-1749)

        B-1 Henry Wenger, Sr. (A22) Second Generation in America (1716-1802)

            C-1 Abraham Wenger (A222) Third Generation in America (1767-1845)

                D-1 Peter Henry Winger (A2226) Fourth Generation in America (1806-1889)

                    E-1 Joseph Levi Robinson Winger (A22269) Fifth Generation in America
b. July 17, 1848, Darke County, Ohio
d. Dec. 31, 1928, bur. Swamp College
m. Nancy Jane Woods, Apr. 5, 1868, Versailles, Ohio
  b. June 29, 1849, Darke County
  d. Mar. 16, 1911, bur. Swamp College

                        F-1 Ida Mae Winger (A222694-6th)
b. Dec. 21, 1873, Darke County
d. July 25, 1875, Darke County
(No issue)

                        F-2 Amanda Ellen Winger (A222696-6th)
b. Aug. 9, 1878, near Osgood, Ohio
d. Aug. 8, 1959, Dayton, Ohio
m. Frank J. Pierstorff, Sept. 6, 1894, Celina, Ohio
  b. Dec. 23, 1871, near Celina
  d. Oct. 27, 1954, bur. Swamp College

                            G-1 Rolland Franklin Pierstorff (A2226961-7th)
b. Apr. 13, 1896, Celina, Ohio
d. Dec. 28, 1969, Acapulco
m. Edna Cecilia Watson, Apr. 22, 1922, Lima, Ohio
  b. Jan. 24, 1899

G-2 Robert John Pierstorff (A2226962-7th)
  b. Aug. 29, 1900, Celina, Ohio
  d. Feb. 4, 1966, Dayton, Ohio
  m. Ursula Carey, Detroit, Michigan

  H-1 Ellen Ursula Pierstorff (A22269621-8th)

F-3 Henrietta (Attie) Winger (A222697-6th)
  b. May 20, 1880, Osgood, Ohio
  d. Feb. 10, 1969, Celina, bur. North Grove
  m. George Nelson Hoenie,
    Sept. 5, 1900, Celina, Ohio
    b. Jan. 15, 1877
    d. July 16, 1965, bur. North Grove

  G-1 Esther Mary Hoenie (A2226971-7th)
    b. June 8, 1901, Celina, Ohio
    m. Homer Everet Deitrick, Feb. 4,
      1924, Celina (1st)
      b. May 15, 1902, Celina, Ohio
      d. Dec. 16, 1945, Celina, Ohio
    m. Clarence August Lymes, Oct. 18,
      1948, Lexington, Ky. (2nd)
      b. June 19, 1898, Celina, Ohio

    H-1 Kenneth Eugene Deitrick
      (A22269711-8th)
      b. Mar. 7, 1925, Celina, Ohio
      m. Mary Elizabeth Schulte, May 18,
        1948, Celina, Ohio
        b. Apr. 23, 1924, Osgood, Ohio

      I-1 Nancy Kay Deitrick (A222697111-9th)
        b. Jan. 14, 1949, Celina, Ohio

      I-2 Susan Elaine Deitrick
        (A222697112-9th)
        b. Jan. 12, 1951, Celina, Ohio

      I-3 Linda Lee Deitrick (A222697113-9th)
        b. Apr. 12, 1955, Celina, Ohio

      I-4 Karen Luedna Deitrick
        (A222697114-9th)
        b. June 23, 1956

G-2 Ruth Nelson Hoenie (A2226972-7th)
    b. Oct. 3, 1903, Celina, Ohio
    m. Belva Thos. Mendenhall, Aug. 24,
    1926, Pioneer, Ohio
    b. Oct. 15, 1904, Osgood, Ohio
    d. June 10, 1964, Celina, Ohio

  H-1 William Thomas Mendenhall
    (A22269721-8th)
    b. July 20, 1927, Celina, Ohio
    m. Phyllis Jane Guyer, June 7, 1954,
    Greenville, Ohio
    b. Dec. 30, 1932, Findlay, Ohio

    I-1 Thomas William Mendenhall
      (A222697211-9th)
      b. Jan. 1, 1956, Cambridge, Ohio

    I-2 Donald Edward Mendenhall
      (A22269712-9th)
      b. Oct. 21, 1957, Findlay, Ohio

    I-3 Julie Ann Mendenhall
      (A22269713-9th)
      b. Nov. 28, 1959, Findlay, Ohio

  H-2 Donald Homer Mendenhall
    (A22269722-8th)
    b. May 23, 1930, Wapakoneta, Ohio
    m. Unmarried

  H-3 Jerry Edward Mendenhall
    (A22269723-8th)
    b. Apr. 21, 1932, Celina, Ohio
    m. Unmarried

G-3 Russel Edward Hoenie (A2226973-7th)
    b. Feb. 6, 1909, Celina, Ohio
    d. Apr. 9, 1911, Celina,
    bur. North Grove

CHAPTER EIGHTEEN

Della Frances Winger of Indiana

DELLA FRANCES WINGER (A222692) of the sixth generation was born December 21, 1870, on the Joseph Winger (A22269) farm near Osgood in Patterson Township, Darke County, Ohio. She was the daughter of Joseph Levi Winger (A22269), the granddaughter of Peter Henry Winger (A2226), the great-granddaughter of Abraham Wenger (A222), the great-great-granddaughter of Henry Wenger, Sr. (A22), and the great-great-great-granddaughter of Christian Wenger (A2). The full account of her earlier life and that of her children, Harriett (A2226921) and Joseph (A2226922), is recorded with that of the parents, brothers and sisters in the chapter giving the story of Joseph Levi Winger (A22269).

Della Frances Winger (A222692) first married David Edward Evans in Decatur, Indiana, June 27, 1889. After his loss, as reported earlier, she married John Adam Fetzer in Decatur, Indiana, June 12, 1899. After less than four years John A. Fetzer passed away, February 11, 1903. She remained a widow for 14 years, and then married Irvin Ianthus Pyle, December 28, 1917.

To Della Frances (A222692) and David Evans two children of the seventh generation were born. Harriett Cecelia (A2226921) was born on a farm near Decatur (Monmouth), Indiana, September 2, 1890. Joseph Evans (A2226922) was born on the same farm, February 15, 1892. He died September 15, 1897, in Decatur, and is buried in the family cemetery on the farm, but is memorialized in Maplewood Cemetery, Decatur, with the Fetzer family.

A Series of Letters

Della Frances (A222692) after the loss of her husband, David Evans, received a number of letters from her family. Her brothers, Frank (A222693) and Charles (A222695), moved to Decatur to be of help. A digest of the communications between the Winger brothers and sisters, as well as the parents, showed the deep family regard and love that passed between them. On one occasion, Joseph Winger (A22269) ·wrote that Nancy Jane, his wife, was ill and that they would have to postpone their visit. He said he was homesick to see his boys and girls. Later Charles (A222695) wrote that he was coming to Decatur and asked Della Frances (A222692) to meet him at the train. He said he had a lot to tell her.

Left to right: Henrietta (Attie) Winger Hoenie (A222697), Della Frances Winger Evans Fetzer (A222692) and Amanda Ellen Winger Pierstorff (A222696).

Frank Pierstorff, the husband of Amanda (A222696), stated that his wife was ill and could not write. He reported that as he was writing, all the Winger family was attending Sunday afternoon dinner. He spoke of a land transaction entered into by Joseph Winger (A22269) that had not turned out satisfactorily and that "Grandpa was dissatisfied." At another time Amanda (A222696) wrote a letter of thanks to Della Frances (A222692) for an Easter hat. On another occasion Amanda wrote that she feared there was illness because she had not heard from Della Frances (A222692) and also that she had been disappointed that the folks did not come to visit on Decoration Day. Another letter from Frank Pierstorff said that Amanda (A222696) had a good cry when she found out that Della Frances (A222692) would not be able to make a scheduled visit.

Several letters from Attie Hoenie (A222697) indicate her love and concern for the welfare of Della Frances (A222692) and the children. Attie always wrote concerning Pa (A22269) and Mom Winger and, of course, there were references to her family and brothers. There was always concern for Ed (A222699) who had proclivities for misfortune.

Frank (A222693) and his wife, Belle Winger, returned to Celina after having been married and living in Decatur. One letter asked Della Frances (A222692) to inquire of Buck Baker if he had a job available in Decatur for Frank Winger (A222693). He said that he had had experience on the C.H.&D. Railroad. Frank (A222693) was out of work because the saw mill in Celina was being torn down and shipped to the southern part of the United States. The letter stated that Emma, the wife of Charles (A222695), had traded her house in an arrangement that did not turn out satisfactorily and, as a result, she was having "smothering spells." Another said, "You ought to be here. We have wonderful roasting ears, beans and cabbage. The pickles have turned out just fine." Frank (A222693) at another time complained about his kidney trouble and that he had been to seven different doctors without relief. It would seem that the vicissitudes of those times reflect problems of living not unlike those of today.

John A. Fetzer

The meeting of Della Frances (A222692) and John A. Fetzer may be of some interest. John A. Fetzer had come to Decatur from Uniondale, Indiana, in the fall of 1898. He established a business which was advertised as "Dealer In Bicycles And Sundries, Repairing, Reenameling, Vulcanizing, Braising And Lathe Work." By hard work he established his shop and became a part of the business community.

The Decatur band had earned quite a reputation for itself. As time passed, the band was in real demand and made regular trips to nearby communities. This was in addition to the regular band concerts which were held in Decatur. In December 1898, the band was invited to give a concert in Fort Wayne, Indiana. My mother,

Della Frances Winger (A222692), was on her way to Fort Wayne to do some Christmas shopping. She, together with friends by the name of Stoneburner, boarded the train that was carrying the Decatur band to Fort Wayne.

Della Frances Winger Fetzer (A222692)

Her friends knew John A. Fetzer and introduced him to my mother. I often heard her say how impressed she was with Mr. John A. Fetzer. She said, "He was real nice and was he ever handsome." A few days later, on January 2, 1899, Mother received a letter from John A. Fetzer. Among other things, it said:

> Please pardon me for addressing you and my awkward letter; however, since our introduction it seems as though I would like to become better acquainted with you. If this is satisfactory, when or where can I see or meet you. Will you kindly inform me by return mail?
>
> Yours very respectfully,
> *John A. Fetzer*

On January 3rd my mother replied: "Dear Friend: Your note received with pleasure and I can only say that I, too, would like to become more acquainted with you." The letter went on to arrange a meeting for the following Saturday night. Two days later another letter came from my father confirming the date and, of course, that was the beginning of the romance that led to engagement and marriage. The wedding ceremony took place June 12, 1899. Since my

John Adam Fetzer

father was a member of the Lutheran Church, they were married in that church in Decatur. Jim Ball, Harriett's (A2226921) step-grandfather, was the principal witness.

Family Circle

The new couple established a home at 312 North Tenth Street, Decatur. Since both had been married previously, life started in earnest when young Homer L. Fetzer at the age of six and Harriett C. Evans (A2226921) at the age of nine united in the family circle to become brother and sister. In no time the parents were as devoted to the two children as if each were the parent of both. The children attended school with the usual family successes, failures, kid pranks and what-have-you. The stories are legion concerning the activities of Homer and Harriett.

312 North Tenth Street, Decatur, Indiana.

Mother looked out the window one day and saw the minister of her church coming to pay a visit. The two children were in the house. Mother, feeling that the house was not presentable due to the cleaning process, decided that she would not respond when the minister knocked on the door. In the meantime, she warned both children that they should remain very quiet. Both of them were on the floor immediately next to the door. After knocking several times, the minister concluded that no one was at home, whereupon he took from his wallet his calling card, stooped and pushed it under the door. Young Homer, seeing the card coming through, immediately reached down, got hold of the card and pulled it the rest of the way.

Another family episode came about when my mother was visiting her family in Ohio. Apparently my father had stayed home to tend his business. On June 13, 1900, he wrote to my mother in Ohio as follows: "Everything looks natural around the place except the weeds are getting a good start in the cucumber patch." In the same letter he advised Mother, who was not feeling too well at the time, to "take Purina, that will take the wrinkles out of you." He then said, "This week end I shall come to Celina if I can. I will ride my 'wheel' over there." The distance to Celina was 15 miles over rough roads. The bicycle he was to ride was the large front wheel affair like the "wheel" he had ridden as a boy to Logan, Ohio, a distance of 175 miles.

Father Out of Town

On another occasion my father had gone to Wilshire, Ohio, to handle some engineering matters. In October he  wrote to my mother expressing concern that he had not heard from her. He said that Halloween was coming up and that she should get a neighbor woman to stay with her that night. He also said that she should keep an eye out the back window "for you never can tell when the boys will come along and push over 'you-know-what.'"

In the sequence of events, my father and mother were discussing possible names to be assigned to their forthcoming child. Both parents hoped it would be a boy. To be prepared, however, they selected a number of names for both boys and girls. Mother was having some difficulty reaching agreement with my father concerning the name for a boy. After days, and near exhaustion, Mother realized that the name John A. Fetzer wanted was none other than John. On March 25, 1901, a boy was born. His name became John Earl Fetzer. That boy was the writer.

John A. Fetzer Takes an Engineering Course

During the year of 1901, my father, who had wanted to be an engineer and had never had the opportunity for formal training, decided to take a correspondence course from the International Correspondence Schools of Scranton, Pennsylvania. In his papers I found one of his lessons on gas engines and mathematics which had been graded by his instructor, F. H. Healy, on February 20th of that year. He received a grade of 100 on that particular lesson and received the following letter from his instructor: "On examining your work on Section 1, we find it to be very satisfactory. We trust you will retain a like interest throughout the remainder of your course. Wishing you success, we are Yours very truly, International Correspondence Schools, School of Mathematics."

Father Builds an Auto

At the time my father was trying to build a career, the horseless carriage was just coming into being. In 1901 there were already experimenters in the field. Such names as Olds, Ford, Maxwell, Apperson, Stanley, White, Franklin and others were known in their

342

own areas as makers of the "auto carriage." John A. Fetzer joined
the others when he designed and built a "buggy with a one-lung
motor." It caused a lot of excitement in Decatur, Indiana. As time
went on, he developed a set of plans purported to be "an advanced
design." From time to time he would go over these plans with my
mother. Together they would plan their future on the manufacture
of this vehicle.

While this was transpiring in Decatur, Indiana, Elwood G.
Haynes, a prosperous businessman in Kokomo, Indiana, had designed and had engaged the Apperson brothers to build a "fine-

This creature of the "horseless carriage" age is a reminder that some technological progress has been made.

working model car." Haynes, a Johns Hopkins graduate in science,
not only was making progress with his "carriage," but he managed to
hold a position as Field Superintendent of the Natural Gas Company
of Kokomo. From time to time, while in the field, he would come to
Decatur where he learned of my father's success with his own
"horseless carriage." Mr. Haynes came to see my father and suggested a merger of their interests so they could take advantage of
their combined talents. My father declined, stating that he had
plans to go either to Detroit or possibly California to start his development. Within a matter of weeks my father was dead. Mr.
Haynes went on to considerable success for his day. Some in the
community say that after my father's death, the plans found their
way into the Haynes development, but this is completely without
foundation in fact, as based in the record. There does seem to be
considerable mystery about the disposition of the plans. They never
could be located among my father's effects.

John A. Fetzer was descended in the tenth generation of Fetzers,
as follows: Bastian Fetzer (1550-1625, 1st), George Fetzer (1591-
1660, 2nd), George Fetzer (1624-1705, 3rd), Paul Fetzer (1652-1735,

4th), Paul Fetzer (1693-1735, 5th), Jacob Fetzer (1733-1803, 6th), Jacob Frederick Fetzer (1768-1821, 7th), Jacob Frederick Fetzer (1806-1880, 8th), John Adam Fetzer (1840-1882, 9th), John Adam Fetzer (1870-1903, 10th). For a full account of the Fetzer family, see *One Man's Family* by John E. Fetzer.

My father, John A. Fetzer, after a short illness, died from pneumonia February 11, 1903. He is buried in the Maplewood Cemetery, Decatur. Ten weeks after my father's death, Walter Adam Fetzer (A2226924), was born April 25, 1903. Walter (A2226924) died August 14th that same year. He, too, is buried in the Maplewood Cemetery, Decatur.

Della Frances (A222692) Enters Business

After my father's death, Mother Della (A222692) entered the millinery business. She established her own hat shop in the same building that previously had been my father's establishment. She had some degree of success in spite of the fact that the total family load was hers. We lived in Decatur until I reached the age of six years.

The Dave Sprunger Horseless Carriage

The one highlight I can remember as a child was the day my sister Harriett's (A2226921) Uncle Dave Sprunger, a descendant of the well-known Bern, Indiana, Swiss family, bought a new "motocycle." This was the four-wheel horseless carriage made by the Reeves Pully Company of Columbus, Indiana. The steering mechanism was operated from the high back seat. This "motocycle" was being developed at the same time Haynes was working on his horseless carriage in Decatur.

Uncle Dave invited Mother, my sister Harriett and me to ride in the horseless carriage to the German picnic 12 miles away. We started at 11 o'clock in the morning, allowing ourselves one hour for the trip. Of course, all of the other German families were going by horse and buggy, so they left quite early in the morning. On the way to the picnic we passed a few horses and buggies on the road and, of course, they were forced into clouds of dust. There was the usual rearing of horses and excitement galore.

We got along just fine until we pulled over the hill to the old wooden bridge crossing the St. Marys River. In the middle of the bridge the chain-driven car crashed into the side of the wooden bars because of a broken chain. It took Uncle Dave quite a while to repair the chain and put the car on the road again. In the mean-

John E. Fetzer at the age of five after the famous ride in the "motocycle" and shortly before life in Decatur, Indiana, was terminated.

time the horses and buggies passed us by and we did not reach the picnic until most of the show was over. The car did cause a great deal of excitement with the onlookers.

When we started back Uncle Dave could not get the motor to go. One horse and buggy after the other pulled out and we were left alone. The occupants of each buggy, as they proudly drove by, gave us rather haughty looks and knowing smiles. Uncle Dave, speaking quite broken English, had some uncomplimentary things to say about the pontifical air of the "darned Dutch." Eventually he got the car started and we went flying to town on the old gravel road. We soon overtook the horses and buggies and let them eat our dust. As I looked back there was "weeping and wailing" and a goodly number of clenched fists were beating the air. When we got back to Decatur, the car developed ignition trouble and Uncle Dave could not stop the motor, so we drove round and round the court-house until the motor ran out of gas. Naturally all of this gave me the thrill of my life as a child. I well recall that my mother took a dim view of the whole thing. She advised Uncle Dave not ever to invite us again to take a ride in his "motocycle." The next week Uncle Dave sold his horseless carriage and never mentioned it again.

A Series of Moves

Shortly thereafter, we moved to Frankfort, Indiana, where my mother established a store near the center of the town. About 1908 the local newspaper carried a story which gives a glowing description in the terms of that day:

Mrs. Della Fetzer, Milliner

There is one among the many fine stores of Frankfort that fills a large place in the estimation of all the matrons and maids of this city and county. It is the millinery parlors conducted by Mrs. Della Fetzer on the west side of South Main Street, just two doors from the public square. There are reasons for its popularity among the ladies of the town and country. Mrs. Fetzer is a past mistress in the millinery art — it is really one of the fine arts — and in her parlor are found ever the latest creations.

Mrs. Fetzer each season makes a business trip embracing the big cities of the East to learn at first hand just what fashion has decreed to be the proper thing in millinery wear and Frankfort ladies get the benefit of what she has learned and approved. She has the creative instinct herself in large measure and when she designs an adaptation of a prevailing fashion it must be admitted to be an improvement artistically on the original.

In her parlors are seen all the differing styles of hats in materials and trimmings. In her workshop Mrs. Fetzer employs eight milliners and all of them are kept busy at their art under her instructions and direction. She has succeeded in her business and is prospering because of her practical knowledge of it and the needs of her customers. Her counsel to those who seek it regarding the hat most fitting to their respective requirements is scarcely less valuable than the quality of her stock is meritorious. Her stock of pretty trimmings in flowers and ribbons of the fitting combinations and colors is extensive, giving the widest range in choice and all of them are good serviceable and durable. She knows just what the fashionable belles of New York and Baltimore and Washington are wearing this fall and will wear this winter and all the prevailing color-tones and trimming materials favored of fashion can be examined in the parlors of Mrs. Fetzer. It is good in many ways for the ladies of Frankfort and Clinton County that such a millinery store and such a clever woman in her art are in this community.

Harriett Cecelia Evans (A2226921)

The early life of Harriett (A2226921), first-born and only daughter of Della ·Winger (A222692) Evans, has been recorded in detail in earlier chapters. It had been the intention of John A. Fetzer, after his marriage to Della (A222692), to legally adopt Harriett (A222-6921). However, his premature death prevented its fulfillment. Harriett (A2226921) always affirmatively considered John A. Fetzer her father. Through the years she has referred to him as "papa" and literally worshiped the ground he walked.

As a young woman, Harriett (A2226921), helped to operate the millinery establishment, sometimes directing the trimmers, sometimes the sales. Among the employed personnel were Delia Woods, Zulah Miller and Margaret Deal. The latter was the sister of Charlie Deal, third baseman for the Detroit Tigers. He was later to become

Back row: Harriett Evans (A2226921), Margaret Deal and Delia Woods. Front row: Zulah Miller and Della Frances Winger Fetzer (A222692).

Harriett Evans Ribble
(A2226921)

my hero after Detroit traded him to the Boston National League Club which won the World Series in 1914. In due course Harriett (A2226921) met Frederick Lloyd Ribble, a dispatcher on the Wabash Railroad. They were married November 1, 1911, in the Grace M.E. Church in Stewart, Illinois. Since Fred Ribble was stationed in Lafayette, Indiana, their married life was begun in West Lafayette, Indiana. As a boy of 11, I moved from Frankfort, Indiana, to West Lafayette, where I lived with Harriett (A2226921) and Fred Ribble while my mother remained in Frankfort to dispose of her millinery business. This she did and the next year Mother (A222692) and I established our home on Wallace Avenue in Lafayette. Harriett (A2226921) and Fred Ribble built a new home next door.

Harriett (A2226921) had her only child, Mary Elizabeth Ribble (A22269211), August 15, 1912. Unfortunately, she died that same day. She is buried in the Springdale Cemetery, Lafayette. Frederick Ribble was born March 7, 1883, at West Lebanon, Indiana. He died May 22, 1942 and is buried in the Logansport, Indiana, cemetery.

Most of her adult life, Harriett (A2226921) spent in service to others. She took a hiatus from Lafayette to associate herself with the Fetzer Broadcasting Company, WKZO, Kalamazoo, Michigan. Here she became Traffic Supervisor while indulging herself in an interesting hobby. While she was associated with the broadcasting business, she was known as "Aunt Hattie." The following account appeared in a Kalamazoo newspaper while she was with WKZO:

Harriett Ribble, Hobbyist

Hobbies, hobbies everywhere!

Wherever your hobby writer chances to stray he finds someone with an interesting hobby. Kalamazoo is certainly becoming hobby-conscious.

This week I chanced to stray into the studios of WKZO. There I overheard Harriett Ribble discussing her collection of dishes. Thereupon I set to work, delving into the history of her hobby.

Mrs. Ribble inherited her love of beautiful dishes from her mother, who for many years collected china and glassware from all parts of the country.

Haviland China had always interested her more at the age of 18. She added several sets of gold band Haviland dishes. As you collectors of Haviland know, it has almost become impossible to buy gold-band dishes now. Which, of course, makes these sets priceless.

Gradually she has added more beautiful and unusual pieces until now she has two china closets filled and many more dishes stored away, totalling almost 400, a complete service for 50 persons. One set is of the most beautiful deep wine-colored glass, she says; another is of a deep, aquamarine shade.

"Aunt Hattie's" great-great-great-grandmother collected a set of midnight blue dishes at her home in Germany. These she passed on to her daughter and so on down the line to Mrs. Ribble. To quote Aunt Hattie: "Never have I seen dishes of such a beautiful shade. It is difficult to explain the color — sometimes it is navy blue — then again a hint of purple seems to display itself." This is one of the oldest sets in her collection and we believe she can be rightfully proud of it.

"I wouldn't know what to do without this hobby of mine," she says. "It gives me so much satisfaction and the large variety of beautiful glassware provides me with dishes for every occasion and every style of food."

Members of the WKZO staff say her beautiful glassware fits in perfectly with the excellent meals she serves. "She is one grand cook," we are told, and these beautiful dishes do justice to the perfectly delightful foods which she prepares.

Returns to Lafayette

Due to the advanced age of our mother, Della (A222692), Hattie (A2226921) and I agreed that she should return to Lafayette to look after her. She returned to Mother's (A222692) home at 1808 Thompson Street where she was to remain a number of years. Here she met and married Peter Edward Nash, June 19, 1944. They were married in the First Baptist Church, Lafayette. Among the members of the family in attendance was Mother Della's (A222692) sister, Amanda

Winger (A222696) Pierstorff. There was a warm family reunion. Peter Nash was a trade union executive and a gentleman of the first order. His marriage with Harriett proved to be compatible and happy. However, misfortune struck again. Peter Nash was injured in a construction accident, developing internal injuries that resulted in death. He died February 25, 1947, in the Methodist Hospital in Indianapolis. Even though he was born in Pittsburgh, June 1, 1882, spending most of his life in the midwest, he chose to be buried in Lafayette where he and Hattie (A2226921) will lie side by side in the Rest Haven Cemetery.

Scott Hutchins Thomas (born May 20, 1878), a brother-in-law of Fred Ribble, Harriett's (A2226921) first husband, had lost his wife. He and Harriett (A2226921) had known each other for forty years. Both had reached the age in life when marriage seems to enhance one's sense of security. They were married July 21, 1949, in the First Baptist Church, Lafayette. Again misfortune struck. After a long illness, Scott Thomas died August 19, 1955, and is buried in the Spring Hill Cemetery, Danville, Illinois.

Thomas Family

It may be of some interest to note that William Sidney Thomas, the brother of Scott Thomas, helped in the capture of Geronomo in the Apache Indian War with General Miles. Fort Thomas in Arizona was named after him. His grandfather was a close personal friend of Abraham Lincoln when the latter was Attorney General for the State of Illinois. Benjamin Morris Thomas, a first cousin of Scott Thomas, was Lieutenant Governor of New Mexico. The Thomas family came from Wales to the United States in 1712. The ancestor of Scott Hutchins Thomas was Elder William Thomas, a minister of the Baptist Church in Llanwarnath, Momouthshire, Wales. He was born in 1678. The Baptist Church in that city was organized in 1652 and rededicated in 1695 while Elder William Thomas was minister. This branch of the Thomas family first settled in Hilltown, Bucks County, Pennsylvania. A complete genealogy of this branch of the Thomas family was written in the earlier days.

My wife, Rhea Yeager Fetzer, and I visited this church in Llanwarnath, Momouthshire, Wales, in 1952.

Della Frances (A222692) Marries Irvin Pyle

In the meantime Mother Della (A222692), after 14 years, had married Irvin Ianthus Pyle. They were married in St. Joseph, Michigan, December 28, 1917, five years after we had moved to Lafayette, Indiana. As a young woman, she had known the Pyle family in Decatur, Indiana. Irvin Pyle was Superintendent of the Waterworks in West Lafayette, Indiana.

Della Frances Winger (A222692) at the age of 85.

Pyle Family

The ancestors of Irvin I. Pyle were Isaac and Mary Pyle, who came from Holland to the state of Pennsylvania as a young couple. They moved from Pennsylvania to Darke County, Ohio, and then to Celina, Ohio, and thence to Decatur, Indiana. This was a coincidental itinerary to that of our branch of the Winger family. Isaac and Mary Pyle had a family of nine among whom was Washington Pyle, the father of Irvin I. Pyle, and Joshua Pyle, the father of Earl William Pyle, who adopted Ernie Pyle, the famous war correspondent of World War II. Washington Pyle (1844-1936) was a member of Company G of the 13th Indiana Cavalry of the War between the States. He is buried in the Maplewood Cemetery, Decatur, Indiana, as is Irvin Ianthus Pyle, who was born March 19, 1869. He died at the age of 95 on April 13, 1964.

My sister, Harriett (A2226921), spent many years of her life in devoted care of Mother, nursing her through her terminal illness.

Mother passed away at the age of 87 on February 12, 1958, in La-fayette, Indiana. She was placed beside my father in the Maplewood Cemetery, Decatur, Indiana, where I had erected an appropriate ancestral monument.

See the Della Frances Winger (A222692) of Indiana Family Tree immediately following the chapter entitled John Earl Fetzer (A222-6923) of Michigan.

At Maplewood Cemetery, Decatur, Indiana.

CHAPTER NINETEEN

John Earl Fetzer of Michigan

SKETCHES OF my earlier life are found throughout this chronicle. There were three great influences in my life. The first was my mother, Della (A222692), and the second was my sister, Harriett Thomas (A2226921). The third was Frederick Lloyd Ribble, the first husband of my sister, Harriett (A2226921). As for the latter, I must give him credit for introducing me to the field of radio. Moreover, it was he who cultivated my love for baseball, and more particularly for the Detroit Tigers.

Fred Ribble was a dispatcher on the Wabash Railroad. He taught me Morse Code and, as a wireless amateur, taught me much of the early wonders of radio, so much so that it shaped my life toward a professional career in that field.

As for baseball, he and nearly everyone else on the Old Wabash were Tiger fans. As a railroad dispatcher, he kept the wires hot giving play-by-play accounts of Tiger games in Detroit. As a boy, I joined the railroaders as an avid follower of Ty Cobb and his Detroit Tigers. I had already been introduced to baseball by Margaret Deal, the sister of Charlie Deal, third baseman for the Detroit Tigers. From the days of the Wabash Railroad excursions to Detroit to see the Tigers play, to the present time as owner of the club, I give Fred Ribble, long since gone, a salute for retaining those qualities which to me have been matters of first importance.

Hattie (A2226921) has always been much more than my sister. She has been a second mother to me, representing all of the good things that the Wingers have stood for. One time I made a speech before the law school at the University of Michigan. Hattie (A222-6921) read my remarks and said, "John, that was outstanding, I couldn't be more proud than I am right now. I can't tell you how much I love you. I always have. Remember, whatever may happen,

I will always be with you." Even though her summation was over-stated, her devotion is typical of all the Winger women. They are famous for overprotecting their own.

JOHN E. FETZER

Picture of an oil portrait presented by Mr. Yetsuo Higa, prominent Tokyo business leader, to John E. Fetzer in November, 1962, while he was heading the Detroit Tiger delegation on the baseball tour of Japan. It is the custom in Japan for politicians, businessmen and other prominent figures to gather at their favorite tea houses to discuss many aspects of their business operations. The presentation was made by Mr. Higa in the usual Japanese tradition at the famous Nakagawa Tea House in Toyko.

A Mother's Letters

As for my mother (A222692), it was she who made a lifelong sacrifice on behalf of her children and for me, in particular. She wrote me scores of letters through my school days and middle life that brought heartwarming memories as I reviewed them in preparation for this book.

On March 30, 1925, she quoted Washington Irving as follows: "There is an enduring tenderness in the love of a mother to a son that transcends all affections of the heart." On February 10, 1926, she said, "Keep your heart free from hate." In a letter dated November 24, 1942, she said, "No one ever had a better son than you. It is my prayer that in the next world we will have the time, which has been denied to us here, to say all the things that our hearts cry to deliver." On May 15, 1943, she said, "No matter where you are, you will always be in my heart." Other letters from 1944 to 1948 alluded to my success in life, but always warned that possessions can blight a life. In November 1948, she said, "I pray for you each morning and each night. I thank God for a blessed son." She went on to say, "I am lonesome for you. At times I feel that I can reach out and touch you. Sometimes I hear your voice." In her last letters, she expressed concern that I should lead an affirmatively spiritual life. Finally, as she could scarcely hold a pen in hand, she indicated some twenty Biblical scriptures that I should read that would cover every vicissitude of life. Her final words to me as I saw her for the last time were, "Pray, John, pray."

It was she who encouraged the writer to finish high school in West Lafayette, Indiana, and spend a time in the Electrical Engineering School of Purdue University, studying such special radio communication courses as Professor R. V. Achetz could provide. Later she pressed me to continue my education even against great odds. Her influence is easily summed up in a poem by an unknown author. As a Winger mother would, she framed it and kept it on my bedroom wall for many years.

To My Son

Do you know that your soul is of mine such a part
That it seems to be fibre and core of my heart
None other can please me, as you, dear, can do;
None other can love me, or praise me, as you.

Remember the world will be quick with a blame,
If shadow or stain ever darkens your name.
"Like mother, like son," is a saying so true,
The world will judge largely the mother by you.

Be yours then the task, if task it may be,
To force the proud world to do homage to thee;
Be sure it will say, when its verdict you've won,
"She reaped as she sowed. Lo! This is her Son."

Who's Who in America

The material concerning the author, John Earl Fetzer, is a secretarial compilation from *Who's Who in America*, the *International Yearbook and Statemen's Who's Who, Eminent Americans, Michigan Through the Centuries* and *One Man's Family, a History and Genealogy of the Fetzer Family*, by John E. Fetzer.

John E. Fetzer (A2226923) is president and owner of Fetzer Broadcasting Company and the Detroit Baseball Club of the American League of Professional Baseball Clubs. He was born March 25, 1901, in Decatur, Indiana, the son of John Adam and Della Frances (Winger) Fetzer (A222692). Mr. Fetzer (A2226923) married Rhea Maude Yeager on July 19, 1926, in Benton Harbor, Michigan. His educational background includes attendance at Purdue University in 1921, where he studied radio communications. In 1926 he graduated from the National Radio Institute in Washington, D.C. Mr. Fetzer (A2226923) attended Andrews University of Michigan, where he received the B.A. degree in 1927. In 1929 he did graduate work at the University of Michigan, studying electronics and modern physics. In 1930 he took extension courses in mathematics at the University of Wisconsin. In 1958 he received an honorary LL.D. from Western Michigan University. Mr. Fetzer's (A2226923) entire business career has been devoted to the field of radio, television and professional baseball.

From 1918 to 1920 he did laboratory and experimental work. In 1921 he was general manager of the radio department of Wolever Electric Company of Indiana and in 1923 he designed, built and operated the first educational radio broadcasting station, known as KFGZ, to be installed in Michigan.

In 1925 Mr. Fetzer (A2226923) studied abroad the economic, sociological and engineering aspects of European broadcasting systems, covering radio stations in England, Holland, Germany, Switzerland and France. In 1926 he built station WEMC of Andrews University of Michigan; in 1930 Mr. Fetzer purchased this station, changed the call letters to WKZO, and moved it to Kalamazoo, Michigan. Mr. Fetzer (A2226923) personally constructed WKZO at Kalamazoo from studio to transmitter. In 1945 he established radio station WJEF at Grand Rapids, and in 1950 inaugurated television station WKZO-TV at Kalamazoo-Grand Rapids. In 1951, Mr. Fetzer (A2226923) established the world's largest frequency modulation station, WJFM, after experimental operation in this field for a period of ten years. In 1953 he established a trusteeship for the benefit of the University of Nebraska, donating to this institution one of the foremost educational television stations in the country. From this beginning a chain of educational television stations covering the entire state of Nebraska has been developed.

National in Scope

John E. Fetzer enterprises, national in scope, are represented by offices in most principal cities of the country. A variety of personal holdings in radio, television, film production, background music franchises, Arizona land development and general enterprises require an extremely versatile management team.

Mr. Fetzer (A2226923), in 1952, became the first chairman of the Television Code Review Board of the National Association of Radio and Television Broadcasters, Washington, D.C. This board administers the program of self-regulation within the television industry, corresponding to the Office of Censorship of the Motion Picture Association of America. During World War II, Mr. Fetzer (A2226923) was in Washington as the United States Censor of Radio. In this position he supervised high-level security matters in the regulation of the four national radio networks and over 900 domestic radio stations in addition to 26 overseas short-wave stations.

European Theatre

In 1945, at the invitation of General Eisenhower and under the auspices of the War Department, Mr. Fetzer (A2226923) joined a study group in the European Theatre of Operations as a war correspondent analyzing the use of radio in the rehabilitation of the German people, as well as postwar communication problems, involving international radio between the United States, England, France, Russia, Germany, Italy and other European countries.

In 1952 he received a special assignment as foreign correspondent to the radio, television and newspaper editors' mission covering Europe and the Middle East, including interviews with Mayor Ernest Reuter of Berlin; Chancellor Konrad Adenauer and High Commissioner John J. McCloy, Bonn, Germany; Chancellor Leopold Figl, Vienna, Austria; Premier Marshal Tito, Belgrade, Yugoslavia; King Paul and Queen Frederika, Athens, Greece; President Celal Bayar, Istanbul, Turkey; The Shah of Iran and Premier Mohammed Mossadegh, Teheran, Iran; Premier David Ben Gurion, Tel Aviv, Israel; Pope Pius XII, Vatican City; Defence Minister Renè Pleven, Secretary of State Maurice Schumann and General deGaulle, Paris, France; General Dwight D. Eisenhower, SHAPE Headquarters, and Prime Minister Winston Churchill and Foreign Secretary Anthony Eden, London, England. Mission Radio Free Europe, Munich, Austro-Hungarian border, observing revolutionary forces, 1956. Broadcasters' good-will mission to Latin America under auspices State Department, spring 1962, where he conferred with many important heads of state, including Adolfo Lopez Mateos, President of Mexico; Dr. Manuel Prado, President of Peru; Jorge Alessandri, President of Chile; Arturo Frondizi, President of Argentina, and Eduardo Victor Haedo, President of Uruguay.

Baseball

On June 13, 1956, Mr. Fetzer (A2226923) organized the 11-man syndicate which was the successful bidder in the purchase of the Detroit Baseball Club of the American League of Professional Baseball Clubs. As one-third owner he became the first chairman of the board of directors. On November 10, 1960, he purchased control of the club by acquiring an additional one-third interest at which time he assumed the presidency of the club. On January 31, 1962, he purchased the final one-third interest and became sole owner. Mr. Fetzer (A2226923) is a member of the board of directors of the American League, as well as chairman of the radio-television committee of the Major Leagues. He also was a member of the pension committee of baseball and for many years sat on the executive council, the controlling body of baseball under the chairmanship of the Commissioner of Baseball. He headed the Detroit Tiger baseball tour of Japan, Okinawa and Korea, as special guest of the Mainichi

Tiger Stadium, Detroit.

Newspapers and the Japanese government including the Crown Prince and Princess and under the auspices of the State Department, fall 1962. Developed the World Champion Detroit Tigers in 1968.

Business and Civic Activities

Since 1947, Mr. Fetzer has been a member of the board of directors of The American National Bank and Trust Company of Michigan; a member of the board of trustees, Kalamazoo College, since 1954; a member of Alpha Kappa Psi fraternity since 1957; a member of the Michigan Economic Expansion Council since 1963; a member of the board of directors, International Village, Detroit, 1963, and a past member of the President's Advisory Council, Western Michigan University, 1963.

Since 1953, Mr. Fetzer (A2226923) has been president and owner of Cornhusker Television Corporation, licensee of KOLN-TV, Lincoln, Nebraska, and KGIN-TV, Grand Island, Nebraska; chairman of the board, Parkway Development, Inc., 1957. In 1958 he dedicated a modern television studio building, Broadcast House; established and became president of Fetzer Music Corporation and Fetzer Television, Inc., including WWTV, Cadillac, Michigan. In 1961 WWTV-FM was established and in 1962 WWUP-TV, Sault

Ste. Marie, was added to Fetzer Television, Inc. Also in 1961, the world's most modern television transmitting station for WKZO-TV, Kalamazoo-Grand Rapids, was dedicated. Established Fetzer Cablevision and Wolverine Cablevision in 1967. Dedicated Broadcast

John E. Fetzer with the World Championship trophy presented to him and the Detroit Tigers by the Commissioner of Baseball. The Detroit Baseball Club defeated the St. Louis Cardinals for the Championship in 1968.

Place, a new office and studio building for WKZO-TV, WJEF and WJFM, Grand Rapids, Michigan. Station WWAM was added to Fetzer Television, Inc., in Cadillac, 1968. Established and became president of John E. Fetzer, Inc., in Detroit, 1968. Acquired and became president of Medallion Broadcasters, Inc., licensee of KMEG-TV, Sioux City, Iowa, 1969, established Fetzer Television Corporation, Kalamazoo, 1970, and Fetzer Communications, Inc., Lincoln, Nebraska, 1971.

Committees, Boards and Associations

Mr. Fetzer (A2226923) served as chairman of the board of Vitapix Corporation, Hollywood, California, 1952-56; chairman of the board of WMBD, Inc., Peoria, Illinois, 1952-56; contributor to Radio and Television Oral History Project, Columbia University, 1953; chairman of CBS Radio Business Standards Committee, 1952-1953; was appointed by Secretary Forrestal to the Broadcasters Advisory Panel of Office of Civil Defense Planning, 1948; member of the advisory board, North American Service, Radiodiffusion Francaise, Paris,

Headquarters of Fetzer operations in the Midwest. Tower in background is master antenna for cable television. The foreground tower is an electronic weather station.

1946-47; member of the citizens committee of Michigan National Guard and member of Michigan Committee for Constitutional Amendment on Aviation, 1946; delegate to Advertising Federation of America, 1945; member of broadcasters advisory committee, Office of War Information, 1942; Broadcasters Victory Council (member, board of directors, 1942); president, alumni association, Andrews University, 1928; and National Radio Institute, 1926.

Mr. Fetzer (A2226923) is a member of the National Association of Broadcasters (member, ethics committee, 1928-1929; engineering committee, 1935-1939; board of directors, 1938-1946, 1956-1960; chairman, war committee, 1942; employer-employee committee and national music committee, 1946; freedom of radio committee, 1947); Michigan Broadcasters Association (vice president, 1936); United States Chamber of Commerce (national councillor); Kalamazoo Chamber of Commerce (member, board of directors, 1940-1950; president, 1944); fellow, Royal Society of Arts, London, England; member, National Genealogical Society; author *One Man's Family*, a history of the Fetzer Family, 1964; member, Associated Press Mission to Europe, 1966; member, Academy of Political Science; Institute of Electrical and Electronics Engineers (life member); American Society of Military Engineers; International Radio and Television Executives Society and Broadcast Pioneers, New York; Broadcasters Club, Washington, D.C.

Awarded citations by National Board of Fire Underwriters, 1943; Office of Censorship, 1945; United States Marine Corps, 1946; Fifth Army, 1947; Golden Ear Award, 1962; American League, 1964; Michigan Legislature, 1968; Nebraska Educational Television System, 1968; recipient, Broadcast Pioneers Award, 1968; Distinguished Service Award of National Association of Broadcasters, the highest award of the broadcasting industry, 1969; The Wolverine Frontiersman Award from Governor Milliken of Michigan, 1969, and the "Top Man" Award, Andrews University, 1969.

A member of the Presbyterian Church, he is also a Mason (32°, 33°, Shriner) and an Elk; and member of the following clubs: Park (president, 1953), Kalamazoo Country Club, Gull Lake Country Club of Kalamazoo, Peninsular Club of Grand Rapids; Detroit Athletic Club, Detroit Club, Press and Economic Clubs of Detroit; and Tucson Country Club.

Fetzer Ancestry

Mr. Fetzer's (A2226923) ancestral line dates to 1550. The line is as follows: Bastian (1550-1625, 1st), George (1591-1660, 2nd), George (1624-1705, 3rd), Paul (1652-1735, 4th), Paul (1693-1735, 5th), Jacob (1733-1803, 6th), Jacob Frederick (1768-1821, 7th), Jacob Frederick (1806-1880, 8th), John Adam (1840-1882, 9th), John Adam (1870-1903, 10th) and John Earl Fetzer (born 1901, 11th). His great-grandfather, Jacob Frederick Fetzer (1806-1880, 8th), came from the Village of Denkendorf, Wurttemberg, Germany, to near Deavertown, Morgan County, Ohio, in 1832. He and his family moved near Logan in Hocking County, Ohio, in 1842. A further move to near Uniondale, Wells County, Indiana, was made in 1867. Members of the family have grown to large numbers throughout the United States including Ohio, Indiana, Illinois, Nebraska, New Jersey, Colorado, Michigan, California and Florida.

Mr. Fetzer's (A2226923) grandmother, the wife of John Adam Fetzer (1840-1882, 9th), was Mary Brodt Fetzer. Her ancestry is authentically traced to 1570, centered around the Villages of Unterheinriet, Untergruppenbach, Grossaspach and Klein Ingersheim, all in Wurttemberg, Germany. Her ancestral line is as follows: Michael Brodt (1570-1644, 1st), Hans Brodt (1614-1693, 2nd), Hans Michael Brodt (1658-1729, 3rd), Hans Michael Brodt (1682-1743, 4th), Albrecht Brodt (1707-1780, 5th), John Jakob Brodt (1741-1812, 6th), Jacob Frederick Brodt (1773-1850, 7th), Gottlieb Brodt (1803-1871, 8th), and Mary Brodt Fetzer (1836-1882, 9th). Gottlieb Brodt (1803-1871, 8th) came to America in 1832. His family first settled in Tuscarawas County, Ohio, then in Hocking County, Ohio, and finally in Wells County, Indiana.

The book, *One Man's Family*, has a 212 page detailed account of the history and genealogy of the Fetzer family.

Rhea Yeager Fetzer

Rhea Yeager Fetzer was born June 7, 1901, in Augusta, Michigan. She is a graduate of Andrews University with the B.A. degree in 1926. She did graduate work at the University of Michigan in 1929. She has been in numerous civic and philanthropic activities including membership on the board of directors of Family Service Center, Kalamazoo Community Chest, Community Concert Association, Senior Citizens Fund, Kalamazoo Symphony Society, Committee

The Fetzer home in
Kalamazoo, Michigan.

The Fetzer home at
Otter Lake in Northern
Michigan.

The Fetzer ranch nea
Tucson, Arizona.

on Aging, Kalamazoo County Council of Social Agencies, First Presbyterian Church, Bronson Methodist Hospital, John E. Fetzer Foundation, Inc. and Kalamazoo Foundation.

Paternal Ancestry

Rhea Maude Fetzer, the wife of John E. Fetzer, on the paternal side comes from a long line of active people. The Yeager family of German ancestry was founded in America in the 18th Century in the state of Pennsylvania by Jacob Yeager, the first known ancestor. Jacob and his wife, Margarette Yeager, lived in Lancaster County, Pennsylvania, and had a family of 21 children.

In 1821 this family went to Rain Township, Haldimand County, Ontario, Canada, and established a farm near the village of Selkirk. Mathias Yeager, the oldest son of Jacob and Margarette Yeager, of the second generation was born and married in Lancaster County. He, his wife and four sons went to Canada with his parents. His wife, Catherine Kestler Yeager, passed away in 1825 at the age of 29. Mathias Yeager then married Mary Hoover, a descendant of Abraham Hoover, also from Lancaster County, Pennsylvania.

Rhea Yeager Fetzer, wife of John E. Fetzer (A2226923).

Mathias and Mary Hoover Yeager had a family of ten. In 1852 this family left Canada and settled on a farm near North Webster, Tippecanoe Township, Kosciusko County, Indiana.

Among the children of this marriage was Abraham Yeager (1830-1910) of the third generation. Abraham Yeager married Mariah Ritter. They had four children of the fourth generation. Of these, Dr. William Nelson Yeager, born December 6, 1870, in Kansas, married Loena Maude Lawrence, October 26, 1897, in Battle Creek, Michigan. Dr. Yeager died October 30, 1939, in Berrien Springs, Michigan. Loena Maude Yeager was born August 16, 1876, in Macomb County, Michigan, and died May 12, 1960, in Kalamazoo, Michigan. Dr. Yeager was a Doctor of Dentistry.

The Yeagers had three children of the fifth generation. These were Paul LeMont Yeager, born November 2, 1905, who married Alice Olsten, born May 2, 1908, and had a daughter, Svea Alice, born October 4, 1938. He died January 5, 1939, as a senior in medical college. Dr. Charles LeVant Yeager, born September 12, 1907, married Emily Usborne, born August 2, 1908, and had a family of two. The children, LeVant Nelson, born September 30, 1935, and Loena Carol, born December 13, 1937, were in a fatal airplane accident August 7, 1954.

Dr. Chas. L. Yeager, M.D., Ph.D., is Senior Psychiatrist and Director of the Electroencephalography Laboratory of the Langley Porter Neuropsychiatric Institute in the California Department of Mental Hygiene. He is a Professor of Psychiatry in Residence at the University of California in the School of Medicine and is a consultant to all State of California hospitals, the U.S. Air Force and the Veterans Administration, as well as author of many scientific papers, publications and periodicals. Rhea Maude Fetzer, the wife of John E. Fetzer (A2226923), was the eldest child.

The summary of these Yeager generations is as follows: Jacob Yeager (1st), Mathias Yeager (2nd), Abraham Yeager (3rd), Dr. William Nelson Yeager (4th) and Rhea Yeager Fetzer (5th).

The Lawrence Family

On the maternal side, Rhea Yeager Fetzer is a descendant of John Lawrence, who came to America and settled in Watertown, Massachusetts, before 1635. He probably came from England in the company with Governor Winthrop in 1630. His first wife, Elizabeth, and he had 12 children born at Watertown. In 1660 the family moved to Groten, Massachusetts, and shortly thereafter the wife, Elizabeth, died. Thereafter, John Lawrence married a widow, Mary Batchelder of Boston, by whom he had two more children.

The posterity of John Lawrence developed a great-grandson by the name of Abbott Lawrence who gained great eminence in the political, professional, commercial and industrial life of Boston. Thereafter, the Hon. Abbott Lawrence became American Minister to the Court of St. James. While in England, he developed an interest in his family history and engaged an attorney, Horatio Somerby, to trace the English ancestry of John Lawrence of Watertown.

In spite of the fact that some Lawrence families have not been in full agreement with the English genealogical line, a pedigree was formulated showing John Lawrence of Watertown and Groton as a descendant of "Sir Robert Lawrence of Ashton Hall in Lancashire, who in 1191 was knighted by Richard Coeur de Lion for his good services at Acre." He was given a coat-of-arms, viz. "Silver, a ross raguly gules." John Lawrence of Watertown and Groton appears as 17th in descent from Sir Robert Lawrence of Ashton Hall.

However, for our purposes it is an established fact that John Lawrence of Watertown and Groton, Massachusetts, was the first confirmed ancestor of the Lawrence line incident to the family of Rhea Yeager Fetzer.

In the second generation of fourteen children, of principal interest to us is Isaac Lawrence. He was the ninth-born child of John and Elizabeth Lawrence, being born in Watertown about 1658. He was married April 19, 1682, at Cambridge, Massachusetts, to Abigail Bellows. They with their son, Isaac, Jr., of the third generation, removed to Norwich, Connecticut, about 1700.

Isaac Lawrence, Jr., married Susanna Read, April 15, 1708, at Norwich. They had four known children of the fourth generation. Samuel Lawrence, the first-born child, is of interest.

Samuel Lawrence was born May 27, 1710, in Norwich, Connecticut. Samuel and his wife, Mary, had ten children of the fifth generation. Their sixth child was John Lawrence who was born February 19, 1746, in Norwich. In 1768, at the age of 22, he removed to Bennington, Vermont. It is believed he married Mary Penfold, February 27, 1776. After his death, October 27, 1825, the Vermont Gazette said, "John Lawrence, 80 years old, was one of the first settlers of Bennington and was a genuine whiz during the Revolutionary struggle. He was a minute man in the Battle of Bennington."

Chasing a Phantom

May we parenthetically report that in later years John Lawrence of Bennington was affirmatively reported by members of the Lawrence family as the son of Johnathan Lawrence, a native of Holland, and of English parentage. This Johnathan Lawrence was reported as the son of John and Mary (Townley) Lawrence. The father of Mary Townley Lawrence disinherited her, and she and her husband John sailed for America, where young Johnathan was reared in Worcester, Massachusetts.

This report of John Lawrence's parentage is entirely erroneous. A will of John Lawrence in Bennington, Vermont, Book 12, page 371, and proven in 1826, definitely establishes him as the son of Samuel Lawrence who was a great-grandson of John Lawrence of Watertown, Massachusetts.

Lawrence families all over America were tied to this John and Mary (Townley) Lawrence story because of an estate in Great Britain that was up for grabs. Lawrence families everywhere were relieved of considerable sums of money chasing this phantom fortune.

Vermont to New York to Michigan

John and Mary Lawrence had six children of the sixth generation, all born in Bennington. Of these, John Lawrence, Jr., was born January 7, 1786, and married Susannah Stanton in 1806. Shortly thereafter, they removed from Bennington to Spafford, Onondago County, New York. They lived there about 12 years and then removed to Cortland County, New York. Again in 1835 they moved to Washington Township, Macomb County, Michigan.

John Lawrence, Jr., and Mary Stanton Lawrence had eight children of the seventh generation. Russell Johnson Lawrence, the fourth child, was born February 22, 1813, in Spafford, New York. He married Lucinda Thompson in 1838. He died April 26, 1900, and she died January 10, 1897. They had a family of 12 in the eighth generation, all born in Michigan. Most of this family was identified with religious activity.

Nehemiah Lawrence, the fifth-born child of Russell Johnson and Lucinda (Thompson) Lawrence was born March 7, 1848, and died May 12, 1924. In 1868 he married Lydia Carey. They had a family

The final resting place prepared for the Fetzers at the Mountain Home Cemetery, Kalamazoo, Michigan.

of five in the ninth generation. Of these, their third daughter, Loena Maude Lawrence, was born August 16, 1876, and married Dr. William N. Yeager October 26, 1897, in Battle Creek, Michigan. As reported in the Yeager family data, they had three children of the tenth generation, including Rhea Maude (Yeager) Fetzer, the wife of John E. Fetzer (A2226923).

The summary of these Lawrence generations is as follows: John Lawrence (1st), Isaac Lawrence (2nd), Isaac Lawrence (3rd), Samuel Lawrence, Jr., (4th), John Lawrence (5th), John Lawrence, Sr., (6th), Russell Johnson Lawrence (7th), Nehemiah Lawrence (8th), Loena Maude Lawrence Yeager (9th) and Rhea Yeager Fetzer (10th).

The Fetzers have no children. Their homes are at 2714 Clovelly Road, Kalamazoo, at Otter Lake in Benzie County, northern Michigan, and on the Fetzer ranch near Tucson, Arizona. His offices are at Fetzer Broadcasting Company, 590 West Maple Street, Kalamazoo, and Detroit Baseball Club, Tiger Stadium, Detroit.

The John Earl Fetzer (A2226923) of Michigan Winger Family Tree immediately follows.

Della Frances Winger (A222692) of Indiana Family Tree
and
John E. Fetzer (A2226923) of Michigan

1st Hans Wenger (b. About 1430) Blumenstein, Thun
2nd Burkhard Wenger (b. About 1450) Forst, Thun
3rd Peter Wenger (b. About 1470) Wattenwil, Seftigen
4th Peter Wenger (b. About 1490) Wattenwil, Seftigen
5th Rudolfus Wenger (b. About 1510) Wattenwil, Seftigen
6th Hans Wenger (b. About 1530) Wattenwil, Seftigen
7th Rudolfus Wenger (Ch. April 5, 1566) Wattenwil-Thurnen,
     Seftigen
8th Peter Wenger (Ch. Dec. 13, 1607) Wattenwil-Thurnen, Seftigen
9th Hans Wenger (Ch. May 30, 1633) Wattenwil-Thurnen, Seftigen
     A   Christian Wenger (A2) First Generation in America
         (1688-1749)
         B-1   Henry Wenger, Sr. (A22) Second Generation in
               America (1716-1802)
             C-1   Abraham Wenger (A222) Third Generation in
                   America (1767-1845)
                 D-1   Peter Henry Winger (A2226) Fourth
                       Generation in America (1806-1889)
                     E-1   Joseph Levi Robinson Winger (A22269)
                           Fifth Generation
                           b. July 17, 1848, Darke County, Ohio
                           d. Dec. 31, 1928, Celina, Ohio
                             bur. Swamp College
                           m. Nancy Jane Woods, Apr. 5, 1868,
                             Versailles, Ohio
                             b. June 29, 1849, near Versailles, Ohio
                             d. Mar. 16, 1911, Celina, Ohio,
                               bur. Swamp College
                         F-1   Della Frances Winger (A222692-6th)
                               b. Dec. 21, 1870, near Osgood, Ohio
                               d. Feb. 12, 1958, Lafayette, Ind.
                                 bur. Maplewood Cemetery,
                                 Decatur, Indiana
                               m. David Edward Evans, June 27, 1889,
                                 Decatur, Ind.
                                 b. May 6, 1870, Monmouth, Ind.
                                 d. Unknown

m. John Adam Fetzer, June 12, 1899,
Decatur, Ind.
b. Aug. 4, 1870, near Uniondale, Ind.
d. Feb. 11, 1903, Decatur, Ind.
m. Irvin Ianthus Pyle, Dec. 28, 1917,
St. Joseph, Michigan
b. Mar. 19, 1869, Decatur, Ind.
d. Apr. 13, 1964, Frankfort, Ind.
bur. Maplewood Cemetery,
Decatur, Ind.

G-1   Harriett Cecelia Evans (A2226921-7th)
b. Sept. 2, 1890, Monmouth,
near Decatur, Ind.
m. Frederick Lloyd Ribble, Nov. 1,
1911, Stewart, Ill.
b. Mar. 7, 1883, West Lebanon, Ind.
d. May 22, 1942, Logansport, Ind.
bur. Logansport Cemetery
m. Peter Edward Nash, June 19, 1944,
Lafayette, Ind.
b. June 1, 1882, Pittsburgh, Pa.
d. Feb. 25, 1947, Indianapolis, Ind.
bur. Rest Haven Cemetery,
Lafayette, Ind.
m. Scott Hutchins Thomas,
July 21, 1949
b. May 20, 1878, Williamsport,
Warren Co., Ind.
d. Aug. 19, 1955, Lafayette, Ind.
bur. Spring Hill Cemetery,
Danville, Ill.

H-1   Mary Elizabeth Ribble
(A22269211-8th)
b. Aug. 15, 1912, Lafayette, Ind.
d. Aug. 15, 1912, Lafayette, Ind.
bur. Springdale Cemetery,
Lafayette, Ind.

G-2   Joseph Lawrence Evans (A2226922-7th)
b. Feb. 15, 1892, Monmouth,
near Decatur
d. Sept. 15, 1897, Decatur, Ind.

G-3 John E. Fetzer (A2226923-7th)
  b. Mar. 25, 1901, Decatur, Ind.
  m. Rhea Maude Yeager, July 19, 1926,
  Benton Harbor, Mich.
  b. June 7, 1901, Augusta, Mich.
G-4 Walter Adam Fetzer (A2226924-7th)
  b. Apr. 25, 1903, Decatur, Ind.
  d. Aug. 14, 1903, Decatur, Ind.
  bur. Maplewood Cemetery

PART II

AMERICA'S AGONY

by

John E. Fetzer

CHAPTER ONE

A Mark of Destiny

AS THIS story began in a time of political and religious revolution, so the prospect for continued revolt, lasting another half-century, is indicated in 1969 as the temper of our times. Henry Wenger (A1) and Christian Wenger (A2), our two brothers from Switzerland, were exiled because they repudiated long-established doctrines born out of bitter antipathies engendered by a period of fervid religious dissention. They sought peace and tranquility in a new land which guaranteed that the freedoms they espoused would find fertile soil. There was clear indication that they and their children, and the generations that were to follow, would find such an environment.

As for Christian Wenger (A2), his was the opportunity to help convert a wilderness into a garden and at the same time practice the tenets of a religious conviction that was soul-satisfying. His oldest son, John Henry Wenger, Sr. (A22), for a time continued to enjoy the fruits of the land and of the spirit that had been planted by his father. Long years after Christian Wenger (A2) had been laid to rest in the Wenger family burying ground in Upper Leacock Township of Lancaster County, the new country began to develop unrest that soon led to revolt.

Words of Life

Henry Wenger, Sr. (A22), due to force of circumstances, was a soldier in that conflict which continued the revolutionary theme his father had experienced in the Old World.

It must be remembered that in that conflict the shoeless, ill-fed and poorly equipped American army, including Henry Wenger's (A22) 10th militia, met a series of reverses in 1777. As a result, General Washington retreated to Valley Forge to pass the winter of 1777. What happened in Valley Forge is astounding to many Americans. I wish to quote from a report first published by Wesley Bradshaw and copied from a reprint in the *National Tribune,* Volume 4, No. 12, December 1880. It was originally narrated by Anthony Sherman:

> The last time I ever saw Anthony Sherman was on the 4th of July, 1859, in Independence Square. He was then 99 years old and becoming very feeble. But though so old, his dimming eyes rekindled as he gazed upon Independence Hall, which he came to visit once more.

> Let us go into the hall, he said. I want to tell you an incident of Washington's life — one which no one alive knows of except myself; and, if you live, you will before long see it verified.

> From the opening of the Revolution we experienced all phases of fortune, now good and now ill, one time victorious and another conquered. The darkest period we had, I think, was when Washington, after several reverses, retreated to Valley Forge where he resolved to pass the winter of 1777. Ah, I have often seen the tears coursing down our dear commander's careworn cheeks as he would be conversing with a confidential officer about the condition of his poor soldiers. You have doubtless heard the story of Washington's going to the thicket to pray. Well, it was not only true, but he used often to pray in secret for aid and comfort from God, the interposition of whose Divine Providence brought us safely through the darkest days of tribulation.

> One day, I remember it well, the chilly winds whistled through the leafless trees. Though the sky was cloudless and the sun shone brightly, he remained in his quarters nearly all the afternoon alone. When he came out I noticed that his face was a shade paler than usual and there seemed to be something on his mind of more than ordinary importance. Returning just after dusk, he dispatched an orderly to the quarters of the officer I mention who was presently in attendance. After a preliminary conversation of about half an hour, Washington, gazing upon his companion with that strange look of dignity which he alone could command, said to the latter:

> "I do not know whether it is owing to the anxiety of my mind, or what, but this afternoon, as I was sitting at this table engaged in preparing a dispatch, something seemed to disturb me. Looking up, I beheld standing opposite me a singularly beautiful female. So astonished was I, for I had given strict orders not to be disturbed, that it was some moments before I found language to inquire the cause of her presence. A second, a third, and even a fourth time did I repeat my question but received no answer from my mysterious visitor except a slight raising of her eyes. By this time I felt strange sensations spreading through me. I would have risen but the riveted gaze of the being before me rendered volition impossible. I assayed once more to address her but my tongue had become useless. Even thought itself had become paralyzed. A new influence, mysterious, potent, irresistible, took possession of me. All I could do was to gaze steadily, vacantly at my unknown visitant. Grad-

ually the surrounding atmosphere seemed as though becoming filled with sensations and grew luminous. Everything about me seemed to rarefy, the mysterious visitor herself becoming more airy and yet more distinct to my sight than before. I now began to feel as one dying, or rather to experience the sensations which I have sometimes imagined accompany dissolution. I did not think. I did not reason. I did not move; all were alike impossible. I was only conscious of gazing fixedly, vacantly at my companions.

"Presently I heard a voice saying, 'Son of the Republic, look and learn.' While at the same time my visitor extended her arm eastwardly. I now beheld a heavy white vapor at some distance rising fold upon fold. This gradually dissipated and I looked upon a strange scene. Before me lay spread out in one vast plain all the countries of the world — Europe, Asia, Africa and America. I saw rolling and tossing between Europe and America the billows of the Atlantic, and between Asia and America lay the Pacific. 'Son of the Republic,' said the same mysterious voice as before, 'Look and learn.' At that moment I beheld a dark, shadowy being like an angel standing, or rather floating, in mid-air between Europe and America. Dipping water out of the ocean in the hollow of each hand, he sprinkled some upon America with his right hand while with his left hand he cast some on Europe. Immediately a cloud raised from these countries and joined in mid-ocean. For a while it remained stationary, and then moved slowly westward until it enveloped America in its murky folds. Sharp flashes of lightning gleamed through it at intervals and I heard the smothered groans and cries of the American people. A second time the angel dipped water from the ocean and sprinkled it out as before. The dark cloud was then drawn back to the ocean in whose heaving billows it sank from view. A third time I heard the mysterious voice saying, 'Son of the Republic, look and learn.' I cast my eyes upon America and beheld villages and towns and cities springing up one after another until the whole land from the Atlantic to the Pacific was dotted with them. Again I heard the mysterious voice say, 'Son of the Republic, the end of the century cometh, look and learn.'

"At this the dark shadowy angel turned his face southward, and from Africa I saw an ill-omened spectre approach our land. It flitted slowly over every town and city of the latter. The inhabitants presently set themselves in battle array against each other. As I continued looking, I saw a bright angel on whose brow rested a crown of light on which was traced the word 'Union,' bearing the American flag which he placed between the divided nation, and said, 'Remember ye are brethern.' Instantly the inhabitants, casting from them their weapons, became friends once more and united around the National Standard.

"And again I heard the mysterious voice saying, 'Son of the Republic, look and learn.' At this the dark, shadowy angel placed a trumpet to his mouth and blew three distinct blasts; and taking water from the ocean, he sprinkled it upon Europe, Asia and Africa. Then my eyes beheld a fearful scene; from each of these countries arose thick, black clouds that were soon joined into one. And throughout this mass there gleamed a dark red light by which I saw hordes of armed men who, moving with the cloud, marched by land and sailed by sea to America which country was enveloped in the volume of cloud. And I dimly saw these vast armies devastate the whole country and burn the villages, towns and cities that I beheld springing up. As my ears listened to the thundering of the cannon, clashing of swords and the shouts and cries of millions in mortal combat, I again heard the mysterious voice saying, 'Son of the Republic, look and learn.' When the voice had ceased, the dark shadowy angel placed his trumpet once more to his mouth and blew a long and fearful blast.

"Instantly a light as a thousand suns shown down from above me, and pierced and broke into fragments the dark cloud which enveloped America. At the same moment the angel, upon whose head still shone the word 'Union,' and who bore our national flag in one hand and a sword in the other, descended from the heavens attended by legions of white spirits. These immediately joined the inhabitants of America, who I perceived were well nigh overcome but who, immediately taking courage again, closed up their broken ranks and renewed the battle. Again, amid the fearful noise of the conflict, I heard the mysterious voice saying, 'Son of the Republic, look and learn.' As the voice ceased, the shadowy angel for the last time dipped water from the ocean and sprinkled it upon America. Instantly the dark cloud rolled back, together with the armies it had brought, leaving the inhabitants of the land victorious.

"Then once more I beheld the villages, towns and cities springing up where I had seen them before, while the bright angel, planting the azure standard he had brought in the midst of them, cried with a loud voice:

" 'While the stars remain, and the heavens send down dew upon the earth, so long shall the Union last.' And taking from his brow the crown on which blazoned the word 'Union' he placed it upon the Standard while the people, kneeling down, said, 'Amen.'

"The scene instantly began to fade and dissolve, and I at last saw nothing but the rising, curling vapor I at first beheld. This also disappearing, I found myself once more gaping upon the mysterious visitor who, in the same voice I heard before, said, "Son of the Republic, what you have seen is thus interpreted.

" 'Three great perils will come upon the Republic.

" 'The most fearful is the third passing, which the whole world united shall not prevail against her. Let every child of the Republic learn to live for his God, his land and Union.' With these words the vision vanished and I started from my seat and felt that I had seen a vision wherein had been shown me the birth, progress and destiny of the United States."

Such, my friends, concluded the venerable narrator, were the words I heard from Washington's own lips and America will do well to profit by them.

Since the beginning of our civilization man has had an insatiable desire to look into the future. History is replete with prophetic utterances, many of which seemed to have a degree of validity. It is a dangerous business to interpret the symbolism of events to come, even though the above narration seems to have recorded considerable history of our country with uncommon accuracy. In any event, let us examine the course of events from the standpoint of a strict constructionist, even though speculative and not necessarily predestined.

A Period of Distress

George Washington, the father of our country, through a strange phenomenon, was privileged to know the destiny not only of his mission but that of a great people, even though he had some reservations. The interpretation indicated that three great perils or stages of development would transpire. It is highly probable that we have passed through the first two stages, which involved many Wengers, and that we presently are in the third stage. In order that we may profit from our past experiences and prepare ourselves for that which may lie ahead, it seems altogether fitting that we should categorically look at the future as an echo from the past. Many historians believe that the past is prologue.

The Roman Empire

Let us attempt to bring Washington's experience into focus by reviewing the condition of the Roman Empire prior to its fall. Rome had reached powerful military superiority over foreign aggressors, thus assuring the safety of its people. All citizens were equally liable for military service. Economic competition was the order of the day. The middle class was an abundant source or wellspring of progress. As a result, idleness was rampant and political rewards were party politic. The masses exchanged their votes for public welfare programs. Since domestic institutions were ennobled, frugality, gravity, piety and patriotism did not commend themselves to sophisticated philosophies. This, plus the pampering of the pleasure-seeking populace, produced major opposition to service in the military. The academics and idle rich, fattened on the social and economic system, advocated its destruction and reform. There was a revolt against the established order. Riots and fires destroyed the cities. Confiscatory taxation followed. Prices rose and inflation debased the currency. Throughout it all, the Empire stood by the commitments to its allies. Ultimately Rome had to retreat from her forward position. Complacency set in. As Rome grew weaker, her strongest allies defected and ultimately attacked their benefactor. In the end Rome was completely and irretrievably overrun and ravaged. Rome was no more. The history of the Roman Empire is expressed in the following cycle:

> From Bondage to Spiritual Faith
> From Spiritual Faith to Great Courage
> From Courage to Liberty
> From Liberty to Abundance
> From Abundance to Selfishness
> From Selfishness to Complacency
> From Complacency to Apathy
> From Apathy to Dependency
> From Dependency back again into Bondage

"Son of the Republic, look and learn." The parallel is altogether too apparent. It is not necessary to name the bench marks. The beginning illustration, wherein members of the Wenger clan and vast members of like-minded people fought to break the chains of bondage, showing spiritual faith and courage, finds its likeness in Rome. History witnessed liberty-seeking, pious people coming to these western shores to create a nation in a land of abundance. Following that, we have witnessed a great deal of complacency, apathy and dependency, which has been translated into high-sounding terms accredited to government and the full gamut of institutionalism. "Son of the Republic, look and learn."

The First Two Cycles

The first two perils of our nation seem to have been completed almost as a copy of the Roman Empire. The third is beginning at the present time. The messenger indicated that we would not follow the course of Rome to bondage but, instead, would respond to a "Light shown down from above — as a thousand suns." The destiny of the United States of America is to lead itself and the world into the era of peace on earth. Through the maze of combat which is here and now, and more to come, "the groans and cries of the American people" will be heard. Even though the whole world shall be against us, "They shall not prevail."

History is also replete with prophecies that have gone awry. The destiny of our nation depends upon the fiber of our people. If we respond to the call, as did many of our forefathers, including the Wengers, then we shall meet the test of time. However, if we remain on our present course, we could go to oblivion as did the Roman Empire.

The Technological Revolution

What is the temper of our age which has brought us to the brink of so adverse a destiny? Time or space does not permit us to penetrate deeply enough to find completely satisfying answers. The length and breadth of the technological revolution simply is overwhelming. Basically, scientific advancement is changing the face of the world and the space around it to a point beyond comprehension.

To select one facet of the problem, the computer age has arrived. These electrical and mechanical wizards are measuring man's performance for the sociologists, statisticians in government, librarians, members of congress, school records, health, taxes, army records, employment records, mortgages and business records, marriage and divorce records and legal records. Most of the States of the Union exchange computerized tax data with the Internal Revenue Service, the police, the National Crime Information Center and private credit bureaus. In short, we now have a national data center which ultimately will control all industry and much of the educational process with complete sociological overtones. It is estimated that 50 per cent of today's labor force will be relocated by computer technology.

In the field of medicine, the computer will give the symptoms of hard-to-diagnose illnesses. Doctors will carry portable computers that will couple the phone line to a master computer that will supply virtually all the wanted information.

In colleges and universities, the computer will supplement libraries to the point that practically all recorded material will be instantly available.

Outer Space

The exploration of outer space is under way. The ability to traverse outer space, to install space stations and to interface the basic sciences will enlarge our horizon far beyond the scope of our present-day world. The research already done brings obsolescence to many of our time-worn concepts.

There are presently known sources of concentrated energy scattered across the Universe at distances of up to ten billion light years. These sources radiate electronic light waves of fantastic intensity. Such an incredible out-pouring of electrical energy seems to indicate a mass of material at the source comparable to that of an entire galaxy of 100 billion stars! Even so, this Laser beam enormity in space is infinitesimal when compared to the whole, which makes up the great and infinite cosmos.

Our planetary universe was created over ten billion years ago, probably from other gigantic planetary units, as a result of what some refer to as the "big-bang" theory. This is but one of many such universes that rotate around a gigantic Central Sun. This Sun is so colossal that each of the universes rotating around it in perfect order and sequence is as small in comparison as the electrons that spin around the nucleus of an atom. It takes our universe over 26,800 years to make one turn of its orbit around this great Central Sun. There are believed to be at least 100 million galaxies. The Milky Way alone, which includes our sun, has approximately three billion similar stars or suns that have at least one satellite planet each, where *life-forms* have the capacity to exist.

While it is only speculation as to what form of life exists, the contemplation of an encounter with a civilization that may be millions of years in advance of ours is overwhelming. In this connection, the United States, British and Soviet scientific community is receiving radio signals from outer space that represent a considerable body of evidence indicating intelligent transmission. Vitali Ginzburg, physicist member of the Soviet Academy of Sciences, urges a crash program to determine if intelligent life exists elsewhere in the universe, even though it may be 100 light years away.

Primal Cause

We of the older generation have too often been inclined to say a little knowledge is a dangerous thing. On the other hand, this new age in which we live probably has advanced more scientifically in the last twenty years than the last 1,000 years. This new era of technology and science, automation and communications, almost defies comprehension. Something has happened to behavioral processes at all levels of society. The sudden advent of the space age has plunged peoples of the world into impatience with social structures, an impatience which portends change. This social revolution is visible in every aspect of life. The complexities of today are well beyond the range of earlier social systems. We crash through one frontier after another and our scientific friends call it the "quantum jump" — an enormous leap ahead. In short, a revolution is in the making, and it is worldwide. The sophistication of the young people of the world is developing a new sense of direction. With it is a re-examination of our social structures. Methodology pursues every institution in the present-day society with relentless fury. There is no escape — all peoples and institutions are identified with it, either offensively or defensively.

Wenger Participation

May we say, parenthetically, many Wenger people have been identified with the action, wherever it has been found. I seriously suspect many of them will be in the forefront of the existing struggle. Let us hope that their participation will be with honor and distinction.

It is my hope that the young Wenger people, who are caught up in the generation gap, will find a degree of meaning to themselves in this family history. An honest appraisal of the past can sharpen the capacity to understand. The popular concepts of the young seem to lend very little credence to their fathers, let alone their family ancestors. Far too many modern youngsters say that looking back "is not my bag." They are frank to say that if you want to talk about the present, "that's my thing."

Perhaps a visit to Wenger localities of the past would do much to reduce this "hang-up." A well-organized trip to Wattenwil, Thurnen, Blumenstein, Mettlieggen, Martisegg, Uetendorf, Buchholterberg, Huberhof or Zweibrücken would expose them to many warmhearted people. The thrill of visiting the home sites of many of our ancestors, where a stable society still exists, with the preservation of many of the ancient landmarks, wholly and totally transcends our distorted environment of today.

In all of these places are to be found many Wenger cousins whose demeanor is a photocopy of our sires — beautiful, considerate people, who still carry an inborn heritage of hundreds of years.

If the young of today could know and feel the spirit of our forefathers as radiated from these present-day relatives in Switzerland

and Germany, they could not help but know that our fathers are listening with compassionate concern for the world today. We can only express a sincere desire that the young of our clan will shake the shackles of a distorted discipline and find some degree of pride in the noble achievements of their sires.

CHAPTER TWO

The World of Dissent

THE YOUNG of the world are adamant about the Atomic Age, the Computer Age and the Space Age, and now are indulging in a meticulous cybernetics of their own. It is happening in Capitalistic America, Communist Russia and Poland, Fascist Spain, Socialist India, Black Africa, White France and Yellow Japan; in Protestant Germany, Catholic Italy, Socialist Sweden and Merry Old England. The majority of youngsters want world peace, they want to feed the starving and clothe the naked. They want better schools for themselves and their children and, above all, the opportunity to make a dignified living. A swelling tide of young people are rejecting the authority of the ruling generation, what they call the "establishment," that is more properly defined as the political, economic, educational, religious and military structures of our social order. Basically, these are the issues. In the United States the depth of student feeling is against war and the ecological crisis at home. Students are against military service and for the civil rights movement. The environment of violence is such that the young accept it as normal. The world record is 128 wars of various kinds since 1898. Furthermore, 73 of these conflicts have taken place in the last 20 years. It is truly a record of shame.

In general, students indicate that many modern universities are engaged in depersonalization of the human personality. Many students find the experience of higher education as meaningless due to the shameful vacillation of some administrators. Too often some of the universities are struck with gloom that pervades the whole community. Students rail against specialization and want to give free reign to emotions and creativity. The more enlightened seem to equate limited experience in terms of credential excellence which the schools cannot recognize. The students believe higher education has a penchant for conformity and the status quo. They say there is a lack of adjustment to new ideas, particularly if they do not readily lend themselves to the usual methods of assessment. They say that too many teachers do not teach but that their principal concern is for self-aggrandizement, a trademark of their "private club." The charge is often heard that honorary degrees are tendered only to those intellectuals who already have too many such honors. Students contend this lends beautiful adornment to the commencement exercise, but is of little academic value.

There can be no doubt that the students are rebeling against the scientific culture and are anticipating something beyond the reign of technocracy. They look with awe at the DNA Age, the discovery of the genetic key which unlocks the secret of life and may determine whether man should be tall or short, smart or stupid or the tint of his skin. They want to seize control over technology before it irreversibly seizes control over them. Using glib rhetoric, they consider old ideologies incapable of coping with their lifestyle and in general with 20th Century problems. They seem to want a new secular theology, something "that will turn them on." Rightly or wrongly, they want to cast aside theological concepts which seem irrelevant to life. Six out of ten students say they want more from life than their parents required at the same age. It is apparent that most of them have tackled all problems in sight, believing that they can find ready solutions. There seems to be ignorance of the prayer of one from their own ranks, namely the late Reinhold Niebuhr, the theologian, who said, "Grant me serenity to accept the things I cannot change; courage to change the things I can; and wisdom to know the difference."

A New Definition of Goals

Youth storms at the present-day materialism and the capitalistic system. Ecology and the needs of our environment, including population control, are coming under critical examination. The young are demanding industrial reform. Internally, they seek a redefinition of goals in order to eliminate pollution of our land, sea and air. While science is in disagreement about the facts, they point out that it took nature hundreds of millions of years to produce the oxygen in our air and that man has already stripped nature's ability to repair the damage to that supply. It is clear that man through neglect is destroying animal and plant life on a scale never dreamed of;

worse, human life will come to a foreseeable end unless the present rate of pollution is reversed.

Nine out of ten students believe that big business is overly concerned with profits rather than the quality of its product. Beyond that youth wants the companies to reach more into community problems, using talents, capital and organizational skill to repair the nation's social machinery. They deride older people who are concerned for security; the young are not concerned about security for themselves. We want "to do our thing, now," they say. Six out of ten believe it is necessary to become "uptight" and disobey the law in varying degrees. Four out of ten say they enjoy their individualism, as indicated by hair styles and dress.

There is a widespread belief that in racial questions there is a complete insensitivity to the real demands and needs of the American black. It is easy to gain the impression that the kids have come to worship the gripe, rather than praise. They simply do not want to live with inherited troubles of this "out-of-touch world" any longer. Probably the most appropriate summary is the sign painted on a large classroom building of a midwestern university, "Due to a lack of interest, tomorrow has been cancelled."

The Activists

Basically, the majority of young people are "spooked" and believe that a complete face-lifting of society can be accomplished through the dialogue of persuasion and debate; many have deep "hang-ups" and believe that peaceful demonstrations are necessary. However, the more extreme student activists are out to destroy the country with force. More than a few of these are subversive. These are the ones who use fabrication, falsification and distortion to radicalize fair-minded students with the hope of shutting down the schools. All Americans who love their country and are opposed to the revolutionary tactics are to be cut down. These extremes of the left could find equal reaction from the right. The lessons of world upheaval should not be lost. This lesson teaches that there is neither safety nor refuge in extremes. The genuine road to freedom and democracy lies toward the center.

Self-Criticism

Too many of our institutions have proceeded on the partial truth that the advocacy of self-criticism is a means of self-improvement.

It is certainly true that our educational system must provide and encourage dissent. Intellectual challenge to yesterday's values and assumptions must be unfettered. Liberty dictates the probing of prevailing political and economic systems. But even this can be and recently has been carried to annoying extremes. Dr. Weimer K. Hicks states the case most appropriately:

> We have made a fetish of identifying the ills of the world and judging the worth of a man by his ability to ferret out weaknesses. A positive attitude seems almost an evidence of weakness, or even capitulation. Thousands of youth have fallen under the spell of this negative thinking. Thus our country, its institutions, and its leaders are suspect.

We are in fact experiencing an age of surplus of moral energy. It has brought an avalanche of simplistic moralism. This attitude which we have all but deified has us lurching from crises to crises with reckless abandon. Many are defending our complex society with patterns of behavior that completely defy rationality. Such moralism drives out thoughtful analysis, even though it is done with eloquent speech. The result has been a myth and countermyth, broadside, that has created expectations that cannot be satisfied. This is the great temptation in the world today. Such corruption must be resisted with all candor and honesty.

The Mass Media

The promulgation of this catechism of failure through the mass media has had the effect of a crushing bastinado on the thinking of the American masses. The spirit and confidence of our people has been and continues to be undermined. Constant negative nagging is rapidly bringing our country to a state of national morbidity. People seem overwhelmed at the advocacy for rapid adaptation. They are becoming depressed, apathetic, aggressive, irritable or actually ill. The mind-jangling and change of pace so challenges our adaptive capacities that we are in an emotional shock on a vast scale.

An example of this is the operation of The Union Rescue Mission in Los Angeles. It has operated for 78 years in the skid row of the city. It reports that the average age of the down-and-outer served by that organization once was more than 60 years. Now it is age 38. They say young men despair more easily in these times of rapid change. Among the "regulars" are men who failed as engineers, doctors, lawyers and teachers because the pressures of this complex society brought tragedy into their lives.

Today as never before there is a longing for some degree of liberation from America's agony. I have personally witnessed this frustration among corporation, college and university presidents; among the professions including doctors, lawyers, clergymen, teachers, journalists, writers, broadcasters and in baseball from the ranks of players to those of ownership. The search goes on interminably in this acrimonious society.

A realistic look at human behavior the world over raises the question of whether there is any hope for mankind. The divisiveness of our species puts man where he seems unable to pull "the driftwood of wisdom from the muddy rivers of time" and seems doomed to hate and be hated, to kill and be killed.

America today is divided more than any time during the last one hundred years. One minority group after another is asserting its identity and power.

Italians are protesting organized crime slurs against them as a group. The Jewish Defense League has been organized "to protect Jewish lives." Negro militants proclaim "black is beautiful." Spanish-speaking citizens press for more recognition. Women's Lib has developed a worldwide program.

Ethnic groups protest in almost every imaginable form. America's 13.2 million welfare recipients are being mobilized by the National Welfare Rights Organization for bigger payments with fewer restrictions. A sub-culture of the elderly is developing to exert "senior power" because inflation is destroying the value of their fixed incomes.

There are easy riders, earth people, new leftists, swingers, squares, cop-outs, youth worshippers, mod fashions, radical chics, black panthers, the shrink, the fun cult and the bell-bottomed paradisers. You name it — we have it. This is a national identity crises and, as of now, it is a cultural pluralism of astronomical proportions.

We can only conclude that we are nearing the time of the unfulfilled Valley Forge Vision of Washington which states that "the angel upon whose head still shone the word 'Union' and who bares our national flag in one hand and a sword in the other descends from the heavens attended by legions of white spirits."

There is Hope

Even though America is fraught with student anarchy, racial strife, negative ecology, crime and dissent, there is hope. Moreover, our strength lies in the fact that the majority of Americans show themselves to be morally strong and spiritually responsible. I cannot condone the charge that the majority of older people are looking for a fake Messiah, one who will "vindicate their selfishness as a way of life, and make them comfortable within their prejudices and preconceptions." In my opinion it is irresponsible, shortsighted and unfair to permit all older people to suffer from melodramatic publicity given to individual cases of abuse and lack of concern. Maturity would insist that the tools of public reporting be fairly used to achieve balanced judgment. I believe the majority are committed to intellectual honesty, rational and humanistic concern and compassion for mankind.

For the most part, our senior citizens are disgusted with confused, pampered, spineless, malcontented kids who more often than not are the product of disintegrated suburban homes. These are the ones with too much money, very big on love and synthetic ideals, but short on the will to do. Older people are galled at the pandering to radical youth and the failure to protect authentic academic integrity. They are revolted at the throwing of missiles, fire bombs, and guerrilla tactics via arson and vandalism. As long as this style is rewarded, it will continue to exist, is the verdict of many. They see persons committed to the forceful overthrow of our constituted governmental authority receive not only a respectful hearing on our college campuses, but paid honoraria for the doing.

Elmer Von Feldt, editor of "Columbia," puts it this way:

> Academic freedom does not permit students or professors to impose on others through any type of physical coercion their values, preferences or judgments. Convictions, however sincere, and feeling, however strong, are no mandate to violate the freedom and rights of others. Realism demands patient tolerance of intellectual dissent, but firmness in the face of violence and disruption. There is reason for being soft-hearted with youth; but never for being soft-headed.

A Respite is Necessary

After the successful onslaught of recent times, a respite is necessary to consolidate the gains and restore a constructive stability.

Thereafter social evolution is desirable in consonance with balanced advocacy so that new liberties and their acceptance become established customs of life and living. Orderly progress is conducive to the educational process and the development of a counter culture.

A noted commentator sums it up rather succulently by saying:

"We've listened to the extremists long enough – and rather politely. Personally I can find nothing of value in what they are saying. They are shockingly ill-equipped in history, philosophy, classic literature, political science, or economics. I find them to be arrogant, ill-mannered boors, each in such hot pursuit of his own inflated ego that there is no consensus. They have no affirmative program – only a tantrum."

The way to progressive reform is through the establishment. Most legitimate institutions of modern society will welcome respected members who may become advocates of constructive change. But first the quality of experience will furnish guidelines for the young that could and should bring change for the better. Protest can never win without mature judgment that is the result of self-identity. One must handle himself first before he can contribute to the betterment of his fellow man.

We must conclude that the activists have had too much prime time. Most of the young are a credit to themselves and, although they stand for reformation, they want to build, not destroy. It is time we move the majority of the young highly intelligent adults to front-center. In my view the solidarity of our people will prevail against this chaos, destruction by violence and cataclysmic cycle. In the long run, let the activists know that Americans have the habit of solving problems. The problems born out of extremity, either to the left or to the right, will melt away as a result of the stable middle, then both extremities will be out of a job. True, psychic exhaustion has forced itself upon the populous as a prelude to replacing the age-old ways of attempting to solve problems by war, hate or revenge by a new social order. A. J. Rydholm summed it up best when he said, "The alchemy of world psychology, working beneath the surface of life, is gradually rearranging values in the total human consciousness, though not without considerable anguish. But these are, on the whole, unavoidable growing pains, not irreparable derangements."

We, as a generous people, are reappraising our priorities and are spending billions to erase poverty and racial inequality at home and more billions to help other nations. When one looks at the record, it is far from being completely sordid. Last year Americans donated 14 billion dollars to charitable causes and 50 million Americans contributed time to such charitable operations. Minority Americans have achieved the greatest progress in the shortest period of time in the history of any republic. It is amazing to see the thousands upon thousands of blacks that have moved up into the middle class. As a group, these 22 million less privileged Americans have a gross national income which is approximately that of some 53 million people in Italy! There are more black millionaires in America than the rest of the world combined. In college, black students comprise 7 per cent of the student population while they constitute 11 per cent of the total population. This represents an increase of 110 per cent in the last five years. Fifty-eight per cent of minority groups are at least high school graduates during the present day. Truly a remarkable accomplishment. Forty-five million children of all races are in our schools and 24 million graduate every year. Nearly eight million students attend our colleges.

Given time, our industry will use the science that is held in contempt by so many to clean up our pollution and help create a healthy environment.

Internationally, many nations of the world are beginning to cast longing eyes toward the solution of problems by peaceful means rather than by war.

Efforts at Communication

Since the two world wars, parents progressively have spent less time with their children. Urbanization, the working mother, the delegation and professionalization of child care, all have contributed to the decrease in relationship between parent and child. Youngsters could not have parental contact so they have resorted to their peers. This age segregation was bound to bring social disruption in its wake. One learns qualities such as trust, cooperation and social responsibility from his parents, and he, in turn, conveys it to his children.

As oldsters we have to find the heartbeat and pulse of the young and meet them on their ground and show them that we care. We must develop mutual respect and a willingness to listen to each other. The young, who comprise 20 per cent of our population and will soon be running the nation, are asking us to listen. In so doing,

I believe we can encourage a constructive outlook with the hope that we can save our society, not destroy it.

The students who desperately want to believe in something that is credible must be shown that a constructive belief will prove to be a self-fulfilling prophecy that will bring about the reformations they seek. They must be shown that evaluations of our country, whether true or false, will materialize if they are *believed* by enough people. Negative evaluations can be dissipated if enough people *refuse* to believe them and, instead, believe and act on good and constructive assumptions. We must turn around the national morbidity, which has been foisted on us, to a positive, constructive and forward-looking *action drive.*

Billy Graham, one of the great evangelists of our time, recently said, "If we could get the eight million young people going back to the campus this fall to study and read the Bible, it could change the picture overnight from one of pessimism to optimism." He went on to say that the youth of today want something to believe in and they want moral guidelines by which to live, even though they might not be conscious of it. Tolstoi once said, "Each of us is stuck with a God-shaped blank and unless this blank is filled with a faith in God, then life has no meaning and modern education will stumble from crisis to crisis until the return to the faith of our fathers."

A Search for Truth

As far as the majority of students are concerned, they seem to want a return of love and they turn to the intuitive, ecstatic, impressionistic sensibilities of man. It is an effort to fill in the "God-shaped blank." We know that young people are angry at the failure of its practitioners to relate to a religious philosophical code that is in keeping with the vast new body of knowledge. "Science has failed to eliminate war and it doesn't seem to respond to most of man's needs," they say. Some day, "Pure rationalism just isn't rational, because man is more than reason, and religion knows that, even if positive science doesn't." Many of the young people at this point are at a tragic impasse because they believe our science has brought us to an era of impersonality. With them it is a matter of life or death. Clearly, the crisis of our time is essentially a religious crisis. Life hides an illusive meaning that is eternally inaccessible. The inquisitive spirit that seeks it is caught in the dilemma; he cannot find or classify life's meaning, yet he dare not renounce the quest as hopeless. It is an identity crises. Perhaps this is a fundamental aspect of the Jesus people.

Many who are in the vanguard of this search are trying to find it through drugs, psychedelics and mysterious music. They are in a desperate hunt for a transcendental experience. This quest has led approximately 61 per cent of the college students to experiment with drugs. Drugs seem to bring the experience that amalgamates the material and the spiritual and with it a flicker of light that man is an eternal being and not mortal after all. Some have called the movement the new pursuit to the sacred.

It seems appropriate to go back to the 1840s to a description of Theophile Gautier, a colleague of Baudelaire. The following from DeRopp's *Drugs and the Mind* describes the precipitate effect of a "cosmic trip."

> A certain numbness overcame me, my body seemed to dissolve and I became transparent. Within my breast I perceived the hashish I had eaten in the form of an emerald, scintillating with a million points of fire. My eye-lashes elongated indefinitely, unrolling themselves like threads of gold on ivory spindles, which spun of their own accord with dazzling rapidity. Around me poured streams of gems of every color in ever-changing patterns like the play within the kaleidoscope. My comrades appeared to be disfigured, part men, part plants, wearing the pensive role, air of Ibiscus. So strange did they seem that I writhed with laughter in my corner and, overcome by the absorbity of the spectacle, flung my cushions into the air, making them turn and twist with the rapidity of an Indian juggler. The first attack passed and I found myself again in a normal state.

This old order description of our new discovery age is altogether too vivid in its appeal. If this is the reality experienced by the inquisitive minds of today, it is no wonder we have almost a mass drug problem.

But many have found that a chemically-induced mystical experience is more like a road block than a discovery that leads to cosmic experience. The artificial experience brings on further frustration and sometimes temporary schizophrenia. The psychedelic effect is likened to a perverted consciousness; it will end in disillusionment. Drug orientation is passive and leads to disengagement from active life. It is rapidly developing a drop-out subculture.

We must pursue every possible avenue to discover a path of excellence that will reject the synthetic. The goal must lead to the Infinite Spirit and self-identity. Let us explore!

Chapter Three

Science and Divinity

THERE IS a genuine scientific path for those students of the majority who are prepared to pay the price of self-discipline. One such course offers the possibility of finding a satisfying experience because it can be earned and retained as one's own. For many it will bring to the surface one's inner-self through Divine precept.

The writer has spent many years researching and interviewing the scientific community in an effort to ascertain the association between science and matters of spiritual concern. During this period, he has exchanged views with scientists in universities, the space program, the electronics industry, the medical profession and the technical services. Many of the latter have been prominent in laboratories of research covering a wide spectrum, not only in the United States, but in Europe, Asia and the Middle East. While a review of my material shows a variety of data and views, there is complete agreement on many of the basic precepts. When the parts are put in place, the structure for a thesis develops. I lay no claim that my conclusions are universal, but I do find a surprising number of scientific men and members of the clergy who are in agreement with the conclusions recorded herein. My role here is to serve in the capacity of a reporter.

Dr. Wernher von Braun

To introduce this approach, Dr. Wernher von Braun, who has played a major role in America's space program, deplores and seems baffled by those who suggest that modern science has discredited belief in God. He says, "There certainly is no scientific reason why God cannot retain the same position in our modern world as He had before we began proving His creation with the telescope and cyclotron." He feels that many young people are confused by the pathetic caricatures of God which have been constructed by human limitation. He goes on to say, "Any effort to visualize God, to reduce Him to our comprehension, to describe Him in our language, beggars His greatness."

Dr. von Braun says, "I find it best to accept God as an intelligent will, perfect in goodness, revealing Himself in the world of experience more fully down through the ages as man's capacity for understanding grows."

Thus, in this age of space travel, men must enlarge their concept of God and recognize that He is not a local deity of this planet but "the creator and master of everything" in the universe.

Dr. von Braun said he believes in "the continuity of our spiritual existence after death" for essentially scientific reasons. "Science has found that nothing can disappear without a trace. Nature does not know extinction. All it knows is transformation. Now, if God applies this fundamental principle to the most minute and insignficant parts of His universe, doesn't it make sense to assume that He applies it also to the masterpiece of His creation — the human soul? I think it does."

The Relationship

The basic problem of our time is the search for personal fulfillment in the light of our scientific advancement. Therefore, it seems altogether appropriate that we should examine the relationship between science and religion. If we are fortunate enough to find an appropriate association, as Dr. von Braun suggests, it might make the basis for discussions with the young. In order to achieve this, it is my view that we must chart a new path that will lead the young people directly to God, the Scientific Father, and his Son, the Master.

It is the view of many scientists that there is a desperate need the world over for a new concept concerning the extraterrestrial order of things in relation to individual spiritual needs. For the most part, they subscribe to this concept as a partial approach to this need without making any attempt whatsoever to prove the thesis. They contend that there is far too much confusion in the average mind between "logic" and "credibility" for the undertaking of such an onerous task. In the end one either does or does not believe, based upon his past or his absorption-quotient to spiritual ideas, whether new or old.

Many scientists believe that the utter contempt for status quo in the world today is symptomatic of a new force which is influencing the mass mind, either for good or evil, depending upon the understanding of and the use to which that force is employed. They are equally sure that a new race of thinkers is marching to the foray. They are ready and willing to break with the past and join a move in keeping with the new view. Many of these are bracing themselves for the interplanetary environment. These are the ones who recognize that soon we may be confronted with a brand-new set of facts which may rock the foundations of scientific and theological principles as we have known them. Indeed, a one-world exigency may be thrust upon us, requiring the acceptance of a completely new life style.

It is a majority view that scientific and spiritual forces find initial unification in the cosmos of outer space.

Outer Space

It has been said that millions of light years from our universe there is a spheroidal solar nucleus, originally established as an Alpha Electromagnetic Field. Its source is unknown. In the space around this sphere is a huge electronic ring which flashes in perpetual motion and brilliancy, as though a thousand million suns were being woven into it, to produce its transcendent luster. From every part of this ring dart long broad shafts of light, sometimes forming into circles, small or great, whirling around the enormous girdle of the intelligent, scintillating, jewel-like opal-tinted flame of the Central Nebulous within. *It is this Nucleus of the great Sun-Globe itself, revolving upon its own axis, that constitutes the sublime scene — the Center of the Universes, the Cause of all Creation, Energy Intelligence, the Universal Mind, the Supreme Principle, the Primal Cause, the Cosmic Field, the Divine Spirit, Infinite Intelligence, God the Father!*

Creation and Re-Creation

For endless ages the Central Sun of our Universe and the Suns of Universes without end have absorbed out of the complex Cosmos this throbbing, pulsating, harmonious emanation of electronic energy from this original Spheroidal Solar Nucleus.

From this concentrated source, electromagnetic radiation produced high-energy light fields of photons forming ultimate combinations of electrons, protons, neutrons, positrons and neutral particles. By the combining of certain protons and electrons, the principal element of matter, namely hydrogen atoms, were formed. It appears that all other elements of matter were formed from the hydrogen blocks. From these elements the universes were formed. Through the combination of hydrogen and helium under radiation pressure, dust clouds in the form of gases were formed around the Central Nucleus. These gases produced swirls in concentric rings surrounding the Central Magnetic Field. Particles and heavier atomic nuclei gradually formed into segments which solidified and turned into dense fields of solid matter in the shape of disks.

Einstein's theory of relativity states that "where there is a movement of mass and its velocity is accelerated to the approximate speed of light, it serves to increase the original mass many fold." This mass thus became swirling hot blobs of stars which threw off smaller hot stars which in turn spun and cooled until planets stabilized in orbit like satellites around the Central Suns of the Universes. Thus the entire process of cosmic gases solidifying into terra firma resulted from the original source of Energy Intelligence, which is a form of low frequency radiation.

All the spheres, including our Earth, continue as the recipients of this First Cause known as interplanetary radiation. These waves are thrown into space in all directions and cast as microwave transmissions. They perform every intelligent act of form, creation and re-creation. They stabilize the suns and planets of the universes by maintaining orbital sequences and create the environment for life on millions of planets. They create the material worlds and the people thereon, not only for basic life in the physical realm, but in counterpart electronic forms which produce worlds of greater magnitude which surround the basic planets.

While the original worlds and the people thereon are created from low frequency radiation, the surrounding worlds exist in higher and higher frequency forms as do the extraterrestrial people thereon. This original electronic and chemical creative process further developed compounds specific to living things forming proteins from nucleic acids and enzyme action. These proteins were endowed with genetic properties. Life, both plant and animal, seems to have been propagated, universally, through the seeding of all planets including our earth.

Those planets capable of supporting life-forms continue the process of survival, multiplication and replenishment, as has been the case in our earthly environment. Thus man was literally formed from the "dust of the earth." At the point of creation of physical man, he was endowed with the equipment to regenerate man. He had the proclivities to rise from a lower form to a higher plateau through his intellectual resonance with Energy Intelligence, God the Father.

Regeneration

Even though the *why* of this great force of God is beyond the knowledge of mankind, the *how* can and will be understood through scientific knowledge. There and there alone lies reality. This Wise Intelligence that pervades all space is consolidated by our Central Sun where it undergoes continuous regeneration and rebirth. It is the cosmogenesis of all forms, both physical and spiritual. All life is motion, flow, rise and fall, wax and wane, vibration, oscillation and change. It is a mass of molecules divided into atoms that bounce up and down, circling all around as does the cosmos, the moons and the worlds. All in constant motion, nothing is still. It is perfection. It is the sum of the all in all and is everywhere. It assumes and becomes the great "I Am."

Man has been created from and is a counterpart of this Source of Power. He is coexistent with it and draws to himself these electronic emanations from this aqueous reservoir — the Universal Intelligence, God the Father. Moreover, the accumulation of knowledge by all the intelligent beings of the planets of the Universe is pooled at this Universal Source. By thinking, it converts mass to electromagnetic energy and continues the process of recreation, both material and biological. Furthermore, it continues to extend superconscious knowledge to all mankind. To understand the use to which man employs this electronic intelligence, it is helpful to reference the conscious and subconscious minds, although the mechanics of such understanding are secondary to practical usage.

The Conscious Mind

The conscious mind is your center of control. The cerebrospinal system of the conscious mind, centered in the frontal portion of the brain, is known as the cerebrum. This cerebrum is the supreme ruler or high command of our mental world. Through this, our power to think, to will, to know, to choose and to deal with all impressions gathered through the senses are demonstrated. Since the conscious mind is the creature of the senses, it generates its reality through materialization of what appears to be data from its environment. As you look around a room you may see a desk, perhaps a table, a chair and numerous objects that give you a concluding impression. In reality you are "looking" at thoughts or ideas that have come into being as material things. It is the thought which precedes the form. Every material thing is the result of conscious creative thinking. Everything you do is preceded by a conscious thought. The way you talk, your manner of speech, your personal conduct, your relations with people, every move is a reflection of your thinking in the conscious mind. If you think positively, your life can be a success; if you think negatively, it can be a distaster. Therefore, be careful how you employ this reasoning power.

Since the conscious mind executes all of the commands of your life, which result from inherited and environmental conditions, proper classification and refinement is a condition precedent to the execution of orders. Milton said of the Conscious Mind, "The Mind is its own place and in itself can make a Hell of Heaven or a Heaven of Hell."

The Subconscious Mind

The physical man is an intricate electronic device with a set of transistor-like cells built in from head to toe. The human body is composed of over eighty trillion such electric cells. Each and every one of them vibrates with cosmic energy and is a permanently adjusted miniature *receiver of electronic wave-forms from the Central Source — the Universal Mind*. The confederation of intelligent entities or cells which biologically formulates the total human anatomy, from the first to the last, is connected through the nervous system to the more sensitive cells of the brain, and culminates in a concentrated center in the frontal dome of the head. This, in the East, is known as the "Thousand Petaled Lotus," but, in the West, as a high-gain parabolic antenna of supreme sensitivity, *which is electronically tuned to the incoming rays of the Infinite Intelligence* as referred to above. This concentration of Universal Energy is transmitted from this vital nerve-ending antenna to the cerebellum, in the back portion of the brain, and in turn to the ganglionic cellular mass at the back of the stomach, known as the solar plexus or abdominal brain. This mass in the solar plexus is an electronic marvel. It weighs only fifty ounces and consists of over 10 billion intelligent cells. *This entire body system is known as the subconscious mind. Thus the subconscious mind of man is in complete attunement with and has every attribute of the Universal Mind at all times.* Every member of the human family without exception is the recipient of this omnipresent flow of electronic Infinite Goodness.

The foremost characteristic of the all-powerful subconscious mind is likened to a gigantic computer, fed by the all-encompassing information of thought-form intelligence. It is impersonal, undisturbed and fearless. It knows all, sees all, and is the sum total of all past, present and future knowledge because of its resonance with the great storehouse of information, the Universal Mind.

The subconscious has the eyes and ears of the video and audio tape recorder. According to one well-known electronic engineer, it faithfully records every impact of the conscious mind, every shade of mind-sight, every form of expression. All is indelibly impressed for preservation and future use through electronic processing. Through reflex action, any portion of the tape spontaneously may be played back at any time or, through the action of the will, absolute recall is at your command. This power placed at the disposal of man is an unlimited resource — no problem is too big to defy solution. If you bring proper application to bear, it will leap to your defense, particularly in time of crisis. It has the faculty of placating the antagonist and virtually pours "oil on troubled waters." It takes a turbulent sea of troubles and converts them into the placid waters of contentment and self-assurance. Its creative powers are unlimited.

The Two Minds

The conscious and the subconscious minds have an electronic complex for interaction so that thoughts may pass between the two systems as reflexes. Therefore every mental action constitutes a molecular impact on the twofold nervous systems of the conscious and the subconscious minds.

As an example of this reflex or molecular action between the two minds, the conscious mind can take command of the heretofore inert cells of the subconscious mind by superimposing mental images upon its mechanism. The conscious mind issues a reasoned command and the subconscious mind fulfills the creative order. The subconscious mind will find the solution to specific problems, but in doing so requires that complete preparation for mental activity be stipulated by the conscious mind. The object to be achieved must be clearly defined, analyzed and dissected as the basic material or the data to be processed for subconscious computer action and solution. When the subject under investigation or new knowledge is inspired within, you learn to investigate it; reason with it; examine it, to see if it has the freedom of truth. Your developed intuition will indicate the degree of its validity.

If you feel the intuitive ideas found in the conscious mind lack maturity, you may return them to their source in the subconscious for refinement. Since the subconscious has electronic contact with all knowledge, it continues to research your problem. After an appropriate time-lag, the total concept by reflex action is returned to the conscious mind in final and concise form, ready for practical use and *immediate* action.

De-Emphasize the Technical

The single most important effort in the life of the individual in quest of advancement is to develop an awareness of this unified relationship between the two minds. Your goal must be to understand that the function of the two minds in reality is one efficient and automatic amalgamation, under the guidance of Infinite Intelligence. When you acquire knowledge and understanding of your mental mechanism, you are well on the way to the elimination of your inhibitions. With the removal of repression you free every thinking cell to perform a constructive function. Then you can abandon the mechanics and concern yourself with operations. Your position is that of a driver of an automobile. You drive with confidence knowing that the carburetor, the engine, the transmission, and a hundred other electrical and mechanical devices are functioning perfectly, as a unified whole, in order to assist you to reach your destination. In reaching your goal, it is not necessary to dwell on the mechanical function of the car because that would interfere with your concentration as the driver. As the operator you simply use the gearshift and the accelerator to ensure the forward motion or the brakes to slow it down. *So it is with your comprehension of unified cosmic consciousness. Once understood, this enables you to de-emphasize technical and philosophical explanations of the functions of the two minds and you possess the magic of knowing and believing. Your absorbing interest is in the complete spiritual unification of life. You now know that you can use your conscious and subconscious minds and the interrelation thereof to achieve your goals in life on the road to Divinity. It is illumination!*

CHAPTER FOUR

The Art of Meditation

ONE CAN comprehend this unification best through the deep *silent* and *secret* meditative discipline from the center of his being which is tantamount to illumination. The fact remains that illumination is a legacy awaiting all mankind; more particularly those who desire it enough to work for it. One must master the art of self-discipline. It is here that one cannot submit to the inclination to use psychedelic drugs. If one stands firm, even though assimilation comes slowly, comprehension will bring qualities of observation that will ultimately bloom in the attainment of the desired goal.

The ultimate objective of meditation is to *experience* true serenity and tranquility. It is not an intellectual theory that is sought, but perception and total Wisdom. Divine knowledge is *realized*, not taught. *It is attained by concentration which disciplines one's conscious mind to remain quiescent and allow his subconscious to perceive the radiation from Universal Mind to bring the peace and security. It cannot be overly emphasized that the conscious mind must be isolated and not allowed to encumber the subconscious in its quest for Wisdom.* One must transcend it through concentrative meditation. If the conscious mind, which travels from thought to thought, is unbridled, it will rationalize or reject one's subconscious experience.

The practice of meditation must be conducted in a quiet environment. It requires relaxation and a position of repose. Toss all thoughts from the conscious mind aside, stop thinking. Hold this technique as long as you can. Practice will extend the holding time. Some achieve this by looking at some one object in the room which becomes a concentration mark. At first the conscious mind will trick you. Be firm and shut it off. By practicing this concentration on a central object daily, one will soon be able to cut off the conscious mind at will, then one will have an *experience* which will lead him to the Universal Mind. No amount of reason, thought, argument, debate or logic of the conscious mind will give you the liberation, freedom and tranquility you want. This is attainable only through the subconscious in attunement with Universal Principle.

One must practice this relaxation daily. Do not become impatient in the lag-time. Success will be yours if you remain steadfast, attentive, with purpose and willpower. You will become strong and positive. One's conscious mind manufactures problems. By surrounding it on an island of its own, it becomes less active, less frantic, absencing itself from interference. Every moment put into meditation will give reward beyond imagination.

Science Studies the Meditative Discipline

There is a genuine hope that a technique will be developed which will, through electronic processing, bring meditative discipline to the average person which would ease the presently required concentration cycles and yet achieve complete attunement.

Control of the mind, its moods and behavior and learning, is under study. Early experimentation at the University of California and elsewhere report preliminary results through the application of tiny electrodes placed in the skull of the participant. Through these electrodes a low voltage electric current is applied to the brain. Aside from a brief "prickling" sensation at first, it is painless. When a negative feeling sweeps over one, all he need do is to push a button on a mechanism attached to his waist and instantly serenity is substituted for the depression. The same system is used to control any number of emotional responses. The ultimate goal is to liberate the anxieties and create the meditative environment by putting one in touch with his inner self.

In recent years scientists have performed electronic experimentation to ascertain the reaction of the mind while in meditation. In an early stage of relaxation, slowing alpha waves appear intermittently. However, as deeper relaxation is achieved, the brain produces larger and slower alpha rhythms. At the same time there is an absence of beta waves which are associated with intense mental activity or anxiety of the conscious mind. The so-called alpha state bears remarkable similarity to the states of meditation well known to Eastern religions. Translated to practical application of this scientific evidence, the participant seems to be experiencing each moment of life anew and is uninfluenced by memories of past events or concerned with future activity. This actually is a confirmation on the part of science to that which can be achieved by prolonged concentration in the normal methodology of meditation. *Meditation may soon be understood in terms of control of brain activity through electronic processing.* It gives strong indication of being safe and predictable and, among other things, some believe it may completely replace drugs. Experimental results indicate that it can overwhelm numerous psychosomatic ills and illuminate the mind by defining and extending the dimensions of the inner man.

Direct Control of Alpha Rhythm

It is also noteworthy that science has developed a system by which the "teacher" can inform the student of his state of consciousness of the moment. Through this technique, studies are under way which will chart the relations between the psychological and the physiological, and a definition of states of consciousness during meditation — states of attention, reaction time, level of anxiety, effects on sleep, etc.

The object of this research is to develop a technique by which ordinary people can learn to control their alpha rhythms. Indeed, this method among others has been under study by Dr. Joe Kamiya at the Langley Porter Neuropsychiatric Institute at the University of California. This method of bio-feedback or auto-control demonstrates that one can achieve a state of calm, relaxed alertness while in a state of meditation, quickly and easily. Inside of six to ten one-hour sessions, most subjects can learn to alter their states of consciousness from normal to that of relaxation and serenity, as achieved in full meditation.

Scores of American and Soviet medical scientists are using sophisticated feedback equipment, enabling them to study a complete array of physiological functions. Much of this is devoted to the retrieval of information deposited in the brain's memory bank, a necessary ingredient when one is attempting to confront his inner self.

Yale University's Dr. José Delgado says a future society has to become "psycho-civilized" through the application of electronic stimulation of the brain. Dr. Arthur Koestler, noted psychologist-philosopher, categorically states that this process cannot begin soon enough. He calls it a race against the clock in order to insure the rational cortex over the irrational of the human brain. He further says that it is a matter of "stabilizing people, of harmonizing them without sterilizing them mentally."

The Researchers

This research, originally undertaken as a part of a program by Dr. Charles L. Yeager, Dr. Joe Kamiya and Dr. Robert Ornstein at the University of California, is of tremendous importance. If this effort is successful, it may be possible to re-direct the psychedelic enigma of the youth cult. It might reduce the generation gap. Moreover, it is an ethical scientific effort to discover new frontiers of the mind, a challenge for man to know more about himself. When a large cross section of our people reach apperception, the state of awakened knowing, it will be only a foretaste of greater and more enthralling developments to come. The Western scientific approach is to discover any method that will improve the lag-time in the achievement of full illumination, hopefully "A Quantum Jump to Nirvana."

Many years ago the great scientist, Charles Steinmetz, after a laboratory session in which he had been studying the composition of matter, said, "Fifty years from now the world will be studying the laws of the spirit. They will take love into the laboratory and find more power in love than there is in electricity." There is every likelihood that his prophecy will be fulfilled.

The Rewards

Scientists and clergymen alike state that understanding the proper application of meditation enables one to travel his appointed course without the limitations of world thought to hinder. One pushes ahead toward a program of successful living in every pursuit of life. One can shed the character image of the past and live life in a new context. One loses the sense of importance of conflicts of the material world and ignores distractions by increasing his power of concentration. One can cut off the mental supply line which feeds his fears, his prejudices, his disbeliefs, his personality conflicts.

In candor, one reviews his mental makeup including emotional reactions and all those repressed painful memories back to the time of his childhood. In this mental outcropping by free association one repeats to himself whatever comes into his mind, irrespective of the subject matter. It becomes a confrontation with self. He learns that this impersonal review discards a judgment of right or wrong because he is being completely honest with himself. He realizes the end result is to bring relief from frustration and bitterness and establish a habit of thinking that will make life a joy. His demeanor becomes translucent, because the inflow of Wisdom has set him free.

Power cannot be asserted over one without his acquiescence. Nothing has importance to him that he does not assign to it. The irritating part of a condition is not the situation itself, but bestowing it with *overly* important qualities. One refuses to accept a phobia, an obsession or an illness as a weapon or excuse in an attempt to solve life's problems. When one rebels against his suffering without the reason of truth, he intensifies it. In an emotional state the gateway to the subconscious is completely receptive. Under such conditions the conscious mind, if not cut off, plants ideas and thoughts deep in the subconscious, whether they are desirable or not.

What one imagines, he brings forth. Fear, hate, jealousy and anger precipitate harmful patterns and are completely destructive. In-fighting produces out-fighting. Exalt your enemy, then "lose him and let him go." Thereafter, you have fulfilled your duty and you, as well as the adversary, are free. The truth cannot be established within until you have banished all self-imposed negative concepts implanted by the conscious mind. One can achieve this by maintaining nonattachment to the fruits of hostile action, which is one way to avoid sorrow and a heavy heart. Above all, it will bring release from the guilt associated with aggression. "Be still and know that I am God." Peace of mind is the result. Thus, you already are making a contribution to a better world through self-improvement. This is the kind of peaceful demonstration that brings benevolent results.

Creative Presence

Many religious leaders say, "Look within to see God's presence." Far too often our early training has led us to seek far and wide for this Supreme Force as a person or image. When one personalizes, he idolizes. Thus he has an empty idol and loses the ideal. The surest way to bring aid under meditation is to use the full impact of the cosmic power within his being. There he designates in his subconscious mind's eye, as on the television screen, that which he desires.

By speaking aloud, one may reinforce his desire to make the picture vivid and clear. This is known as creative prayer — to completely outline the image. It opens up a whole new line of communication between one and the Father of Radiation through the Central Source. To create the image is to modulate the electronic waves of radiation, which bathe his being into a picture form. The Universal Substance which permeates every cell within is molded and fashioned through believing and knowing, and becomes a form of answered prayer. The desire is placed in true form and instantly finds fulfillment. It will give a foundation that will be plausible enough so that the leap of faith will take along the whole man.

Speak Affirmatively

"In the ordinary walks of life one should speak affirmatively of serenity, life, peace, harmony and indicate a forward-looking philosophical treatment of great truths," says a French psychologist. The following are excellent examples. "The Divine Spirit of the assured self transcends all distortion." "I am completely capable of succeeding in every effort that I truthfully affirm." "I am in resonance with the intelligence and wisdom that guides all my endeavors into correct and profitable channels."

If we anticipate harmonious solutions in the attitude of prayer, we get harmonious results, not only guiding people to us in large numbers, but overcoming every distasteful experience of life. It leads to love and the sorting and forgiving process, separating the positive from the negative. Thus one takes conscious constructive control of his life and learns to dominate his environmental and inherited tendencies, achieving self-mastery and eventually Supreme Wisdom.

"In this state, the healing Force is now converting every cell, tissue, nerve, muscle and bone according to the excellence of the pattern established in the subconscious mind, and the vitality of the life principle is manifest in every atom of one's being which restores health, harmony and peace," according to a prominent educator. His life is above turmoil; it is quiet, contemplative and compulsive, leading to joy, security, completeness, perfection, infinity, eternity. The body becomes young and vibrant. He ceases to measure life by years and measures it only by itself. It is eternal, ever present and limitless. It provides the base of integration for the reality of personal experience. He becomes conscious of the unfathomable — the complete totality of God. In this state one develops the force of mind, heart, faith, hope, material wealth, inspiration and love by pouring out a quickening spirit to uplift humanity. One assimilates the balanced channel of intuition to create the necessary harmony to lift up all men in a reformed society.

The Divine Monitor

In this state one has a divine monitor and learns to meditate in gratitude and to cultivate a sense of deep perception. The miracles of yesterday become his normal experiences of today. The progressive comprehension of this equation constitutes and reinforces creative prayer. The understanding of the principle indicates the love of God, within. To see manifestations of this principle in others is to completely remove the veil and he recognizes "the Divinity of the Father in every face." It is demonstrated as the first principle of "Love thy neighbor as thyself." The elders sense a new channel of communication that leads to the accomplishment of all of the life goals of the young. This is the ultimate aim for all of humanity — the path to attainment. The world can only change when each soul that comprises it becomes a new being. The aggregate of the whole brings to light a new society.

The goals of all religious thinking are the same — to find Divinity under Universal Law. Each shade of religious construction has rightly satisfied millions on this planet Earth. However, there can be only one set of facts — only one truth about the whole. Nothing can impede or destroy Truth. Truth is the essence of Infinity. There is only one Intelligence, one Consciousness, one Substance; all in one and one in all. This Wisdom Philosophy is the concept that will lift stumbling man, whether he be a Protestant, Catholic, Jew, Mohammedan, Buddhist or a member of any other religious faith, and enable him to channel Supreme Diety into the orthodoxy of his own faith.

A summary of these spiritual truths is expressed in this free translation of the *Idyll of the White Lotus:*

410

The soul of man is immortal, and its future is eternal, with a growth and splendor that has no limit. The principle which gives life dwells within and without and is undying as well as eternally beneficent; is not heard, nor seen, nor felt, but is perceived by the man who desires illumination.

Each man is his absolute Lawgiver, the dispensor of glory or gloom to himself, the decreor of his life, his reward, his punishment.

On the scientific side, we have attempted here to extend the explanation of Einstein's Quantum Theory in the establishment of laws by induction, an approach to electronics as the basis of life. Namely, there can be no effective religion, science, social or philosophical structure, or satisfying living, outside the indisputable and basic fact that there is oneness in all things. Thus the spiritual forces united with the scientific in outer space now become the essence of the inner life force of man.

Furthermore, one's growth is in direct proportion to his degree of enlightenment concerning this Universal Principle. This is the truth of God. This is the natural law of science. This is the road to eternity. "Son of the Republic, look and listen!"

CHAPTER FIVE

A New Age Epilogue

OBVIOUSLY, OUR concept of this New Age spiritually goes far beyond the anthropomorphic concept of God in that He encompasses the total universe as One Being. Understanding of this thesis reveals the true meaning of the assertion of one of the Greatest Scientists of all time, the Master Prophet, when he said that all, along with him, are Sons of God and that no one at any time has seen the Father. The Father's attributes are made evident through the electronic experience of Divinity, not as a personality. You now know that you were created in the image that God-Mind decreed. You understand for a certainty that he who sees God in man has seen the handiwork of the Father, the Universal Mind. You will know then for a certainty that the miracles of the Masters were accomplished through their scientific knowledge. Their use of electronic forces, applied to the atomic structure of all things physical, led to the control of matter through thought energy, Controlled Molecular Orientation. Man becomes the sole expression of the Infinite Creator. "I and the Father are One," becomes a truism. It goes without saying that this knowledge greatly contributes to the extension and explanation of orthodox understanding.

In this time of advanced enlightenment over that of the jungles of the past, man is ready and willing to find the full meaning of Sacred Writings. Evidence abounds in these Greatest Works of all time, which sustain and explain the meditative art in the language of this century. Here is a new road from darkness to light, a final proof that God is not dead.

Practiced by Leaders

While I cannot fully testify to a personal experience with this meditative art, I am immensely intrigued with the application of this force as applied by political, scientific and religious leaders. Such political and religious leaders as Churchill and Gandhi, particularly in periods of stress, in various degrees were moved and guided to action by segments of this Supreme Principle. Washington at Valley Forge, Franklin at the Continental Congress, and Lincoln in the struggle between the states, as well as other leaders throughout the world, both past and present, have had similar experiences testifying to the impact of such Eternal Wisdom.

Einstein, Edison and Tesla, to name only a few recent-day scientists, freely admitted to inspired ideas through the subconscious mind. Some space scientists feel the presence of silent partners as did Captain Edgar D. Mitchell, the Apollo 14 astronaut. He says, "I think of the Universe as an ordered place with an intelligent motivating force . . . synonymous with Infinite Wisdom and perfect altruism." Lt. Col. James B. Irwin, our astronaut on the Apollo 15 mission to the moon, put it this way:

> While I was on the moon, in fact, I felt a sense of inspiration, a feeling that someone was with me and watching over me, protecting me. There were several times when tasks seemed to be impossible. But they worked out all right every time. We were able to accomplish almost all of our objectives, and I believe it helped to have someone there watching over me.

Such understanding has a depth of meaning which prepares man for the coming new era of change, a new man in a postmodern world.

The End of the Third Peril

It has been thus interpreted. Three important cycles mark the periods of formation of the great United States of America. The third phase of this development "was to try men's souls." In fact, it may be America's darkest hour. This vision partially foretells events which after great trials the United States must overcome, trials that caused the downfall of earlier civilizations including the Roman Empire. "Let every child of the Republic learn to live for his God, his land and Union." We shall prevail against the enemies of the Republic. "While the stars remain, and the heavens send down dew upon the earth, so long shall the Union last."

The Fruits of Understanding

When the third peril is finished and man has discovered that science and spiritual forces through Meditative Wisdom have led him to the path of attainment and complete personal fulfillment, he will then discover his new world of peace, the Golden Era of Earth.

In the new age that lies in the century ahead, through improved electronic instrumentation, direct communication between persons on the earth plane and those in the extraterrestrial plane will become commonplace. This will solve forever the efficacy of the reality of life in other vibratory forms and the eternity of the human soul. It will be a coming of the faith of our fathers whose prophets freely communicated with other realms. Science abounds with experimental evidence that will soon bring this process of inter-global communication completely into focus.

The new age education will be totally relevant. Through the electronic tube, off-campus training will give recognition for experience outside the classroom for students and teachers alike. The educational process will not be confined to the young but will include all ages, granting major degrees through revised curricula. The emphasis will be on the totality of the cognitions given through perception, intellectually assimilated. Practical experience will be infused with the totally integrated educational process. Thus the dignity of occupational balance and erudition will be restored.

A New Power Discovery

The era will see the abandonment of the use of thermonuclear energy. Due to the hazard to humanity of high level radioactive wastes which must remain sealed away for as long as 500,000 years, a substitute will be sought. A new power will be discovered through the scientific application of universal spiritual forces.

At that time and not until then, through spiritual intuition from Energy Intelligence, science will break through and discover a whole new branch of physics in the realm of anti-matter that will truly extend man into every part of the universe.

Man will find a system of electronic physics dealing with wave forms in which each half-wave consists of a negative cycle becoming half positive and a positive cycle becoming half negative. Force and anti-force.

Carl Anderson, Nobel prize winner, discovered in a field of electrons that there are anti-electrons, a forerunner to the thesis that where matter exists there is anti-matter. This not only will be expressed in the physical but the anti-physical, a channel to another dimension of the Cosmic, and *will lead to the discovery of new dimensions in the use of solar energy.* Indeed, communication satellites are already using elementary solar power to run the electronic equipment of these "stars of the sky" which bring us worldwide telephone and television service.

The coming of solar power will be available in unlimited quantities for all the peoples of the world. It will be there for the taking, to run our cars, trains, planes. It will light, heat and air condition our homes. Water generators will bring an unlimited supply of water and deserts will be turned into gardens. It will furnish mass-produced products at low cost for the benefit of all. Every material and spiritual want of man can be satisfied.

A New Order

This solar power discovery of Infinite Intelligence will revolutionize industry and introduce new basic scientific laws in physics that will extend our horizon to unbelievable heights.

In the wake of this industrial revolution, great social changes will follow. Freedom of enterprise will be universal because of the diffusion of industry. Prosperity will be universal because of the ease with which production can be developed in all parts of the world. Competition for world markets by the power nations will be eliminated. As a result, the law of the jungle will pass, and through spiritual dynamics, the necessity for armed conflict will be eliminated. The world at peace with almost unlimited resources will solve ecological problems.

Nations will unite under the banner of a one world Hierarchy and universal brotherhood will be achieved. Human concern for all races will grow harmoniously with the new environment. Science and spiritual forces will unite under the aegis of Energy Intelligence, Solar Planetary Power, God the Father. Thus the earth will be resurrected, re-formed and raised into a higher dimension. Then all the people of the world will unite to express the truths, central to all major religions.

The Great Invocation

From the point of Light within the Mind of God
Let Light stream forth into the minds of men.
Let Light descend on Earth.

From the point of Love within the Heart of God
Let Love stream forth into the hearts of men.
May Christ return to Earth.

From the center where the Will of God is known
Let Purpose guide the little wills of men —
The Purpose which the Masters know and serve.

From the center which we call the race of men
Let the Plan of Love and Light work out.
And may it seal the door where evil dwells.

Let Light and Love and Power restore the Plan On Earth.

Terminus Ad Quem

It is hoped that within the next 200 years enlightened members of the Wenger family will want to update this history. From the present, we have looked with honor at much of the tradition born out of the Wenger past. In all probability future Wenger historians will not neglect traditionalism but will add to that record the value of change. That record will, among other things, reveal a change from ritual to relevance and from authority to participation. As suggested earlier, ideologies will bring action and decision making, and personal knowledge could well alter objective truth. Much will be recorded showing a change in human relationships from violence to creativity, politeness to honesty, self-righteousness to openness. In short, because of the new man, a total change in the methodology of communications will be a part of our history.

It may be apparent upon future review that progress has gone far beyond that which would be creditable in our times. I am sure the record will show that members of the clan will have made continuing contributions toward the solution of environmental problems, both scientific and spiritual, and that peace on earth will have been achieved as a spiritual legacy of Christian Wenger (A2) who came to these shores in 1718.

The Wengers have been found on many paths to Eternity. The Path contained herein is a necessary course for those Wengers and a large cross section of mankind who have been cut adrift, seeking their identity. There is nothing here intended as a deprecation to the many alternative paths to Divinity. If you have had a satisfying spiritual experience on another path, this thesis is sufficiently flexible to render a partial need, or until such time as it becomes a demonstrated truth, it will accept outright rejection. Each person must find his own. We all seek an experience, not a theorem. That alone is self-determination which is the spiritual legacy of all men.

Finally, let me quote a passage of Flora R. Matthews:

> Whatever happens, do not be afraid. When the earth shakes, it is but birth pains of the New Age. When the earth bears a New Age, it comes in trembling. A New Age is being born . . . an age of peace, an age of serenity and beauty. The birth is painful and the birth pangs may be violent, but it is a chosen child of God, this New Age. This is to be an age of no more fear, no more turmoil, no more war . . . an age of love in man, for man, through man, of love of God, of love of all His creatures, and, above all, of love for his fellow man. This is the secret . . . man's love for his fellow man is the measuring stick of his love of God.

"Son of the Republic, look and listen!"

Omega

Appendix

The Family Tree Analysis

The following system is used to identify the generations in America. The system is identical for all charts without regard to family branch.

A   Christian Wenger, 1st generation in America

B-1, B-2, B-3, etc., 2nd generation in America

C-1, C-2, C-3, etc., 3rd generation in America

D-1, D-2, D-3, etc., 4th generation in America

E-1, E-2, E-3, etc., 5th generation in America

F-1, F-2, F-3, etc., 6th generation in America

G-1, G-2, G-3, etc., 7th generation in America

H-1, H-2, H-3, etc., 8th generation in America

I-1, I-2, I-3, etc., 9th generation in America

J-1, J-2, J-3, etc., 10th generation in America

K-1, K-2, K-3, etc., 11th generation in America

Previous researchers have used the York System as defined above. These Wenger historians have assigned York numbers to Henry Wenger (A1) and Christian Wenger (A2). Hence, the York System numbers apply to all American research on this family line, past, present and future.

The York System

The following illustrates the number plan of the York System for easy identification.

Christian Wenger, the first American immigrant, was given A2. (His brother, Henry, was given A1.) Each generation in America is indicated by capital letters, starting with A and ending with K. The numeral indicates the order of birth in each family of the person being cataloged, such as first, second, third, etc. The tenth-born child is indicated with a zero (0), the eleventh with an (A) and the twelfth with a (B). As the family increases in number, the thirteenth child is indicated as (C), the fourteenth as (D), the fifteenth as (E), etc. This is an illustration of the York System.

Christian Wenger	(A2)	Christian Wenger is the first generation.
Henry Wenger, Sr.	(A22)	Second-born child of Christian (A2)
Abraham Wenger	(A222)	Second-born child of Henry, Sr. (A22)
Peter Henry Winger	(A2226)	Sixth-born child of Abraham (A222)
Joseph Levi Winger	(A22269)	Ninth-born child of Peter Henry (A2226)
Della Winger Fetzer	(A222692)	Second-born child of Joseph (A22269)
John Earl Fetzer	(A2226923)	Third-born child of Della Winger Fetzer (A222692)

In the family tree sections included here, a generation number is included. In connection with the York identification number assigned to each descendant, it appears as follows: Christian Wenger (A2-1st) or Peter Henry Winger (A2226-4th) or Della Frances Winger (A222692-6th), which indicates Christian Wenger (A2-First Generation in America), Peter Henry Winger (A2226-Fourth Generation in America), or Della Frances Winger (A222692-Sixth Generation in America).

If you wish to determine your generation number as a descendant from our first known Swiss ancestor, simply take your American generation number and add nine to it. Thus, Christian Wenger (A2-1st) means he was the first generation in America. Add nine (1 + 9) to indicate the generation number in question which is ten as a descendant from the first known ancestor. Again, Peter Henry Wenger (A2226-4th) means he was the fourth generation in America. Add nine (4 + 9) to indicate that his generation number is thirteen as a descendant from the first known ancestor.

The Christian Crusade Arms Design

There is an alternate coat of arms which is emblematic of the early Christians or pilgrims who were of the Crusaders during the Christian Crusade. All Wengers who are philosophically a part of the Christian Crusade may adopt this coat of arms.

When the Christian churches were burned or turned into stables, and the pilgrims were mocked and persecuted at every turn, the Christians buckled on their armor and fought faithfully for the right to defend their religion. Men fastened crosses upon their clothing and painted crosses upon their shields to indicate that they enlisted in the cause to defend their rights. This movement was known as the Crusade. It was an expedition under the banner of the Cross by Christians to recover the Holy Land. It was a vigorous concerted action for the defense of their cause.

Wenger Coat of Arms

The Emblem

The helmet is a defensive covering for the head. It was used long before heraldry was known. Some helmets were made of white metal argent (silver); others were made of leather. Argent signifies peace and sincerity. Some were made of iron and had a green color, or vert, which signifies hope, joy and loyalty.

The shield is a broad piece of defensive armor consisting of a plank as of metal, wood or leather and carried on the arm or held in the hand by a handle; for the protection of the body in battle, it consists of gule, or red shield, which denotes military fortitude and magnanimity; it also signifies "the martyr's colour." Upon the shield is painted a cross of silver (or argent) which signifies peace and sincerity. The cross is an emblem or ensign of the Christian religion.

The bandeau or wreath appears on the top of the helmet and is made of ribbons twisted in the form of a rope. The colors of the ribbons are the same as the colors that appear on the shield, gule or

422

red, argent or silver. The wreath or bandeau supports the crest on the helmet. It was probably adopted from the Sacacens by the Crusaders, who found that it afforded additional protection to the head from the heat of the sun and the blows of the enemy.

The crest is that part of an achievement of arms which appears above the helmet. In the early period of heraldry, crests were highly esteemed as they could be obtained only by actual service in the field. They were generally composed of leather and were worn upon the helmet (Melbourne). The crest is of very ancient origin (Cussons). The colors are the same as the charger, gule or red, argent or silver.

The mantling is a decorative accessory which appears behind the helmet; it encircles the upper part and almost the whole of it. The colors are the same as the shield, gule or red, argent or silver.

The Blumenstein Arms

On the occasion of the erection of an official building in 1755, Jacob Wenger, the Mayor of Blumenstein, dedicated his coat of arms which had been placed in a stained glass window. This has

The Coat of Arms adopted in 1755 by Mayor Jacob Wenger of Blumenstein.

been preserved in the Bern Historical Museum. It shows as figures in the coat of arms a green Dreiberg in a red escutcheon which was the shield of the family. On this shield is a silver rose and two golden stars. This is unlike the eagle and lion arms used by other Wenger families in Blumenstein.

Bitzius Wenger established himself at Pohlern, a community near Blumenstein. Here he adopted a coat of arms identical to that of Jacob Wenger above.

In Germany

In Germany there were two brothers of Palatinate nobility. Emanuel Franz Wenger, who became President of the Court Church of St. Cajetan at Munich, and his brother, John Emanuel Clemens Wenger, are recorded in the register of the nobility of the Kingdom of Bavaria. They were granted the diploma in 1788. The arms includes the escutcheon quartered one and four of silver and black and a diagonally divided sinister with a unicorn of changed color. Two and three are in blue, showing a fallen spike with a blue lily and two stars.

Henry Wanger (A1) Family Tree

1st Hans Wenger (b. About 1430) Blumenstein, Thun
2nd Burkhard Wenger (b. About 1450) Forst, Thun
3rd Peter Wenger (b. About 1470) Wattenwil, Seftigen
4th Peter Wenger (b. About 1490) Wattenwil, Seftigen
5th Rudolfus Wenger (b. About 1510) Wattenwil, Seftigen
6th Hans Wenger (b. About 1530) Wattenwil, Seftigen
7th Rudolfus Wenger (Ch. April 5, 1566) Wattenwil-Thurnen, Seftigen
8th Peter Wenger (Ch. Dec. 13, 1607) Wattenwil-Thurnen, Seftigen
9th Hans Wenger (Ch. May 30, 1633) Wattenwil-Thurnen, Seftigen
    A   Henry Wanger (A1) (Ch. Feb. 3, 1680) Wattenwil, Switzerland
          d. 1753, bur. E. Coventry Mennonite Cemetery
          m. Elsi (Elsbeth) Blum before 1705
        B-1 Hans Wanger (A11)
             b. 1706, Wattenwil, Switzerland
             Ch. Feb. 17, 1709, Rothenbach, Switzerland

B-2   Heinrich Wanger (A12)
  b. 1708, Wattenwil, Switzerland
  Ch. Feb. 17, 1709, Rothenbach, Switzerland
B-3   Barbara Wanger (A13)
  b. New Hanover Township, Pennsylvania
  m. John Heistand
 C-1   Isaac Heistand (A131)
 C-2   Anna Heistand (A132)
 C-3   Abraham Heistand (A133)
 C-4   Jacob Heistand (A134)
 C-5   Henry Heistand (A135)
 C-6   John Heistand (A136)
 C-7   David Heistand (A137)
 C-8   Magdalena Heistand (A138)
 C-9   Veronica Heistand (A139)
 C-10 Elizabeth Heistand (A130)
B-4   Eva Wanger (A14)
  b. New Hanover Township, Pennsylvania
B-5   Hannah Wanger (A15)
  b. New Hanover Township, Pennsylvania
  m. Edward De Haven
 C-1   John De Haven (A141)
 C-2   Margaret De Haven (A142)
 C-3   Herman De Haven (A143)
 C-4   Hannah De Haven (A144)
 C-5   Mary De Haven (A145)
 C-6   Edward De Haven (A146)
 C-7   Abraham De Haven (A147)
B-6   Jacob Wanger (A16)
  b. New Hanover Township, Pennsylvania
  m. Barbara
 C-1   Abraham Wanger (A161)
 C-2   Magdalena Wanger (A162)
 C-3   Elizabeth Wanger (A163)
B-7   Magdalina Wanger (A17)
  b. New Hanover Township, Pennsylvania
  m. M. Wisler
 C-1   John Wisler (A171)
 C-2   Jacob Wisler (A172)
 C-3   Mary Wisler (A173)
 C-4   Susanna Wisler (A174)

C-5 Esther Wisler (A175)

C-6 Abraham Wisler (A176)

B-8 Abraham Wanger (A18)
       b. New Hanover Township, Pennsylvania

C-1 Anna Wanger (A181)

C-2 Barbara Wanger (182)
       m. Koch Brower

B-9 John Wanger (A19)
       b. 1726, New Hanover Township
       d. Jan. 6, 1803, Berkes County, Pennsylvania
       bur. East Coventry Mennonite Cemetery
       m. Margaret Rebecca
         b. April 1, 1734
         d. Aug. 1, 1793

C-1 Elizabeth Wanger (A191)

C-2 Abraham Wanger (A192)

  D-1 Jacob Wanger (A1921)

  D-2 Magdalena Wanger (A1922)

  D-3 Elizabeth Wanger (A1923)

  D-4 Hannah Wanger (A1924)

  D-5 Magdalena Wanger (A1925)

  D-6 John Wanger (A1926)

  D-7 Samuel Wanger (A1927)

  D-8 Abraham Wanger (A1928)
         m. Susannah, d. Mar. 18, 1793

    E-1 Abraham Wanger (A19281)
           b. Dec. 11, 1787
           d. April 23, 1861
           m. Mary Magdalena Berge
             b. April 2, 1798
             d. Feb. 28, 1878

      F-1 Susanna Wanger (A192811)

      F-2 Henry Wanger (A192812)

      F-3 Peter Wanger (A192813)

      F-4 Elizabeth Wanger (A192814)

      F-5 Rebecca Berge Wanger (A192815)
           b. Aug. 26, 1830
           d. Nov. 1, 1911
           m. Wm. Bishop Stanford, Jan. 1, 1851

      F-6 Mary Wanger (A192816)

      F-7 Abraham Wanger (A192817)

F-8 Annie Wanger (A192818)

F-9 Susanna Wanger (A192819)

F-10 George Wanger (A192810)
m. Rebecca Price, d. Dec. 30, 1876

G-1 Newton Wanger (A1928101)

G-2 George Price Wanger (A1928102)

G-3 Joseph Price Wanger (A1928103)

G-4 Irving Price Wanger (A1928104)
b. March 5, 1852
m. June 25, 1884, Emma C. Titlow

H-1 Rebecca Wanger (A19281041)

H-2 Rebecca Wanger (A19281042)

H-3 Lincoln Wanger (A19281043)

H-4 George Wanger (A19281044)

H-5 Ruth Wanger (A19281045)

H-6 Marion Wanger (A19281046)

C-3 Samuel Wanger (A193)

C-4 Jacob Wanger (A194)

C-5 Magdalena Wanger (A195)

C-6 Hannah Wanger (A196)

C-7 John Wanger (A197)

C-8 Magdalena Wanger (A198)

B-10 Elizabeth Wanger (A10)
b. New Hanover Township, Pennsylvania
m. Mr. Souder

B-11 Veronica Wanger (A1A)
b. New Hanover Township, Pennsylvania
m. John Switzer

C-1 Hannah Switzer (A1A1)

C-2 Mary Switzer (A1A2)

C-3 Jacob Switzer (A1A3)

C-4 Esther Switzer (A1A4)

C-5 Magdalena Switzer (A1A5)

C-6 John Switzer (A1A6)

C-7 Elizabeth Switzer (A1A7)

C-8 Veronica Switzer (A1A8)

C-9 Barbara Switzer (A1A9)

George Wanger (A192810) Family

George Wanger (A192810) of the above Henry Wanger (A1) Family Tree married Rebecca Price and was a well-known farmer of North Coventry. He distinguished himself as a zealous worker in the anti-slavery cause, having made his house a station on the underground railroad. He was also actively engaged in the temperance movement and other reforms. His brother, Abraham (A192817), was a well-known member of the Chester County Bar and was District Attorney from 1872 to 1875. His son, Irving Price Wanger (A1928104), became a member of the United States Congress from the 7th Pennsylvania District. Irving Price Wanger (A1928104) was reared on the old Wanger homestead. He was educated in the public schools of Pottstown where he later taught school. He studied law at Morristown, Pennsylvania, in 1872 with Franklin March, a distinguished member of the Montgomery County Bar. He was admitted to the Bar in December 1875. He became a member of the law firm Wanger and Knip and built up a large law practice in his city.

In 1880, as a Republican, he was elected District Attorney for Montgomery County. That same year he was a delegate to the Republican National Convention and in 1889 he became Chairman of the Republican County Committee. In 1890 he was unanimously nominated for Congress by the Republicans of the 7th District. Again in 1892 he campaigned for Congress and was elected. He stayed in the 53rd Congress and was on the Committee of Public Lands, Railways and Canals. He was renominated in 1894 and re-elected as a member of the 54th Congress. He was considered one of the most able congressmen of his time and the fact that he was re-elected was emphatic testimonial of the regard and confidence in which he was held by his fellow citizens. The Honorable Irving Price Wanger married Emma C. Titlow and had a family of five children. He was a member of the Episcopalian Church, the Odd Fellows, the Order of Red Men and most of the Masonic bodies, being Grand Commander of the Knights of Templar of Pennsylvania.

A Companion Volume

Much of the detailed American family history for Henry Wanger (A1), has been reported in the text. It would be a significant contribution if his American descendants would undertake the publication of a volume companion to this one. Since the European ancestral background is common to both brothers, a companion history covering Henry Wanger's (A1) American descendants could bring together traditions, background and biographical data that would significantly enhance the total record.

A number of collateral Wanger histories of considerable worth, have been published; however, many of these do not give enough weight to the past connections of their first known American ancestor. We feel sure that many of these Wenger families, which have partial documentation, merge with the unsolved male line of descendants indicated here.

Research in Switzerland

List of the communes, districts and parishes in the state of Bern in which Wenger families had hereditary citizenship before 1800. (*Familiennamenbuch der Schweiz*, 1940, Vol. II, 823)

Commune	District	Parish	Registers
Gürbenthal:			
Amsoldingen	Thun	Amsoldingen	1662
Forst	Thun	Amsoldingen	1662
Höfen	Thun	Amsoldingen	1662
Längenbühl	Thun	Amsoldingen	1662
Blumenstein	Thun	Blumenstein	1561
Pohlern	Thun	Blumenstein	1561
Oberstocken	Niedersimmental	Reütigen	1698
Thierachern	Thun	Thierachern	1570
Uebeschi	Thun	Thierachern	1570
Uetendorf	Thun	Thierachern	1570
Gurzelen	Seftigen	Gurzelen	1555
Rüeggisberg	Seftigen	Rüeggisberg	1581
Thurnen	Seftigen	Thurnen	1549
Wattenwil	Seftigen	Wattenwil	1649
Bern and Schwarzenburg:			
Köniz	Bern	Köniz	1552
Oberbalm	Bern	Oberbalm	1549
Guggisberg	Schwarzenburg	Guggisberg	1591
Rüschegg	Schwarzenburg	Rüschegg	1661
Rüschegg	Schwarzenburg	Guggisberg	1591
Wahlern	Schwarzenburg	Wahlern	1577
Albligen	Schwarzenburg	Albligen	1607

Bernese Oberland:

Grindelwald	Interlaken	Grindelwald	1557

Emmenthal: Signau and Thun

Buchholterberg	Thun	Oberdiessbach	1588
Oberlangenegg	Thun	Schwarzenegg	1693
Oberlangenegg	Thun	Steffisburg	1552
Röthenbach	Signau	Röthenbach	1570

Seeland:

Rapperswil	Aarberg	Rapperswil	1567

Voluminous Records

From the preceding list of parish records, it may be seen that our investigations at Thurnen, Wattenwil, Rothenbach and Oberdiessbach reveal only a small fraction of the total records available concerning Wenger families of Swiss extraction. Our research at Thurnen for the period 1597 to 1674 covered 84 Wenger families with 470 entries of individuals. At Wattenwil we searched the records between 1659 and 1751. This covered 40 Wenger families with 185 separate records of individuals. At Oberdiessbach when we searched for Christian Wenger (A2) between 1664 and 1710, we found 16 Wenger families with more than 70 entries of individuals. At Rothenbach between 1570 and 1619 we found 19 families by the name of Wenger encompassing 80 individual listings. All Wenger records found there were in the State Church. For the most part, Wengers in the Emmental district, who went there to hide in the hills, remained anonymous to the church records.

All our Swiss research, particularly the working papers, will in due course be made available to principal genealogical libraries throughout the United States.

European Wenger Authors

Below is a partial list of European Wenger authors and the dates of their publications as compiled by Roger D. Winger:

Dr. A. Wenger (Dr. Ing A. Wenger), Berlin, 1908
Dr. Albert Wenger, Zurich, 1919
Dr. Alfred Wenger, Strassburg, Germany, 1900
Dr. Fritz Wenger, Marburg, 1928
Dr. Fritz Wenger, Zurich, 1915

Dr. Ernest Wenger, Bern, 1910
Dr. Friedrich Wenger, Leipzig, 1915
Dr. Hans Wenger, Bern, 1939
Dr. Henri Leon Wenger, Strassbourg, no date
Dr. Johannes Martin Wanger, Konigsburg, 1928
Dr. Robert Wenger, Leipzig, 1915
Dr. Walter Rudolph Wenger, 1931, Basel
Dr. Willo Wenger, Stuttgart, 1946
Dr. Joseph Wenger, Munich, 1926
Dr. Julius Wenger, Breslau, 1927
Dr. Karl Wenger, Bern, 1905
Dr. Leon Wenger, Paris, 1945
Frau Liza Wenger, famous novelist,
    Bern, Zurich, Berlin
    1938 on. (24 novels)
Dr. Paul Eugene Etienne Wenger, Geneva, 1948
Dr. Pierre Wenger, Geneva, 1942
Dr. Oscar Winger, Berlin, 1927

Partial List of Known Wenger Immigrants

Name	Year of Arrival
Henry Wenger (A1)	1717
Christian Wenger (A2)	1718
Christian Wenger	1727
Henry Wenger	1727
John Jacob Wenger	1733
Hans Wenger	1734
Jacob Wenger	1735
Lazarus Wenger	1736
Karl Michael Wenger	1736
Hans Wenger	1737
Hans Wenger	1748
Michael Wenger	1749
Christian Wenger	1749
Hans Wenger	1751
Joseph Wenger	1754
Casper Wenger	1764
Jacob Wenger	1801
Christian Wenger	1810
John Winger	1822

Christian Wenger	1824
George Wenger	1838
Jacob Wenger	1847
John Wenger	1851
Christian Wenger	1860
Jacob Wenger	1860
Conrad Wenger	1861
Frederick Wenger	1868

For Future Researchers

The following is a list of male Wengers of our line whose descendants are not completely known as this is written. Future family researchers may well find the links to these Wengers that will solve multitudinous family genealogies. By consulting the York numbers, it will be easy enough for each searcher to identify the family patterns of each ancestor.

Abraham Wenger	(A23)
Christian Wenger	(A24)
Michael Wenger	(A25)
Jacob Wenger	(A2214)
Samuel Wenger	(A2224)
David Wenger	(A2227)
John Wenger	(A2231)
Jacob Wenger	(A2232)
Jacob Wenger	(A2246)
George Wenger	(A2247)
Ameziah Wenger	(A22121)
Henry Wenger	(A22212)
Jacob Wenger	(A22244)
John Wenger	(A22245)
Abraham Wenger	(A22281)
Aldus J. Wenger	(A222111)
John Wenger	(A222426)
Amsa Wenger	(A2211111)
Angus Wenger	(A2211112)
Raymond Morley Wenger	(A2211141)
Russell Elmo Wenger	(A2211142)
Melvin Wenger	(A2211161)
Harry Glouner Wenger	(A2221418)
David L. Wenger	(A222131111)

The John Barr Sale

The handbill advertising the John Barr sale in Lancaster County, Pennsylvania, is reproduced on page 193. John Barr was the father of Anna Barr Winger, wife of Peter Henry Winger (A2226). The following shows the conditions of sale and the names of the purchasers:

> The conditions of the present public vendue, held on the premises of Jacob Neff by John Barr, the 7th day of February, 1835, are as follows: The highest and best bidder shall be the buyer. Persons purchasing articles of this sale not amounting to the value of 5 dollars shall pay cash; but if at, or exceeding the sum of 5 dollars, shall have four months credit by giving their notes of hand, before the removal of the goods, with approved security.
>
> Persons purchasing articles at this sale, who are not willing to comply with the above terms, shall return them to the crier before the sale closes, and make good any deficiency that may happen in the price at the second bidding. Any article struck off, and claimed by two or more persons, shall immediately be put up at a former bid.

Purchasers' Names

Andrew Ashon
Jacob Barge
Leonard Barge
Henry Barr
Samuel Barr
John Bassler
Rev. Henry Bowman
Daniel Brubaker
Benjamin Buckwalter
H. Bushman
Martin Bushman
Daniel Cleck
Robert Crawford
John Eleman
David Eshelman
Jacob Eshelman
George Fagon
Richard Fisher
Frederick Fry
Henry Goodhart
Abrm Groff
John Groff

Jonas Harnish
John Hasson
Adam Hefener
Abrm Herr
Christian Herr, Jr.
Elias Herr
Jacob Herr
Martin Herr
Jacob Hess
Charles Huber
Christian Huber
John Huber
David Hummel
Daniel John
Samuel Kendig
Thomas Kennedy
Michael Kiester
Joseph Leaman
John C. Lemon
Edmond Martin
John Martin
John Massen

Henry Miller, Jr.
John Morton
David Musser
Dr. M. Musser
Samuel Myers
Daniel Mylin
Francis Peoples
Hiram Pierce
James Reed
Samuel Ressler
John L. Riley
David Rush
Christian Snievely
John Stanton
Samuel String
David Strohm
James Warren
John Warren
John Whisler
Benjamin Winick
John Witmer
Samuel Yeager

Correspondents

The following is a partial list of my correspondents who have involved themselves in Wenger research:

Lucinda Wenger Oaks
West Milton, Ohio

M. Luther Heisey
237 North Lime Street
Lancaster, Pennsylvania

Mable Van Dyke Baer
4513 Brandywine St., N.W.
Washington, D.C.

Dr. J. C. Wenger
Goshen College
Goshen, Indiana

Mrs. Harold Waters
Rural Route 1
New Ross, Indiana

Mrs. Joseph McConville
235 East Walnut Street
Ephrata, Pennsylvania

Miss Mary A. Ranck
Lancaster County Historical Society
307 North Duke Street
Lancaster, Pennsylvania

Mrs. Dorothy W. Thalmer
242 Oak Street
Pottstown, Pennsylvania

Mr. Henry Wenger
15111 Wyoming Avenue
Detroit, Michigan

Mr. Samuel S. Wenger
42 North Duke Street
Lancaster, Pennsylvania

Mr. Emmert L. Wingert
Attorney at law
1 West Main Street
Madison, Wisconsin

Ezra Wenger
Fredericksburg, Pennsylvania

Mr. Rolla S. Wenger
348 Clifford Avenue
Union City, Indiana

Mr. Robert M. Winger
State of Michigan
Department of Public Instruction
Lansing, Michigan

Mr. Paul Winger
Superintendent of Schools
Sturgis, Michigan

Mrs. Claude D. Locke
333 West Fourth Street
Greenville, Ohio

Mr. R. E. Wenger
119 East Third Street
Greenville, Ohio

Mr. Ralph L. Wingard
Johnstown, Pennsylvania

Miss Luella B. Wenger
734 Southwest End Avenue
Lancaster, Pennsylvania

Mr. Fritz Allimann
Wabersackerstrasse 24
CH3097 Liebefeld-Bern
Switzerland

Dr. Robert Oehler
Aebnitstrasse 35
3073 Gumligen
Switzerland

Dr. Fritz Braun
675 Kaiserslantern
Germany

Mr. Ira D. Lardis
Lancaster Mennonite Historical Society
2215 Mill Stream Road
Lancaster, Pennsylvania

Mr. Earle K. Wenger, Sr.
68 Hannah Street
Battle Creek, Michigan

Mr. Allen C. Wenger
Wayland, Iowa

Mr. Raymond J. Wenger
207 Baer Building
Reading, Pennsylvania

Mrs. Robert Hager
58 Marathon Avenue
Dayton, Ohio

Mr. L. K. Funkhouser
27 North Summit Street
Dayton, Ohio

Dr. Delbert Gratz
Bluffton College
Bluffton, Ohio

Mrs. Nettie L. Major
2231 Bancroft Place, N.W.
Washington, D.C.

Miss Winifred M. McLachlan
4497 South 3200 West
Salt Lake City, Utah

Grace W. Wenger
130 Main Street
Landisville, Pennsylvania

Norman W. Nauman
Route 4, Box 23
Manheim, Pennsylvania

Maude S. Yuninger
Lancaster, Pennsylvania

Madelene Howland
505 North Swarthmore Avenue
Swarthmore, Pennsylvania

Harriett C. Thomas
1130 State Street
Lafayette, Indiana

Mr. Joseph A. Winger
635 North Owl Drive
Sarasota, Florida

Mr. Clyde Foster
2818 Winthrop Avenue
Racine, Wisconsin

Mr. Charles Sanders Foster
1050 Northwest 128 Terrace
Miami, Florida

Mr. Russell Winger
Omaha Street
Bellfountain, Ohio

Mr. Lawrence F. Winger
980 Wilmington Avenue
Dayton, Ohio

Mr. Ralph Winger
425 Dayton Towers Drive
Dayton, Ohio

Mr. Wm. R. Wenger
200 Lonsdale Avenue
Dayton, Ohio

Mrs. Della Frances Winger Pyle
1808 Thompson Street
Lafayette, Indiana

Mr. John Winger
McGrawsville, Indiana

Mr. John Winger
4322 St. James Street
Dayton, Ohio

Mrs. Alice McKee
602 South Main Street
Ansonia, Ohio

Mrs. Floyd R. Detrick
R.R. 1
West Melton, Ohio

Rolland Pierstorff
R.R. 3
Lebanon, Ohio

W. K. Finton
Rural Route 5
Greenville, Ohio

Mrs. Ralph J. Smith
1418 North Jay Street
Kokomo, Indiana

Mrs. Agnes Watters
2226 25th Avenue
Fort Wayne, Indiana

Mrs. Blanche Passwater
122 Park Boulevard
New Haven, Indiana

Mrs. Forrest Hager
1121 East Lordman
Kokomo, Indiana

Mrs. Edna Doss
55 Ward Street
Dayton, Ohio

Dallas O. Watters
717 Prospect Avenue
Fort Wayne, Indiana

Joseph R. Frey
Conover/Cohn Roads
Yorkshire, Ohio

Aldus Seldomridge
Rural Route 1
Lancaster County, Pennsylvania

Charles Swann
218 Eastern Drive
Chesterfield, Indiana

Mr. Gerald Hess
R. R. 3
Versailles, Ohio

Mrs. Maude Hess
Rossburg, Ohio

Mr. Charles Wenger
Route 3
Versailles, Ohio

John W. Waymire
4230 Cherokee Avenue
San Diego, California

Mr. Joseph Seacrest
Lincoln, Nebraska

Mrs. Esther Lime
320 South Walnut Street
Celina, Ohio

Mrs. Ruth Mendenhall
114 East Warren Street
Celina, Ohio

Mrs. Amanda Pierstorff
Lebanon, Ohio

Mrs. Nelson Hoenie
515 Wayne Street
Celina, Ohio

Mr. Charles Wenger
144 Bel Air Avenue
Dayton, Ohio

Mrs. Mildred Foster
930 North Tamiami Trail
Sarasota, Florida

James W. McCowan
R.F.D. 2
Coatesville, Pennsylvania

Mrs. Wilma Beertema
1031 Ashley Drive
Kalamazoo, Michigan

Ira R. Barr
Yellow Springs, Ohio

R. Thomas Mayhill
27 North Jefferson St.
Knightstown, Indiana

Mrs. Mary S. Streeter
P.O. Box 59
East Orleans, Mass.

Wenger Historian Files

Wenger historians, including Samuel Wenger who descends from Christian Wenger (C) of 1727, Norman Nauman of the Hans Wenger (K) line of 1748 and Rev. Roger D. Winger through the same line from the Martin Wenger (K17) family, have volumes of genealogical material. All of this data, as well as much of the material collected by the writer including Swiss working papers, will ultimately reside among others with the Mennonite Conference Historical Archives in Lancaster, Pennsylvania. Dr. Winger probably has the most voluminous files of any of the Wenger historians. He is listed in the *Dictionary of International Biography, Who's Who in the Mid-West, Who's Who in the Protestant Clergy* and the *Inter-*

national Platform Association. All of his massive correspondence and records are being microfilmed by the genealogical society of the Mormons and will be placed in their archives. Over 50,000 items and 6,000 index cards will be available there. These include much data on 150 Wenger immigrants to America and on European Wenger history. It also contains a directory of 10,000 Wengers and variants. Dr. Winger estimates that his records include information about more than 75 branches of Wenger families and hundreds of others who have been interested in information concerning their ancestors.

Dr. Roger D. Winger, the author of *Wenger Clan Notes,* states that the Mormons have hundreds of researchers in Europe and throughout the United States gathering records. He indicates that their files probably will encompass one billion microfilms including complete filming of all colonial records. Many Winger family genealogies or parts thereof will be included. It hardly needs to be said that Dr. Winger has a fine professional record and his *Wenger Clan Notes* has been one of the leading family genealogical publications in the country. It also should be noted that during 1963 Dr. Winger offered his Clan Notes to libraries in America and Europe.

Wenger Clan Notes

Volume I — 1954-1956

Volume I of *Wenger Clan Notes* comprises a journal of research on the history of the Wenger Clan. In it are twelve quarterly issues with 48 large book pages of compact historical material touching on most of the topics that would interest a student of family history.

Below is a summary of the General Index of the volume to give the reader an orderly arrangement of facts. It is the only printed material now available on the general history of the Wenger Clan.

The General Index

Authors: Wenger Clan

Biographies: "Who's Who" among the Clan

Cemeteries: Those bearing clan names.

Daughters of the American Revolution: How to apply and carry on research for membership.

Folk Lore and Anecdotes:

Government and the Clan: Persecutions, revolutionary soldiers, assignments.

Historians: Suggestions for genealogists and a list of over 40 in research.

History of the Wenger Clan: General items, lineages, names and their origins, etc.

Illustrations and Portraits:

Immigrant Ancestors to America: 27 immigrants in chronological order of their arrival.

Immigration: Causes and effects; to and from where; use of serial letters, etc.

Landmarks Bearing Wenger Names: Villages, mountains, glaciers, cemeteries.

Press References: "We See By The Papers."

Publications and Manuscripts: On general subjects; and Wengerology.

Relationship: How to determine it.

Relics: Reminders of the past.

Religion and the Clan: Persecution episodes; denominations; etc.

Research: Methods and suggestions.

Reunions, Wenger Clan: General items; list of Wenger, Wingard, Winger, and Wingert Family Associations and history of each.

Revolutional War Wengers: Qualifying for membership in D.A.R.

Wengers in Germany: A list of them.

Wengers in Switzerland: Habitat of and a list of Wengers.

Wenger and Variant Names: A history of, and interesting facts about each of the following names: Wanger, Wengen, Wenger, Wengerd, Wengert, Winagard, Wingard, Winger, Wingerd, Wingert, Winget, Wynegar, and Wyngart. This index mentions landmarks, origins, publications, religion, reunions, root meanings and stems, use of suffixes, reasons for variation, etc.

Wenger and Variant Names: An alphabetical list of several hundred persons mentioned in the 12 issues of Wenger Clan Notes. The large number of families and branches covered will impress you with the prodigious amount of research that has been and is being carried on to make possible such a comprehensive volume of facts about Wengerology.

438

Wenger Clan Notes

Volume II — 1957-1959
(In Progress)

With Volume I of *Wenger Clan Notes* completed, this unique periodical is now making Volume II. Inasmuch as most of the information in *Wenger Clan Notes* will not be found elsewhere in print, it will be a favor to your posterity to have a complete file to hand down from your household. Address all inquiries to: Wenger Family Associations, Rev. Roger D. Winger, Historian, 2750 Read Street, Omaha, Nebraska 68112.

A Christian Wenger Humanities Center

As this Wenger history was being prepared, Elizabethtown College near Lancaster, Pennsylvania, made a proposal to the writer that a memorial to Christian Wenger (A2) and Christian Wenger (C) would be a fitting tribute to the contributions of the two founders of our pioneer Wenger families.

The Christian Wenger Humanities Center, at the far right, is a memorial to our Christian Wenger (A2) and Christian Wenger (C). The building on the left and center is the new Social Science Center. Both buildings are on the campus of Elizabethtown College near Lancaster, Pennsylvania.

Subsequently the writer made a substantial challenge gift to the College representing the descendants of Christian Wenger (A2).

The gift was made with the proviso that the descendants of Christian Wenger (C) would contribute sufficient funds to complete the Christian Wenger Humanities Center.

Samuel S. Wenger, Esquire, Administrator of Elizabethtown College and a descendant of Christian Wenger (C), accepted the challenge in behalf of his ancestor and will undertake the drive to secure the additional funds.

Suitable plaques commemorating the two progenitors will grace the entrance hall to the Center.

Some Traditional Stories

The following traditional stories made research in our family line most difficult since it was discovered that some of these stories occurred in several unrelated Wenger families whose ancestors resided in Lancaster County, Pennsylvania.

It has been indicated that one Wenger ancestor was ship-wrecked off the coast of Ireland. He went ashore, stayed long enough to marry an Irish girl and the two of them came to America. This was proven inaccurate as applied to our Emanuel Wenger (A2221). Stories abound of Irish and English births of certain Wenger ancestors whose fathers came to Ireland and England, stayed for a time and then came to America. There are many stories which state that all of the family did not come at the same time.

We were led to investigate the German Palatinate, more particularly Zweibrücken, because of an Ohio family story which said, "One ancestor was brought to America at the age of two from his place of origin in Germany." Our investigation was fruitful in that we found the connecting link to Christian Wenger (A2).

A Cousin

An interesting sequel to the John H. Winger (A22267) of Ohio story is the fact that Lt. Hezekiah Winger of Springfield, Ohio, was also a member of Company E along with our John Winger (A22267) during the Civil War. Johnson Block, a real estate agent in Springfield, Ohio, was a member of the same Company. He stated years later that he recollected that a cousin (John Winger A22267) to their Hezekiah Winger was a member of Company E. The fact that these Winger Boys referred to each other as cousins implies a relationship

440

between two separate lines of Winger families. The founder of this line of Wingers, namely Christian Wenger (A2), had a son by the name of Michael Wenger (A26). Some researchers have indicated that this Michael Wenger (A26) was the same as Karl Michael Wenger who came to Lancaster County from Switzerland in 1736. He was the ancestor of a long line of Wengers residing in Lebanon and Franklin Counties in Pennsylvania. Members of the Winger family residing in Franklin County ultimately went to Springfield, Clark County, Ohio, as well as Lincoln, Lancaster County, Nebraska. Joseph Winger of Franklin County, Pennsylvania, was the forebear of Joseph W. Seacrest, distinguished publisher in the state of Nebraska. Karl Michael Wenger was the ancestor of the Wengers in Springfield, Ohio, including the Hezekiah Winger referred to as a member of Company E.

It goes without saying that this cousin link in Ohio and the Pennsylvania traditional story of the relationship between Karl Michael Wenger and our Christian Wenger (A2) progenitor is not substantial enough evidence upon which to draw final conclusions. This is especially true because Michael Wenger (A26) died before 1762, reportedly without issue, according to previously cited documentary evidence. Therefore, there is some doubt that the Karl Michael Wenger referred to above is one and the same with our Michael Wenger (A26). It is highly probable that the above line of Wengers is descended from Christian Wenger of 1727. There is some indication that this line did merge with our Christian Wenger (A2) line, possibly in Switzerland, although there is no documentary proof.

Jacob Wenger

Jacob Barr, who is a descendant of John Barr, the father of Anna Barr Winger, now lives on the old John Barr farm in Bath Township, Greene County, Ohio. In 1945 he told the writer the following: Peter Winger (A2226) had a brother, Jacob Winger, and two sisters, who lived for a time in Greene County. He stated that Jacob Winger, known as Jake, established a tavern near Bradford in Darke County. For a number of years a search was made to find these relatives, but without success. The documentary evidence discovered in Chester County, Pennsylvania, definitely established the Peter Henry Winger (A2226) family pattern. From this we conclude that Peter Winger (A2226) had no brother by the name of Jacob. As a result, we conclude that these relatives were not brothers and sisters, but probably cousins who remain undocumented. Peter Winger (A2226) had at least two Winger cousins by the name of Jacob.

In the research for Jacob Winger, who was presumed to have been a brother of our Peter Henry Winger (A2226), we discovered another Jacob Winger of some interest. This Jacob Winger has no relationship to our family. In any event, it led us to the town of Miamisburg located south of Dayton on the east bank of the Miami River. In early times it was known as "Hole's Station." The town was incorporated February 11, 1832. At that time it had a population of 500. The first election of the town officers was held at the home of Jacob Winger which later became known as the Washington House. That was May 7, 1832. At that time Gooding Hollaway was elected mayor and other officers were chosen as recorder and town council. Eighty-four votes were cast.

Jacob Winger was proprietor of the Washington House for many years after 1830. He sold it to Samuel Zehring. Jacob Winger was born about 1795. He died in 1863 and is buried in the Miamisburg Cemetery. His first wife was Catherine who was born in 1792 and died January 8, 1851. Later that same year he married a woman by the name of Maria Adeline. Jacob Winger had a daughter by the name of Mary E. Winger who married Samuel Zehring, August 13, 1893. This is the same Samuel Zehring who purchased the Washington House from Jacob Winger. One record indicates that the French Counsel in Cincinnati owed Jacob Winger $102. The debt apparently was not collected. Other data indicates that Samuel Zehring was appointed administrator of the Jacob Winger estate July 11, 1863. Jacob Winger was born in France in 1799 and was drafted into the French Army at the age of fifteen. He was a member of Napoleon Bonaparte's Imperial Guard and a member of the French Legion of Honor. He became an American citizen in 1825. Originally, he bought the Washington House tavern from Peter Hetzel in 1832 for $800.

In Montgomery County, Ohio

Charles Winger (A222671), the son of John H. Winger (A22267), reported to the writer many years ago that Peter Henry Winger (A2226) had relatives who lived in Montgomery County, Ohio. He stated that at one time he thought that Peter Henry Winger (A2226) had had some connection with the Church of the Brethren in Christ in Stillwater Valley. A search of those church records never disclosed any evidence of his connection.

In any event, it is interesting to note that in the *History of Montgomery County, Ohio,* by W. H. Beers & Company, there is an item to the following effect: The Reverend John Winger was born in Lancaster County, Pennsylvania, February 26, 1807. He remained at home with his father until he was 27 years of age and learned the business of manufacturing woolens. He moved to Ohio with his parents in 1827 and settled in Montgomery County, Ohio, where he remained until his death January 28, 1879. He is buried beside his first wife, Sarah. He organized the Church of the Brethren in Christ in Stillwater Valley. He entered the ministry in 1840 under the guidance of the River Brethren and the church was organized. He preached for 39 years and never asked or received any pay. He was twice married, having eight children by his first wife, and two by his second. In 1947 the writer exchanged several letters with a Charles Winger who lived in Clayton, Montgomery County, Ohio. His communication stated that at an early time there were four Winger brothers who came to Montgomery County, Ohio. These were Christian Winger, John Winger, Joseph Winger and Tobias Winger. He stated that their father was one of seven boys that came to Lancaster County, Pennsylvania, from the Palatinate of Germany. It is very possible that the Reverend John Winger referred to above is from this latter family. An extensive correspondence with Mrs. Pearl Swartz, clerk of the church, who lived in Tipp City, Ohio, indicated that she could find no trace of our Peter Henry Winger in their records. She did indicate, however, that there was a Winger cemetery south of the church in Polk Grove. Later the writer visited that cemetery and found a cluster of Winger graves.

In 1944 the writer had extensive correspondence with John W. Waymire of San Diego, California. His line of Wingers was sired by Hans Winger who came to this country on the ship, *Charming Nancy,* in 1837. He stated then that many of the early Wingers from his line went to Montgomery County, Ohio. It seems probable, therefore, that some of the these families may be from the Hans Winger lineage. Many other Winger families in this county state their line to be that of Christian Wenger of 1727.

Darke County, Ohio

In Darke County, Ohio, there were several other Wenger families residing there at the same time our Peter Winger (A2226) resided in that county. Josph and Lydia Wenger resided in Washington Township in 1850. They had the following children: Israel, David, Aaron, Sarah, William, Samuel and Joseph. Also in the same township resided Elias and Catherine Wenger. They had the following children: Matilda, Isaah, Abraham, Franklin, William, Mary Catherine, Margaret, Josiah, Sarah and Hiram. Our data indictes that these families are descended from Hans Wenger of Bern, Switzerland, whose son, Hans, arrived in the New World in 1748.

There were several other Wenger families living in Darke County about 1850. These were George Wenger, William Wenger, David Wenger, Ezra Wenger and Christian Wenger. None of these families, insofar as could be ascertained, had any relationship with our branch of the Winger family.

Reflections

Busy people simply do not have time to write a book, except at the cost of tremendous sacrifice. Every spare moment for years has been devoted to this compulsive project. Someone has said that there is no such thing as an original idea. Much of this script falls in that category, even though supplementary data has been added. If I have inadvertently quoted without specific credit or misquoted another, please know that this has not been my intention. I have only wanted to state a thesis based on historical fact and a philosophy pertaining to great sociological questions.

When I wrote *One Man's Family*, I found that no sooner had the ink dried than I found a word, a line, a paragraph, a little discordant. I suspect it would be hoping for too much for the author to avoid feeling the same way about the present work.

Through the years, there has been considerable correspondence with Norman W. Nauman, Samuel S. Wenger and Rev. Roger D. Winger, as well as many other Winger historians, concerning my branch of Wingers. Much of this material in my earlier correspondence was follow-up on leads that led nowhere. Should these files ever find their way into a library, they should be evaluated in the light of later material which in the meantime has been incorporated in this work.

I should like to take this opportunity to acknowledge the faithful work and typing of this script by my secretary, Wilma Beertema. To her, my thanks and appreciation.

It should be noted that some birth and death dates in a few generations of Wengers are only projections. Death dates through wills and estate papers are more readily obtained; however, the birth dates for the most part had to be established by playing the role of detective. By constantly looking for little items, a pattern was established which seems to be reasonably credible.

The pictures of Christian Wenger (A2), Henry Wenger (A22), Abraham Wenger (A222) and Peter Henry Wenger (A2226) and some wives as well as others are photographs of drawings made by the well-known artist, Elaine Journet. Some of these were identified, others partially and a few are simply a calculated guess. From the Peter Henry Wenger (A2226) papers and effects we secured pictures and tintypes, oil paintings and descriptive material, much of which was poorly preserved. Several Canadian Wengers in the Adam Wenger (A221) line made contributions. The artists and architects had to use photo psychometry, so to speak, to produce some of the pictures. While we did not use the carbon test, we do believe these photographs are within credible range.

One of my reviewers of this script, a Doctor of Philosophy, expressed the view that this book shows a depth of research and importunity comparable to that of many a candidate for a doctor's degree at his university. He expressed the proposition that the message in this work is so in touch with our times it should be suggested reading on every university campus.

As a businessman, I can say these are very kind words, coming from an academician. In fact, even though this assertion may be biased, I find it rewarding. This is especially true since I chose to write this book of limited exposure instead of another that some publishers said would have been a popular best seller.

That book would have been my baseball story, a field far removed from the subject matter here. However, in spite of a momentary urge, I did resist the opportunity to talk shop. That is the way it is with this baseball owner who, among other proprietors, was recently defined by a writer "as an unregenerate skinflint who underpays his players, overcharges his customers, resists change, covers over scandal and does it all cloaked in the American flag, apple pie, Mom, peanuts and crackerjack, homemade fudge and hot dogs."

See what I mean — really this *is* the end!

INDEX TO BIOGRAPHICAL SKETCHES

446